student
ATLAS

First Canadian Edition 2004
04 05 06 6 5 4 3 2 1
Copyright © 1998, 2002, 2004 Dorling Kindersley Limited

Dorling Kindersley is represented in Canada by
Tourmaline Editions Inc.
662 King Street West, Suite 304
Toronto, Ontario M5V 1M7

National Library of Canada Cataloguing in Publication

Student atlas [cartographic material] / David Lambert,
educational consultant. – Canadian ed.

Includes index.
ISBN 1-55363-035-1

1. Children's atlases. 2. Atlases, Canadian. I. Lambert, David

G1021.S78 2004   j912   C2003-905971-5

Reproduction by Colourscan, Singapore, and The Printed Word, London.
Printed and bound in China by Toppan Printing Co. (Shenzen) Ltd.

ACKNOWLEDGEMENTS
The publishers are grateful for permission to reproduce the following photographs:
t=top, b=bottom, a=above, l=left, r=right, c=centre

Axiom: J Spaull 84br. **Bridgeman Art Library**: Hereford Cathedral, Trustees of the Hereford Mappa Mundi 8tr.
J Allan Cash: 104cr. **Bruce Coleman Ltd**: C Ott 28cr (below); Dr E Pott 4bc; H Reinhard 19cr; J Murray 114bl; Peter Terry
19crr. **Colourific**: Black Star/R Rogers 49br; Frank Herrmann 103bc. **Comstock**: 17tc. **James Davis Travel Photography**: 44tr,
103tr. **Robert Harding Picture Library**: 6tr (below), 21c, 21cr, 22br, 84cr (above), 28bl, 30cr, 30br, 31bl, 102bl; A Tovy 104br;
Adam Woolfitt 54br; C Bowman 48tr; Charcrit Boonson 82cr (below); David Lomax 20tr; Franz Joseph Land 19tr; G Boutin
104cl (below); G Renner 17c, 102cr(above); Gavin Hellier 31tr; H P Merten 23tl; Jane Sweeney 23bl; Louise Murray 85tr; Peter
Scholey 83tr; Robert Francis 23cr; Schuster/Keine 54cr (above); Simon Westcott 82br. **Hutchison Library**: A Zvoznikov 19cl; J
Nowell 85bl; R Ian Lloyd 10cl. **Image Bank**: Carlos Navajas 17bl; M Isy-Schwart 17bc; P Grumann 56cr (below); Steve Proehl
30cr (below); Terje Rakke 17br. **Images Colour Library**: 19c, 54cr (below), 102br. **Impact**: Jeremy Nicholl 105cl (below); Mark
Henley 20bl; Paul O'Driscoll 55cr; Robin Lubbock 102br. **Frank Lane Picture Agency**: D Smith 19bc; W Wisniewsli 17cr.
Magnum: Chris Steele Perking 104tr (below); Ian Berry 56br; Jean Gaumy 57cl. **N.A.S.A**: 9tc. **N.H.P.A**: M Wendler 4cl, 46bl.
Oxford Scientific Films: Konrad Wothe 19tc; L Gould 4tr; Nobert Rosing 28cl. **Panos Pictures**: Alain le Garsheur 84cr; Alain
le Garsmeur 31cl (below); Alberto Arzoz 55tr; Bruce Paton 105bl; Jeremy Hartley 104bl; Maria Luiza M Cavalho 48cl (below);
Paul Smith 47cr; Rhodri Jones 49bl; Ron Gilling 103cr; Trygve Bolstad 22bl. **Edward Parker**: 17cr (above). **Pictor
International**: 4tc, 10bc, 18tr, 20br. **Planet Earth Pictures**: J Waters 49bc. **South American Pictures**: Robert Francis 29br;
Tony Morrison 46cr, 47cl. **Spectrum Colour Library**: 29br. **Frank Spooner Pictures**: Gamma/E Baitel 83cl. **Still Pictures**: J
Frebet 49cr; R Seitre 82cr (above). **Tony Stone Images**: 17tr, 48cl; A Sacks 28cr; Alan Levenson 84cr; D Austen 131cr; D
Hanson 17cl; Donald Johnson 54bc; Earth Imaging 6tr (above); G Johnson 82bl; H Strand 49tr; J Jangoux 19bcr; J Warden
46bc; John Garrett 105br; L Resnick 105tr; P Chesley 114tr; Randy Wells 19br; Robert Frerck 57tr; Tony Craddock 57cr.
Telegraph Colour Library: 29tr. **Travel Ink**: Colin Marshall 22bc. **Trip**: A Kuznetsov 84bc; H Rogers 82cr; M Barlow 48bl; N
Ray 10tr; Robert Belbin 92bl; V Kolpakov 85cr (below); V Sidoropolev 56cr; W Jacobs 114cl. **World Pictures**: 131tr. **ZEFA
Picture Library**: 19bcl, 19cll, 55bc; Bramaz 30bl; Damm 103cl; Heilman 46cr (below); K Siewert 46cl; Kitchen 19bll; Sunak
83cr; Surpress 47tr. **Jacket**: Front cover image: Science Photo Library/NOAA

Discover more at
www.dk.com

CONTENTS

LEARNING MAP SKILLS

THE WORLD

THE WORLD ATLAS

NORTH AMERICA

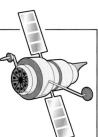

SOUTH AMERICA

EUROPE

ASIA

AFRICA

AUSTRALASIA & OCEANIA

POLAR REGIONS

AMAZING EARTH

Earth is unique among the nine planets that circle the Sun. It is the only one that can support life, because it has enough oxygen in its atmosphere and plentiful water. In fact, seen from space, the Earth looks almost entirely blue. This is because about 70% of its surface is under water, submerged beneath four huge oceans: the Pacific, Atlantic, Indian and Arctic oceans. Land makes up about 30% of the Earth's surface. It is divided into seven landmasses of varying shapes and sizes called continents. These are, from largest to smallest: Asia, Africa, North America, South America, Antarctica, Europe and Australia.

WATERY WORLD

The Earth's oceans and seas cover more than 367 million sq km – that is twice the surface of Mars and nine times the surface of the moon.

Beneath the ocean waves lies the biggest and most unexplored landscape on Earth. Here are coral reefs, enormous, open plains, deep canyons, and the longest mountain range on Earth – the Mid-Atlantic Ridge – which stretches almost from pole to pole.

THE SHAPE OF THE EARTH

Photographs taken from space by astronauts in the 1960s, and more recently from orbiting satellites, have proven beyond doubt what humans had already worked out long ago – that the Earth is shaped like a ball. But it is not perfectly round. The force of the Earth's rotation makes the world bulge very slightly at the Equator and go a little flat at the North and South poles. So the Earth is actually a flattened sphere, or a 'geoid'.

HEIGHTS AND DEPTHS

The Pacific Ocean contains the deepest places on the Earth's surface – the ocean trenches. The very deepest is Challenger Deep in the Mariana Trench which plunges 10,923 m into the Earth's crust. If Mount Everest, the highest point on land at 8,850 m, was dropped into the trench, its peak wouldn't even reach the surface of the Pacific.

WATER

Over 97% of the Earth's water is salt water. The total amount of salt in the world's oceans and seas would cover the whole of Europe to a depth of five km. Less than 3% of the Earth's water is fresh. Of this, 2.24% is frozen in ice sheets and about 0.6% is stored underground as groundwater. The remainder is in lakes and rivers.

COASTS

The total length of the Earth's coastlines is more than 500,000 km – that is the equivalent of 12 times around the globe. A high percentage of the world's people live in coastal zones: of the ten most populated cities on Earth, eight are situated on estuaries or the coast.

WET EARTH

Tropical rainforests grow in areas close to the Equator, where it is wet and warm all year round. Although they cover just 7% of the Earth's land, these thick, damp forests form the richest ecosystems on the planet. More plant and animal species are found here than anywhere else on Earth.

DRY EARTH

Deserts are among the most inhospitable places on the planet. Some deserts are scorching hot, others are freezing cold, but they have one thing in common – they are all dry. Very few plant and animal species can survive in these harsh conditions. The world's coldest and driest continent, Antarctica (*left*), is a cold desert.

BIODIVERSITY

Today, almost six hundred million humans, approximately one million animal species and 355,000 known plant species depend on the air, water and land of planet Earth.

VANISHING FORESTS

10,000 years ago, thick forests covered about half of the Earth's land surface. Today, 33% of those forests no longer exist, and more than half of what remains has been dramatically altered. During the 20th century, more than 50% of the Earth's rainforests have been felled.

DIFFERENT WORLD VIEWS

Because the Earth is round, we can only see half of it at any one time. This half is called a hemisphere, which means 'half a sphere'. There are always two hemispheres – the half that you see and the other half that you don't see. Two hemispheres placed together will always make a complete sphere.

PLANET WATER, PLANET LAND

The Earth can also be divided into land and water hemispheres. The land hemisphere shows most of the land on the Earth's surface. The water hemisphere is dominated by the vast Pacific Ocean – from this view, the Earth appears to be almost entirely covered by water.

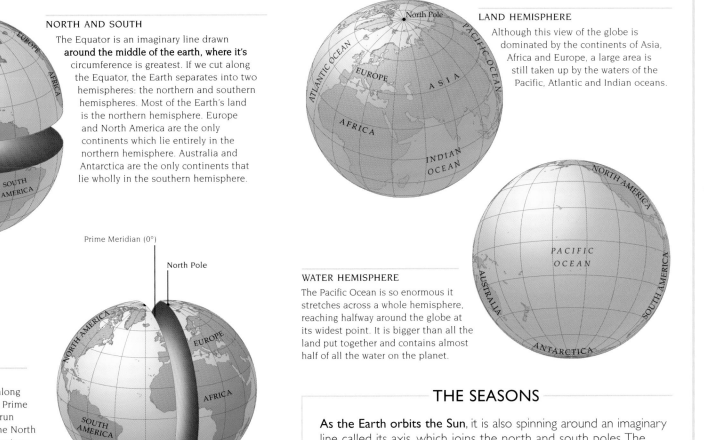

NORTH AND SOUTH

The Equator is an imaginary line drawn **around the middle of the earth, where it's** circumference is greatest. If we cut along the Equator, the Earth separates into two hemispheres: the northern and southern hemispheres. Most of the Earth's land is the northern hemisphere. Europe and North America are the only continents which lie entirely in the northern hemisphere. Australia and Antarctica are the only continents that lie wholly in the southern hemisphere.

The southern hemisphere contains three of the Earth's four great oceans: the Pacific, Indian and Southern oceans.

EAST AND WEST

The Earth can also be divided along two other imaginary lines – the Prime Meridian (0°) and 180° – which run opposite each other between the North and South poles. This creates eastern and western hemispheres. The continents in the eastern hemisphere are traditionally called the Old World while those in the western hemisphere – the Americas – were named the New World by the Europeans who explored them in the 15th century.

LAND HEMISPHERE

Although this view of the globe is dominated by the continents of Asia, Africa and Europe, a large area is still taken up by the waters of the Pacific, Atlantic and Indian oceans.

WATER HEMISPHERE

The Pacific Ocean is so enormous it stretches across a whole hemisphere, reaching halfway around the globe at its widest point. It is bigger than all the land put together and contains almost half of all the water on the planet.

THE SEASONS

As the Earth orbits the Sun, it is also spinning around an imaginary line called its axis, which joins the north and south poles. The Earth's axis is not quite at right angles to the Sun, but tilts over at an angle of 23.5°. As a result, each place gradually moves closer to the Sun and then further away from it again. Summer in the northern hemisphere is when the north is closest to the Sun. In winter, the northern hemisphere tilts away from the Sun, receiving far less heat and light. In the southern hemisphere the seasons are reversed, with summer in December and winter in June.

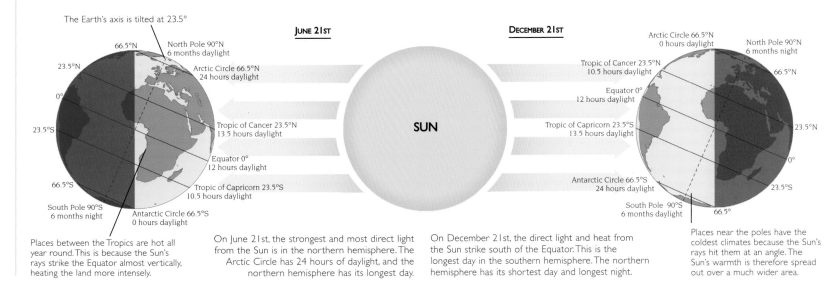

Places between the Tropics are hot all year round. This is because the Sun's rays strike the Equator almost vertically, heating the land more intensely.

On June 21st, the strongest and most direct light from the Sun is in the northern hemisphere. The Arctic Circle has 24 hours of daylight, and the northern hemisphere has its longest day.

On December 21st, the direct light and heat from the Sun strike south of the Equator. This is the longest day in the southern hemisphere. The northern hemisphere has its shortest day and longest night.

Places near the poles have the coldest climates because the Sun's rays hit them at an angle. The Sun's warmth is therefore spread out over a much wider area.

MAPPING THE WORLD

The main purpose of a map is to show, or locate, where things are. The only truly accurate map of the whole world is a globe – a round model of the Earth. But a globe is impractical to carry around, so map-makers (cartographers) produce flat paper maps instead. Changing the globe into a flat map is not simple. Imagine cutting a globe in half and trying to flatten the two hemispheres. They would be stretched in some places, and squashed in others. In fact, it is impossible to make a map of the round Earth on flat paper without some distortion of area, distance or direction.

MODELS OF THE WORLD

Satellite images can show the whole world as it appears from space. However, this image shows only one half of the world, and is distorted at the edges.

A globe (*right*) is the only way to illustrate the shape of the Earth accurately. A globe also shows the correct positions of the continents and oceans and how large they are in relation to one another.

LATITUDE

We can find out exactly how far north or south, east or west any place is on Earth by drawing two sets of imaginary lines around the world to make a grid. The horizontal lines on the globe below are called lines of latitude. They run from east to west. The most important is the Equator, which is given the value 0°. All other lines of latitude run parallel to the Equator. and are numbered in degrees either north or south of the Equator.

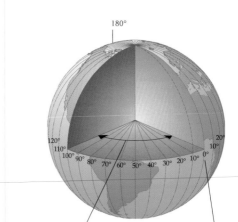

North Pole – 90°N

The value of each line of latitude increases from 0° to 90° as you move towards the North or South poles.

90° 80° 70° 60° 50° 40° 30° 20° 10° 0° 10° 20° 30° 40° 50° 60°

Equator 0°

South Pole – 90°S

Lines of latitude are measured from the centre of the Earth. An angle is then measured from here in relation to the Equator.

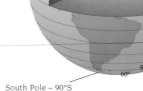

One degree of latitude is approximately 113 km.

Lines of latitude divide the world into 'slices' of equal thickness on either side of the Equator.

LONGITUDE

The vertical lines on the globe below run from north to south between the poles. They are called lines of longitude. The most important passes through Greenwich, London and is numbered 0°. It is called the Prime Meridian. All other lines of longitude are numbered in degrees either east or west of the Prime Meridian. The line directly opposite the Prime Meridian is numbered 180°.

180°

120° 110° 100° 90° 80° 70° 60° 50° 40° 30° 20° 10° 0°   20° 10°

Prime Meridian – 0°

Lines of longitude are also measured from the centre of the Earth. This time, the angle is taken in relation to the Prime Meridian.

Lines of longitude divide the world into segments, like those of an orange – wide near the Equator, but narrow at the poles.

WHERE ON EARTH?

When lines of latitude and longitude are combined on a globe, or as here, on a flat map, they form a grid. Using this grid, we can locate any place on land, or at sea, by referring to the point where its line of latitude intersects with its line of longitude. Even when a place is not located exactly where the lines cross, you can still find its approximate position.

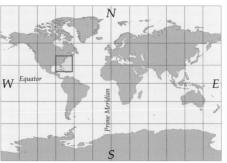

N

W   *Equator*   E

Prime Meridian

S

The map above is of the eastern USA. It is too small to show all the lines of latitude and longitude, so they are given at intervals of 5°. Miami is located at about 26° north of the Equator and 80° west of the Prime Meridian. We write its location like this: 26°N 80°W.

MAKING A FLAT MAP FROM A GLOBE

Cartographers use a technique called projection to show the Earth's curved surface on a flat map. Many different map projections have been designed. The distortion of one feature – either area, distance, or direction – can be minimized, while other features become more distorted. Cartographers must choose which of these things it is most important to show correctly for each map that they make. Three major families of projections can be used to solve these questions.

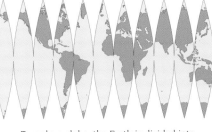

To make a globe, the Earth is divided into segments or 'gores' along lines of longitude.

1 CYLINDRICAL PROJECTIONS

These projections are 'cylindrical' because the surface of the globe is transferred onto a surrounding cylinder. This cylinder is then cut from top to bottom and 'rolled out' to give a flat map. These maps are very useful for showing the whole world.

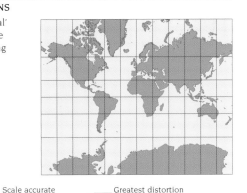

The cylinder touches the globe at the Equator. Here, the scale on the map will be exactly the same as it is on the globe. At the northern and southern edges of the cylinder, which are furthest away from the surface of the globe, the map is most distorted. The Mercator projection (*above*), created in the 16th century, is a good example of a cylindrical projection.

Scale accurate at Equator

Greatest distortion

Greatest distortion

2 AZIMUTHAL PROJECTIONS

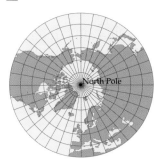

North Pole

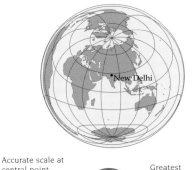

New Delhi

Azimuthal projections put the surface of the globe onto a flat circle. 'Azimuthal' means that the direction or 'azimuth' of any line coming from the centre point of that circle is correct. Azimuthal maps are useful for viewing hemispheres, continents and the polar regions. Mapping any area larger than a hemisphere gives great distortion at the outer edges of the map.

Accurate scale at central point

Greatest distortion

The circle only touches the globe's surface at one central point. The scale is only accurate at this point and becomes less and less accurate the further away the circle is from the globe. This kind of projection is good for maps centering on a major city or on one of the poles.

3 CONIC PROJECTIONS

Conic projections are best used for smaller areas of the world, such as country maps. The surface of the globe is projected onto a cone which rests on top of it. After cutting from the point to the bottom of the cone, a flat map in the shape of a fan is left behind.

The conic projection touches the globe's surface at one latitude. This is where the scale of the map will be most accurate. The parts of the cone furthest from the globe will be the most distorted and are usually omitted from the map itself.

Greatest distortion

Most accurate scale

PROJECTIONS USED IN THIS ATLAS

The projections which are appropriate for showing maps at a world, continental or country scale are quite different. The projections for this atlas have been carefully chosen. They are ones that show areas as familiar shapes and ensure that they are distorted as little as possible.

1 World Maps

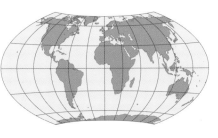

The Wagner VII projection is used for our world maps as it shows all the countries at their correct sizes relative to one another.

2 Continents

The Lambert Azimuthal Equal Area is used for continental maps. The shape distortion is relatively small and countries retain their correct sizes relative to one another.

3 Countries

The Lambert Conformal Conic shows countries with as little distortion as possible. The angles from any point on the map are the same as they would be on the surface of the globe.

HOW MAPS ARE MADE

New technologies have revolutionized map making. Computers and information from satellites have replaced drawing boards and drafting pens, and the process of creating new maps is now far easier. But map making is still a skilled and often time-consuming process. Information about the World must be gathered, sorted and checked. The cartographer must make decisions about the function of the map and what information to select in order to make it as clear as possible.

THE MAPPA MUNDI

Maps have been made for thousands of years. The 13th century Mappa Mundi, meaning 'known world' shows the Mediterranean Sea and the Don and Nile rivers. Asia is at the top, with Europe on the left, and Africa to the right. The oceans are shown as a ring surrounding the land. The map reflects a number of biblical stories.

HISTORICAL MAP MAKING

This detailed hand-drawn map of the southern coast of Spain was made in about 1750. The mountains are illustrated as small hills and the labels have been hand lettered.

For centuries, maps were drawn by hand. Very early maps were no more than a pictorial representation of what the surface of the ground looked like. Where there were hills, pictures were drawn to represent them. Later maps were drawn using information gathered by survey teams. They would carefully mark out and calculate the height of the land, the positions of towns and other geographical features. As knowledge and techniques improved, maps became more accurate.

NEW TECHNIQUES

Computers make it easier to change map information and styles quickly. This map of the southern coast of Spain, made in 1997 has been made using digital terrain modelling (see below) and traditional cartography.

Today, cartographers have access to far more data about the Earth than in the past. Satellites collect and process information about its surface. This is called remote-sensed data. Further information may be drafted in the traditional way. Locations can be verified by GPS (Global Positioning Systems) linked to satellites. Computers are now widely used to combine different sorts of map information. Any computerized map is produced using a GIS (Geographical Information System).

MODERN MAP MAKING

1 **Measuring the Earth's surface**
The surface of the Earth is divided up into squares. Satellites take measurements of the height of the land in each square. The data collected can then be manipulated on a computer to produce a digital terrain model (DTM).

3 **Adding detail to the land surface**
The height of the land can be shown using bands of colour, or by contour lines, which are applied to the digitally-created surface of the Earth. Colour can also be used to show different kinds of vegetation, such as deserts, forests and grasslands.

2 **Making a terrain model**
Using the grid produced from the height data, a detailed 3-D model of the Earth can be built in the memory of a powerful computer. Software can then recreate the effects of the sun shining onto mountains and into valleys so that they can be seen much more clearly.

4 **Adding map detail**
Features such as roads, rivers, towns and cities can now be added to the map. They are selected, and compiled and scanned digitally into the computer. The information can then be 'draped' on top of the terrain model to create a map.

SHOWING INFORMATION ON A MAP

A map is a selective diagram of a place. It is the cartographer's job to decide what kind of information to show on a map. They can choose to highlight certain kinds of features – such as roads, rivers and land height. They can also show other features such as sea depth, place names, and borders which would be impossible to see either on the ground or from a photograph. The information that can be shown in a map is influenced by a number of factors, most notably by its scale.

This is a satellite photograph of the harbour area of Rio de Janeiro in Brazil. Although you can see the bay and where most of the housing is, it is impossible to see roads or get any sense of the position of places relative to one another.

This is a map of the same area as you can see in the photograph. Much of the detail has been greatly simplified. Towns are named and marked; contours indicate the height of the land; and roads, railways and borders between districts have been added.

SCALE

To make a map of an area it needs to be greatly reduced in size. This is known as drawing to scale. The scale of the map shows us by how much the area has been reduced. The smaller the scale, the greater the area of land that can be shown on the map. There will be far less detail and the map will not be as accurate. The maps below show the different kinds of information that can be shown on maps of varying scales.

WAYS TO SHOW SCALE

When using a map to work out what areas or distances are in reality, we need to refer to the scale of that particular map. Map scales can be shown in several ways.

1 **Representative fraction**
One unit on the map would be equal to 1,000,0000 units on the ground.

1:1,000,000

2 **Linear scale**
The line is marked off in units which represent the real distances of the map, given in both miles and kilometres.

SCALE BAR

0 km   10   20

0 miles   10   20

3 **Statement of scale**
It means that 1 mm on the map represents 1 km on the ground.

1 mm represents 1 km

LONDON 1:21,000,000

This small-scale map shows the position of London in relation to Europe. Very little detail can be seen at this scale – only the names of countries and the largest towns.

LONDON 1:5,500,000

At a scale of 1 to 5,500,000 you can see the major road network in the southeast of the UK. Many towns are named and you can see the difference in size and status.

LONDON 1:900,000

This map is at a much larger scale. You can see the major roads that lead out from London and the names of many suburbs, places of interest and airports.

LONDON 1:12,500

This is a street map of central London. The streets are named, as are places of interest, train and underground stations. The scale is large enough to show plenty of detail.

READING MAPS

Maps use a unique visual language to convey a great deal of detailed information in a relatively simple form. Different features are marked out using special symbols and styles of print. These symbols are explained in the key to the map and you should always read a map alongside its key or legend. This page explains how to look for different features on the map and how to unravel the different layers of information that you can find on it.

PHYSICAL FEATURES

All the regional and country maps in this atlas are based on a model of the Earth's surface. The computer-generated relief gives an accurate picture of the surface of the land. Colours are used to show the relative heights of the land; green is for low-lying land, and yellows, browns and greys are for higher land. Water features like streams, rivers and lakes are also shown.

1 WATER FEATURES

On this map extract, the blue lines show a number of rivers, including the Salween and the Irrawaddy. The Irrawaddy forms a huge delta, splitting into many streams as it reaches the sea.

2 RELIEF

These mountains are in the north of Southeast Asia. The underlying relief on the map and the coloured bands help you to see the height of the land.

HUMAN FEATURES

Maps also reveal a great deal about the human geography of an area. As well as showing where towns and roads are, different symbols can tell you more about the size of towns and the importance of a road. Borders between countries or regions can only be seen on a map.

3 BORDERS

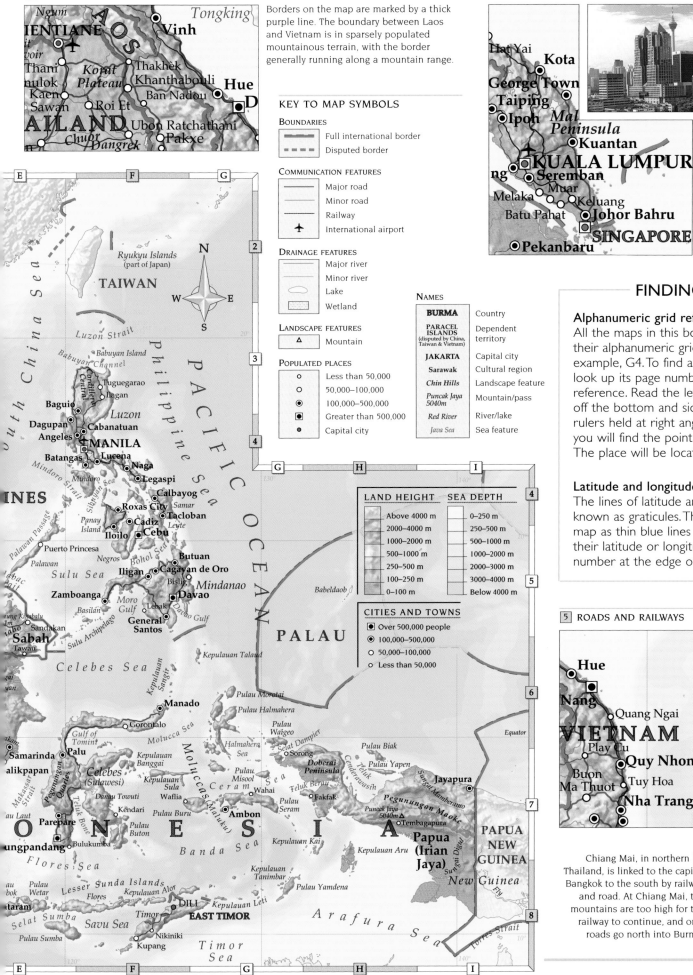

Borders on the map are marked by a thick purple line. The boundary between Laos and Vietnam is in sparsely populated mountainous terrain, with the border generally running along a mountain range.

Map labels: Ngum, LAOS, Vinh, Tongking, IENTIANE, voir, Thani, nulok, Kaen, Sawan, Korat Plateau, Thakhèk, Khanthabouli, Ban Nadou, Hue, D, Roi Et, AILAND, Ubon Ratchathani, Pakxe, Chuor, Dangrek

KEY TO MAP SYMBOLS

BOUNDARIES

———	Full international border
- - -	Disputed border

COMMUNICATION FEATURES

——	Major road
——	Minor road
——	Railway
✈	International airport

DRAINAGE FEATURES

	Major river
	Minor river
◯	Lake
▭	Wetland

LANDSCAPE FEATURES

△	Mountain

POPULATED PLACES

◦	Less than 50,000
○	50,000–100,000
◉	100,000–500,000
▣	Greater than 500,000
●	Capital city

NAMES

BURMA	Country
PARACEL ISLANDS (disputed by China, Taiwan & Vietnam)	Dependent territory
JAKARTA	Capital city
Sarawak	Cultural region
Chin Hills	Landscape feature
Puncak Jaya 5040m	Mountain/pass
Red River	River/lake
Java Sea	Sea feature

4 SETTLEMENTS

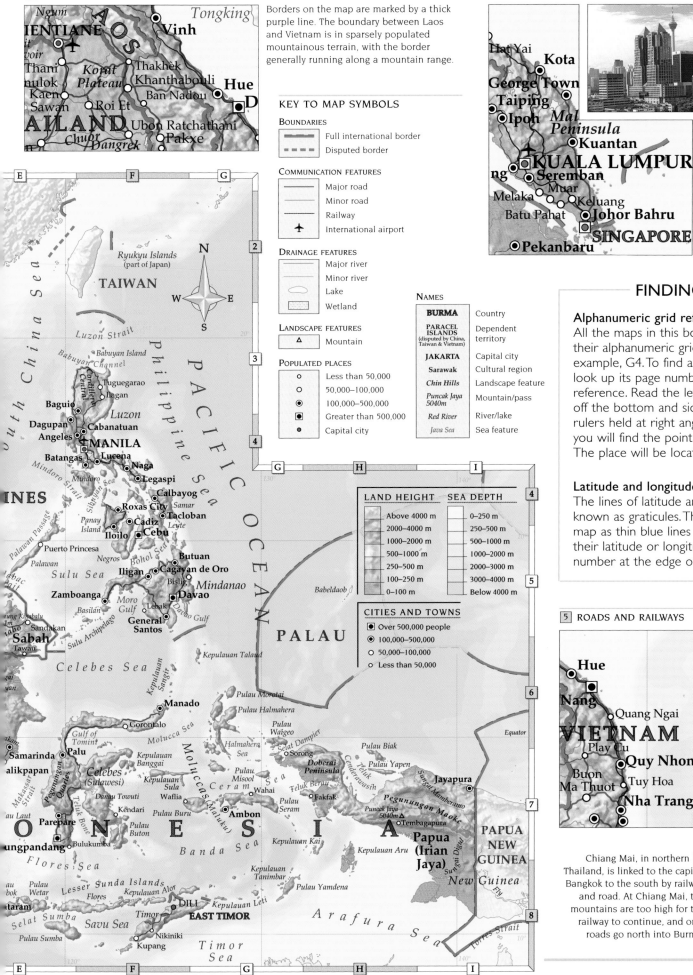

Map labels: Hat Yai, Kota, George Town, Taiping, Ipoh, Mal Peninsula, Kuantan, KUALA LUMPUR, Seremban, Muar, Melaka, Keluang, Batu Pahat, Johor Bahru, SINGAPORE, Pekanbaru, ng

The symbol for a settlement can tell you its position, population and political status. Most towns are shown by a circle or a square. These represent the size of their population. Where a town is coloured red, this shows that it is a capital city such as Kuala Lumpur in Malaysia.

LAND HEIGHT

	Above 4000 m
	2000–4000 m
	1000–2000 m
	500–1000 m
	250–500 m
	100–250 m
	0–100 m

SEA DEPTH

	0–250 m
	250–500 m
	500–1000 m
	1000–2000 m
	2000–3000 m
	3000–4000 m
	Below 4000 m

CITIES AND TOWNS

▣	Over 500,000 people
◉	100,000–500,000
○	50,000–100,000
◦	Less than 50,000

FINDING PLACES

Alphanumeric grid references

All the maps in this book are indexed using their alphanumeric grid reference – for example, G4. To find a place you must first look up its page number and then its grid reference. Read the letters and numbers off the bottom and side of the grid. Using rulers held at right angles to one another you will find the point where the lines meet. The place will be located within this square.

Latitude and longitude references

The lines of latitude and longitude are known as graticules. They are shown on the map as thin blue lines with the value of their latitude or longitude given as a blue number at the edge of the map.

5 ROADS AND RAILWAYS

a The major road and railway links between Hue and Nha Trang hug the Vietnamese coast. A string of coastal towns is often connected by road and rail in this manner.

Map labels: Hue, Nang, Quang Ngai, VIETNAM, Play Cu, Buon Ma Thuot, Quy Nhon, Tuy Hoa, Nha Trang

Chiang Mai, in northern **b** Thailand, is linked to the capital Bangkok to the south by railway and road. At Chiang Mai, the mountains are too high for the railway to continue, and only roads go north into Burma.

Map labels: Chiang Mai, Mae Nam Nan, Sirikit Reservo, Udon Th, Phitsanu, Khon K, Nakhon S, THAILAN, Mae Nam Ping, BANGKOK

Main map labels: Ryukyu Islands (part of Japan), TAIWAN, South China Sea, Luzon Strait, Babuyan Island, Babuyan Channel, Cordillera Central, Tuguegarao, Ilagan, Baguio, Dagupan, Cabanatuan, Angeles, Luzon, MANILA, Batangas, Lucena, Naga, Mindoro, Mindoro Strait, Legaspi, Calbayog, Samar, Roxas City, Panay Island, Cadiz, Tacloban, Iloilo, Cebu, Leyte, Puerto Princesa, Palawan, Negros, Bohol Sea, Butuan, Sulu Sea, Iligan, Cagayan de Oro, Bislig, Mindanao, Zamboanga, Basilán, Moro Gulf, Lebak, Davao, Davao Gulf, General Santos, Sulu Archipelago, Sandakan, Sabah, Tawau, Celebes Sea, PHILIPPINES, LINES, Philippine Sea, PACIFIC OCEAN, PALAU, Babeldaob, Sibuyan Sea, Palawan Passage, Manado, Gorontalo, Gulf of Tomini, Molucca Sea, Pulau Morotai, Pulau Halmahera, Pulau Talaud, Kepulauan Sangir, Kepulauan Talaud, Pulau Waigeo, Equator, Samarinda, alikpapan, Palu, Celebes (Sulawesi), Kepulauan Banggai, Kepulauan Sula, Danau Towuti, Waflia, Kendari, Pulau Buru, Halmahera Sea, Selat Dampier, Sorong, Doberai Peninsula, Pulau Misool, Teluk Berau, Fakfak, Teluk Cenderawasih, Pulau Biak, Pulau Yapen, Sungai Mamberamo, Jayapura, Parepare, Teluk Bone, Pulau Buton, Ceram Sea, Wahai, Pulau Seram, Ambon, Puncak Jaya 5040m, Tembagapura, Pegunungan Maoke, Sungai Digul, PAPUA (Irian Jaya), PAPUA NEW GUINEA, New Guinea, ungpandang, Bulukumba, Banda Sea, Kepulauan Kai, Kepulauan Aru, Sungai Fly, Fly, Flores Sea, Lesser Sunda Islands, Kepulauan Tanimbar, Pulau Yamdena, O NESIA, lok, Pulau Wetar, Flores, Kepulauan Alor, Kepulauan Leti, DILI, Timor, EAST TIMOR, Arafura Sea, Selat Sumba, Savu Sea, Pulau Sumba, Timor Sea, Nikiniki, Kupang, Torres Strait

USING THE ATLAS

This Atlas has been designed to develop map-reading skills and to introduce readers to a wide range of different maps. It also provides a wealth of detailed geographic information about the world today. The Atlas is divided into four sections: **Learning Map Skills**; **The World About Us**, covering global geographic patterns; the **World Atlas**, dealing with the world's regions, and an **Index-Gazetteer**.

LEARNING MAP SKILLS

Maps show the Earth – which is three-dimensional – in just two dimensions. This section shows how maps are made; how different kinds of information are shown on maps; how to choose what to put on a map and the best way to show it. It also explains how to read the maps in this Atlas.

THE WORLD ABOUT US

These pages contain a series of world maps which show important themes, such as physical features, climate, life zones, population and the world economy, at a global scale. They give a worldwide picture of concepts which are explored in more detail later in the book.

Text introduces themes and concepts in each spread.

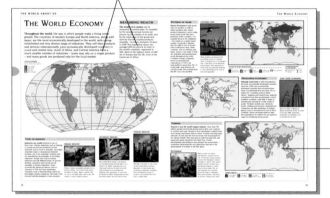

Photographs illustrate examples of places or topics shown on the main map.

World maps show geographic patterns at a global scale.

Introduction to projections: different projections and how they work.

Choosing the best projections: the map projections used in this book.

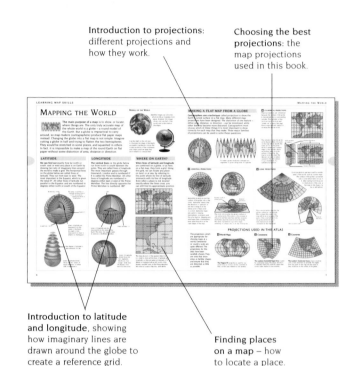

Introduction to latitude and longitude, showing how imaginary lines are drawn around the globe to create a reference grid.

Finding places on a map – how to locate a place.

CONTINENTAL MAPS

A cross-section through the continent shows the relative height of certain features.

A detailed physical map of the continent shows major natural geographic features, including mountains, lakes and rivers.

Photographs and locator maps illustrate the main geographic regions and show you where they are.

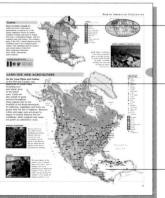

The industry map shows the main industrial towns and cities and the main industries in each continent. It also shows the wealth of each country relative to the rest of the world.

The political map of the continent shows country boundaries and country names.

CONTINENTAL GEOGRAPHY PAGES

Humans have colonized and changed all the continents except Antarctica. These pages show the factors which have affected this process: climate, the availability of resources such as coal, oil, and minerals, and varying patterns of land use. Mineral resources are directly linked to many industries, and most agriculture is governed both by the quality of the land and the climate.

The climate map shows the main types of climates across the continent and where the hottest and coldest, wettest and driest places are.

The mineral resources map shows where the most important reserves of minerals, including coal and precious metals, are found.

The land use map shows different types of land and the main kinds of farming that take place in each area.

CONTINENTAL PAGES

These pages show the physical shape of each continent and the impact that humans have made on the natural landscape – building towns and roads and creating borders between countries. They show where natural features such as mountain ranges and rivers have created physical boundaries, and where humans have created their own political boundaries between states.

REGIONAL MAPS

The main part of the Atlas contains detailed maps of countries and regions. Each of these is accompanied by a series of small thematic maps, models and charts, which give information about the climate, where people live, how they use the land, the different kinds of industry, and important environmental issues.

TERRAIN MODEL

A computer-generated landscape model shows what the land really looks like. There are no roads or towns to mask the physical geography of the country or region. Mountain ranges, plains and river basins can be easily seen.

COLOURED THUMB TAGS

Each section has its own colour code.

Learning Map Skills

The World About Us

Europe

Asia

North America

South America

Africa

Australasia and Oceania

Antarctica and the Arctic

CLIMATE MAPS

These maps show the temperature and rainfall patterns in January and July. Coloured bands indicate temperatures: blue for low temperatures, orange for high ones. Rainfall is represented by black lines with a number giving the average amount of rain. These are called isohyets.

Isohyets show the rainfall patterns in millimetres per year. The areas between the lines are either over or under the figures shown on the ishohyets.

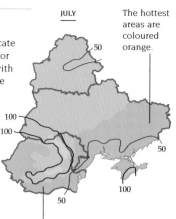

JULY

The hottest areas are coloured orange.

Here the rainfall is between 50 and 100 mm per year.

JANUARY

LOCATOR GLOBE

This shows the location of the country or region both within its continent, and in relation to the rest of the world.

MAP GRID

Each main map has a grid. Using the grid will help you to find a place on the map. Grid references are expressed as letters (running from left to right across the frame), and numbers (running from the top to the bottom of the frame), for example, A 4, G 6. Everything on the map is referenced in the **Index-Gazetteer** at the back of the book.

REGIONAL MAPS

The main map on each regional page shows the main topographical features of the area: the height of the land, the major roads, the rivers and lakes. It also shows the main cities and towns in the region – represented by different symbols.

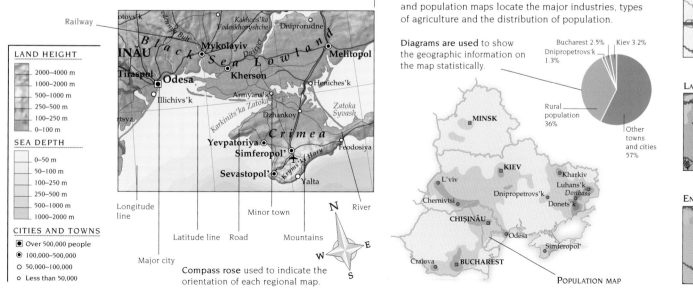

LAND HEIGHT

- 2000–4000 m
- 1000–2000 m
- 500–1000 m
- 250–500 m
- 100–250 m
- 0–100 m

SEA DEPTH

- 0–50 m
- 50–100 m
- 100–250 m
- 250–500 m
- 500–1000 m
- 1000–2000 m

CITIES AND TOWNS

- Over 500,000 people
- 100,000–500,000
- 50,000–100,000
- Less than 50,000

Railway

Longitude line

Latitude line

Road

Mountains

Minor town

Major city

River

Compass rose used to indicate the orientation of each regional map.

THEMATIC MAPS

These small maps show various aspects of the geography of the country or region. The environment maps cover topics such as the effects of pollution. Industry, land use and population maps locate the major industries, types of agriculture and the distribution of population.

Diagrams are used to show the geographic information on the map statistically.

Bucharest 2.5%   Kiev 3.2%
Dnipropetrovs'k 1.3%

Rural population 36%

Other towns and cities 57%

POPULATION MAP

INDUSTRY MAP

LAND USE MAP

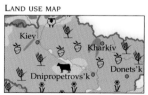

ENVIRONMENT MAP

THE PHYSICAL WORLD

This map shows the main physical features of the world: the mountain ranges, the great rivers and lakes, deserts, grassland plains, seas and oceans. No human settlements are named on this map – only the physical or landscape features.

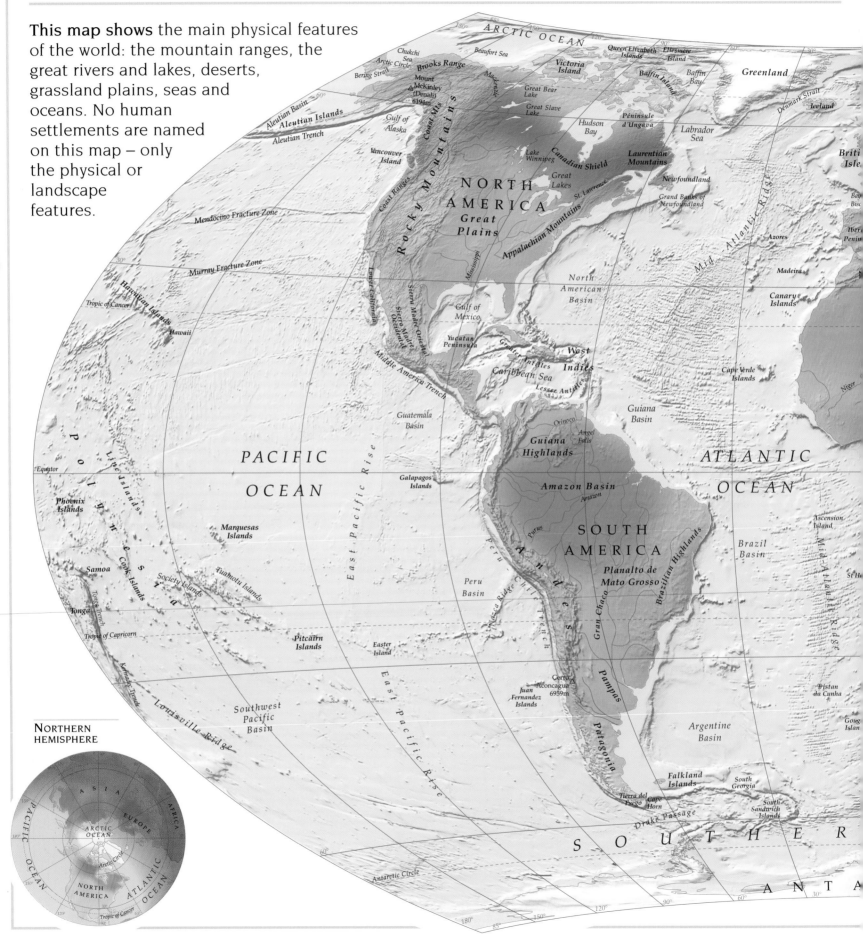

ARCTIC OCEAN

Chukchi Sea
Beaufort Sea
Queen Elizabeth Islands
Ellesmere Island
Arctic Circle
Bering Strait
Brooks Range
Victoria Island
Baffin Island
Baffin Bay
Greenland
Mount McKinley (Denali) 6194m
Mackenzie
Great Bear Lake
Great Slave Lake
Hudson Bay
Péninsule d'Ungava
Labrador Sea
Denmark Strait
Iceland

Aleutian Basin
Aleutian Islands
Aleutian Trench
Gulf of Alaska
Coast Mtns
Vancouver Island

Lake Winnipeg
Canadian Shield
Laurentian Mountains
Newfoundland

NORTH AMERICA

Mendocino Fracture Zone

Murray Fracture Zone

Hawaiian Islands

Tropic of Cancer

Hawaii

Rocky Mountains
Coast Ranges
Lower California
Sierra Nevada
Sierra Madre Oriental
Sierra Madre Occidental

Great Plains
Great Lakes
St. Lawrence
Appalachian Mountains
Mississippi

North American Basin

Grand Banks of Newfoundland

Mid-Atlantic Ridge

Azores
Madeira

Canary Islands

Briti Isle

Iber Penin

Bay Bisc

Gulf of Mexico
Yucatan Peninsula
Greater Antilles
Caribbean Sea
Lesser Antilles
West Indies

Middle America Trench

Guatemala Basin

Guiana Basin

Cape Verde Islands

Niger

PACIFIC OCEAN

Equator

Polynesia
Phoenix Islands

Line Islands

Marquesas Islands

Samoa

Cook Islands

Society Islands

Tuamotu Islands

Tonga
Tonga Trench

Tropic of Capricorn

Pitcairn Islands

Easter Island

Galapagos Islands

East Pacific Rise

Orinoco
Angel Falls

Guiana Highlands

Amazon Basin
Amazon

SOUTH AMERICA

Planalto de Mato Grosso

ATLANTIC OCEAN

Ascension Island

Brazil Basin

Mid-Atlantic Ridge

St He

Purus

Peru Basin

Peru-Chile Trench

Nazca Ridge

Andes

Brazilian Highlands

Gran Chaco

Pampas

East Pacific Rise

Southwest Pacific Basin

Louisville Ridge

Kermadec Trench

Cerro Aconcagua 6959m
Juan Fernandez Islands

Patagonia

Argentine Basin

Tristan da Cunha

Goug Islan

Falkland Islands

South Georgia

South Sandwich Islands

Tierra del Fuego
Cape Horn
Drake Passage

SOUTHER

Antarctic Circle

ANTA

NORTHERN HEMISPHERE

ASIA
EUROPE
AFRICA
PACIFIC OCEAN
ARCTIC OCEAN
ATLANTIC OCEAN
NORTH AMERICA
Arctic Circle
Tropic of Cancer

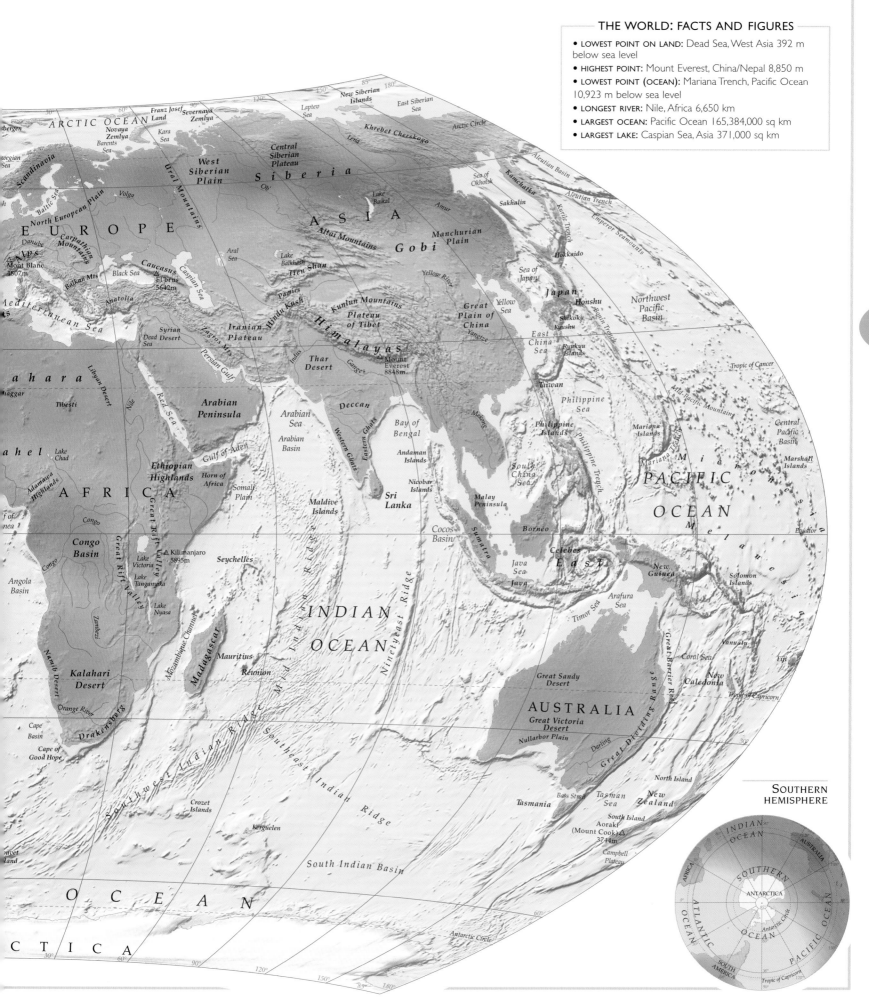

- **LOWEST POINT ON LAND:** Dead Sea, West Asia 392 m below sea level
- **HIGHEST POINT:** Mount Everest, China/Nepal 8,850 m
- **LOWEST POINT (OCEAN):** Mariana Trench, Pacific Ocean 10,923 m below sea level
- **LONGEST RIVER:** Nile, Africa 6,650 km
- **LARGEST OCEAN:** Pacific Ocean 165,384,000 sq km
- **LARGEST LAKE:** Caspian Sea, Asia 371,000 sq km

ARCTIC OCEAN

Spitsbergen
Franz Josef Land
Severnaya Zemlya
Novaya Zemlya
Barents Sea
Kara Sea
Laptev Sea
New Siberian Islands
East Siberian Sea
Arctic Circle
Khrebet Cherskogo

Norwegian Sea
Scandinavia
Baltic Sea
North European Plain
Ural Mountains
West Siberian Plain
Central Siberian Plateau
Siberia
Lena
Sea of Okhotsk
Kamchatka
Aleutian Basin

EUROPE
Danube
Carpathian Mountains
Alps
Mont Blanc 4807m
Balkan Mts
Black Sea
Caucasus
El'brus 5642m
Anatolia
Volga
Aral Sea
Lake Balkhash
Tien Shan
Altai Mountains
ASIA
Gobi
Manchurian Plain
Amur
Sakhalin
Hokkaido
Kurile Trench
Aleutian Trench
Emperor Seamounts

Mediterranean Sea
Caspian Sea
Hindu Kush
Pamirs
Kunlun Mountains
Plateau of Tibet
Yellow River
Great Plain of China
Yellow Sea
Sea of Japan
Japan
Honshu
Northwest Pacific Basin

Sahara
Syrian Desert
Dead Sea
Iranian Plateau
Zagros Mts
Himalayas
Mount Everest 8848m
Ganges
Yangtze
East China Sea
Shikoku
Kyushu
Ryukyu Islands
Tropic of Cancer

Ahaggar
Tibesti
Nile
Red Sea
Arabian Peninsula
Indus
Thar Desert
Deccan
Taiwan
Philippine Sea
Mid-Pacific Mountains
Central Pacific Basin

Sahel
Lake Chad
Gulf of Aden
Arabian Sea
Arabian Basin
Western Ghats
Eastern Ghats
Bay of Bengal
Andaman Islands
Mekong
Philippine Islands
Philippine Trench
Mariana Islands
Marshall Islands

Gulf of Guinea
Ethiopian Highlands
Horn of Africa
Somali Plain
Maldive Islands
Sri Lanka
Nicobar Islands
South China Sea
Malay Peninsula
PACIFIC OCEAN
Mariana Trench

Adamawa Highlands
AFRICA
Great Rift Valley
Congo
Congo Basin
Lake Victoria
Kilimanjaro 5895m
Seychelles
Cocos Basin
Sumatra
Borneo
Celebes
Java Sea
New Guinea
Solomon Islands
Equator
Melanesia

Angola Basin
Lake Tanganyika
Lake Nyasa
Zambezi
Mozambique Channel
Madagascar
Mauritius
Réunion
INDIAN OCEAN
Ninetyeast Ridge
Mid Indian Ridge
Java
East Indies
Arafura Sea
Timor Sea
Coral Sea
Vanuatu
Fiji
New Caledonia

Namib Desert
Kalahari Desert
Orange River
Drakensberg
Great Sandy Desert
Great Barrier Reef
Tropic of Capricorn

Cape Basin
Cape of Good Hope
Southwest Indian Ridge
Southeast Indian Ridge
AUSTRALIA
Great Victoria Desert
Nullarbor Plain
Darling
Great Dividing Range

Crozet Islands
Kerguelen
South Indian Basin
Tasmania
Bass Strait
Tasman Sea
New Zealand
North Island
South Island
Aoraki (Mount Cook) 3744m
Campbell Plateau

OCEAN
ANTARCTICA

INDIAN OCEAN
AUSTRALIA
AFRICA
SOUTHERN OCEAN
ANTARCTICA
ATLANTIC OCEAN
PACIFIC OCEAN
Antarctic Circle
SOUTH AMERICA
Tropic of Capricorn

THE EARTH'S STRUCTURE

The shape and position of the Earth's oceans and continents make a familiar pattern. This is just the latest in a series of forms which the Earth has taken in the hundreds of millions of years since its creation. Massive forces inside the Earth cause the continents and oceans to move apart and together again, forming larger landmasses and then breaking them apart – a process known as plate tectonics. The movement is very slow – but over millions of years, the changes can be enormous.

DYNAMIC EARTH

The heart of the Earth is a solid core of iron surrounded by several layers of very hot – sometimes liquid – rock. The crust is relatively thin and is made up of a series of 'plates' which fit closely together. Movement of the molten rock deep within the mantle of the Earth causes the plates to move, creating changes in the surface features of the Earth.

THE EARTH'S PLATES

Continental plate

Oceanic plate

Plate boundary or margin

Continental and oceanic plates are tectonic plates – made from crustal rock on which continents or oceans float

INSIDE THE EARTH

Rocky crust

Outer core – liquid iron and nickel

Inner core – made of iron

Mantle – made from solid and molten rock

TECTONIC PLATES, VOLCANOES AND EARTHQUAKES

▲ Volcanic zone

▨ Earthquake zone on land

⇨ Direction of plate movement

ⵥⵥⵥ Rift valley

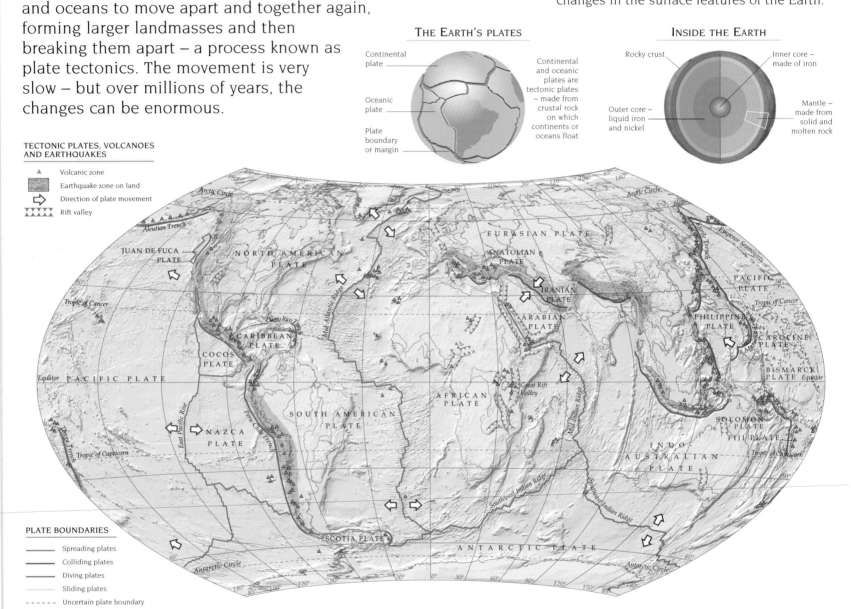

PLATE BOUNDARIES

— Spreading plates

— Colliding plates

— Diving plates

— Sliding plates

- - - Uncertain plate boundary

PLATE BOUNDARIES

The point where two plates meet is known as a plate boundary. As the Earth's plates move together or apart or slide alongside one another, the great forces which result cause great changes in the landscape. Mountains can be created, earthquakes occur and there may be frequent volcanic eruptions.

SPREADING PLATES

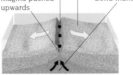

Earthquake zone

Ocean floor

Magma pushed upwards

Solid mantle

As plates move apart, magma rises through the outer mantle. When it cools, it forms new crust. The Mid-Atlantic Ridge is caused by spreading plates.

COLLIDING PLATES

Colliding plate

Mountains thrust upwards

Earthquake zone

When two plates bearing landmasses collide with one another, the land is crumpled upwards into high mountain peaks such as the Alps, and the Himalayas.

DIVING PLATES

Earthquake zone

Mountains

Ocean plate

Continental plate

When an ocean-bearing plate collides with a continental plate it is forced downwards under the other plate and into the mantle. Volcanoes occur along these boundaries.

SLIDING PLATES

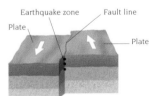

Earthquake zone

Fault line

Plate

Plate

As two plates slide past each other, great friction is set up along the fault line which lies between them. This can lead to powerful earthquakes.

SHAPING THE LANDSCAPE

The Earth's surface is made from solid rock or water. The land is constantly re-shaped by external forces. Water flowing as rivers or in the oceans erodes and deposits material to create valleys and lakes and to shape coastlines. When water is built up and compressed into solid sheets of ice, it can erode more deeply, creating deeper, wider valleys. Wind also has a powerful effect; stripping away vegetation and transporting rock particles vast distances.

RIVERS

Most rivers have their sources in mountain areas. They flow fast through the mountains, eroding deep V-shaped valleys. As they reach flatter areas they begin to meander in great loops, both eroding and then depositing rock particles as they slow down.

GLACIERS

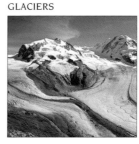

In cold areas, close to the poles or on mountain tops, snow is built up into rivers of ice called glaciers. They move slowly, eroding deep U-shaped valleys. When the glacier melts, ridges of eroded rock called moraines are left at the sides and end of the glacier.

SEA ACTION

The oceans change the landscape in two major ways. They batter cliffs, causing rock to break away and the land to retreat, and they carry eroded material along the coast, to make beaches and sand bars.

WIND

Wind can erode and break down rock into smaller boulders and stones and eventually into sand. Desert sand dunes are shaped by the force of the wind and vary from ripples to hills 200 m high.

LANDSLIDES

Heavy rain can loosen soil and rock beneath the surface of slopes. As this moves, the top layers slip forward, to form heaps of rubble at the base of the slope.

THE WORLD'S OCEANS

Just over two-thirds of the Earth's surface is covered by water and more than 98% of this water is contained in the oceans. Movements within the Earth shape the ocean floor in the same way as they do the land surface, creating mountain ranges, trenches and plateaus, and changing the shape and size of the oceans. The difference between an ocean and a sea is simply its size; oceans are much bigger.

POLAR OCEANS

The Southern and Arctic Oceans contain large icebergs, that have broken away from the ice shelf.

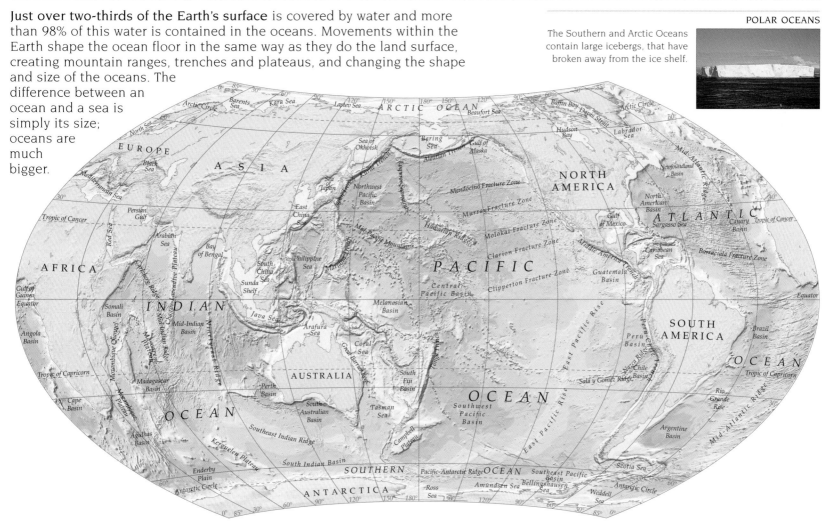

INDIAN OCEAN

The Indian Ocean covers about 20% of the world's surface. Ocean swells, starting deep in the Southern Ocean, often cause flooding in Sri Lanka and the Maldives.

PACIFIC OCEAN

The Pacific is the largest and deepest ocean in the world. It contains an arc of volcanic islands, including Japan, Indonesia and New Guinea, known as the 'Ring of Fire'.

ATLANTIC OCEAN

The Atlantic Ocean was formed about 180 million years ago. The land which now forms Europe and Africa pulled apart from the Americas to create an ocean 3,000 km wide.

CLIMATE AND LIFE ZONES

This map shows the different climates found around the world. Climates are particular combinations of temperature and humidity. Climates are affected by latitude, the height of the land, winds and ocean currents. Climates can change, but not overnight. Weather is local and consists of short-term events such as thunderstorms, hurricanes and blizzards.

HURRICANES

Hurricanes are violent cyclonic windstorms, driven by heat energy gathered from tropical seas. The Caribbean islands and the east coast of the USA are particularly prone to hurricanes.

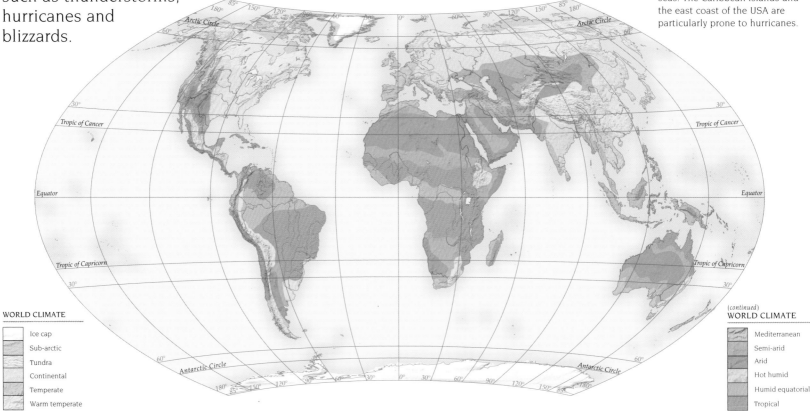

WORLD CLIMATE

- Ice cap
- Sub-arctic
- Tundra
- Continental
- Temperate
- Warm temperate

(continued) WORLD CLIMATE

- Mediterranean
- Semi-arid
- Arid
- Hot humid
- Humid equatorial
- Tropical

WINDS

All over the Earth there are a series of large-scale wind patterns called prevailing winds which have a direct effect on weather and climate. The direction of the wind depends on global air pressure. Winds travel from areas of high pressure to areas of low pressure. The westerlies, polar easterlies, and the northeast and southeast trade winds are all prevailing winds. The Equator is known for its light winds – known as the Doldrums. Changes in the direction of the prevailing winds can have a serious impact on the weather all over the planet.

WINDS

- Cool wind
- Warm wind

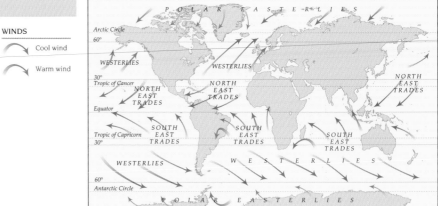

OCEAN CURRENTS

Ocean currents help to distribute heat around the Earth and have a great influence on climate. Convection currents circulate massive amounts of warm and cold water around the oceans. Warm water is moved away from the tropics to higher latitudes and cold water is moved toward the tropics.

OCEAN CURRENTS AND SURFACE TEMPERATURES

- Cold currents
- Warm currents
- El Niño
- 20 – 30°C
- 10 – 20°C
- 0 – 10°C
- Sea-water –2° – 0°C
- Sea-ice (average) below –2°C

LIFE ZONES

The map below shows the Earth divided into different biomes – also called biogeographical regions. The combination of climate, the type of landscape, and the plants and animals that live there, are used to classify a region. Similar biomes are found in very different places around the world.

POLAR REGIONS
The North and South poles are permanently covered by ice. Only a few plants and animals can live here.

TUNDRA
Tundra is flat, cold and dry with few trees. Plants such as mosses and lichens grow close to the ground.

DESERTS
Very little rain falls in desert areas, whether they are hot deserts such as the Sahara or cold deserts like the Gobi.

NEEDLELEAF FORESTS
Tall coniferous trees such as pine and spruce, with spines or needles instead of leaves, grow in the far north of Scandinavia, Canada and the Russian Federation.

BROADLEAF FORESTS
Broadleaf or deciduous forests once covered temperate regions over most of the northern hemisphere. They contain trees of many varieties – all of which shed their leaves every year.

TEMPERATE RAINFORESTS
Evergreen, broadleaved trees need a warmer, wetter climate than deciduous trees. They are known as temperate rainforests.

MEDITERRANEAN
Close to the shores of the Mediterranean Sea, the vegetation consists mainly of herbs, shrubs and drought-resistant trees.

BIOME TYPES

- Mountains
- Polar regions
- Tundra
- Tropical rain forests
- Dry woodlands
- Savanna
- Temperate grasslands

(continued)
BIOME TYPES
- Mediterranean
- Needleleaf forest
- Temperate rainforest
- Broadleaf forest
- Cold desert
- Hot desert
- Wetlands

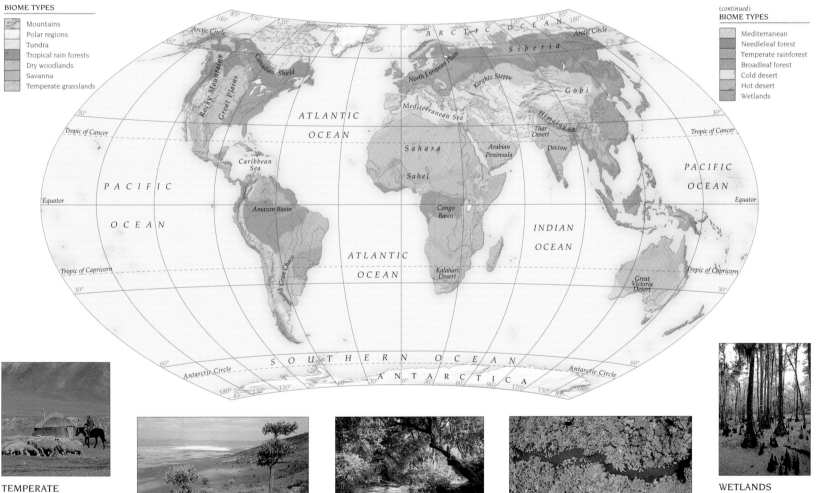

TEMPERATE GRASSLANDS
Grasslands cover the central areas of the continents. They are known in the middle latitudes as prairies, steppe and pampas.

SAVANNAH
The savannah consists of woodland, interspersed with grassland. These regions lie between the tropical rainforest and hot desert regions.

DRY WOODLANDS
Dry woodlands are found at the edge of grasslands. They contain small trees and shrubs adapted to dry conditions.

TROPICAL RAINFORESTS
Around the Equator, where temperatures are high and there is plenty of rain, tropical rainforests can flourish. Trees grow continuously and are tall with huge, broad leaves.

WETLANDS
Low-lying swamps and marshes are known as wetlands. They are often home to a rich variety of animal, plant and bird species.

WORLD POPULATION

There are now nearly six thousand million people on Earth. The population has increased more than three times since 1900. Before that date, the number of people increased slowly as people were born and died at similar rates. With improved living conditions, better medical care and more efficient food production, more people survived to adulthood and the population began to grow much faster. If growth continues at the present rate, the world's population is likely to reach 8.5 billion by the year 2020.

OVERCROWDING

Favelas – or shanty towns – have grown up many South American cities because of overcrowding.

POPULATION STRUCTURES

Measuring the numbers of old and young people gives the age structure of a country or continent. If there are large numbers of young people and a high birth rate, the population is said to be youthful – as is the case in many African, Asian and South American countries. If the birth rate is low but many people survive into old age, the population distribution is said to be ageing – this is true of much of Europe, Japan, Canada and the USA. Extreme events like wars can distort the population, leading to a loss of population in certain age groups.

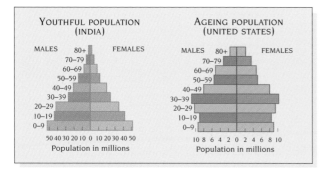

YOUTHFUL POPULATION (INDIA)

MALES   80+   FEMALES
         70–79
         60–69
         50–59
         40–49
         30–39
         20–29
         10–19
         0–9
50 40 30 20 10 0 10 20 30 40 50
Population in millions

AGEING POPULATION (UNITED STATES)

MALES   80+   FEMALES
         70–79
         60–69
         50–59
         40–49
         30–39
         20–29
         10–19
         0–9
10 8 6 4 2 0 2 4 6 8 10
Population in millions

POPULATION DENSITY

The main map (centre) and the map below both show population density – the number of people who live in a given area. The map below shows the average population density per country. You can see that European countries and parts of Asia are very densely populated. The large map shows where people actually live. While the average population density in Brazil and Egypt is quite low, the coasts of Brazil and the areas close to the River Nile in Egypt are very densely populated.

DENSE POPULATION

Huge crowds near the Haora Bridge in Kolkata (Calcutta), India – one of the world's most densely populated cities.

POPULATION DENSITY

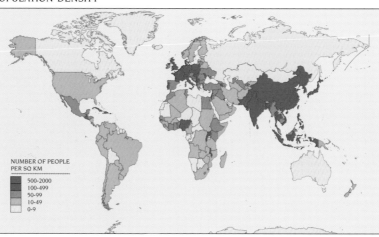

NUMBER OF PEOPLE PER SQ KM

500–2000
100–499
50–99
10–49
0–9

SPARSE POPULATION

The cold north of Canada has one of the lowest population densities in the world. Some people live in extreme isolation, separated from others by lakes and forests.

URBAN GROWTH

The 20th century has seen a huge increase in the number of people living in cities. This has led to more large cities and the development of some 'super cities' such as Mexico City and Tokyo, each with more than 20 million people. In 1900, only about 10% of the population lived in cities. Now it is closer to 50% and soon the figure may be nearer two in three people. Some continents are far more 'urbanized' than others: in South America nearly 80% of people live in cities, whereas in Africa the figure is only about 30%.

LEVELS OF URBANIZATION

URBANIZATION
- 90-100%
- 60-89%
- 40-59%
- 0-39%
- data unavailable

POPULATION GROWTH

The rate of population growth varies dramatically between the continents. Europe has a large population but it is increasing slowly. Africa is still sparsely populated, but in some countries such as Kenya, the population is growing very rapidly, increasing pressure on the land. China and India have the world's largest populations. Both countries now have laws to try and curb the birth rate.

CONTROLLING GROWTH

In 1980, fewer than 25% of women in less developed countries used birth control. Education programmes and more widely available contraceptives are thought to have doubled this figure. But many families still have no access to contraception.

AN AGEING POPULATION

In some countries, a low birth rate, and an increasingly long-lived elderly population has greatly increased the ratio of old people to younger people, putting a strain on health and social services. For example, in Japan, most people can now expect to live to at least 80 years of age.

POPULATION DENSITY
(People per sq km)
- Below 1
- 1–5
- 6–10
- 11–20
- 21–50
- 51–100
- 101–200
- Above 200

BIRTH RATE

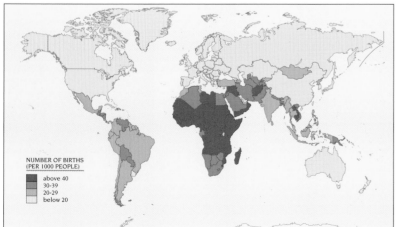

**NUMBER OF BIRTHS
(PER 1000 PEOPLE)**
- above 40
- 30-39
- 20-29
- below 20

LIFE EXPECTANCY

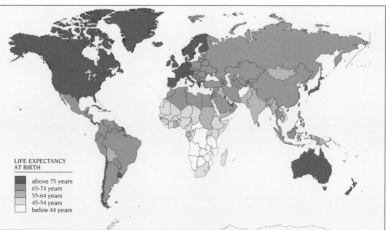

**LIFE EXPECTANCY
AT BIRTH**
- above 75 years
- 65-74 years
- 55-64 years
- 45-54 years
- below 44 years

THE WORLD ECONOMY

Throughout the world, the way in which people make a living varies greatly. The countries of western Europe and North America, along with Japan, are the most economically developed in the world, with a long-established and very diverse range of industries. They sell their products and services internationally. Less economically developed countries in south and central Asia, much of Africa, and Central America have a much smaller number of industries – some may rely on a single product – and many goods are produced only for the local market.

MEASURING WEALTH

The wealth of a country can be measured in several ways: for example, by the average annual income per person; by the volume of its trade; and by the total value of the goods and services that the country produces annually – its Gross Domestic Product or GDP. The map below shows the average GDP per person for each of the world's countries, expressed in $US. Most of the highest levels of GDP are in Europe and the US; most of the lowest are in Africa.

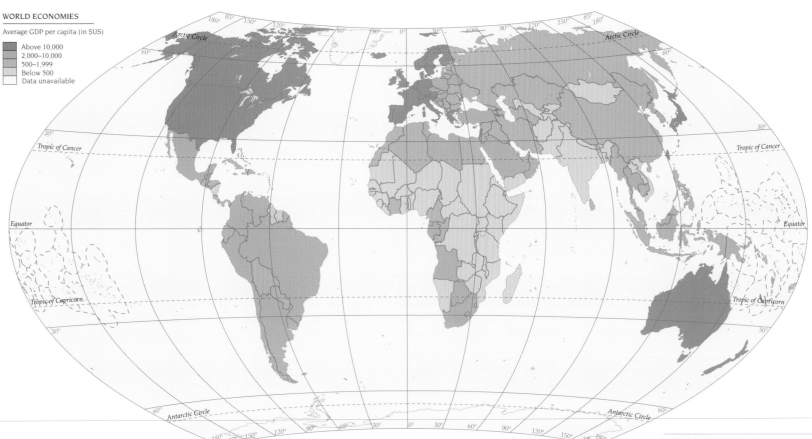

WORLD ECONOMIES

Average GDP per capita (in $US)

- Above 10,000
- 2,000–10,000
- 500–1,999
- Below 500
- Data unavailable

TYPES OF INDUSTRY

Industries are usually defined in one of three ways. Primary industries such as farming or mining involve the production of raw materials such as food or minerals. Secondary industries make or manufacture finished products out of raw materials: clothing and car manufacture are examples of secondary industries. People who work in tertiary industries provide different kinds of services. Banking, insurance and tourism are all examples of tertiary industries. Some economically advanced nations such as Germany or USA now have quaternary industries such as biotechnology which are knowledge-creation industries, devoted to the research and development of new products.

PRIMARY INDUSTRY

Tobacco leaves are picked and laid out for drying in Cuba, one of the world's great producers of cigars. Many countries rely on one or two high-value 'cash crops' like tobacco to earn foreign currency.

SECONDARY INDUSTRY

This skilled Thai weaver is producing an intricately patterned silk fabric on a hand loom. Fabric manufacture is an important industry throughout South and Southeast Asia. In India and Pakistan, vast quantities of cotton are produced in highly mechanized factories, but many fabrics are still hand woven.

TERTIARY INDUSTRY

The City of London is one of the world's great finance centres. Branches of many banks and insurance companies, including the world famous Lloyds of London, are clustered into the City's 'square mile'.

PATTERNS OF TRADE

Almost all countries trade goods with one another in order to obtain products they cannot produce themselves, and to make money from goods they have produced. Some countries – for example those in the Caribbean – rely mainly on a single export, usually a foodstuff or mineral, and can suffer a loss of income when world prices drop. Other countries, such as Germany and Japan, export a vast range of both raw materials and manufactured goods throughout the world. A number of huge companies, known as transnational corporations or TNCs, are responsible for more than 70% of world trade, with divisions all over the world. They include firms like BP, Coca Cola and IBM.

CONTAINER SHIPS

Many products are transported around the world on container ships. Containers are of a standard size so that they can be efficiently transported to their destinations. Some ships are specially designed to carry perishable goods such as fruit and vegetables.

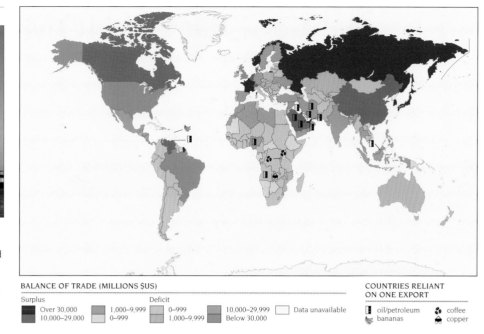

BALANCE OF TRADE (MILLIONS $US)

Surplus		Deficit		
Over 30,000	1,000–9,999	0–999	10,000–29,999	Data unavailable
10,000–29,000	0–999	1,000–9,999	Below 30,000	

COUNTRIES RELIANT ON ONE EXPORT

- oil/petroleum
- coffee
- bananas
- copper

MEXICO
BRAZIL
SINGAPORE
MALAYSIA
INDONESIA
PHILIPPINES
TAIWAN
SOUTH KOREA

DEVELOPING ECONOMIES

Although world trade is still dominated by the more economically developed countries, since the 1970s, less economically developed countries have increased their share of world trade from less than 10% to nearly 20%. Countries such as Brazil, Mexico, Malaysia and South Korea, aided by investment from their governments or from wealthier countries, were able to begin to manufacture and export a wide variety of goods. Products include cars, electronic goods, clothing and footwear. Multinational companies can take advantage of cheaper labour costs to manufacture goods in these countries. Moves are being made to limit the exploitation of workers who are paid low wages for producing luxury goods.

ASIAN 'TIGER' ECONOMIES

The economies of Malaysia, Taiwan and South Korea, boomed in the late 1980s, attracting investment for buildings such as the Petronas Towers.

TOURISM

Tourism is now the world's largest industry. More than 500 million people travel both abroad and in their own countries as tourists each year. People in more developed countries have more money and leisure time to travel. Tourism can bring large amounts of cash into the local economy, but local people do not always benefit. They may have to take low-paid jobs and experience great intrusions into their lives. Tourist development and pollution may damage the environment – sometimes destroying the very attractions that led to the development of tourism in the first place.

ECOTOURISM

These tourists are being introduced to a giant tortoise, one of the many unique animals found in the Galapagos Islands. A number of places with special animals and ecosystems have introduced schemes to teach visitors about them. This not only educates more people about the need to safeguard these environments, but brings in money to help protect them.

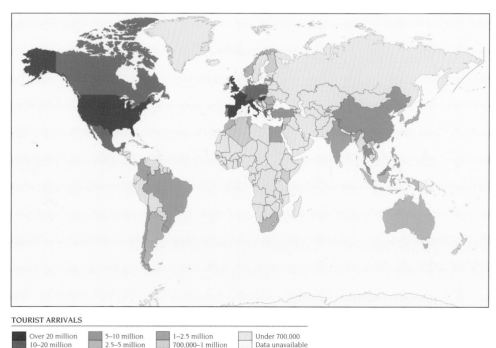

TOURIST ARRIVALS

Over 20 million	5–10 million	1–2.5 million	Under 700,000
10–20 million	2.5–5 million	700,000–1 million	Data unavailable

BORDERS AND BOUNDARIES

There are more countries in the world today than ever before – over 190 – whereas in 1950, there were only 82. Since then, many former European colonies and Soviet states have become independent. The establishment of borders for each of these countries has often been the subject of disagreement.

Military borders
At the end of wars, new borders are often drawn up between the countries – frequently along ceasefire lines. They may remain there for many years. At the end of the Korean War in 1953, North and South Korea were divided close to the 38° line of latitude. This border has remained heavily fortified.

Enclaves
If part of a country's territory has become separated from the rest of the country, and is surrounded by foreign territory, it is called an enclave. Kaliningrad is part of the Russian Federation, but is cut off from it by Lithuania and Belarus.

River borders
Over one-sixth of the world's national borders are formed by rivers. Long stretches of the Danube form natural borders in southeastern Europe.

The longest border
The border between the USA and Canada is the longest continuous border in the world. It cuts through the centre of the Great Lakes. To the west of the Great Lakes, the border runs along the 49° line of latitude.

Mountain borders
Mountain ranges such as the Pyrenees, Alps and Himalayas form natural borders between many countries. In the Andes, border disputes between Chile and Argentina centred on finding the highest point in the mountain range which divided them.

Straight line borders
The borders of many countries in Africa and other former colonial territories are straight lines. This was the simplest solution for colonial administrators, who often knew little of the country's geography or population.

Lake boundaries
Countries which lie next to lakes usually fix their borders in the middle of the lake. Complicated agreements between colonial powers led to the awkward division of Lake Nyasa in Africa.

Territorial disputes
There are still many disputed territories and borders. One of the most serious territorial disputes is between India and Pakistan over Jammu and Kashmir, which has led to three wars since 1947.

THE ATLAS
OF THE
WORLD

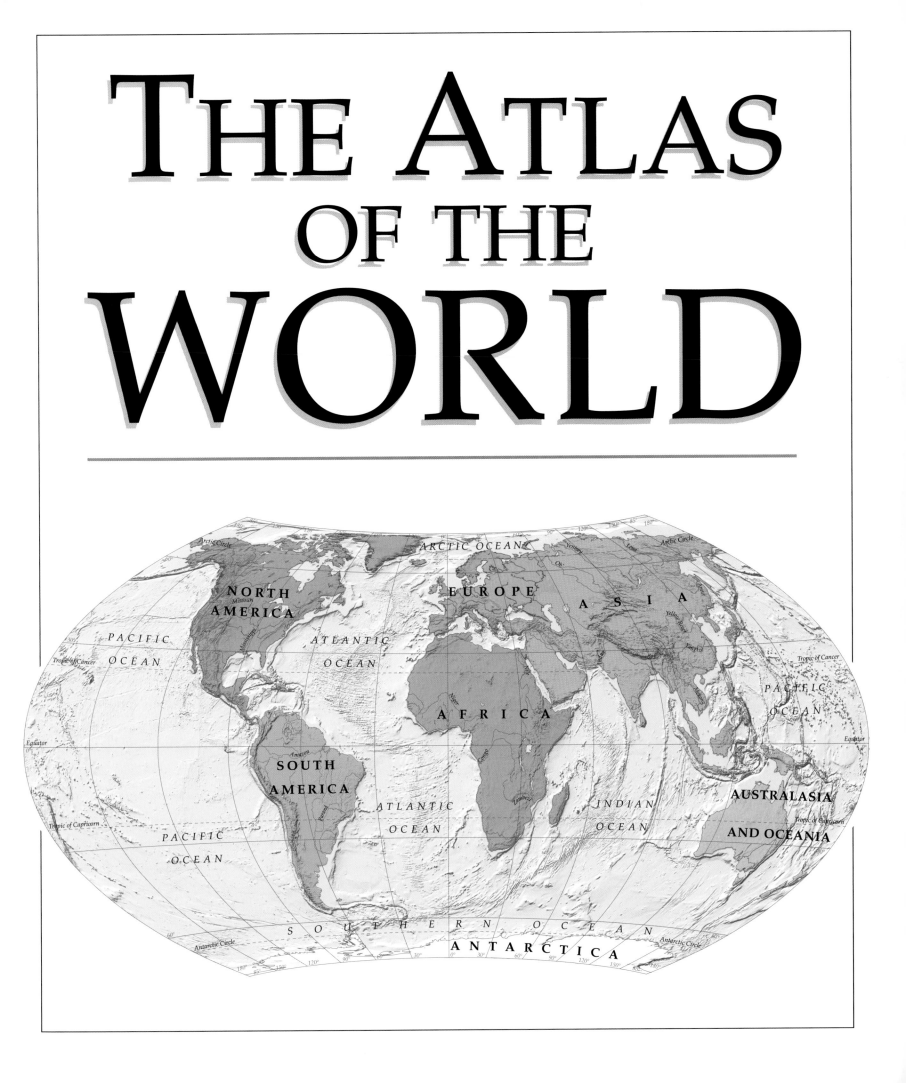

THE NATIONS OF THE WORLD

The world is divided into 193 independent countries, and about 60 overseas territories or dependencies. The largest country is the Russian Federation covering 17,075,200 sq km; the smallest is Vatican City in Rome, with an area of 0.44 sq km.

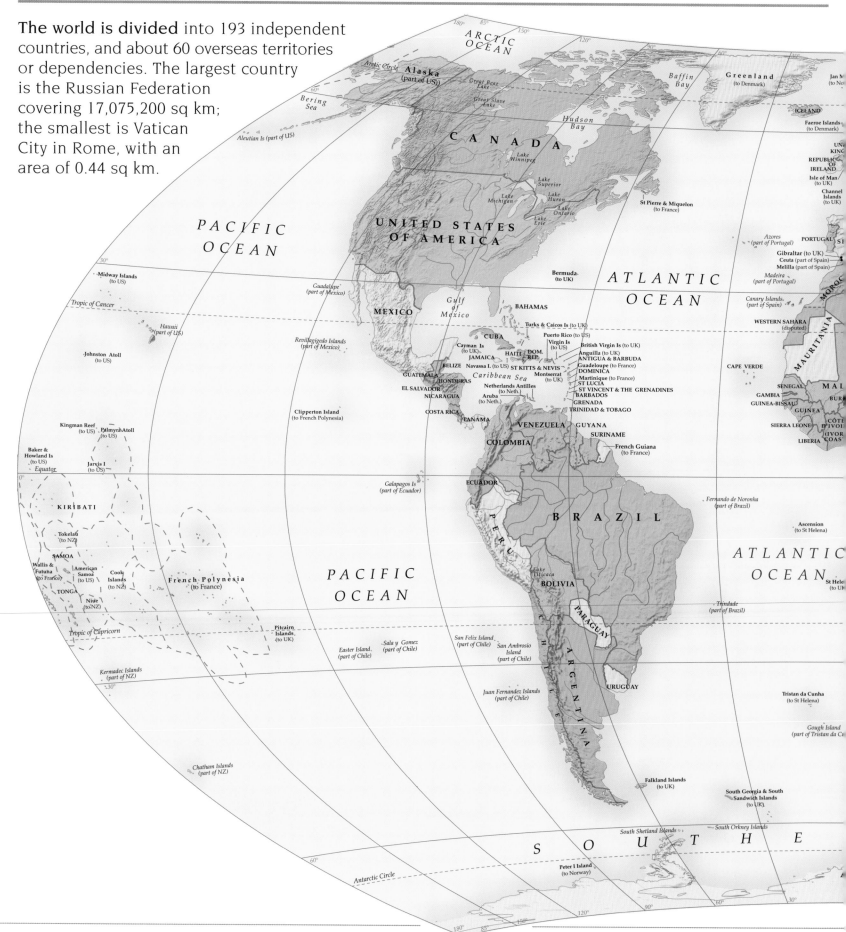

ARCTIC OCEAN

Arctic Circle

Alaska (part of US)

Bering Sea

Aleutian Is (part of US)

Great Bear Lake

Great Slave Lake

CANADA

Lake Winnipeg

Lake Superior

Lake Michigan

Lake Huron

Lake Ontario

Lake Erie

UNITED STATES OF AMERICA

Hudson Bay

Baffin Bay

Greenland (to Denmark)

Jan M (to No

ICELAND

Faeroe Islands (to Denmark)

UN KING

REPUBLIC OF IRELAND

Isle of Man (to UK)

Channel Islands (to UK)

St Pierre & Miquelon (to France)

PACIFIC OCEAN

Midway Islands (to US)

Tropic of Cancer

Hawaii (part of US)

Johnston Atoll (to US)

Guadalupe (part of Mexico)

MEXICO

Gulf of Mexico

BAHAMAS

Bermuda (to UK)

ATLANTIC OCEAN

Revillagigedo Islands (part of Mexico)

Turks & Caicos Is (to UK)

CUBA

Cayman Is (to UK)

JAMAICA

HAITI

DOM. REP.

Puerto Rico (to US)

Virgin Is (to US)

British Virgin Is (to UK)

Anguilla (to UK)

ANTIGUA & BARBUDA

Guadeloupe (to France)

DOMINICA

Martinique (to France)

ST LUCIA

ST VINCENT & THE GRENADINES

BARBADOS

GRENADA

TRINIDAD & TOBAGO

BELIZE

Navassa I. (to US)

ST KITTS & NEVIS

Montserrat (to UK)

GUATEMALA

HONDURAS

EL SALVADOR

NICARAGUA

Caribbean Sea

Netherlands Antilles (to Neth.)

Aruba (to Neth.)

COSTA RICA

PANAMA

Clipperton Island (to French Polynesia)

VENEZUELA

GUYANA

SURINAME

French Guiana (to France)

COLOMBIA

Galapagos Is (part of Ecuador)

ECUADOR

PERU

BRAZIL

Fernando de Noronha (part of Brazil)

Azores (part of Portugal)

PORTUGAL

Gibraltar (to UK)

Ceuta (part of Spain)

Melilla (part of Spain)

Madeira (part of Portugal)

Canary Islands (part of Spain)

WESTERN SAHARA (disputed)

MAURITANIA

MORO

CAPE VERDE

SENEGAL

GAMBIA

GUINEA-BISSAU

GUINEA

SIERRA LEONE

LIBERIA

MAL

BUR

CÔTE D'IVOI (IVOR COAS

Ascension (to St Helena)

ATLANTIC OCEAN

St Hele (to U

Kingman Reef (to US)

Palmyra Atoll (to US)

Baker & Howland Is (to US)

Jarvis I (to US)

Equator

KIRIBATI

Tokelau (to NZ)

SAMOA

Wallis & Futuna (to France)

American Samoa (to US)

Cook Islands (to NZ)

TONGA

Niue (to NZ)

French Polynesia (to France)

PACIFIC OCEAN

Lake Titicaca

BOLIVIA

Trindade (part of Brazil)

Tropic of Capricorn

Pitcairn Islands (to UK)

Easter Island (part of Chile)

Sala y Gomez (part of Chile)

San Felix Island (part of Chile)

San Ambrosio Island (part of Chile)

CHILE

PARAGUAY

ARGENTINA

Kermadec Islands (part of NZ)

Juan Fernandez Islands (part of Chile)

URUGUAY

Tristan da Cunha (to St Helena)

Gough Island (part of Tristan da Cu

Chatham Islands (part of NZ)

Falkland Islands (to UK)

South Georgia & South Sandwich Islands (to UK)

South Shetland Islands

South Orkney Islands

SOUTHE

Antarctic Circle

Peter I Island (to Norway)

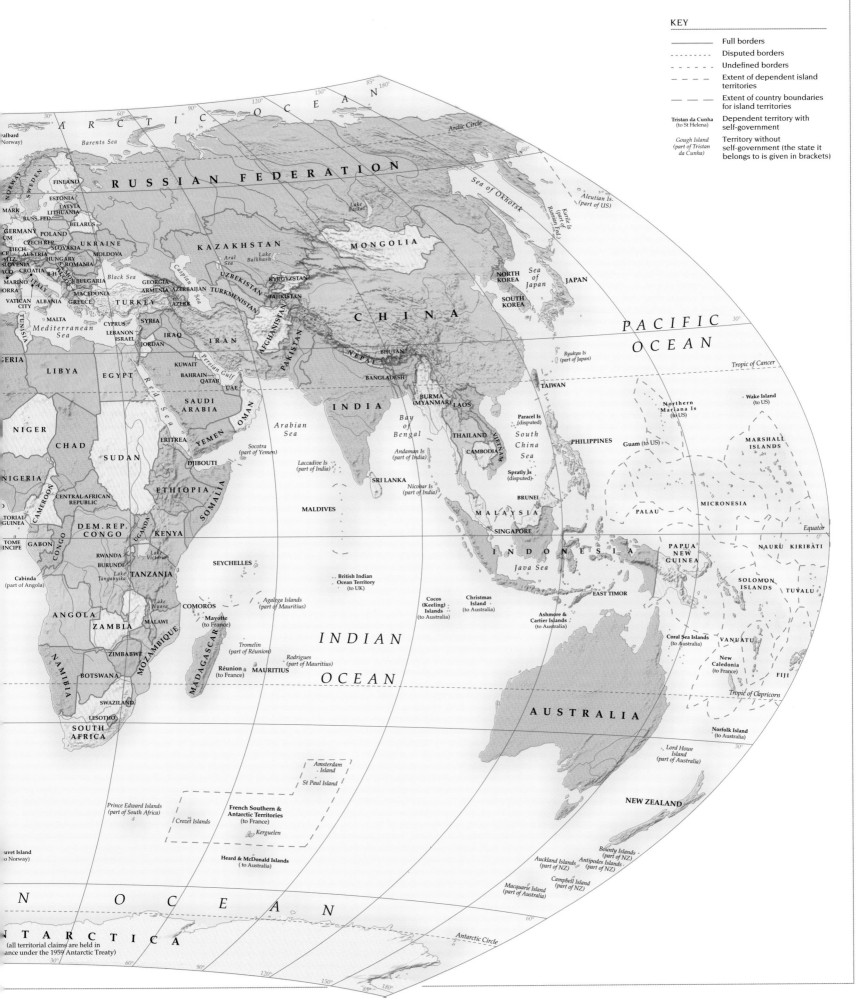

KEY

———————— Full borders

--------- Disputed borders

— — — — Undefined borders

– – – – Extent of dependent island
territories

— — — Extent of country boundaries
for island territories

Tristan da Cunha
(to St Helena)   Dependent territory with
self-government

Gough Island
(part of Tristan
da Cunha)   Territory without
self-government (the state it
belongs to is given in brackets)

ARCTIC   OCEAN

Barents Sea

Arctic Circle

valbard
(part of Norway)

NORWAY

SWEDEN

FINLAND

ESTONIA

MARK

LATVIA
LITHUANIA

RUSS. FED.

BELARUS

GERMANY

POLAND

UM

CZECH REP.

UKRAINE

LIECH.

SLOVAKIA

VITZ.

AUSTRIA

HUNGARY

MOLDOVA

SLOVENIA

ROMANIA

ACO

CROATIA

BH

BULGARIA

MARINO

ITALY

Black Sea

GEORGIA

MARINO

Caspian Sea

MACEDONIA

ARMENIA

AZERBAIJAN

VATICAN
CITY

ALBANIA

GREECE

TURKEY

AZERB.

MALTA

CYPRUS

SYRIA

TUNISIA

Mediterranean
Sea

LEBANON

ISRAEL

IRAQ

JORDAN

ERIA

LIBYA

EGYPT

KUWAIT

Persian Gulf

BAHRAIN
QATAR

UAE

NIGER

CHAD

SUDAN

SAUDI
ARABIA

OMAN

Red Sea

YEMEN

Socotra
(part of Yemen)

ERITREA

DJIBOUTI

NIGERIA

CENTRAL AFRICAN
REPUBLIC

ETHIOPIA

SOMALIA

CAMEROON

TORIAL
GUINEA

TOME
INCIPE

GABON

CONGO

DEM. REP.
CONGO

UGANDA

KENYA

RWANDA

BURUNDI

Lake
Victoria

Cabinda
(part of Angola)

TANZANIA

Lake
Tanganyika

SEYCHELLES

British Indian
Ocean Territory
(to UK)

Lake
Nyasa

COMOROS

Mayotte
(to France)

Agalega Islands
(part of Mauritius)

ANGOLA

ZAMBIA

MALAWI

Tromelin
(part of Réunion)

ZIMBABWE

MOZAMBIQUE

MADAGASCAR

Rodrigues
(part of Mauritius)

Réunion
(to France)

MAURITIUS

NAMIBIA

BOTSWANA

SWAZILAND

LESOTHO

SOUTH
AFRICA

RUSSIAN   FEDERATION

Lake
Baikal

Sea of Okhotsk

KAZAKHSTAN

MONGOLIA

Aral
Sea

Lake
Balkhash

UZBEKISTAN

KYRGYZSTAN

TURKMENISTAN

TAJIKISTAN

AFGHANISTAN

CHINA

NORTH
KOREA

Sea
of
Japan

JAPAN

SOUTH
KOREA

Aleutian Is.
(part of US)

Kurile Is
(part of
Russian Fed.)

IRAN

PAKISTAN

NEPAL

BHUTAN

BANGLADESH

INDIA

BURMA
(MYANMAR)

LAOS

Ryukyu Is
(part of Japan)

PACIFIC
OCEAN

Tropic of Cancer

TAIWAN

Arabian
Sea

Bay
of
Bengal

Andaman Is.
(part of India)

THAILAND

VIETNAM

Paracel Is
(disputed)

South
China
Sea

PHILIPPINES

Wake Island
(to US)

Northern
Mariana Is
(to US)

Laccadive Is
(part of India)

CAMBODIA

Guam (to US)

MARSHALL
ISLANDS

SRI LANKA

Nicobar Is
(part of India)

Spratly Is
(disputed)

MALDIVES

BRUNEI

PALAU

MICRONESIA

MALAYSIA

Equator

SINGAPORE

INDONESIA

PAPUA
NEW
GUINEA

NAURU   KIRIBATI

Java Sea

INDIAN

OCEAN

EAST TIMOR

Cocos
(Keeling)
Islands
(to Australia)

Christmas
Island
(to Australia)

Ashmore &
Cartier Islands
(to Australia)

Coral Sea Islands
(to Australia)

SOLOMON
ISLANDS

TUVALU

VANUATU

New
Caledonia
(to France)

FIJI

Tropic of Capricorn

AUSTRALIA

Norfolk Island
(to Australia)

Lord Howe
Island
(part of Australia)

Amsterdam
Island

St Paul Island

NEW ZEALAND

Prince Edward Islands
(part of South Africa)

French Southern &
Antarctic Territories
(to France)

Crozet Islands

Kerguelen

Bounty Islands
(part of NZ)

uvet Island
(o Norway)

Heard & McDonald Islands
(to Australia)

Auckland Islands
(part of NZ)

Antipodes Islands
(part of NZ)

Macquarie
Island
(part of Australia)

Campbell Island
(part of NZ)

N   OCEAN

NTARCTICA
(all territorial claims are held in
ance under the 1959 Antarctic Treaty)

Antarctic Circle

CONTINENTAL NORTH AMERICA

North America is the world's third largest continent, stretching from icy Greenland to the tropical Caribbean. The first people came from Asia more than 20,000 years ago. Their descendants spread across the continent, ate fish, meat, and wild and cultivated plants, and developed a wide variety of cultures and languages. About 500 years ago, immigrants from Europe, Africa, and Asia began to arrive in North America, bringing their own languages and cultures.

CROSS-SECTION THROUGH NORTH AMERICA

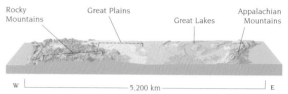

In the west, the land rises from the Pacific Ocean to the coastal ranges and the Rocky Mountains. Further east, the continent flattens into the Great Plains and the Great Lakes – gouged out by glaciers at the end of the last Ice Age. The Appalachian Mountains are older than the Rockies, and very worn down.

PHYSICAL NORTH AMERICA

The high peaks of the Rocky Mountains of Canada and the USA tower above the lower ranges of the western coasts. These ranges stretch from the icy north of Alaska, south to Mexico and Central America. The heart of the continent is flatter, and much of it is drained by the mighty Mississippi-Missouri river system.

1 THE FAR NORTH

Much of Canada's far north is covered by ice and snow. Only in summer, when the ice thaws, can hardy lichens grow. Great pine forests are found further south.

2 THE MOUNTAINOUS WEST

A huge mountain chain runs down the western side of the continent. These mountains are young, and are still being formed.

3 THE GREAT PLAINS

The fertile soils of much of the Great Plains – at the heart of the continent – allow cereal crops like wheat and corn to be grown.

THE DESERT REGIONS 4

The Sonoran Desert, in southwestern USA, is typical of North America's extensive desert regions.

5 THE TROPICAL SOUTH

The Yucatan Peninsula, in Mexico, is full of caves and sinkholes because the humid tropical climate accelerates erosion.

ELEVATION

6000m
5000m
4000m
3000m
2000m
1000m
500m
250m
100m
sea level
below sea level
cross-section

SCALE 1:52,000,000

0 km   500   1000

0 miles 250   500   750   1000

POLITICAL NORTH AMERICA

The USA, Canada and Mexico are all federal countries. This means that political power is shared between the national government and the state or provincial governments. Canada and the USA are democracies with a long history of freedom and equal rights. Governments in the countries south of the USA have been less stable, often ruled by dictators or harsh regimes. Many people have suffered for their political beliefs. Until about 20 years ago many of the Caribbean islands were ruled by European countries as colonies.

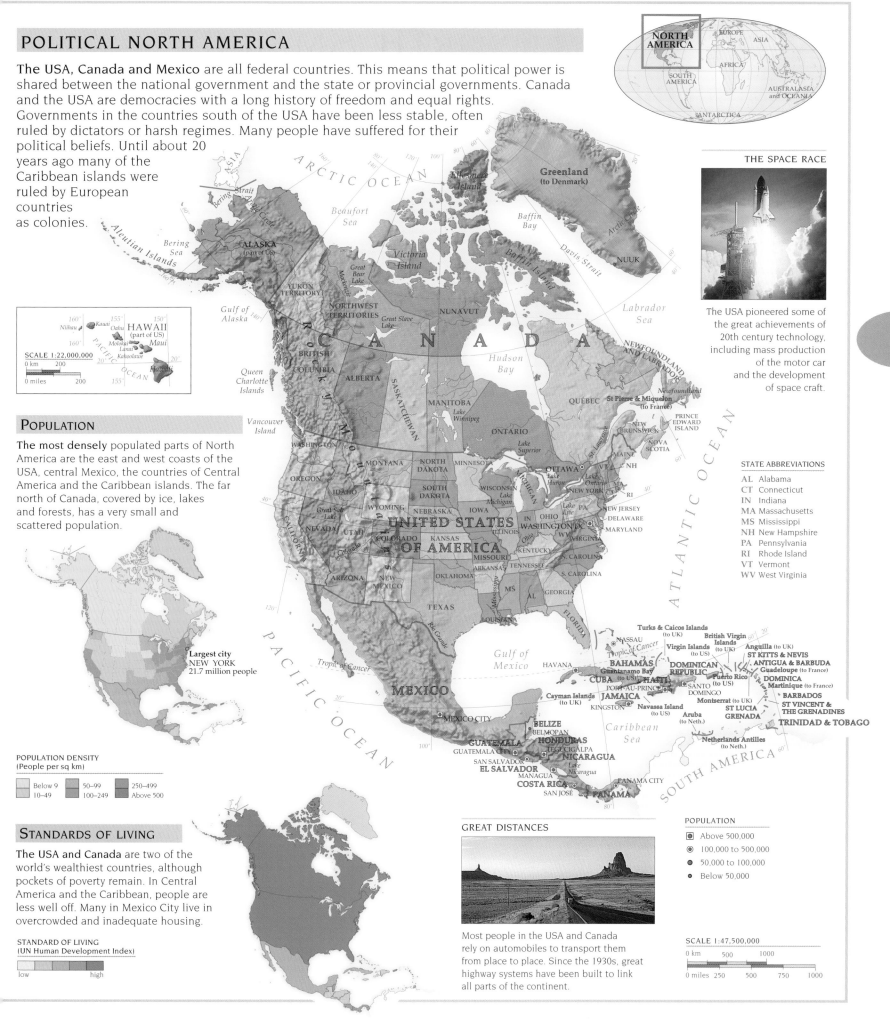

THE SPACE RACE

The USA pioneered some of the great achievements of 20th century technology, including mass production of the motor car and the development of space craft.

POPULATION

The most densely populated parts of North America are the east and west coasts of the USA, central Mexico, the countries of Central America and the Caribbean islands. The far north of Canada, covered by ice, lakes and forests, has a very small and scattered population.

Largest city
NEW YORK
21.7 million people

POPULATION DENSITY
(People per sq km)

- Below 9
- 10–49
- 50–99
- 100–249
- 250–499
- Above 500

STANDARDS OF LIVING

The USA and Canada are two of the world's wealthiest countries, although pockets of poverty remain. In Central America and the Caribbean, people are less well off. Many in Mexico City live in overcrowded and inadequate housing.

STANDARD OF LIVING
(UN Human Development Index)

low   high

GREAT DISTANCES

Most people in the USA and Canada rely on automobiles to transport them from place to place. Since the 1930s, great highway systems have been built to link all parts of the continent.

STATE ABBREVIATIONS

AL Alabama
CT Connecticut
IN Indiana
MA Massachusetts
MS Mississippi
NH New Hampshire
PA Pennsylvania
RI Rhode Island
VT Vermont
WV West Virginia

POPULATION

- ◉ Above 500,000
- ◎ 100,000 to 500,000
- ● 50,000 to 100,000
- • Below 50,000

SCALE 1:47,500,000

HAWAII (part of US)
SCALE 1:22,000,000

NORTH AMERICAN GEOGRAPHY

Canada and the USA are among the world's wealthiest countries. They have rich natural resources, good farmland and thriving, varied industries. The range of different industries in Mexico is growing, but other Central American countries and the Caribbean islands rely on one or two important cash crops and tourism for most of their incomes. They have a lower standard of living than Canada and the USA.

MINERAL RESOURCES

North America still has large amounts of mineral resources. Canada has important nickel reserves, Mexico is renowned for its silver, and bauxite – used to make aluminum – is found in Jamaica. Oil and gas are plentiful, particularly in the arctic northwest by the Beaufort Sea, and further south by the Gulf of Mexico.

INDUSTRY

The USA and Canada have an extremely wide range of industries, from mining and the processing of farm produce, to heavy and light manufacturing and service industries like banking. A variety of goods are produced, including aeroplanes, cars and computers. Oil exports and machine assembly are Mexico's main industries. In Central America and the Caribbean nations, most industry is based on agricultural produce.

MINERAL RESOURCES

- Bauxite
- Copper
- Iron
- Nickel
- Phosphates
- Silver
- Uranium
- ☐ Oil/gas field
- ☐ Coal field

TIMBER PROCESSING

Huge tracts of forest are found toward the north of the continent; over 40% of Canada is covered by forest. Timber is processed to make paper in cities such as Portland and Vancouver.

HI-TECH INDUSTRY

The Santa Clara Valley, just south of San Francisco is also known as Silicon Valley, because of the number of firms producing computer hardware and software and micro-electronics which have set up in the area.

FOOD PROCESSING

Jamaica has been famous for its rum since the 16th century. Syrup is extracted from sugar cane which is then fermented to make rum.

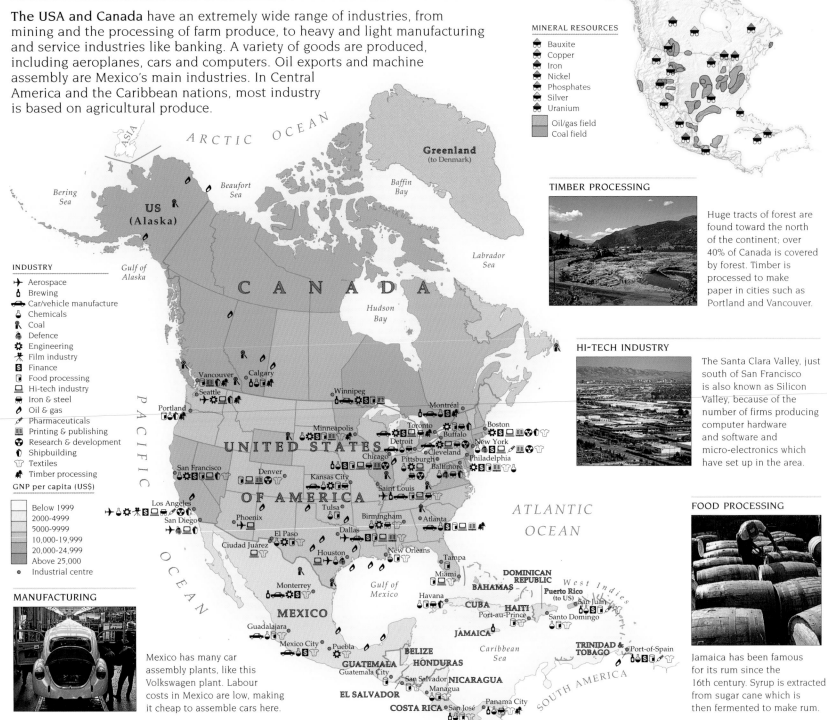

INDUSTRY

- ✈ Aerospace
- ♦ Brewing
- 🚗 Car/vehicle manufacture
- 🜍 Chemicals
- ⚒ Coal
- ⚓ Defence
- ✿ Engineering
- ✈ Film industry
- $ Finance
- ▣ Food processing
- 🖥 Hi-tech industry
- 🚂 Iron & steel
- ♦ Oil & gas
- ⚗ Pharmaceuticals
- ▦ Printing & publishing
- ☢ Research & development
- ⚓ Shipbuilding
- ♈ Textiles
- 🌲 Timber processing

GNP per capita (US$)

- Below 1999
- 2000-4999
- 5000-9999
- 10,000-19,999
- 20,000-24,999
- Above 25,000
- • Industrial centre

MANUFACTURING

Mexico has many car assembly plants, like this Volkswagen plant. Labour costs in Mexico are low, making it cheap to assemble cars here.

CLIMATE

Much of northern Canada lies within the Arctic Circle and is permanently covered by ice or the sparse vegetation known as tundra. Southern Canada and much of central USA have a continental climate, with hot summers and cold winters. The southern parts of the USA, Central America and the Caribbean have a hot, humid tropical climate. The Caribbean and the eastern and central states of the USA often experience hurricane-force winds, waterspouts and tornadoes.

Coldest place
NORTHICE (Greenland)
Temperature -66°C

Wettest place
HENDERSON LAKE (BC, Canada)
Annual rainfall 6650mm

Hottest place
DEATH VALLEY (CA, USA)
Temperature 57°C

Driest place
BATAQUES (Mexico)
Annual rainfall 30mm

EXTREME WEATHER EVENTS

Symbols indicate climatic extremes

CLIMATE

- Ice cap
- Tundra
- Sub-arctic
- Cool continental
- Warm temperate
- Mediterranean
- Semi-arid
- Arid
- Humid equatorial
- Tropical
- Hot Humid

NORTH AMERICA'S HOTTEST PLACE

Death Valley in California is the hottest and driest place in the USA. Strong, dry winds sweep through the valley, constantly reshaping the sand and salt deposits which cover its floor.

LAND USE AND AGRICULTURE

On the great plains and prairies of the USA and Canada, vast quantities of cereal crops, including corn and wheat, grow in the fertile soils. Cattle are also raised on great ranches throughout these regions and on the foothills of the Rocky Mountains. In California, vegetables and fruits are grown with the aid of irrigation. Bananas, coffee and sugar cane are grown for export in Central America and the Caribbean, while sorghum and maize are grown as subsistence crops.

BANANA PLANTATION

Banana plantations are common in the Caribbean and Central America. The fruit is grown for local consumption and for export to the USA and Europe, where they are valued for their flavour and nutritional qualities.

FISHING

The Grand Banks off the eastern coast of Canada were once home to almost limitless fish stocks. Overfishing has reduced the number of fish to very low levels. Quotas limiting the numbers of fish caught are helping numbers to rise.

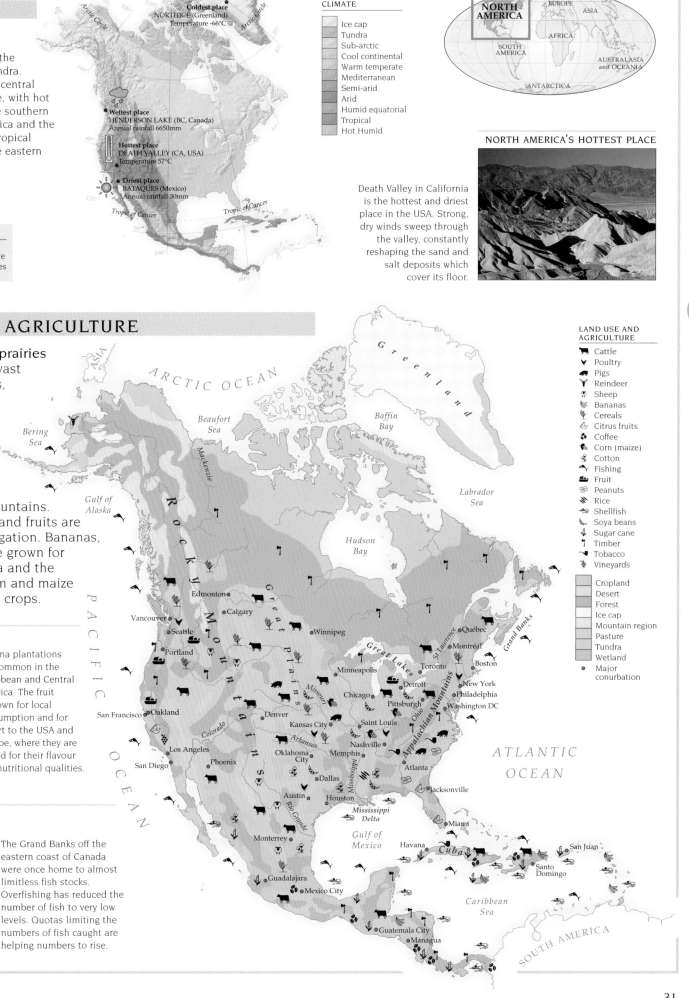

LAND USE AND AGRICULTURE

- 🐄 Cattle
- 🦃 Poultry
- 🐖 Pigs
- 🦌 Reindeer
- 🐑 Sheep
- 🍌 Bananas
- 🌾 Cereals
- 🍊 Citrus fruits
- ☕ Coffee
- 🌽 Corn (maize)
- Cotton
- 🎣 Fishing
- 🍎 Fruit
- 🥜 Peanuts
- Rice
- 🦐 Shellfish
- Soya beans
- Sugar cane
- Timber
- Tobacco
- Vineyards

- Cropland
- Desert
- Forest
- Ice cap
- Mountain region
- Pasture
- Tundra
- Wetland
- ● Major conurbation

EASTERN CANADA

NEW BRUNSWICK, NEWFOUNDLAND AND LABRADOR,
NOVA SCOTIA, ONTARIO, PRINCE EDWARD ISLAND, QUÉBEC

The first European settlements grew up in the Atlantic provinces, and along the St. Lawrence River, where Québec City and Montréal were founded. People gradually migrated further west along the St. Lawrence River and the Great Lakes, establishing other cities including Toronto. Although the majority of Canadians speak English, people in Québec speak mainly French, and both English and French are official languages in Canada.

INDUSTRY

In the Atlantic provinces the traditional fishing industry has declined, causing unemployment. However, Newfoundland has a thriving food processing industry. Ontario and Québec have a wide range of industries, including the generation of hydro-electricity, mining, and chemicals, car manufacture and fruit canning in the great cities. Large amounts of wood pulp and paper are also produced.

STRUCTURE
OF INDUSTRY

Primary 3%
Services 66%
Manufacturing 31%

INDUSTRY

- Car manufacture
- Chemicals
- Fish processing
- Food processing
- Hydro-electric power
- Metal refining
- Mining
- Timber processing
- Hi-tech industry
- Tourism
- Major industrial centre / area
- Major road

FARMING AND LAND USE

The best farmland lies on the flat, fertile plains close to the St. Lawrence River and on the strip of land between lakes Erie and Ontario. It is used to grow fruits such as grapes, cherries and peaches, and to raise cattle. Nova Scotia has fruit farms, and the rich red soils of Prince Edward Island produce a big crop of potatoes. The vast forests that grow across the north are a major source of timber.

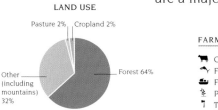

LAND USE

Pasture 2% Cropland 2%
Other (including mountains) 32%
Forest 64%

FARMING AND LAND USE

- Cattle
- Fishing
- Fruit
- Potatoes
- Timber
- Pasture
- Cropland
- Forest
- Tundra
- Major conurbation

ENVIRONMENTAL ISSUES

Acid rain caused by emissions from factories in the USA and along the St. Lawrence River destroys forests and kills marine life. Massive hydro-electric power projects in James Bay on Hudson Bay have flooded huge areas of land, affecting the environment and the local Cree people. Overfishing in the Atlantic has led to limits being set on the number of fish that can be caught.

ENVIRONMENTAL ISSUES

- Depleted fish stocks
- Major dam
- Urban air pollution
- Affected by acid rain
- Major industrial centre

THE LANDSCAPE

A huge, ancient mass of rock called the Canadian Shield lies beneath much of eastern Canada. It is covered by low hills, rocky outcrops, thousands of lakes and huge areas of forest. Much of the Canadian Shield is permanently frozen. The St. Lawrence River flows out of Lake Ontario and on into the Atlantic Ocean. It is surrounded by rolling hills and flat areas of very fertile farmland.

Scoured by ice

About 20,000 years ago, Labrador and northern Québec were completely covered by ice. The glaciers scraped hollows in the rock beneath. When the ice melted, lakes were left in the hollows that remained.

Lake Superior (B 5)

Lake Superior is the largest freshwater lake in the world. It covers an area of 83,270 sq km and lies between Canada and the USA.

St. Lawrence River (E 5)

The St. Lawrence River is 1,197 km long. Parts of it have become silted up, causing it to be 'braided' into many different channels. Between December and mid-April the river freezes over.

Highlands

The highlands of New Brunswick, Nova Scotia and Newfoundland are the most northerly part of the Appalachian mountain chain.

The Bay of Fundy (F 5)

This bay has the world's highest tides. It is shaped like a funnel, and as the Atlantic flows into it, the ever narrowing shores cause the water level to rise 6–15 m at every high tide.

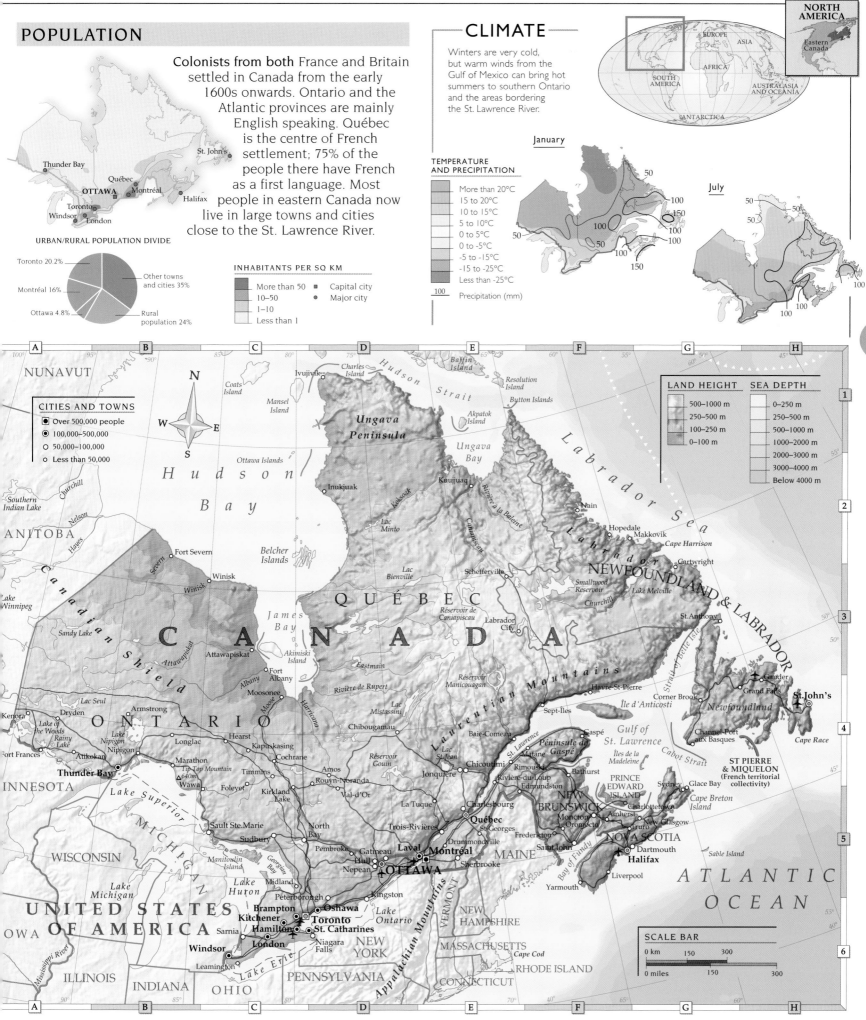

POPULATION

Colonists from both France and Britain settled in Canada from the early 1600s onwards. Ontario and the Atlantic provinces are mainly English speaking. Québec is the centre of French settlement; 75% of the people there have French as a first language. Most people in eastern Canada now live in large towns and cities close to the St. Lawrence River.

Thunder Bay
St. John's
Québec
OTTAWA
Montréal
Toronto
Halifax
Windsor
London

URBAN/RURAL POPULATION DIVIDE

Toronto 20.2%
Other towns and cities 35%
Montréal 16%
Ottawa 4.8%
Rural population 24%

INHABITANTS PER SQ KM

- More than 50
- 10–50
- 1–10
- Less than 1
- ■ Capital city
- ● Major city

CLIMATE

Winters are very cold, but warm winds from the Gulf of Mexico can bring hot summers to southern Ontario and the areas bordering the St. Lawrence River.

NORTH AMERICA
Eastern Canada

EUROPE
ASIA
AFRICA
SOUTH AMERICA
AUSTRALASIA AND OCEANIA
ANTARCTICA

January

TEMPERATURE AND PRECIPITATION

- More than 20°C
- 15 to 20°C
- 10 to 15°C
- 5 to 10°C
- 0 to 5°C
- 0 to -5°C
- -5 to -15°C
- -15 to -25°C
- Less than -25°C

July

—100— Precipitation (mm)

CITIES AND TOWNS

- ■ Over 500,000 people
- ◉ 100,000–500,000
- ○ 50,000–100,000
- ○ Less than 50,000

LAND HEIGHT

- 500–1000 m
- 250–500 m
- 100–250 m
- 0–100 m

SEA DEPTH

- 0–250 m
- 250–500 m
- 500–1000 m
- 1000–2000 m
- 2000–3000 m
- 3000–4000 m
- Below 4000 m

SCALE BAR

0 km — 150 — 300
0 miles — 150 — 300

33

WESTERN CANADA & ALASKA

ALBERTA, BRITISH COLUMBIA, MANITOBA, NORTHWEST TERRITORIES, NUNAVUT, SASKATCHEWAN, YUKON TERRITORY, ALASKA

The first inhabitants of western Canada were the First Nations. Then came the Inuit. By the late 1800s, the Canadian Pacific Railway was completed and European settlers moved west, turning most of the prairie into grain farms. North of the prairies lie the vast, sparsely populated territories. Alaska, part of the USA, has huge oil reserves amidst spectacular wilderness.

POPULATION

Most of western Canada's people live near the Canada/US border, taking advantage of the warmer climate and convenient transport routes. Further north, the population is sparse, with only a few people – mainly the Inuit – per 100 sq km. In Alaska, most people live in the city of Anchorage and in the southern regions.

URBAN/RURAL POPULATION DIVIDE

Vancouver 20%

Edmonton 10.6%

Calgary 9.4%

Other towns and cities 37%

Rural population 23%

INHABITANTS PER SQ KM

More than 10
1–10
Less than 1
● Major city

ENVIRONMENTAL ISSUES

Across the north of the region, the ground is permanently frozen. This is called permafrost. Building on this frozen surface is very difficult, because the heat from houses or roads can cause the ground to melt, and subside. The Trans-Alaskan Pipeline, which brings oil from Prudhoe Bay to Valdez, was built above ground to prevent the permafrost melting.

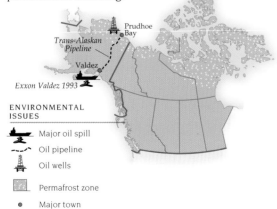

Prudhoe Bay

Trans-Alaskan Pipeline

Valdez

Exxon Valdez 1993

ENVIRONMENTAL ISSUES

🛩 Major oil spill
⌐ Oil pipeline
⚒ Oil wells
▦ Permafrost zone
● Major town

FARMING AND LAND USE

More than 20% of the world's wheat is grown in Canada's prairie provinces: Manitoba, Alberta and Saskatchewan. Beef cattle graze on the ranches of Alberta and British Columbia. Fruits, especially apples, flourish in the sheltered southern valleys of British Columbia, and Pacific salmon and herring are caught off the west coast. Much of the region is heavily forested.

Anchorage

Edmonton

Calgary

Vancouver

Winnipeg

LAND USE

Pasture 5%
Cropland 4%
Forest 38%
Other (including mountains) 53%

FARMING AND LAND USE

🐄 Cattle
🎣 Fishing
🌾 Cereals
🦐 Fruit
🪵 Timber
● Major conurbation

Pasture
Cropland
Forest
Mountain region
Barren
Tundra

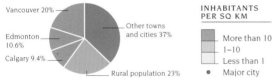

Anchorage

Edmonton
Saskatoon
Vancouver
Calgary
Regina
Winnipeg

THE LANDSCAPE

The prairie provinces are mostly flat. Occasionally, the level plains are broken up by river valleys such as the Qu'Appelle in Saskatchewan. In the west, the jagged peaks and steep passes of the Rocky Mountains are covered in snow for months on end. West of the Rockies and the Coast Mountains, the land descends sharply to the British Columbia coast. Alaska is mountainous, and scattered with plains and many lakes left by glaciers.

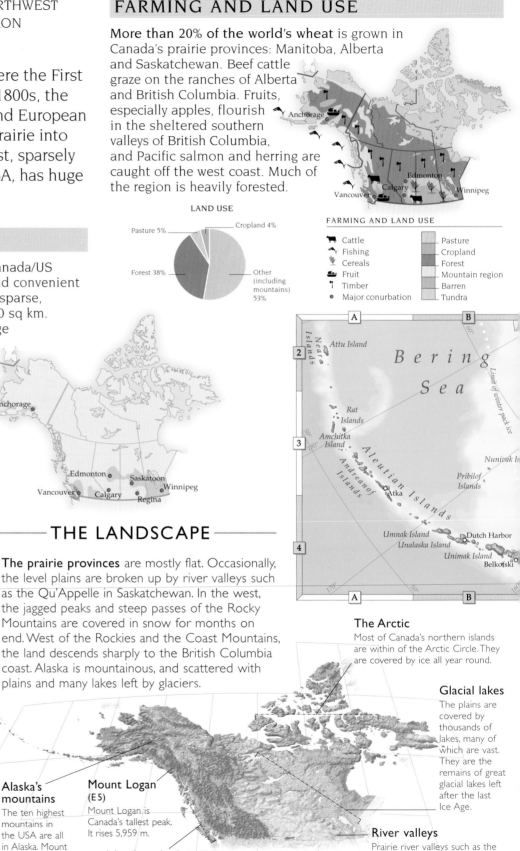

Bering Sea

Near Islands

Attu Island

Rat Islands

Amchitka Island

Andreanof Islands

Aleutian Islands

Atka

Umnak Island

Unalaska Island

Dutch Harbor

Unimak Island

Belkofski

Nunivak Is

Pribilof Islands

Limit of winter pack ice

The Arctic

Most of Canada's northern islands are within of the Arctic Circle. They are covered by ice all year round.

Glacial lakes

The plains are covered by thousands of lakes, many of which are vast. They are the remains of great glacial lakes left after the last Ice Age.

Alaska's mountains

The ten highest mountains in the USA are all in Alaska. Mount McKinley (Denali) (D4) is the highest at 6,194 m.

Mount Logan (E 5)

Mount Logan is Canada's tallest peak. It rises 5,959 m.

Islands and inlets (E 6)

The British Columbia coast is peppered with islands and fjord-like inlets, created by the force of the Pacific Ocean.

River valleys

Prairie river valleys such as the Qu'Appelle (H7) (French for 'who calls') were cut by glacial meltwater thousands of years ago.

INDUSTRY

Alberta and Alaska have huge reserves of fossil fuels and the other provinces are rich in minerals such as zinc, nickel, silver and uranium. Major industries in the prairie provinces are related to agriculture, such as meat-processing in Manitoba. British Columbia's economy depends on manufacturing, especially cars, chemicals and machinery, along with paper and timber industries.

STRUCTURE OF INDUSTRY (Canada)
Primary 3%
Services 66%
Manufacturing 31%

Alaska
Primary 9%
Services 75%
Manufacturing 16%

INDUSTRY

- Car manufacture
- Chemicals
- Engineering
- Food processing
- Metal refining
- Oil & gas
- Mining
- Timber processing
- Tourism
- Major industrial centre / area
- Major road

CLIMATE

Parts of northern Canada and Alaska are frozen all year round. The prairie provinces have warm summers and cold winters. Coastal British Columbia is mild and wet.

TEMPERATURE AND PRECIPITATION
- More than 20°C
- 15 to 20°C
- 10 to 15°C
- 5 to 10°C
- 0 to 5°C
- 0 to -5°C
- -5 to -10°C
- -10 to -15°C
- Less than -15°C
- 100 Precipitation (mm)

January

July

NORTH AMERICA
Western Canada & Alaska

SCALE BAR
0 km 200 400
0 miles 200 400

LAND HEIGHT
- Above 4000 m
- 2000–4000 m
- 1000–2000 m
- 500–1000 m
- 250–500 m
- 100–250 m
- 0–100 m

SEA DEPTH
- 0–250 m
- 250–500 m
- 500–1000 m
- 1000–2000 m
- 2000–3000 m
- 3000–4000 m
- Below 4000 m

CITIES AND TOWNS
- Over 500,000 people
- 100,000–500,000
- 50,000–100,000
- Less than 50,000

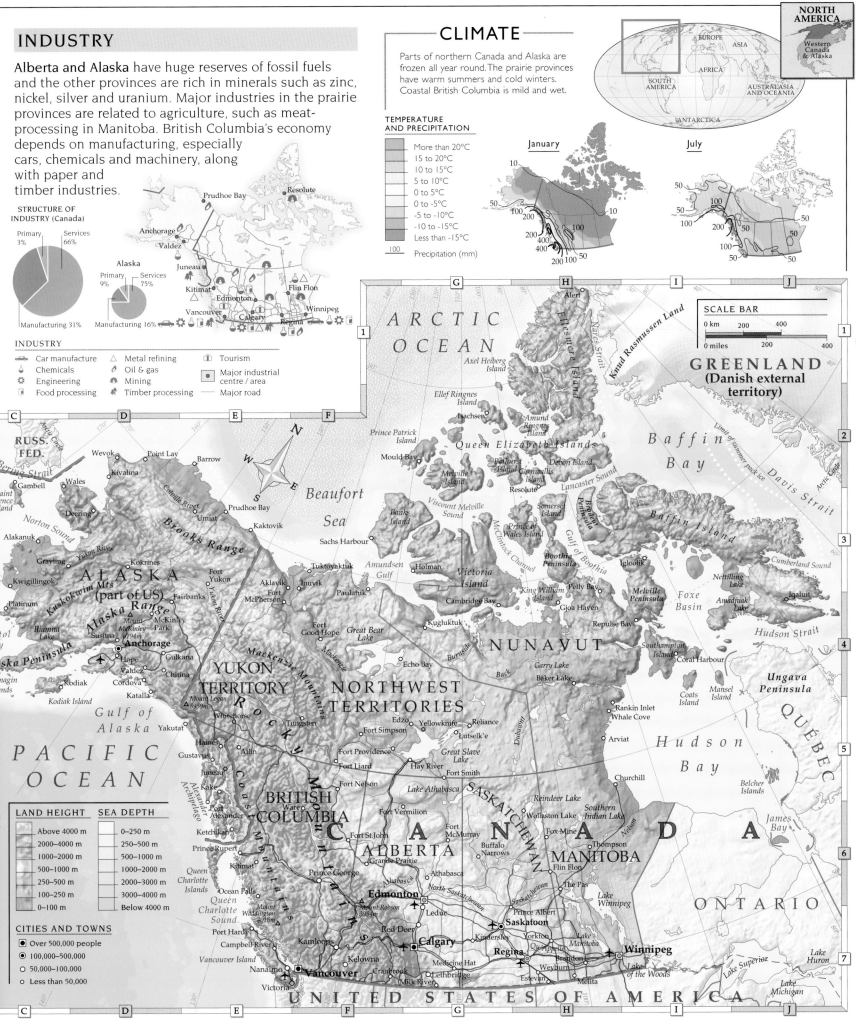

EASTERN USA

The east coast of the USA was settled by European colonists from the 17th century onwards. When the USA became independent in 1776, people gradually spread westwards towards the Mississippi River, and down towards the southern states. In the late 19th and early 20th centuries, thousands of immigrants from all over the world passed through New York on their way to new lives elsewhere in the USA. Today, the eastern USA contains some of the world's most developed and powerful cities.

POPULATION

The northeastern and Great Lakes states are the most populous parts of North America, with people taking advantage of the good transport routes and the availability of jobs. Some of the USA's biggest cities, like New York, are found here, yet in New England many towns have less than 30,000 people. In recent years, many have migrated to the 'Sunbelt' states of the south – especially to Florida.

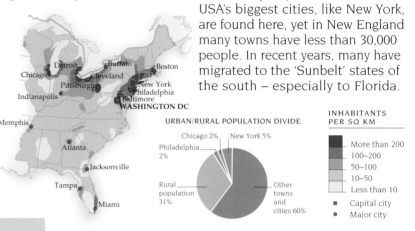

URBAN/RURAL POPULATION DIVIDE

Chicago 2%   New York 5%
Philadelphia 2%
Rural population 31%
Other towns and cities 60%

INHABITANTS PER SQ KM

More than 200
100–200
50–100
10–50
Less than 10
■ Capital city
● Major city

INDUSTRY

The northeast is the USA's industrial heartland. The Great Lakes states are the centre of car manufacturing, but service industries are also developing. Hi-tech industries such as computers and electronics are found around Boston and in New Jersey. New York is the USA's financial capital. Further south, states like North Carolina are centres for research and development and Florida has a successful tourist industry.

INDUSTRY

- 🚗 Car manufacture
- ⚗ Chemicals
- ⚙ Engineering
- 🥫 Food processing
- 🚂 Iron & steel
- 👕 Textiles
- ⛏ Coal
- S Finance
- 💻 Hi-tech industry
- 🔬 Research & Development
- 🏛 Tourism
- ▣ Major industrial centre / area
- — Major road

STRUCTURE OF INDUSTRY

Primary 5%
Services 63%
Manufacturing 32%

THE LANDSCAPE

The Atlantic and Gulf coasts are bordered in the south by a wide and mainly low-lying plain, with many swampy areas. Towards the north, the plain gradually falls away, forming salt marshes, lagoons and offshore sandbars. Inland, the plain is overlooked by the rounded peaks of the Appalachian Mountains. West of the mountains is the vast Mississippi Basin.

Great Lakes
The five Great Lakes were formed during the last Ice Age and contain 20% of the world's fresh water. The area around the lakes is rich in natural resources, including coal, iron, copper and timber.

Appalachian Mountains (E 4)
The forest-covered Appalachians are one of the oldest mountain chains in the world. Over a period of about 400 million years they have been lowered and rounded by erosion. Their eastern side has been worn down to a plain called a piedmont, or 'mountain foot'.

FARMING AND LAND USE

Dairy, livestock and fruit farming are important in New York, Pennsylvania and the Great Lakes states. North Carolina is the USA's biggest tobacco grower. The southeastern states once grew most of the world's cotton; today soya beans and peanuts are the most important crops. Fish are caught in the states bordering the Gulf of Mexico, and Florida is famous for its citrus fruits.

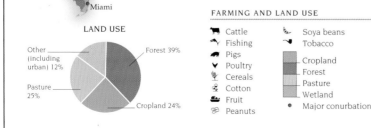

LAND USE

Other (including urban) 12%
Forest 39%
Pasture 25%
Cropland 24%

FARMING AND LAND USE

- 🐂 Cattle
- 🎣 Fishing
- 🐖 Pigs
- 🦃 Poultry
- 🌾 Cereals
- ❀ Cotton
- 🍎 Fruit
- 🥜 Peanuts
- 🌱 Soya beans
- 🍃 Tobacco
- Cropland
- Forest
- Pasture
- Wetland
- ● Major conurbation

Mississippi River (C 4)
The Mississippi is the world's third longest river, and one of its busiest waterways. Goods from the agricultural and industrial regions around the Great Lakes are transported by barge down to the Gulf of Mexico.

The Everglades (E 7)
One-fifth of Florida is covered by swampy tropical wetlands. Part of this area includes the Everglades National Park, which is home to many wild animals and plants, including some endangered species.

Flooded valleys (F 4)
Along the Atlantic coast the lower reaches of many river valleys have been flooded by the sea. This has created large bays and inlets such as Long Island Sound and Chesapeake Bay.

ENVIRONMENTAL ISSUES

Air pollution, caused by emissions from industry and power stations, and car fumes, is a problem in the cities and sprawling built-up areas close to the Great Lakes and along the Atlantic coast. Acid rain affects most of the area, and many of the larger rivers have been polluted by industrial effluent.

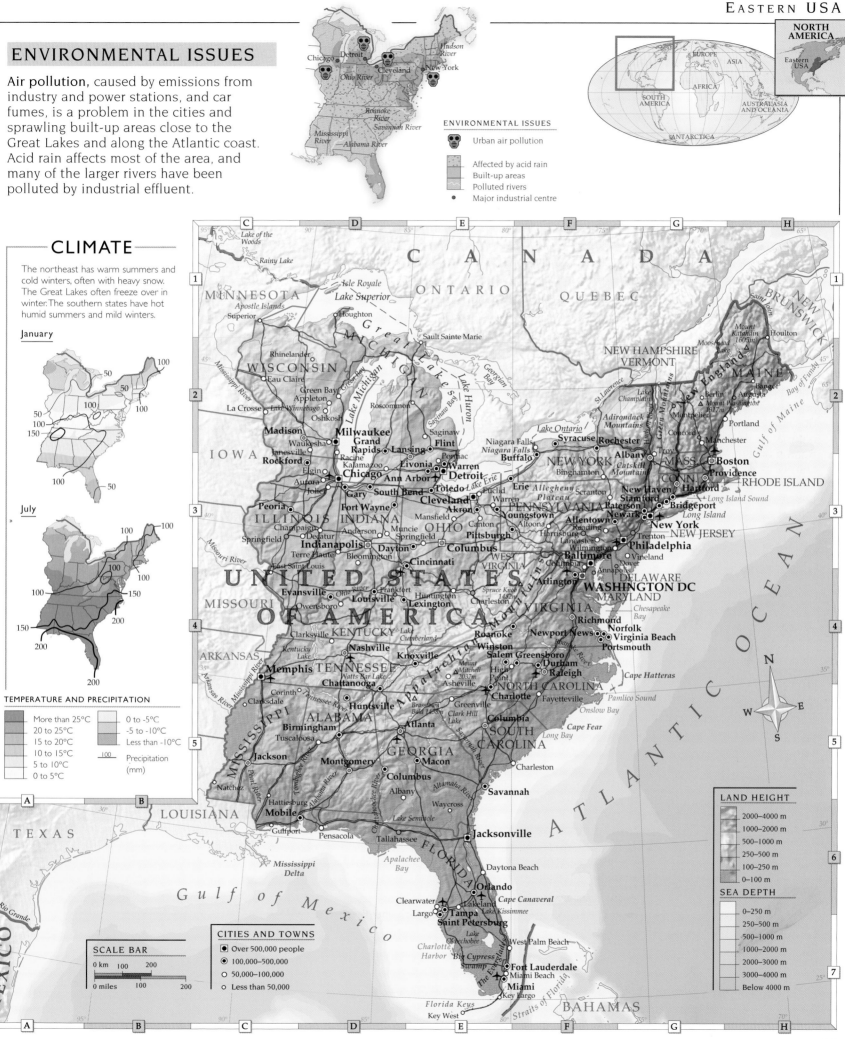

ENVIRONMENTAL ISSUES

- Urban air pollution
- Affected by acid rain
- Built-up areas
- Polluted rivers
- Major industrial centre

NORTH AMERICA

CLIMATE

The northeast has warm summers and cold winters, often with heavy snow. The Great Lakes often freeze over in winter. The southern states have hot humid summers and mild winters.

January

July

TEMPERATURE AND PRECIPITATION

- More than 25°C
- 20 to 25°C
- 15 to 20°C
- 10 to 15°C
- 5 to 10°C
- 0 to 5°C
- 0 to -5°C
- -5 to -10°C
- Less than -10°C
- 100 Precipitation (mm)

LAND HEIGHT

- 2000–4000 m
- 1000–2000 m
- 500–1000 m
- 250–500 m
- 100–250 m
- 0–100 m

SEA DEPTH

- 0–250 m
- 250–500 m
- 500–1000 m
- 1000–2000 m
- 2000–3000 m
- 3000–4000 m
- Below 4000 m

SCALE BAR

0 km 100 200

0 miles 100 200

CITIES AND TOWNS

- Over 500,000 people
- 100,000–500,000
- 50,000–100,000
- Less than 50,000

WESTERN USA

Western USA stretches from the Mississippi Basin across the Great Plains to the mighty Rocky Mountains and the Pacific Ocean. Its dramatic scenery varies from vast evergreen forests and lush valleys in the north, to the huge farming and cattle-ranching prairies of the Midwest and the deserts of the southwest, where temperatures soar over 40°C in summer. The western states have a very racially mixed population. Many people have ancestors from Europe, Africa and Asia, and the southwest is home to communities of native Americans such as the Navajo.

INDUSTRY

Western USA is a major agricultural producer, although its cities have a variety of manufacturing and service industries. Washington has an important aerospace industry, and its forests, along with those in Oregon, supply most of the USA's timber. Oklahoma and Texas have big oil and gas fields, and minerals are mined in Montana and Wyoming. 'Silicon Valley' in California is a world centre for micro-electronics.

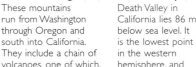

INDUSTRY

✈ Aerospace industry	⚒ Timber processing
🚗 Car manufacture	💻 Hi-tech industry
🜀 Chemicals	☢ Research & development
⚙ Engineering	🏛 Tourism
🏭 Food processing	
👕 Textiles	⊙ Major industrial centre / area
⛏ Mining	— Major road
🛢 Oil & gas	

STRUCTURE OF INDUSTRY

Primary 7%
Services 65%
Manufacturing 28%

POPULATION

California has more people than any other US state. Immigrants from Asia and Latin America, especially Mexico, make up a large, and growing, part of its population. Outside the big cities, most of the other western states are sparsely populated, and people depend on cars to cover the huge distances between places.

INHABITANTS PER SQ KM

■ More than 200	● Major city
■ 100–200	
■ 50–100	
■ 10–50	
□ Less than 10	

URBAN/RURAL POPULATION DIVIDE

Los Angeles 12.8%
Houston 4.9%
Seattle 4.3%
Rural population 20%
Other towns and cities 58%

FARMING AND LAND USE

Huge cereal farms and cattle ranches take up most of the Great Plains. More maize and wheat is produced here than anywhere else in the world. Fruit is grown in the sheltered valleys of Oregon and Washington, and in California, where the fertile but dry land is irrigated almost all year round to produce the country's biggest crop of citrus and other fruits.

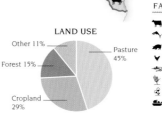

LAND USE

Other 11%
Forest 15%
Cropland 29%
Pasture 45%

FARMING AND LAND USE

🐂 Cattle	🌱 Soya beans
🐟 Fishing	🌲 Timber
🐖 Pigs	
🦃 Poultry	▫ Cropland
🦐 Shellfish	▪ Desert
🌾 Cereals	■ Forest
🌿 Cotton	▪ Pasture
🍎 Fruit	▫ Wetland
	● Major conurbation

THE LANDSCAPE

The Great Plains sweep west from the Mississippi River flood plain. At the western edge of the plains the land rises, becoming the Rocky Mountains. Within this chain there are many high plateaus and basins. Further west are the Sierra Nevada, the Cascade Range, and finally the Coast Ranges, which run along the Pacific seaboard.

Cascade Range (B 2)
These mountains run from Washington through Oregon and south into California. They include a chain of volcanoes, one of which, Mount Saint Helens, last erupted in 1980.

Death Valley (C 3)
Death Valley in California lies 86 m below sea level. It is the lowest point in the western hemisphere, and one of the hottest places on Earth.

Rocky Mountains (D 3)
The Rockies stretch in an almost unbroken chain from Alaska to New Mexico. Some of North America's highest peaks are found here, as well as many active volcanoes.

Badlands (E 2)
About 5,200 sq km of South Dakota is covered by 'badlands'. These are created in dry areas with little or no vegetation; occasional heavy rainstorms wear away the exposed rock to create deep gullies and sharp pinnacles.

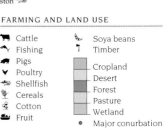

Earthquakes
The San Andreas Fault is a break in the Earth's crust that runs for 1,050 km through California. A sudden movement of land along the fault causes earthquakes, such as the one in 1994 which caused much damage in Los Angeles.

Grand Canyon (C 4)
The Grand Canyon in Arizona is a spectacular gorge cut by the Colorado River. The canyon is about 446 km long, between 8–29 km wide and up to 1,829 m deep.

Great Plains (E 3)
The landscape of the Great Plains is largely treeless farmland. The region was once natural grassland or prairie, grazed by huge herds of buffalo. Being far from any oceans, summers here are very hot and winters freezing.

NORTH AMERICA

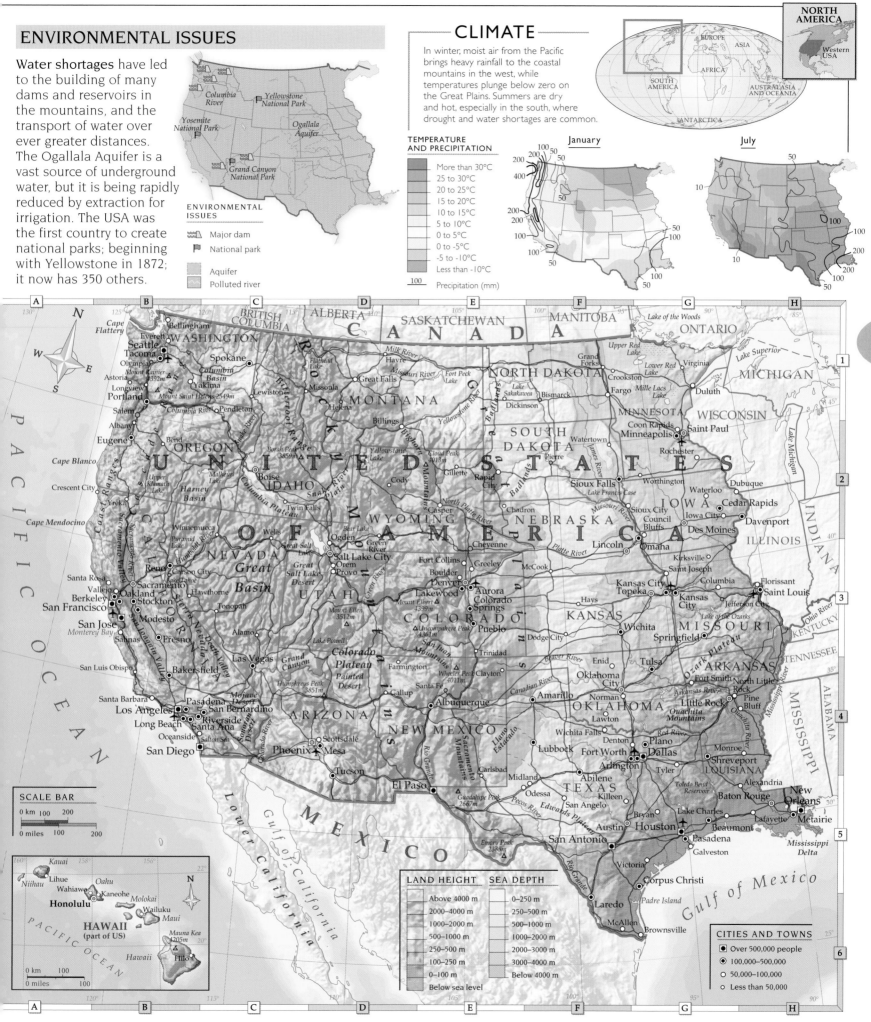

ENVIRONMENTAL ISSUES

Water shortages have led to the building of many dams and reservoirs in the mountains, and the transport of water over ever greater distances. The Ogallala Aquifer is a vast source of underground water, but it is being rapidly reduced by extraction for irrigation. The USA was the first country to create national parks; beginning with Yellowstone in 1872; it now has 350 others.

Columbia River
Yellowstone National Park
Yosemite National Park
Ogallala Aquifer
Grand Canyon National Park

ENVIRONMENTAL ISSUES

- Major dam
- National park
- Aquifer
- Polluted river

CLIMATE

In winter, moist air from the Pacific brings heavy rainfall to the coastal mountains in the west, while temperatures plunge below zero on the Great Plains. Summers are dry and hot, especially in the south, where drought and water shortages are common.

TEMPERATURE AND PRECIPITATION

- More than 30°C
- 25 to 30°C
- 20 to 25°C
- 15 to 20°C
- 10 to 15°C
- 5 to 10°C
- 0 to 5°C
- 0 to -5°C
- -5 to -10°C
- Less than -10°C

100 Precipitation (mm)

January

July

EUROPE ASIA
AFRICA
SOUTH AMERICA
AUSTRALASIA AND OCEANIA
ANTARCTICA
Western USA

SCALE BAR
0 km 100 200
0 miles 100 200

LAND HEIGHT
- Above 4000 m
- 2000–4000 m
- 1000–2000 m
- 500–1000 m
- 250–500 m
- 100–250 m
- 0–100 m
- Below sea level

SEA DEPTH
- 0–250 m
- 250–500 m
- 500–1000 m
- 1000–2000 m
- 2000–3000 m
- 3000–4000 m
- Below 4000 m

CITIES AND TOWNS
- Over 500,000 people
- 100,000–500,000
- 50,000–100,000
- Less than 50,000

HAWAII (part of US)

Kauai
Niihau
Lihue
Oahu
Wahiawa
Kaneohe
Honolulu
Molokai
Wailuku
Maui
Mauna Kea 4205m
Hawaii
Hilo

0 km 100
0 miles 100

MEXICO

Mexico is a large country with a rich mixture of traditions and cultures. The ancient civilization of the Aztecs which flourished here was crushed by Spanish invaders in the 16th century. Spain ruled Mexico until its independence in 1836 and today, the country has the world's largest and fastest growing Spanish-speaking population. Mexico is mostly dry and mountainous, and farm land is limited, so the country has to import most of the basic foods it needs to feed its people.

FARMING AND LAND USE

Most of the land suitable for farming is planted with corn – a big part of the Mexican diet. Along the Gulf coast coffee, sugar cane and cotton are grown on plantations for export. Parts of the dry north are irrigated to grow cotton, but most of the land is taken up by large cattle ranches. Fishing, especially for shellfish such as lobster and shrimp is important in coastal areas.

FARMING AND LAND USE

- 🐄 Cattle
- 🐟 Fishing
- 🐑 Sheep
- 🍌 Bananas
- ☕ Coffee
- 🌽 Corn (maize)
- Cotton
- Fruit
- 🍇 Grapes
- Shellfish
- Sugar cane
- Timber

- Cropland
- Desert
- Forest
- Pasture
- Wetland
- ● Major conurbation

LAND USE

- Cropland 13%
- Other 22%
- Pasture 39%
- Forest 26%

THE LANDSCAPE

Much of Mexico is made up of a high plateau. The climate there is very dry and varies between true desert in the north, and semi-desert further south. The plateau is separated from the coastal plains by two long, rugged mountain chains: the Eastern Sierra Madre and the Western Sierra Madre. Towards the south, the mountain ranges join, meeting in the region of high volcanic peaks that surround Mexico City.

The Rio Grande (D 2)
This river flows from Colorado in the USA and forms much of Mexico's northern border. It crosses a vast arid area on its way to the Gulf of Mexico.

Eastern Sierra Madre (D 5).

Earthquakes and volcanoes
Volcanic activity is common in Mexico. Popocatépetl (F 5) and Volcán El Chichónal (G 5) have erupted recently, and Mexico City was hit by a devastating earthquake in 1985.

Yucatan Peninsula (H 4)
The Yucatan Peninsula is a low, wide tableland, formed by layers of limestone. Limestone absorbs water, so there are few rivers on the peninsula, and the tropical rainforests found there are fed mainly by streams and underground water.

Western Sierra Madre (C 3).

Lower California (B 3)
This long and very dry peninsula, separates the Gulf of California from the Pacific Ocean. The Gulf was formed after the last Ice Age, when the sea rose to flood a major rift valley.

POPULATION

Most of the north is sparsely populated due to the hot, dry climate and lack of cultivable farm land. As people have migrated from the countryside in search of work, the cities have grown dramatically; almost 75% of Mexicans now live in urban areas. Mexico City is home to almost a quarter of the population and is one of the world's largest cities.

INHABITANTS PER SQ KM
- More than 200
- 100–200
- 50–100
- Less than 50
- ■ Capital city
- ● Major city

URBAN/RURAL POPULATION DIVIDE
- Mexico City 21.6%
- Guadalajara 2.4%
- Monterrey 2%
- Other towns and cities 48%
- Rural population 26%

ENVIRONMENTAL ISSUES

Fast, unplanned growth has led to poor sanitation and water supplies in Mexico City, while the wall of mountains which surround the city traps pollution from cars and factories, giving it some of the world's worst air pollution. Much of Mexico's tropical rainforest has been felled, leading to increased soil erosion. Land clearance further north is also causing desertification.

ENVIRONMENTAL ISSUES
- Risk of desertification
- Deforested areas
- Remaining tropical forests
- Path of recent devastating hurricane
- ● Major industrial city
- Volcanic eruption
- Urban air pollution

Mitch 1998
Nevado de Colima 1994
Popocatépetl 1994
Volcán El Chichónal 1994

A
- 115°
CALIFORNIA
1
- Tijuana Mexicali San
- Rosarito
- Ensenada
- 30°
2
- Bahía
- Isla Cedros Sebast Vizca
- Guerrero Neg
3
- 25°
- Tropic of Cancer
4
- 20°
5
- Isla Clarión
6
- 115°
A

NORTH
AMERICA

Mexico

INDUSTRY

Oil and gas on the Gulf coast are the biggest source of income. Mexico is also rich in other minerals; it is the world's top silver producer. Manufacturing is centred around Mexico City and along the US border, where mainly foreign owned factories assemble products for export. Tourism is increasing throughout Mexico.

STRUCTURE OF INDUSTRY

Primary 8%
Services 64%

Manufacturing 28%

INDUSTRY

- 🚗 Car manufacture
- 📺 Electronics
- ⚙ Engineering
- 🏭 Food processing
- 🚃 Iron & steel
- 🛢 Oil refining
- 👕 Textiles
- ⛏ Mining
- 🛢 Oil and gas
- 🧳 Tourism
- ▣ Major industrial centre / area
- — Major road

CLIMATE

Northern Mexico and the peninsula of Lower California are dry, hot and largely desert. Towards the south, rainfall increases, especially in July. Moist, warm conditions allow rainforests to grow.

January

July

TEMPERATURE AND PRECIPITATION

- More than 30°C
- 25 to 30°C
- 20 to 25°C
- 15 to 20°C
- 10 to 15°C
- 5 to 10°C
- Less than 5°C

—100— Precipitation (mm)

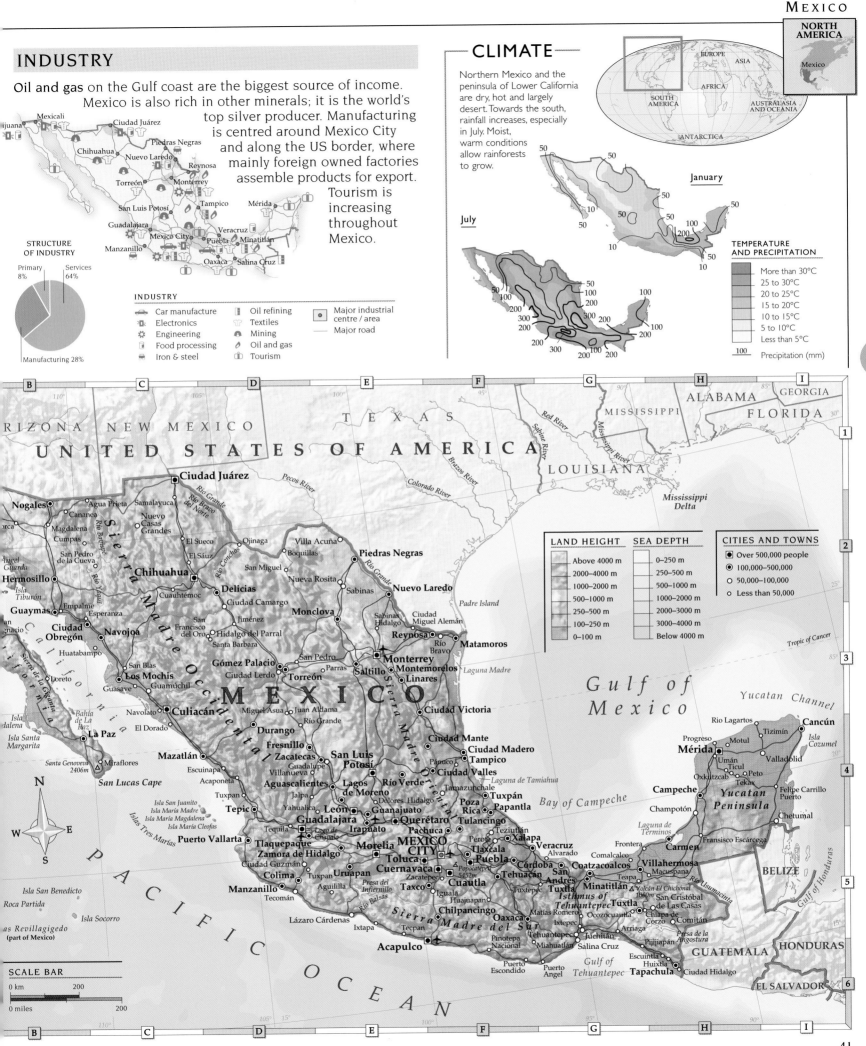

LAND HEIGHT
- Above 4000 m
- 2000–4000 m
- 1000–2000 m
- 500–1000 m
- 250–500 m
- 100–250 m
- 0–100 m

SEA DEPTH
- 0–250 m
- 250–500 m
- 500–1000 m
- 1000–2000 m
- 2000–3000 m
- 3000–4000 m
- Below 4000 m

CITIES AND TOWNS
- ◼ Over 500,000 people
- ◉ 100,000–500,000
- ○ 50,000–100,000
- ○ Less than 50,000

SCALE BAR

0 km   200

0 miles   200

CENTRAL AMERICA

BELIZE, COSTA RICA, EL SALVADOR, GUATEMALA, HONDURAS, NICARAGUA, PANAMA

Central America lies on a narrow bridge of land which links North and South America. All the countries here, except Belize, were once governed by Spain. Today, most of their people are *mestizos* – a mix of the original Maya Indian inhabitants and Spanish settlers. The hot, steamy climate is ideal for growing tropical crops, such as coffee and bananas, which are exported worldwide.

FARMING AND LAND USE

About half of all the agricultural products grown here are exported. The Pacific coast has fertile, well-watered land suitable for growing cotton and sugar cane. In the central highlands are big coffee plantations, and ranches where beef cattle are raised. Bananas grow well along the humid Caribbean coastal plain, and shrimp and lobster are caught offshore.

FARMING AND LAND USE

- 🐄 Cattle
- Shellfish
- Bananas
- Coffee
- Corn (maize)
- Cotton
- Sugar cane
- Timber

- Cropland
- Forest
- Pasture
- Major conurbation

LAND USE

Pasture 28%
Forest 40%
Cropland 14%
Other 18%

ENVIRONMENTAL ISSUES

Central America's rainforests are rapidly being cut down for timber and to make way for farmland and land for building. Over half of Guatemala's forests have been felled, mostly in the last 30 years. The situation is also bleak in Honduras, Costa Rica and Nicaragua. Central America has a line of volcanoes running through the region which are still active.

Mitch 1998
Volcán Tacana 1986
Volcán de Fuego 1974
Volcán de Izalco 1958
Volcán Cerro Negro 1995
Volcán Concepcion 1986
Volcán Arenal 1995

ENVIRONMENTAL ISSUES

- Volcanic eruption
- Deforested areas
- Remaining forests
- Path of recent, devastating hurricane

POPULATION

Central America's people live mainly in the valleys of the central highlands or along the Pacific coastal plains. Despite the threat of volcanic eruptions and earthquakes, towns and cities developed in these areas because of the fertile volcanic soils found there. Just over half the population still live in rural areas, mostly in small villages or remote settlements, but the cities have expanded rapidly and overcrowding has become a serious problem.

BELMOPAN
GUATEMALA CITY
TEGUCIGALPA
SAN SALVADOR
MANAGUA
SAN JOSÉ
PANAMA CITY

INHABITANTS PER SQ KM

- More than 50
- 25–50
- Less than 25
- Capital city

URBAN/RURAL POPULATION DIVIDE

San Salvador 3.3%
Tegucigalpa 3.2%
Managua 3.5%
Other towns and cities 37%
Rural population 53%

THE LANDSCAPE

The Sierra Madre in the north and the Cordillera Central to the south form a mountainous ridge that stretches down most of Central America. Along the Pacific coast north of Panama is a belt of more than 40 active volcanoes. The mountains are broken by valleys and basins with large, fertile areas of rich, volcanic soil.

Coral reef (C 2)
Off the coast of Belize is a 290-km-long coral reef – the second longest in the world. Its waters contain spectacular marine life. In places, the reef has become built up into dozens of small sandy islands called cayes.

Sierra Madre (A 3)

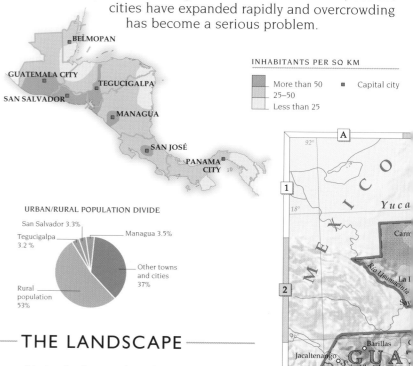

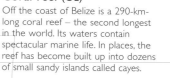

The Mosquito Coast (E 4)
The Mosquito Coast is a remote area of tropical rainforests, lagoons, and rivers lined with mangroves. Most of it is uninhabited by humans, but there is a huge variety of animal species, including monkeys and alligators.

Lake Nicaragua (E 5)
This large freshwater lake contains about 400 islands, some of which are active volanoes like Volcán Concepcion. The lake is also home to the world's only freshwater sharks.

Cordillera Central (G 6)

The Panama Canal (H 6)
The Panama Canal links the Atlantic and Pacific oceans along a distance of 82 km. Half of its route passes through Lake Gatún, a freshwater lake which acts as a reservoir for the canal, providing water to operate the locks.

NORTH AMERICA

Central America

CLIMATE

Temperatures are high all year round, although in January the Caribbean side of Central America is is cooler and wetter than the Pacific side. Summers are generally much wetter, especially in the Sierra Madre in Guatemala and on the Pacific coasts of Costa Rica and Panama.

TEMPERATURE AND PRECIPITATION
- More than 25°C
- 20 to 25°C
- Less than 20°C
- 100 Precipitation (mm)

January

July

INDUSTRY

Coffee, fish, and timber processing, fruit exporting and textile-weaving are typical of the small-scale industries found in Central America. Most industries are based in the capital cities and larger towns. In Panama, many people work at the Panama Canal, which is one of the world's busiest shipping routes. The country is also a major financial centre, with many banking and insurance companies.

INDUSTRY
- Chemicals
- Coffee processing
- Fish processing
- Food processing
- Textiles
- Banana exporting
- Timber processing
- S Finance
- Major industrial centre / area
- Major road

STRUCTURE OF INDUSTRY
Primary 18%
Services 60%
Manufacturing 22%

SCALE BAR
0 km 50 100
0 miles 50 100

CITIES AND TOWNS
- Over 500,000 people
- 100,000–500,000
- 50,000–100,000
- Less than 50,000

LAND HEIGHT
- 2000–4000 m
- 1000–2000 m
- 500–1000 m
- 250–500 m
- 100–250 m
- 0–100 m

SEA DEPTH
- 0–250 m
- 250–500 m
- 500–1000 m
- 1000–2000 m
- 2000–3000 m
- 3000–4000 m
- Below 4000 m

THE CARIBBEAN

The Caribbean Sea is enclosed by an arc of many hundreds of islands, islets and offshore reefs which reach from Florida in the USA round to Venezuela in South America. From 1492, Spain, France, Britain and the Netherlands claimed the islands as colonies. Most of the islands' original inhabitants were wiped out by disease and a wide mixture of peoples – of African, Asian and European descent – now make up the population. The islands are prone to earthquakes, hurricanes and volcanic eruptions.

THE LANDSCAPE

The Bahamas
The Bahamas are low-lying, islands formed from limestone rock. Their coastlines are fringed by coral reefs, lagoons and mangrove swamps. Some of the bigger islands are covered by forests.

The islands are formed from two main mountain chains: the Greater Antilles, which are part of a chain running from west to east, and the Lesser Antilles, which run from north to south. The mountains are now almost submerged under the Atlantic Ocean and Caribbean Sea. Only the higher peaks reach above sea level to form islands.

Hispaniola (F 4)
Two countries, Haiti and the Dominican Republic, occupy the island of Hispaniola. The land is mostly mountainous, broken by fertile valleys.

Cuba (C 3)
Cuba is the largest island in the Antilles. Its landscape is made up of wide, fertile plains with rugged hills and mountains in the southeast.

The Lesser Antilles
Most of these small volcanic islands have mountainous interiors. Barbados and Antigua and Barbuda are flatter, with some higher volcanic areas. Monserrat was evacuated in 1997, following volcanic eruptions on the island.

FARMING AND LAND USE

Agriculture is an important source of income, with over half of all produce exported. Many islands have fertile, well-watered land and large areas are set aside for commercial crops such as sugar cane, tobacco and coffee. Some islands rely heavily on a single crop; in Dominica, bananas provide over half the country's income. Cuba is one of the world's biggest sugar producers.

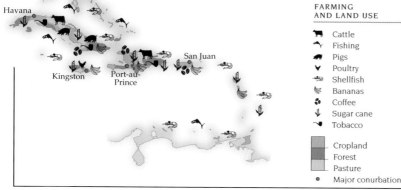

Havana
San Juan
Kingston
Port-au-Prince

FARMING AND LAND USE

- 🐄 Cattle
- 🎣 Fishing
- 🐖 Pigs
- 🦃 Poultry
- 🦐 Shellfish
- 🍌 Bananas
- ☕ Coffee
- Sugar cane
- Tobacco

- Cropland
- Forest
- Pasture
- ● Major conurbation

ENVIRONMENTAL ISSUES

The islands of the Caribbean are often under threat from hurricane storm systems which sweep in from the Atlantic Ocean between May and October. The winds can reach speeds of up to 250 km per hour, devastating everything that lies in their path and causing severe flooding. The storms themselves are enormous; a hurricane can extend outwards for 650 km from its calm centre, which is known as the 'eye'.

TOURISM

Tourism is thriving in the Caribbean, often bringing more income to the region than other, traditional industries. Long sandy beaches, clear, warm waters and the climate are the main attractions. In Cuba and the Dominican Republic, tourism is expanding at some of the fastest rates in North America. As hotel complexes and new roads and airports are developed, the environment is often damaged. Local people who work in the industry often receive little of the extra cash brought in by the tourists.

TOURISM

🏝 Major tourist destinations

Bahamas
Cuba
Jamaica
Puerto Rico
Virgin Islands
Antigua & Barbuda
Dominican Republic
Guadeloupe
St Lucia
Barbados
Aruba
Grenada
Trinidad & Tobago

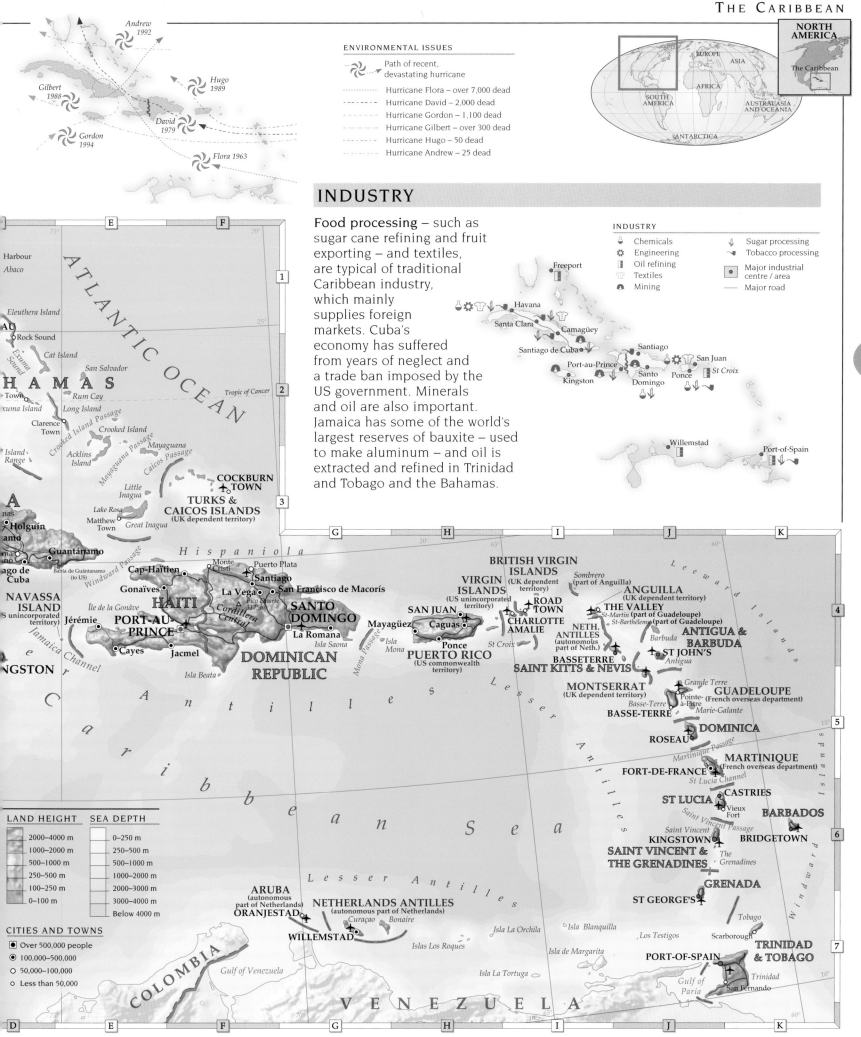

ENVIRONMENTAL ISSUES

- Path of recent, devastating hurricane
- Hurricane Flora – over 7,000 dead
- Hurricane David – 2,000 dead
- Hurricane Gordon – 1,100 dead
- Hurricane Gilbert – over 300 dead
- Hurricane Hugo – 50 dead
- Hurricane Andrew – 25 dead

Andrew 1992
Gilbert 1988
Hugo 1989
David 1979
Gordon 1994
Flora 1963

NORTH AMERICA
The Caribbean

INDUSTRY

Food processing – such as sugar cane refining and fruit exporting – and textiles, are typical of traditional Caribbean industry, which mainly supplies foreign markets. Cuba's economy has suffered from years of neglect and a trade ban imposed by the US government. Minerals and oil are also important. Jamaica has some of the world's largest reserves of bauxite – used to make aluminum – and oil is extracted and refined in Trinidad and Tobago and the Bahamas.

INDUSTRY
- Chemicals
- Engineering
- Oil refining
- Textiles
- Mining
- Sugar processing
- Tobacco processing
- Major industrial centre / area
- Major road

LAND HEIGHT / **SEA DEPTH**
- 2000–4000 m / 0–250 m
- 1000–2000 m / 250–500 m
- 500–1000 m / 500–1000 m
- 250–500 m / 1000–2000 m
- 100–250 m / 2000–3000 m
- 0–100 m / 3000–4000 m
- Below 4000 m

CITIES AND TOWNS
- Over 500,000 people
- 100,000–500,000
- 50,000–100,000
- Less than 50,000

45

CONTINENTAL SOUTH AMERICA

The towering peaks of the Andes stand high above the western side of South America. They act as a barrier to the sparsely inhabited interior of the continent which includes the dense rainforest of the Amazon Basin – one of the Earth's last great wildernesses. Most people live on South America's coastal fringes. Brazil is both the largest country, and the most populous. Over half the continent's land area and half its people are found there.

4,990 km

7,640 km

CROSS-SECTION ACROSS SOUTH AMERICA

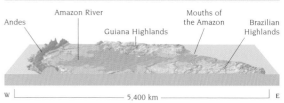

Andes — Amazon River — Guiana Highlands — Mouths of the Amazon — Brazilian Highlands

W ⟵ 5,400 km ⟶ E

The high peaks of the Andes rise up from a narrow strip of land bordering the Pacific Ocean. East of the Andes, the land flattens into a broad, shallow basin into which the Amazon River flows. To the north are the older Guiana Highlands where rock has been eroded to form flat-topped 'table' mountains.

PHYSICAL SOUTH AMERICA

Ancient masses of rocks, like the Guiana and Brazilian highlands, which are known as shields, form the core of South America. The Andes are the solid backbone of the continent. They are relatively young, formed by collisions between different plates of the Earth's crust. The major rivers; the Paraná and the mighty Amazon flow in deep depressions to the east of the mountains.

ELEVATION

6000m
5000m
4000m
3000m
2000m
1000m
500m
250m
100m
sea level
below sea level
⟩⟨ cross-section

SCALE 1:40,000,000

0 km 400 800

0 miles 400 800

5 VOLCANOES

The high Andes are lined with many volcanoes. Cotopaxi in Ecuador at 5,897 m is one of South America's highest active

4 THE AMAZON BASIN

The Amazon River flows through a vast geological depression in the north of the continent, supporting thousands of square kilometres of tropical rainforest.

1 GUIANA HIGHLANDS

The Guiana Highlands are part of the ancient core of the continent. They are heavily eroded, with deep valleys and steep waterfalls.

2 MANGROVE SWAMPS

Dense mangrove swamps grow along the equatorial coast of Brazil, Colombia and Ecuador. The delicate ecosystem of the mangrove swamp is easily destroyed by pollution.

3 THE ANDES

The Andes run the entire length of the continent – over 7,250 km – from the storm-lashed island of Tierra del Fuego to the tropical north. The mountains are on a volcanically active zone, and earthquakes are common.

Caribbean Sea
Gulf of Darien
Lake Maracaibo
Central America
Gulf of Panama
Llanos
Orinoco
Highest waterfall Angel Falls
ATLANTIC OCEAN
Cordillera Occidental
Cordillera Central
Cordillera Oriental
Río Negro
Guiana Highlands
Japurá
Branco
Represa Balbina
Mouths of the Amazon
Equator
Cotopaxi 5897m
Putumayo
Amazon
Amazon
Chimborazo 6310m
Marañón
Amazon Basin
Madeira
Tapajós
Xingu
Tocantins
Gulf of Guayaquil
Nevado Huascarán 6768m
Madre de Dios
Guaporé
Planalto de Mato Grosso
São Francisco
Represa de Sobradinho
Brazilian Highlands
Lake Titicaca
Lago Poopó
Atacama Desert
Pilcomayo
Paraguay
Gran Chaco
Paraná
Mesopotamia
Uruguay
Tropic of Capricorn
Cerro Ojos del Salado 6880m
Salado
Paraná
Lagoa dos Patos
Mirim Lagoon
PACIFIC OCEAN
Highest point Cerro Aconcagua 6959m
Pampas
River Plate
Colorado
Río Negro
ATLANTIC OCEAN
Isla de Chiloé
Chonos
Lowest point Península Valdés -40m
Gulf of San Jorge
Patagonia
Bahía Grande
Falkland Islands
Strait of Magellan
Tierra del Fuego
Cape Horn

POLITICAL SOUTH AMERICA

In the 17th century, explorers from Spain and Portugal claimed most of South America for their rulers in Europe. Their influences are still strong today: Brazilians speak Portuguese, while much of the rest of the continent is Spanish-speaking. The small nations of the north, Suriname and Guyana, were Dutch and British colonies and French Guiana is a French overseas department. The mix of peoples is mainly European, native American and African. Some native peoples still live in the dense Amazon rainforest.

SCALE 1:35,000,000

0 km 400 800
0 miles 400 800

TRANSPORT LINKS

The Pan American Highway is a vital transport link, running from the far south of the continent, northwards along the Pacific coast. Its route takes it through sparsely populated areas like the Atacama Desert.

POPULATION

Many South American countries have a similar pattern of population distribution. The largest numbers of people are found near the coasts. Migration to the coastal cities has led to rocketing population figures, and growing social problems. São Paulo is now the world's third largest city after Mexico City and Tokyo; its outskirts are fringed with sprawling, shantytown suburbs – known as *favelas*.

BORDER DISPUTES

Many of South America's borders have been, or remain, disputed. Bolivia is landlocked as a result of a dispute with Chile in 1883, when it lost its lands bordering the Pacific Ocean.

URBAN GROWTH

Urban growth has transformed São Paulo into a major population and industrial centre. Its rapid growth has created many problems, like traffic congestion, overcrowding, and inadequate sewerage.

POPULATION

Capital cities
◉ Above 500,000
◎ 100,000 to 500,000
● 50,000 to 100,000
○ Below 50,000

Other cities
▣ Above 500,000
▢ 50,000 to 100,000

STANDARDS OF LIVING

There are many inequalities in living standards across South America. Argentina's economy has suffered during the regional recession but living standards are still above those of Guyana and Bolivia, which have weak economies, and are heavily reliant upon trade in raw materials. The booming black market drug trade increases crime and corruption.

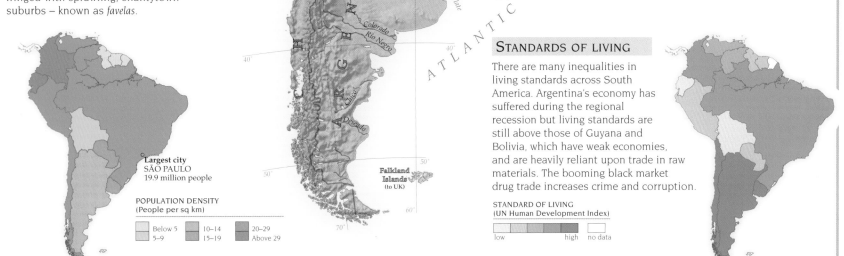

Largest city
SÃO PAULO
19.9 million people

POPULATION DENSITY
(People per sq km)

Below 5
5–9
10–14
15–19
20–29
Above 29

STANDARD OF LIVING
(UN Human Development Index)

low — high — no data

SOUTH AMERICAN GEOGRAPHY

Agriculture is still the most common form of employment in South America. Cattle and cash crops of coffee, cocoa and, in some places, coca for cocaine, provide the main sources of income. Brazil has the greatest range of industries, followed by Argentina, Venezuela and Chile. The large coastal cities such as Rio de Janeiro, Lima and Buenos Aires are where most of the jobs are found. This encourages people to migrate from the country to the city, in search of employment.

INDUSTRY

Brazil is the continent's leading industrial producer and São Paulo the major industrial city. Manufactured products include iron and steel, automobiles, chemicals, textiles, and meat and leather products from the continent's vast cattle herds. In the mountains of Bolivia and Colombia, coca plants are grown to make cocaine, which has created a black market for this illegal drug.

OIL AND GAS

Under the waters of Lake Maracaibo, Venezuela, lie some of South America's biggest oil reserves. Oil exploitation has brought great wealth to Venezuela. The money has helped the country to build new roads and develop other industries.

INDUSTRIAL CENTRE

São Paulo, Brazil, is the largest city in South America and a leading industrial centre. A wide range of goods is manufactured here, including automobiles, chemicals, textiles and electronic products. São Paulo is also a leading financial centre Hundreds of people flock to the city daily in search of work.

TRADE AND EXPORTS

The Chilean port of Valparaíso ships many different products out of South America. Trade is growing with Japan and other countries around the Pacific Ocean.

MINERAL RESOURCES

South America's mineral resources are highly localized. Few countries have both fossil fuels and metallic ores. The richest oilfields are in the north, especially in Venezuela. Coal, however, is scarce. When the Andes formed, heat helped create the many metallic minerals which are mined today.

MINERAL RESOURCES
- Bauxite
- Copper
- Iron
- Lead
- Silver
- Tin
- Oil/Gas field
- Coal field

COPPER MINES

Metallic mineral reserves are abundant in the Andes. Chuquicamata, northern Chile, is one of the world's largest copper mines.

GNP per capita (US$)
- Below 999
- 999-1999
- 2000-2999
- 3000-3999
- 4000-4999
- Above 5000
- Industrial centre

ECONOMIC ACTIVITY
- Aerospace
- Brewing
- Car/vehicle manufacture
- Chemicals
- Coal
- Electronics
- Engineering
- Finance
- Fish processing
- Food processing
- Hi-tech industry
- Iron & steel
- Metal refining
- Narcotics
- Oil and gas
- Pharmaceuticals
- Printing & publishing
- Shipbuilding
- Textiles
- Timber processing
- Tobacco processing

Caribbean Sea

Central America

Barranquilla
Cartagena
Maracaibo
Barquisimeto
Caracas
Valencia
Ciudad Guayana
VENEZUELA
GUYANA
Georgetown
SURINAME
Paramaribo
French Guiana (to France)
Medellín
Bogotá
COLOMBIA
Cali
Quito
ECUADOR
Guayaquil
Belém
Manaús
Fortaleza
Amazon Basin
BRAZIL
Chiclayo
Natal
Recife
Chimbote
Maceió
Lima
PERU
Cusco
BOLIVIA
Salvador
La Paz
Brasília
Arequipa
Santa Cruz
Arica
Sucre
Iquique
Belo Horizonte
Chuquicamata
PARAGUAY
São Paulo
Rio de Janeiro
Antofagasta
Asunción
San Miguel de Tucumán
Corrientes
Curitiba
Porto Alegre
Córdoba
Santa Fe
URUGUAY
Valparaíso
Mendoza
Rosario
Rio Grande
Santiago
Buenos Aires
Montevideo
Talca
Concepción
ARGENTINA
Neuquén
Bahía Blanca
Valdivia

PACIFIC OCEAN

ATLANTIC OCEAN

Comodoro Rivadavia

Falkland Islands (to UK)

Punta Arenas

Cape Horn

CLIMATE

South America has four main climatic regions; tropical, arid, temperate, and the cold climate of the far south. The Amazon Basin, covered by massive rain forests, and the Guiana Highlands have a humid, tropical climate which allows vegetation to flourish. West of the Andes the climate tends to be very dry. Moist air flowing west from the Atlantic Ocean is prevented from reaching the shores of the Pacific Ocean by the Andes and rain falls before it can pass over the mountains. This creates arid deserts like the Atacama.

EXTREME WEATHER EVENTS

Symbols indicate climatic extremes

Wettest place
QUIBDO (Colombia)
Annual rainfall 899cm

Driest place
ARICA (Chile)
Annual rainfall 0.08cm

Hottest place
RIVADAVIA (Argentina)
Temperature 49°C

Coldest place
SARMIENTO (Argentina)
Temperature -33°C

CLIMATE

Subarctic
Cool continental
Warm temperate
Semi-arid
Arid
Temperate
Tropical
Humid equatorial

SOUTH AMERICA

PATAGONIAN ICEFIELDS

Towards the south of the continent, the climate becomes very cold. Large expanses of ice, forming glaciers are found in southern Patagonia and on islands such as Tierra del Fuego at the tip of South America.

LAND USE AND AGRICULTURE

Many plants now found throughout the world originated in South America, like the tomato, potato and cassava. Today, coffee, cocoa, rubber, soya beans, corn (maize), and sugar cane are widely cultivated, and grapes are grown in sheltered valleys in the Andes. Much of the Amazon Basin is covered by dense rainforest and is unsuitable for cultivation, although some farmers practise 'slash and burn' techniques to make land for crops and cattle farming, which destroy ancient forest.

LAND USE AND AGRICULTURE

Cattle
Pigs
Sheep
Bananas
Corn (Maize)
Citrus fruits
Coca
Cocoa
Cotton
Coffee
Fishing
Oil palms
Peanuts
Rubber
Shellfish
Soya beans
Sugar cane
Vineyards
Wheat

Barren land
Cropland
Desert
Forest
Mountain region
Pasture
Wetland
Major conurbation

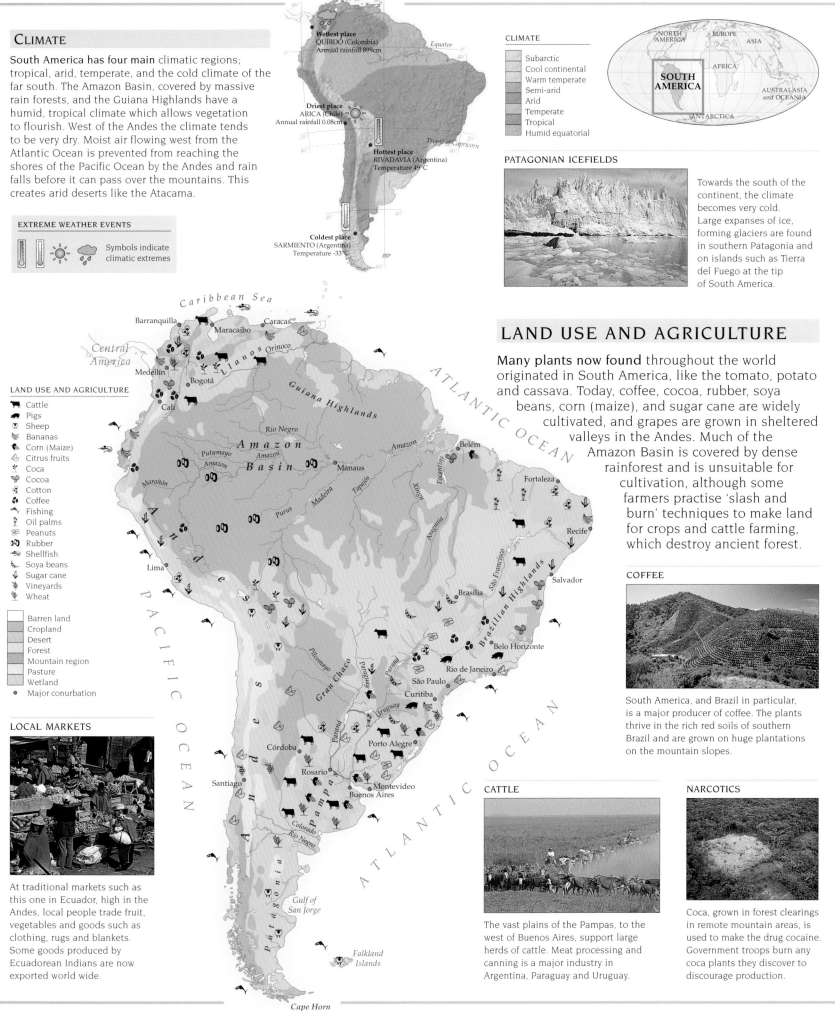

COFFEE

South America, and Brazil in particular, is a major producer of coffee. The plants thrive in the rich red soils of southern Brazil and are grown on huge plantations on the mountain slopes.

LOCAL MARKETS

At traditional markets such as this one in Ecuador, high in the Andes, local people trade fruit, vegetables and goods such as clothing, rugs and blankets. Some goods produced by Ecuadorean Indians are now exported world wide.

CATTLE

The vast plains of the Pampas, to the west of Buenos Aires, support large herds of cattle. Meat processing and canning is a major industry in Argentina, Paraguay and Uruguay.

NARCOTICS

Coca, grown in forest clearings in remote mountain areas, is used to make the drug cocaine. Government troops burn any coca plants they discover to discourage production.

NORTHERN SOUTH AMERICA

BRAZIL, COLOMBIA, ECUADOR, GUYANA, PERU,
SURINAME, VENEZUELA

High mountains, steamy rain forests and hot, grassy
plains cover much of northern South America. From
the 16th century, after the conquest of the Incas, the
western countries were ruled by Spain, while Brazil was
governed by Portugal, Guyana by Britain, and Suriname
by the Dutch. The more recent history of some of these
countries has included periods of civil war and military
rule. Most are still troubled by widespread poverty.

FARMING AND LAND USE

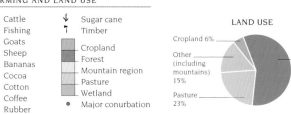

The variety of climates means a wide
range of crops including sugar cane,
cocoa and bananas can be grown for
export. Coffee is the most
important cash crop; Brazil is the
world's leading coffee grower.
Cattle are farmed on the plains of
Colombia, Venezuela and southern
Brazil. Much of the good farmland is
owned by a few rich landowners,
and many peasant farmers do not
have enough land to make a living.

FARMING AND LAND USE

- 🐂 Cattle
- 🐟 Fishing
- 🐐 Goats
- 🐑 Sheep
- 🍌 Bananas
- 🍫 Cocoa
- 🌱 Cotton
- ☕ Coffee
- Rubber
- ↓ Sugar cane
- Timber

Cropland
Forest
Mountain region
Pasture
Wetland
● Major conurbation

LAND USE

Cropland 6%
Forest 56%
Other (including mountains) 15%
Pasture 23%

INDUSTRY

Important oil reserves are found in
Venezuela and parts of the Amazon
Basin; Venezuela is one of the world's
top oil producers. Brazil's cities have
a wide range of industries including
chemicals, clothes and shoes,
and textiles. Metallic minerals,
particularly iron ore, are mined
throughout the area and specially-built
industrial centres like Ciudad Guayana
have been developed to refine them.

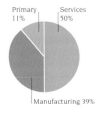

STRUCTURE OF INDUSTRY

Primary 11%
Services 50%
Manufacturing 39%

INDUSTRY

- ⚗ Chemicals
- Food processing
- Iron & steel
- △ Metal refining
- Textiles
- Mining
- Oil
- Timber processing
- Tourism
- Major industrial centre / area
- — Major road

THE LANDSCAPE

The Andes run down the western side of South
America. There are many volcanoes among their peaks,
and earthquakes are common. The tropical rainforests
surrounding the River Amazon take up most of western
Brazil. Huge, dry, flat grasslands called *llanos* cover
central Venezuela and part of eastern Colombia.

Angel Falls (D 2)
Venezuela's Angel Falls is the
world's highest waterfall. Twenty
times as high as Niagara Falls, it
drops 980 m from a spectacular
plateau deep in the Guiana Highlands.

River Amazon (D 4)
The Amazon is the longest
river in South America, and
the second longest in
the world. It flows over
6,439 km from the Peruvian
Andes to the coast of Brazil.
One-fifth of the world's fresh
water is carried by the river.

POPULATION

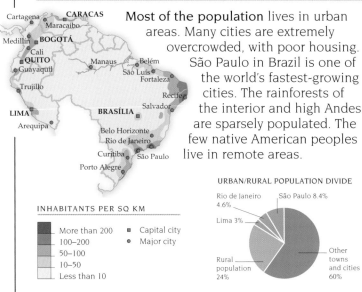

Most of the population lives in urban
areas. Many cities are extremely
overcrowded, with poor housing.
São Paulo in Brazil is one of
the world's fastest-growing
cities. The rainforests of
the interior and high Andes
are sparsely populated. The
few native American peoples
live in remote areas.

INHABITANTS PER SQ KM

- More than 200
- 100–200
- 50–100
- 10–50
- Less than 10
- ■ Capital city
- ● Major city

URBAN/RURAL POPULATION DIVIDE

Rio de Janeiro 4.6%
São Paulo 8.4%
Lima 3%
Rural population 24%
Other towns and cities 60%

Andes (B 5)
The snow-capped
Andes are the
longest mountain
range on Earth.
They stretch
7,250 km down
the whole length
of South America.

Lake Titicaca (C 6)
South America's
largest lake is the
highest navigable
lake in the world
at 3,810 m above
sea level. It lies
across the border
between Peru
and Bolivia.

Pantanal (E 6)
This is the largest area of
wetlands in the world. It spreads
across 130,000 sq km of Brazil.
Many hundreds of plant and
animal species are found here.

Amazon rainforest (D 4)
The enormous rainforest
surrounding the River
Amazon and its tributaries
covers 6,500,000 sq km,
an area almost as big as
Australia. It is estimated
that at least half of all
known living species
are found in the forest.

50

SOUTH AMERICA
Northern South America

SCALE BAR
0 km   200   400
0 miles   200   400

NORTH AMERICA   EUROPE   ASIA
AFRICA
AUSTRALASIA AND OCEANIA
ANTARCTICA

CITIES AND TOWNS
- ■ Over 500,000 people
- ◉ 100,000–500,000
- ○ 50,000–100,000
- ○ Less than 50,000

Caribbean Sea
Gulf of Venezuela
Lesser Antilles
Isla de Margarita
TRINIDAD & TOBAGO
(claimed by Venezuela)

PANAMA
COSTA RICA
HONDURAS
NICARAGUA

Santa Marta
Ríohacha
Coro
Barranquilla
Maracaibo
CARACAS
Barcelona
Maturín
Cartagena
Barquisimeto
Valencia
Sincelejo
Gulf of Darien
Lake Maracaibo
Guanare
El Tigre
Ciudad Guayana
Montería
Mérida
Barinas
Río Orinoco
Ciudad Bolívar
Barrancabermeja
Cúcuta
San Cristóbal
GEORGETOWN
Bello
Bucaramanga
New Amsterdam
Medellín
VENEZUELA
PARAMARIBO
Itagüí
Sogamoso
Linden
Nieuw Nickerie
Kourou
Manizales
Tunja
Angel Falls
CAYENNE
Armenia
BOGOTÁ
Mount Roraima 2810m
SURINAME
FRENCH GUIANA
Tuluá
Villavicencio
Puerto Ayacucho
(French overseas department)
Buenaventura
COLOMBIA
Guiana Highlands
Cali
San José del Guaviare
Boa Vista
Popayán
Caracaraí
(claimed by Surinam)
Florencia
Río Vaupés
Roraima
Amapá
Pasto
Mitú
Pico da Neblina 3014m
Macapá
Ilha Caviana de Fora
Esmeraldas
Tulcán
Río Caquetá
Río Negro
Represa Balbina
Ilha de Marajó
Baía de Marajós
Ibarra
Río Apaporis
Mouths of the Amazon
Latacunga
QUITO
Río Napo
Río Japurá
Manaus
Santarém
Belém
São Luís
Portoviejo
ECUADOR
Río Putumayo
Tefé
Amazon
Parnaíba
Guayaquil
Coari
Altamira
Camocim
Cuenca
Iquitos
Amazon Basin
Fortaleza
Gulf of Guayaquil
Río Marañón
Bacabal
Piripiri
Teresina
Machala
Loja
Río Javari
A m a z o n a s
Itaituba
Maranhão
Mossoró
Tumbes
Imperatriz
Rio Grande do Norte
Talara
Chulucanas
Río Juruá
Río Madeira
Marabá
Floriano
Ceará
Natal
Sullana
B R A Z I L
Humaitá
Río Tapajós
Carolina
Picos
Piauí
Paraíba
João Pessoa
Piura
Chachapoyas
Río Purus
Porto Velho
Balsas
Juazeiro do Norte
Campina Grande
Punta Negra
Cajamarca
Japiim
Feijó
Rio São Manuel
Pernambuco
Recife
Chiclayo
PERU
Acre
Rondônia
Juazeiro
Alagoas
Trujillo
Pucallpa
Rio Branco
Represa de Sobradinho
Maceió
Chimbote
Huaraz
Abunã
Chapada dos Parecis
Rio Xingu
Serra do Cachimbo
Serra dos Carajás
Aracaju
Cerro de Pasco
Huánuco
Puerto Maldonado
Río Guaporé
Serra Formosa
Rio Araguaia
Taguatinga
Estância
Barranca
LIMA
Huancayo
Mato Grosso
Rio Tocantins
Feira de Santana
Callao
Ayacucho
Cusco
Cuiabá
Goiás
BRASÍLIA
Bahia
Salvador
Pisco
Anápolis
Rio São Francisco
Itabuna
Baía de Todos os Santos
Ica
Juliaca
Lake Titicaca
Rondonópolis
Goiânia
Montes Claros
Vitória da Conquista
Canavieiras
Nevado Ampato 6310m
Puno
BOLIVIA
Brazilian Highlands
Arequipa
Volcán Misti 5822m
Jataí
Minas Gerais
Governador Valadares
Tacna
Gran Chaco
Araguari
Uberlândia
Uberaba
Belo Horizonte
Vitória
Mato Grosso do Sul
Campo Grande
Divinópolis
Ribeirão Preto
Espírito Santo
Juiz de Fora
Campos
CHILE
Atacama Desert
Pantanal
Marília
Campinas
Nova Iguaçu
Maringá
Londrina
São Paulo
Santos
Rio de Janeiro
Represa de Itaipú
PARAGUAY
Ponta Grossa
Curitiba
ARGENTINA
Iguazu Falls
Río Iguazu
Joinville
Blumenau
Santa Catarina
Florianópolis
Passo Fundo
Rio Grande do Sul
Santa Maria
Canoas
Porto Alegre
Bagé
Lagoa dos Patos
URUGUAY
Rio Grande
Mirim Lagoon

ATLANTIC OCEAN
PACIFIC OCEAN
Atol das Rocas
Cabo de São Roque
Tropic of Capricorn
Equator

0 km 100
0 miles 100
Isla Darwin
Galapagos Islands (Archipiélago de Colón) (part of Ecuador)
Isla San Salvador
Isla Santa Cruz
Isla San Cristóbal
Isla Isabela
Puerto Baquerizo Moreno
Isla Santa María

LAND HEIGHT
- Above 4000 m
- 2000–4000 m
- 1000–2000 m
- 500–1000 m
- 250–500 m
- 100–250 m
- 0–100 m

SEA DEPTH
- 0–250 m
- 250–500 m
- 500–1000 m
- 1000–2000 m
- 2000–3000 m
- 3000–4000 m
- Below 4000 m

ENVIRONMENTAL ISSUES

The destruction of the Amazon rainforest, which is being reduced by 4 sq km every hour, is the most important environmental issue in this region. This is seriously threatening one of the world's most valuable resources, and wiping out entire species. In 1992, the United Nations held its first Earth Summit in Rio de Janeiro, Brazil, to help highlight this problem.

Colombia all forests destroyed by 2000
Amazon Basin 8 million hectares of forest destroyed every year
Ecuador 50% of forests destroyed by 2000
Atlantic coastal forests 5% of forest remaining

ENVIRONMENTAL ISSUES
- Deforested areas
- Remaining forests

CLIMATE

Lowland areas are hot and humid all year round. The highlands are cooler, and the higher peaks of the Andes are permanently covered by snow.

TEMPERATURE AND PRECIPITATION
- More than 30°C
- 20 to 30°C
- 10 to 20°C
- 0 to 10°C
- Less than 0°

100 Precipitation (mm)

January

July

SOUTHERN SOUTH AMERICA

ARGENTINA, BOLIVIA, CHILE, PARAGUAY, URUGUAY

The southern half of South America forms a long, narrow cone, with landscapes ranging from barren desert in the west, to frozen glaciers in the far south. The whole area was governed by Spain until the early 19th century, and Spanish is still the main language spoken, although the few remaining native American groups use their own languages. Most people now live in vast cities such as Buenos Aires and Santiago.

POPULATION

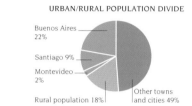

Since the 1950s, there has been a tremendous move from the countryside to the cities, and in Argentina, Chile and Uruguay more than 80% of the people are now city dwellers. The capital cities of all these countries have grown hugely – Buenos Aires now holds a third of Argentina's population, and more than half of Uruguay's people live in the capital, Montevideo.

INHABITANTS PER SQ KM
- More than 100
- 50–100
- 10–50
- Less than 10
- ■ Capital city
- ● Major city

URBAN/RURAL POPULATION DIVIDE

Buenos Aires 22%
Santiago 9%
Montevideo 2%
Rural population 18%
Other towns and cities 49%

INDUSTRY

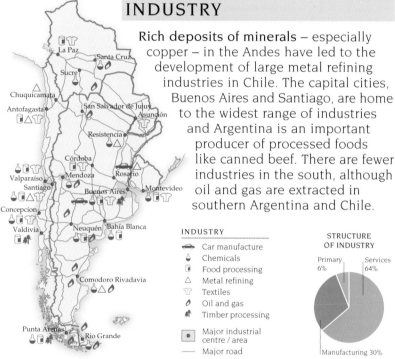

Rich deposits of minerals – especially copper – in the Andes have led to the development of large metal refining industries in Chile. The capital cities, Buenos Aires and Santiago, are home to the widest range of industries and Argentina is an important producer of processed foods like canned beef. There are fewer industries in the south, although oil and gas are extracted in southern Argentina and Chile.

INDUSTRY
- 🚗 Car manufacture
- Chemicals
- Food processing
- △ Metal refining
- Textiles
- Oil and gas
- Timber processing
- ⊡ Major industrial centre / area
- — Major road

STRUCTURE OF INDUSTRY

Primary 6%
Services 64%
Manufacturing 30%

THE LANDSCAPE

Southern South America's landscape varies from tropical forest and dry desert in the north, to sub-Arctic conditions in the south. The towering Andes divide Chile from Argentina. East of the Andes lie forests and rolling grasslands. To the west is a thin coastal strip. The wet, windswept, freezing southern tip of the continent has volcanoes alongside glaciers and fjords.

Gran Chaco (C 3)
This huge stretch of forest and grassland runs from Bolivia, through Paraguay and into Argentina. The south and east provide grazing for cattle.

The Paraná River (C4)
South America's second longest river is the Paraná. It stretches 4,200 km from the Brazilian Highlands, finally flowing into the River Plate near Buenos Aires in Argentina.

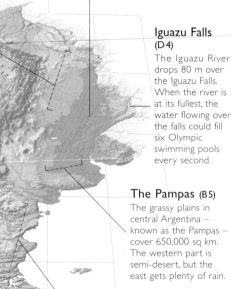

Iguazu Falls (D4)
The Iguazu River drops 80 m over the Iguazu Falls. When the river is at its fullest, the water flowing over the falls could fill six Olympic swimming pools every second.

Atacama Desert (A3)
The Atacama Desert in northern Chile is the driest place on Earth. In some parts, rain has not fallen for hundreds of years.

Chile
The far south of Chile has a dramatic landscape of fjords, lakes, jagged mountain peaks and spectacular glaciers.

The Pampas (B5)
The grassy plains in central Argentina – known as the Pampas – cover 650,000 sq km. The western part is semi-desert, but the east gets plenty of rain.

Patagonia (B8)
The high, windswept plateau of Patagonia covers 770,000 sq km of southern Argentina. The south is dry and freezing cold, with very little vegetation.

ENVIRONMENTAL ISSUES

Many of southern South America's rivers are polluted, particularly close to Buenos Aires. The Itaipú Dam on the Paraná River is the world's largest hydro-electric power project. Deforestation is a persistent problem. In Bolivia, forests are being cut down at a record rate of 200,000 hectares a year. Air quality in Buenos Aires and Santiago is poor, especially in Santiago which is surrounded by mountains, making it difficult for pollution to escape.

ENVIRONMENTAL ISSUES
- Major dam
- Urban air pollution
- Deforested areas
- Polluted river
- ● Major industrial centre

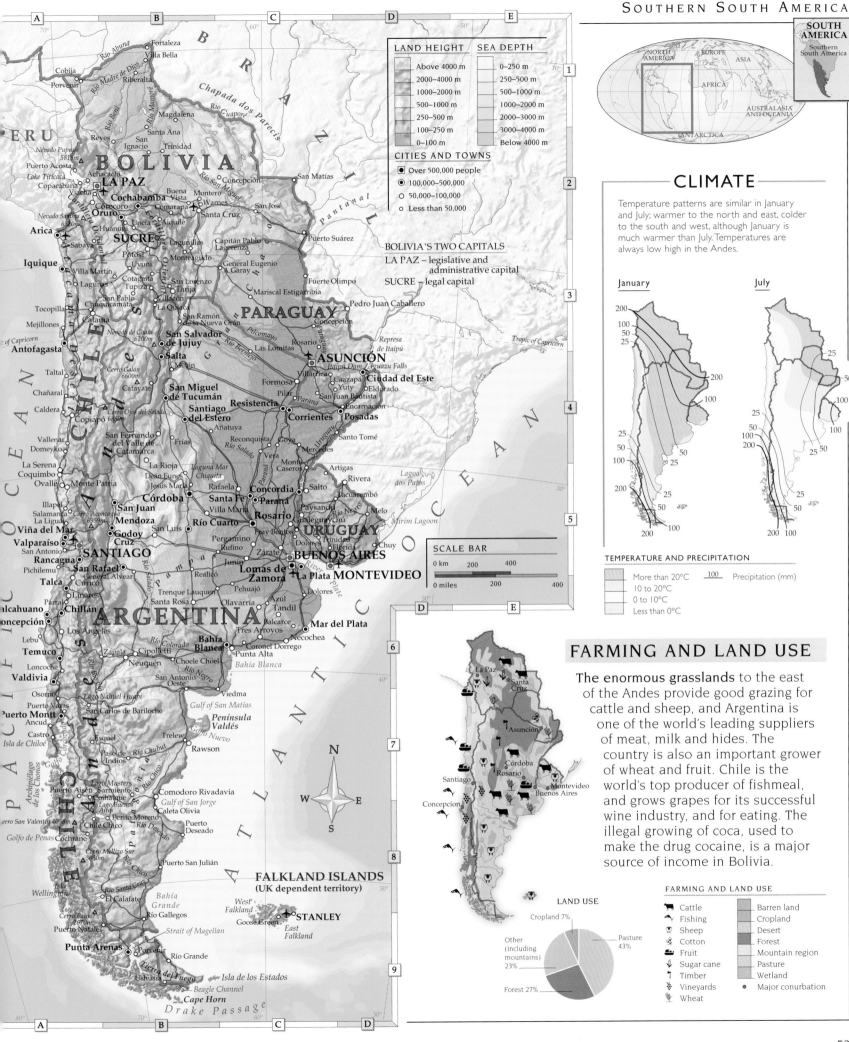

SOUTH AMERICA
Southern South America

LAND HEIGHT
- Above 4000 m
- 2000–4000 m
- 1000–2000 m
- 500–1000 m
- 250–500 m
- 100–250 m
- 0–100 m

SEA DEPTH
- 0–250 m
- 250–500 m
- 500–1000 m
- 1000–2000 m
- 2000–3000 m
- 3000–4000 m
- Below 4000 m

CITIES AND TOWNS
- ■ Over 500,000 people
- ◉ 100,000–500,000
- ○ 50,000–100,000
- ○ Less than 50,000

BOLIVIA'S TWO CAPITALS
LA PAZ – legislative and administrative capital
SUCRE – legal capital

SCALE BAR

0 km   200   400

0 miles   200   400

CLIMATE

Temperature patterns are similar in January and July; warmer to the north and east, colder to the south and west, although January is much warmer than July. Temperatures are always low high in the Andes.

January

July

TEMPERATURE AND PRECIPITATION
- More than 20°C — 100 Precipitation (mm)
- 10 to 20°C
- 0 to 10°C
- Less than 0°C

FARMING AND LAND USE

The enormous grasslands to the east of the Andes provide good grazing for cattle and sheep, and Argentina is one of the world's leading suppliers of meat, milk and hides. The country is also an important grower of wheat and fruit. Chile is the world's top producer of fishmeal, and grows grapes for its successful wine industry, and for eating. The illegal growing of coca, used to make the drug cocaine, is a major source of income in Bolivia.

LAND USE
- Cropland 7%
- Pasture 43%
- Other (including mountains) 23%
- Forest 27%

FARMING AND LAND USE
- Cattle
- Fishing
- Sheep
- Cotton
- Fruit
- Sugar cane
- Timber
- Vineyards
- Wheat
- Barren land
- Cropland
- Desert
- Forest
- Mountain region
- Pasture
- Wetland
- ● Major conurbation

FALKLAND ISLANDS
(UK dependent territory)

CONTINENTAL EUROPE

Europe is the world's second smallest continent, occupying the western tip of the vast Eurasian landmass. To the north and west are old highlands, with the high peaks of the Alps in the south. Most people live on the densely populated North European Plain, which runs from southern England, through northern France, across Germany into Russia.

CROSS-SECTION THROUGH EUROPE

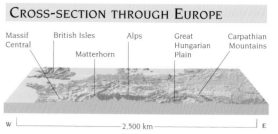

Massif Central | British Isles | Matterhorn | Alps | Great Hungarian Plain | Carpathian Mountains

W ⊢——— 2,500 km ———⊣ E

In the west, the land rises up from the Atlantic coast towards the Massif Central in France, and the high peaks of the Alps. Between the Alps and the Carpathian Mountains is the Great Hungarian Plain, where the River Danube flows on its way to the Black Sea.

PHYSICAL EUROPE

The ancient mountains of northwest Europe were scoured and smoothed by glaciers in the last Ice Age. The Alps are newer and more jagged – pushed up when Africa collided with Europe. In between is the North European Plain, where thick layers of fertile soils allow many different crops to be grown.

1 THE FROZEN NORTH

Europe's northern coastline stretches deep into the Arctic Circle. Here in Norway, icebergs drift into the deep, wide-bottomed fjords.

THE NORTH EUROPEAN PLAIN 2

The North European Plain has low, rolling hills and plains. Much of the area is cultivated and used for growing crops like wheat and sugar beet.

3 ANCIENT HIGHLANDS

Some of the world's oldest rocks are found in northwest Europe. Erosion by glaciers in the last Ice Age created smoothed hills such as the mountains of Wales.

4 THE ATLANTIC COAST

On Europe's Atlantic coast, the force of waves and winds has created striking landforms like this huge sand dune in southwest France.

THE ALPS 5

The Alps are Europe's major mountain chain. They formed about 65 million years ago. The Matterhorn is one of the most dramatic peaks.

ELEVATION

5000m
4000m
3000m
2000m
1000m
500m
250m
100m
sea level
below sea level
⟩—⟨ cross-section

SCALE 1:31,000,000

0 km   300   600
0 miles   300   600

54

POLITICAL EUROPE

Europe's population increased rapidly during the 18th and 19th centuries, following the Industrial Revolution. In the 20th century, Europe suffered a series of wars which redrew the political map. From 1989–1991, communist governments in eastern Europe and the former Soviet Union collapsed, as political reform swept through the countries behind the 'Iron Curtain'. In 2004 the European Union took a further step towards expansion.

EUROPEAN UNION

six original members, 1957

nine further members, 1973 – 1995

ten new members, 2004

REGIONAL IDENTITY

Throughout Europe, there is a growing call to recognize regional cultural identity. The Basque region, bordering southwest France and Spain, is one example.

RURAL LIFE

Away from Europe's bustling cities, traditional rural lifestyles survive. Here in Ireland, a winter shelter is being made for cattle.

POPULATION

Capital cities
- ◉ Above 500,000
- ◉ 100,000 to 500,000
- ● 50,000 to 100,000

SCALE 1:27,500,000

0 km   300   600

0 miles   300   600

POPULATION

More than 700 million people live in Europe, and its population is highly urbanized. In Belgium and the Netherlands, almost 90% of people live in cities. In the south and east, more people still live in rural areas. The northern countries have the smallest populations, because much of the land is too cold to be habitable.

POPULATION DENSITY
(People per sq km)

Below 49   100–149   200–299
50–99   150–199   Above 300

Largest city
MOSCOW
13.2 million people

SPREADING CITIES

Amsterdam, in the Netherlands is part of a conurbation, a large built-up area where several towns or cities have merged together to form a single urban area.

STANDARDS OF LIVING

Living standards are generally much lower in eastern Europe than in the wealthier west. Homelessness and unemployment are still problems, even in the most prosperous countries.

STANDARD OF LIVING
(UN Human Development Index)

low   high

EUROPEAN GEOGRAPHY

Europe is blessed with a temperate climate, ample mineral reserves, and good transport links. During the 18th and 19th centuries the continent was transformed, as new methods of production made industry and farming more efficient and productive. Today, in many countries, 'heavy' industries have been replaced by hi-tech and service industries. Agriculture is still important and many crops thrive on Europe's fertile plains.

INDUSTRY

Western Europe has some of the world's wealthiest countries. In countries such as France, Germany and the UK, traditional industries like iron and steel-making are now being replaced by light industries such as electronics, and services like finance and insurance. In Eastern Europe, industry was subsidized by the communist governments for years. Many factories are old fashioned and need investment to improve their equipment and production methods.

ECONOMIC ACTIVITY

- ✈ Aerospace
- 🚗 Car/vehicle manufacture
- ⚗ Chemicals
- ⛏ Coal
- ⚓ Defence
- 💻 Electronics
- ⚙ Engineering
- Ⓢ Finance
- 🍴 Food processing
- 💻 Hi-tech industry
- 🚆 Iron & steel
- ⚗ Oil and gas
- 📖 Printing & publishing
- 👕 Textiles
- 🌲 Timber processing

GNP per capita (US$)
- Below 1999
- 2000-4999
- 5000-9999
- 10,000-19,999
- 20,000-24,999
- Above 25,000
- Industrial centre

MINERAL RESOURCES

Europe has few sizeable reserves of metallic minerals; most were used up by industry during the 19th century. Oil, gas and coal are found in large quantities – gas in the North Sea and oil in the Volga basin. Coal, though abundant, is being steadily depleted.

MINERAL RESOURCES
- Bauxite
- Chromium
- Copper
- Iron
- Manganese
- Nickel
- Uranium
- Oil/gas field
- Coal field

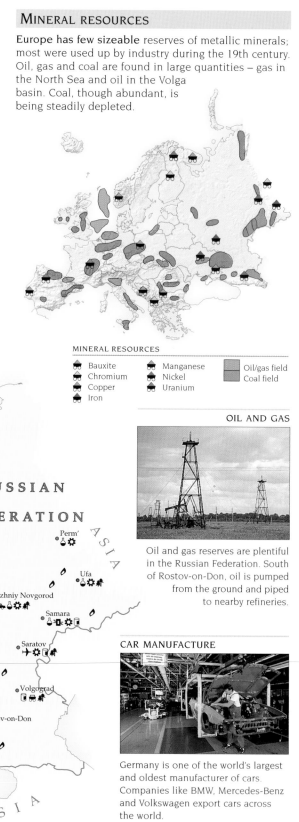

OIL AND GAS

Oil and gas reserves are plentiful in the Russian Federation. South of Rostov-on-Don, oil is pumped from the ground and piped to nearby refineries.

CAR MANUFACTURE

Germany is one of the world's largest and oldest manufacturer of cars. Companies like BMW, Mercedes-Benz and Volkswagen export cars across the world.

FINANCE

London, Frankfurt and Paris are among the most important financial centres in the world. Many banks and financial institutions have their headquarters here. At the London Stock Exchange, people buy and sell stocks and shares.

CLIMATE

Europe's climate is temperate with few climatic extremes. In the far north, Europe extends into the Arctic Circle and the climate is so cold that in the winter, the Baltic Sea freezes over. Towards the Atlantic coast in the west, the climate becomes wetter and warmer because of a warm ocean current, known as the Gulf Stream. Countries such as Italy and Spain which border the Mediterranean Sea, have long, hot summers and low rainfall, which can sometimes lead to problems such as drought.

CLIMATE

- Tundra
- Subarctic
- Cool continental
- Temperate/humid
- Mediterranean
- Semi-arid

Coldest place
UST' SHCHUGOR (Russ. Fed.)
Temperature -55°C

Driest place
ASTRAKHAN' (Russ. Fed.)
Annual rainfall 160 mm

Wettest place
CRKVICE (Serbia & Montenegro)
Annual rainfall 4650 mm

Hottest place
SEVILLE (Spain)
Temperature 50°C

EXTREME WEATHER EVENTS

Symbols indicate climatic extremes

THE MEDITERRANEAN CLIMATE

The mild, warm climate around the Mediterranean Sea allows olives, citrus fruits and grapes to thrive. Long, sunny days also help the fruits ripen. Grapes are harvested and crushed to make many different wines.

LAND USE AND AGRICULTURE

Europe's agricultural heart is the North European Plain, where fertile soils and ample rainfall mean that a variety of crops can be grown. Wheat is the main grain crop, and a wide range of fruit and vegetables are also grown. Dairy and beef cattle are raised for their milk and meat throughout Europe. In the south, the Mediterranean climate allows citrus fruits and olives to grow. Forests cover much of northern Scandinavia, while in the hills of the British Isles, sheep farming is common.

CROPLANDS

Many different crops are grown on the North European Plain. Sunflowers, wheat, and sugar beet – used to make sugar – are amongst the main crops grown there.

FISHING

The north Atlantic Ocean provides a rich marine harvest for fishermen. Today the cod, haddock and mackerel stocks have to be protected from over-fishing.

LAND USE AND AGRICULTURE

- Cattle
- Goats
- Pigs
- Reindeer
- Sheep
- Cereals
- Citrus fruits
- Fishing
- Fruit
- Olive oil
- Potatoes
- Root crops
- Shellfish
- Sunflowers
- Timber
- Vineyards

- Cropland
- Forest
- Ice cap
- Mountain region
- Pasture
- Tundra
- Wetland
- ● Major conurbation

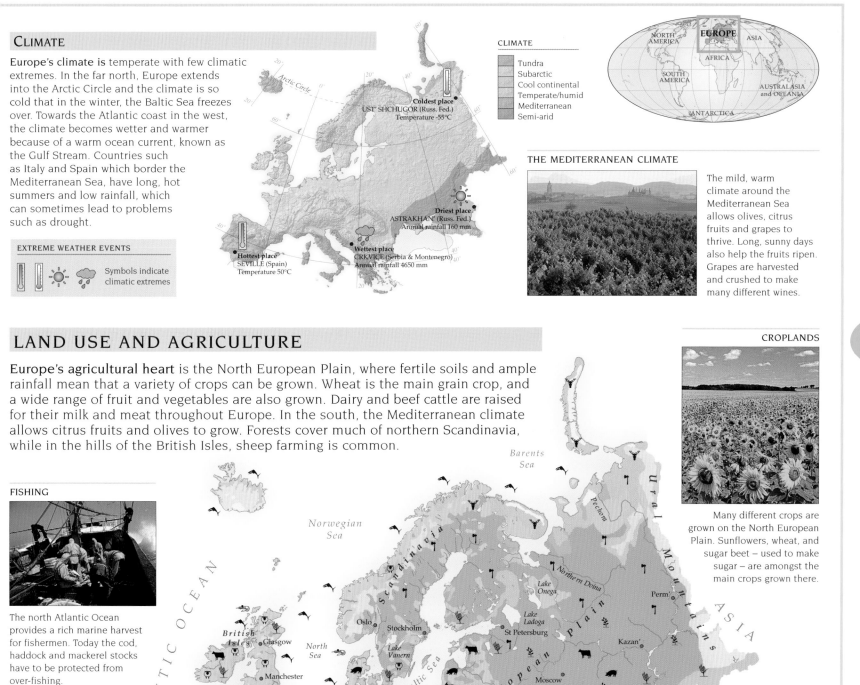

Barents Sea

Norwegian Sea

ATLANTIC OCEAN

British Isles — Glasgow

North Sea

Manchester
Birmingham
Hamburg
London
Brussels
Berlin
Paris
Warsaw
Prague
Munich
Vienna
Milan
Marseille
Barcelona
Rome
Athens

Oslo
Stockholm
St Petersburg
Lake Ladoga
Lake Onega
Lake Vanern
Baltic Sea
Moscow
Kazan'
Perm'
Kiev
Donets'k
Odesa
Bucharest
Istanbul

Scandinavia
North European Plain
Ural Mountains
ASIA

Pechora
Northern Dvina
Volga
Don
Dnieper
Danube
Rhine
Elbe
Loire
Alps
Pyrenees
Tagus
Madrid

Black Sea
Caucasus
Mediterranean Sea
AFRICA
ASIA

DAIRY FARMING

Dairy farming is very common across northern Europe. Cows grazed on rich pastures produce milk – used for making butter and cheese.

NORTHERN EUROPE

DENMARK, ESTONIA, FINLAND, ICELAND, LATVIA, LITHUANIA, NORWAY, SWEDEN

Denmark, Sweden and Norway are together known as Scandinavia. These countries, along with the North Atlantic island of Iceland, have similar languages and cultures. Finland has a very different language and a separate identity from its Scandinavian neighbours. Estonia, Latvia and Lithuania, known as the Baltic states, were part of the Soviet Union until 1989, when each became an independent country.

INDUSTRY

In Scandinavia, many natural resources are used in industry: timber for paper and furniture; iron ore for steel and cars; and fish and natural gas from the seas. Hydro-electric power is generated by water flowing down steep mountain slopes. The Baltic states still rely on Russia to supply their raw materials and energy.

INDUSTRY

- 🚗 Car manufacture
- ⚗ Chemicals
- ⚙ Engineering
- Fish processing
- Hydro-electric power
- Shipbuilding
- Timber processing
- Tourism
- ▣ Major industrial centre / area
- — Major road

STRUCTURE OF INDUSTRY

Primary 4%
Services 65%
Manufacturing 31%

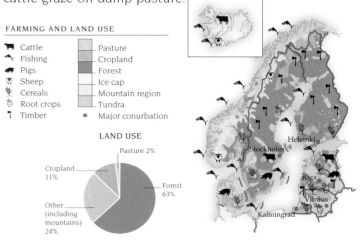

POPULATION

The population is distributed mainly along the warmer and flatter southern and coastal areas. Population totals and densities are low for all of the countries, and Iceland has the lowest population density in Europe, with just three people per sq km. Many Scandinavians have holiday homes on the islands, along the lake shores, or in coastal areas.

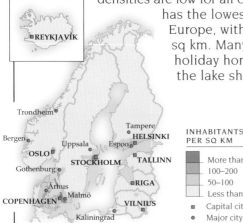

INHABITANTS PER SQ KM

- More than 200
- 100–200
- 50–100
- Less than 50
- ▪ Capital city
- ▪ Major city

URBAN/RURAL POPULATION DIVIDE

Helsinki 1.8%   Stockholm 2.5%
Oslo 1.7%
Other towns and cities 64%
Rural population 30%

FARMING AND LAND USE

Southern Denmark and Sweden are the most productive areas, with pig farming, dairy-farming and crops such as wheat, barley and potatoes. Sheep farming is important in southern Norway and Iceland. In the Baltic states, cereals, potatoes and sugar beet are the main crops and cattle graze on damp pasture.

FARMING AND LAND USE

- Cattle
- Fishing
- Pigs
- Sheep
- Cereals
- Root crops
- Timber
- Pasture
- Cropland
- Forest
- Ice cap
- Mountain region
- Tundra
- ● Major conurbation

LAND USE

Pasture 2%
Cropland 11%
Forest 63%
Other (including mountains) 24%

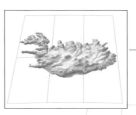

THE LANDSCAPE

The north and west of Scandinavia is extremely rugged and mountainous, with landscapes eroded by ice. In the south of Scandinavia the land is flatter, with fertile soils deposited by glaciers. Much of Finland, Norway and Sweden is covered by dense forests. The Baltic states are much lower, with rounded hills and many lakes and marshes.

The land of ice and fire. Iceland is one of the world's most active volcanic areas. There are about 200 volcanoes on the island, along with bubbling hot springs, mud-holes, and geysers which spurt boiling water and steam high into the air.

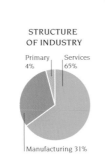

Fjords
Norway has many fjords: deep, wide valleys, drowned by seawater when the ice melted at the end of the last Ice Age.

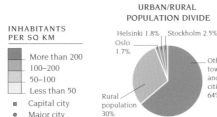

Baltic Sea (D 7)
Ships from Finland, Sweden and the Baltic states use the Baltic Sea as their route to the north Atlantic Ocean. In winter, much of the sea is frozen.

Glacial lakes
Finland and Sweden have many thousands of lakes. During the last Ice Age, glaciers scoured hollows which filled with water when the ice melted.

Courland Spit (D 7)
This wide sandspit runs fo 100 km along the Baltic c of Lithuania and the Russ enclave of Kaliningrad. It encloses a huge lagoon

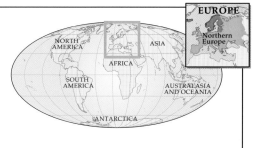

EUROPE
Northern Europe

ENVIRONMENTAL ISSUES

Northern Europe has been badly affected by industrial pollution from other parts of Europe. Polluted air moves north, and mixes with the rain to create acid rain. This poisons forests and lakes, destroying the plants and animals living in them. In Norway and Sweden, electricity is produced by dams that obtain power from the plentiful water supply. Hydroelectric power is a clean, alternative energy source.

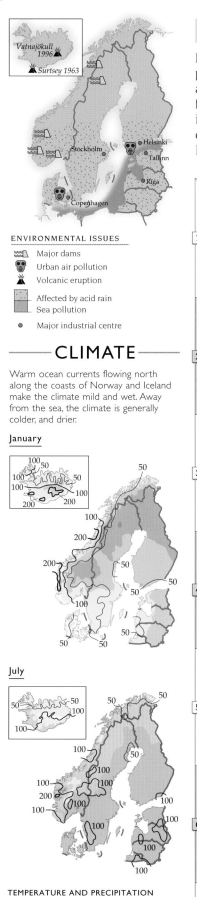

Vatnajökull 1996
▲ Surtsey 1963

Stockholm
Helsinki
Tallinn
Riga
Copenhagen

ENVIRONMENTAL ISSUES

- Major dams
- Urban air pollution
- Volcanic eruption
- Affected by acid rain
  Sea pollution
- Major industrial centre

CLIMATE

Warm ocean currents flowing north along the coasts of Norway and Iceland make the climate mild and wet. Away from the sea, the climate is generally colder, and drier.

January

100
100
100
50
50
100
100
200
200
100
200
50
50
50
50

July

50
50
50
100
100
100
100
200
100
100
100
100
100
100

TEMPERATURE AND PRECIPITATION

More than 15°C	0 to -5°C
10 to 15°C	-5 to -10°C
5 to 10°C	-10 to -15°C
0 to 5°C	Less than -15°C

100
Precipitation (mm)

ICELAND
Norwegian Sea

Bolungarvík
Raufarhöfn
Ísafjardhur
Siglufjördhur
Husavík
Stykkishólmur
Akureyri
REYKJAVÍK
Seydhisfjördhur
Neskaupstadhur
Solfoss
Djúpivogur
Thorlákshöfn
Hvannadalshnúkur 2119m
Surtsey
Vestmannaeyjar
Faxaflói

ATLANTIC OCEAN

Arctic Circle

SCALE BAR

0 km   100   200
0 miles   100   200

LAND HEIGHT
- 2000–4000 m
- 1000–2000 m
- 500–1000 m
- 250–500 m
- 100–250 m
- 0–100 m

SEA DEPTH
- 0–50 m
- 50–100 m
- 100–250 m
- 250–500 m
- 500–1000 m
- 1000–2000 m
- Below 2000 m

CITIES AND TOWNS
- Over 500,000 people
- 100,000–500,000
- 50,000–100,000
- Less than 50,000

North Cape (Nordkapp)
Magerøya
Barents Sea
Sørøya
Varangerhalvøya
Talvik
Latseluv
Tana
Kirkenes
Ringvassøy
Kvaløya
Talvik
Alta
Vadsø
Válljohka
Karigasniemi
Inarijärvi
Tromsø
Senja
Andøya
Kaamanen
Ivalo
Harstad
Kaaresuvanto
Saariselkä
Vesterålen
Finnmarksvidda
Lofoten
Lapland
RUSSIAN FEDERATION
Vestfjorden
Narvik
Torneträsk
Muonio
Bodø
Kebnekaise 2117m
Kiruna
Kolari
Ounasjoki
Sattanen
Sodankylä
Malmberget
Gällivare
Rovaniemi
Komijärvi
Skalka
Arctic Circle
Jokkmokk
Kuusamo
Mo i Rana
Svartis
Boden
Haparanda
Tornio
Kemi
Mosjøen
Arvidsjaur
Luleå
Piteå
Hailuoto
Kempele
Pudasjärvi
Vega
Skellefteå
Raahe
Oulu
Storuman
Oulujoki
Suomussalmi
Namsos
Storuman
Vilhelmina
Lycksele
Umeå
Kokkola (Karleby)
Kajaani
Oulujärvi
Kuhmo
Steinkjer
Verdal
Dorotea
FINLAND
Nurmes
Sotkamo
Levanger
Strömsund
Hoting
Örnsköldsvik
Jakobstad (Pietarsaari)
Iisalmi
Pielinen
SWEDEN
Östersund
Kramfors
Härnösand
Vaasa (Vasa)
Lapua
Siilinjärvi
Kuopio
Joensuu
Trondheim
Stjørdalshalsen
Storsjön
Svenstavik
Timrå
Närpes (Närpiö)
Seinäjoki
Keuruu
Äänekoski
Kallavesi
Molde
Åndalsnes
 Range
Sundsvall
Kankaanpää
Näsijärvi
Jyväskylä
Haukivesi
Ålesund
Ratan
Sveg
Hudiksvall
Pori
Tampere
Päijänne
Lappeenranta
Imatra
Dombås
Femunden
Idre
Ljusdal
Rauma
Nokia
Hämeenlinna
Lake Ladoga
Glittertind 2472m
Ringebu
Bollnäs
Söderhamn
Mora
Hyvinkää
Kouvola
Jotunheimen
Lillehammer
Rättvik
Gävle
Riihimäki
Porvoo
Kotka
Bergen
Gjøvik
Hamar
Leksand
Falun
Sandviken
Hämeenkylä
Turku (Åbo)
Vantaa
Gol
Mjøsa
Malung
Borlänge
Tierp
Salo
Espoo
HELSINKI
Eidfjord
Hønefoss
Hardangervidda
Lillestrøm
Ludvika
Avesta
Sala
Uppsala
Hanko (Hangö)
Kunda
Narva
Leirvik
Sandvika
OSLO
Filipstad
Norrtälje
Åland Islands
Haugesund
Drammen
Ski
Grums
Karlstad
Västerås
Nora
Täby
TALLINN
Kohtla-Järve
Stavanger
Kongsberg
Moss
Sarpsborg
Örebro
Sollentuna
Södertälje
STOCKHOLM
Lake Peipus
ESTONIA
Sandnes
Horten
Halden
Åmål
Säffle
Hjälmaren
Nyköping
Hiiumaa
Pärnu
Tartu
Räpina
Moi
Evje
Fredrikstad
Strömstad
Mellerud
Vänern
Askersund
Mariestad
Norrköping
Vortsjärv
Uulu
Mõisaküla
Võru
Arendal
Lidköping
Vättern
Linköping
Gotland
Saaremaa
Gulf of Riga
Kristiansand
Uddevalla
Trollhättan
Visby
Ventspils
Kolka
LATVIA
Viļaka
Gothenburg (Göteborg)
Borås
Jönköping
Kungsbacka
Oskarshamn
Saulkrasti
Hjørring
Mölndal
Varberg
Borgholm
RIGA
Skrīveri
Ludza
Aalborg
Lasø
Ljungby
Växjö
Öland
Jūrmala
Jelgava
Dagda
Hobro
Randers
Halmstad
Laholm
Kalmar
Liepāja
Pakruojis
Rokiškis
Daugavpils
Holstebro
Viborg
Helsingborg
Karlskrona
Salantai
Dotnuva
Zarasai
Jutland
Lund
Kristianstad
Šiauliai
Panevėžys
Klaipėda
LITHUANIA
Kaunas
Jonava
VILNIUS
BELARUS
Århus
Helsingør
Kattegat
Hanöbukten
Baltic Sea
Neringa
Šilutė
Ukmergė
Giedraičiai
Ringkøbing Fjord
DENMARK
COPENHAGEN (KØBENHAVN)
Malmö
Kaliningrad
Courland Lagoon
Zelenogradsk
Neman
Alytus
Salčininkai
Esbjerg
Kolding
Odense
Slagelse
Zealand
Rønne
Bornholm
Gulf of Danzig
Mamonovo
Veisiejai
Rømø
Lolland
Falster
Nykøbing
KALININGRAD (part of Russian Federation)
GERMANY
POLAND

ICELAND
Norwegian Sea
Atlantic Ocean
North Sea
Norwegian Sea
Skagerrak
Gulf of Bothnia
Gulf of Finland
Arctic Circle

THE LOW COUNTRIES

BELGIUM, LUXEMBOURG, NETHERLANDS

Belgium, Luxembourg and the Netherlands are called the Low Countries because most of their land is flat and low-lying. Much of the Netherlands lies below sea level, and over hundreds of years the Dutch have built dykes and dams to prevent flooding, and have pumped water off large areas of land to reclaim them from the sea. The Low Countries are Europe's most densely populated countries, but most of their people have a high living standard.

ENVIRONMENTAL ISSUES

Huge land reclamation projects in the Netherlands, such as the IJsselmeer project, have created some new land for agricultural use, and also for houses, roads and open spaces. Heavy industry has caused serious air pollution in cities such as Amsterdam and Rotterdam, and added to Europe's acid rain problem.

ENVIRONMENTAL ISSUES

- 🏭 Urban air pollution
- Built-up areas
- Reclaimed land
- Polluted river
- Major industrial centre

CLIMATE

The Low Countries share a similar climate, with mild winters and warm summers. Only in the upland Ardennes region does rainfall increase and temperatures decrease.

January

July

TEMPERATURE AND PRECIPITATION

- More than 15°C
- 10 to 15°C
- 5 to 10°C
- 0 to 5°C
- Less than 0°C

100 Precipitation (mm)

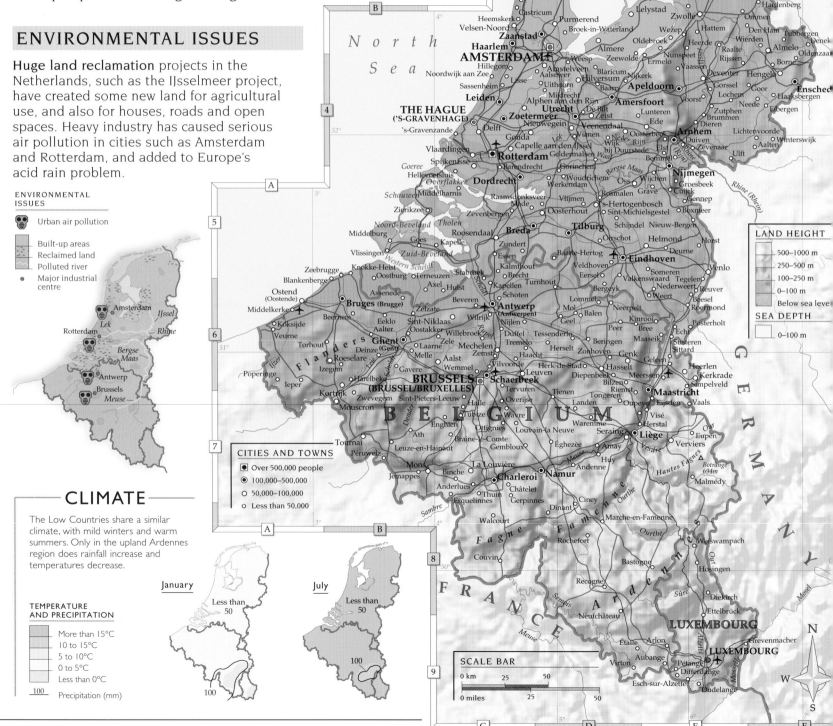

NETHERLANDS' TWO CAPITALS
AMSTERDAM - capital
THE HAGUE - seat of government

LAND HEIGHT
- 500–1000 m
- 250–500 m
- 100–250 m
- 0–100 m
- Below sea level

SEA DEPTH
- 0–100 m

CITIES AND TOWNS
- ■ Over 500,000 people
- ◉ 100,000–500,000
- ○ 50,000–100,000
- ○ Less than 50,000

SCALE BAR
0 km   25   50
0 miles   25   50

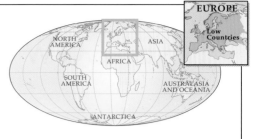

POPULATION

More than 25 million people live in the Low Countries and nine out of every ten people live in a town or city. The largest urban area – known as the *Randstad Holland* – is in the Netherlands. It runs in an unbroken line from Rotterdam in the south, to Amsterdam in the west. Even most rural areas in the Low Countries are densely populated.

INHABITANTS PER SQ KM

- More than 200
- 100–200
- 50–100
- 0–50

■ Capital city
● Major city

URBAN/RURAL POPULATION DIVIDE

Amsterdam 2.8%
Brussels 3.9%
Rotterdam 2.3%
Rural population 8%
Other towns and cities 83%

INDUSTRY

The Low Countries are an important centre for the hi-tech and electronics industries. Good transport links to the rest of Europe allow them to sell their products in other countries. The built-up area stretching from Amsterdam in the Netherlands to Antwerp in Belgium has the greatest number of factories. Luxembourg is also an important banking centre; many international banks have their headquarters in its capital city.

STRUCTURE OF INDUSTRY

Primary 3%
Services 68%
Manufacturing 29%

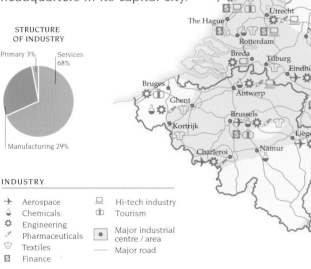

INDUSTRY

✈ Aerospace
⚗ Chemicals
⚙ Engineering
🧪 Pharmaceuticals
👕 Textiles
S Finance
💻 Hi-tech industry
🏛 Tourism
▪ Major industrial centre / area
— Major road

FARMING AND LAND USE

The Low Countries' fertile soils and flat plains provide excellent conditions for farming. The main crops grown are barley, potatoes, and flax for making linen. In the Netherlands, much farmland is used for dairy-farming. The country is also famous for growing flowers, which are exported around the world. Flowers and vegetables are grown either in open fields or in enormous greenhouses, which allow production all year round.

LAND USE

Forest 16%
Pasture 26%
Cropland 29%
Other (including urban) 29%

FARMING AND LAND USE

- 🐄 Cattle
- 🐖 Pigs
- 🌾 Cereals
- Flax
- 🌷 Flowers
- 🐄 Market gardening
- 🌱 Sugar beet
- Pasture
- Cropland
- Forest
- Wetland
- ● Major conurbation

THE LANDSCAPE

The Low Countries are largely flat and low-lying. The ancient hills of the Ardennes, in the far southeast, are the only higher region. They rise to heights of more than 500 m. Two major rivers – the Meuse and the Rhine – flow across the Low Countries to their mouths in the North Sea. At the coast, the River Rhine deposits large quantities of sediment to form a delta.

Polders
In the Netherlands, land has been reclaimed from the sea since the Middle Ages by building dykes and drainage ditches. These areas of land are called polders. They are very fertile.

The River Rhine (E4)
The River Rhine erodes and carries large amounts of sediment along its course. When it reaches the Netherlands it divides into three rivers. As they approach the North Sea, the rivers slow down, depositing the sediment to form a delta.

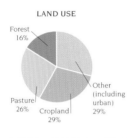

Low-lying Netherlands
Over two-thirds of the Netherlands lies at or below sea level. This makes flooding a constant threat in coastal areas.

Flanders (B6)
The plains of Flanders in western Belgium have fertile soils which were deposited by glaciers during the last Ice Age. They provide excellent land for growing crops.

Heathlands
The heathlands on the Dutch-Belgian border have thin, sandy soils. The only plants which grow well here are heathers and gorse.

The Ardennes (D8)
The hills of the Ardennes were formed over 300 million years ago. They have many deep valleys, which have been eroded by rivers like the Meuse.

THE BRITISH ISLES

UNITED KINGDOM, IRELAND

The British Isles lie off the northwest coast of mainland Europe. They are made up of two large islands and over 5,000 smaller ones. Politically, the region is divided into two countries: the United Kingdom – England, Wales, Scotland and Northern Ireland – and Ireland. Geographically, the British Isles are divided between highlands to the north and west, and lowlands to the south and east.

THE LANDSCAPE

Low rolling hills, high moorlands, and small fields with high hedges are all typical of the British Isles. Ireland is known as the Emerald Isle, because heavy rainfall gives it a lush, green appearance. Scotland and Wales are mountainous; the rocks forming the mountains there are some of the oldest in the world.

Indented coastlines
The west coast of the British Isles faces the Atlantic Ocean, and over 3,000 km of open sea to the North American continent. Storms and high waves constantly batter the hard, rocky coastline, giving it a jagged outline.

Ben Nevis (C 4)
This mountain is the highest point in the British Isles. It is 1,343 m above sea level.

The Lake District (D 5)
The Lake District National Park has England's highest peak, Scafell Pike, at 978 m (E4), its deepest lake, Wast Water (80 m), and its largest lake, Windermere (16 km long).

The Pennines (D 6)
The Pennines are a chain of high hills, topped by moorland. They run for over 400 km, and are known as the 'backbone of England'.

The Burren (A 6)
The Burren is a large area of limestone rock in the west of Ireland. Its flat surfaces are known as limestone 'pavements'. There are also many caves and sinkholes in the area.

Rias
Rias are river valleys that have been drowned by rising sea levels. The southern coast of southwest England has many good examples.

The Fens (E 6)
This is the flattest area in England. Much of the land here has been reclaimed from the sea.

FARMING AND LAND USE

The English lowlands and the wide, flat stretches of land in East Anglia are the agricultural heartland of the United Kingdom. The country is no longer self-sufficient in food, but wheat, potatoes and other vegetables, and fruits, are widely grown. In Ireland, and in central and southern England, dairy and beef cattle feed off grassy pastures. In the hilly and mountainous areas, sheep farming is more usual.

FARMING AND LAND USE

- 🐂 Cattle
- 🐟 Fishing
- 🐑 Sheep
- 🌾 Cereals
- 🐄 Market gardening
- 🥕 Root crops
- ▢ Pasture
- ▢ Cropland
- ▢ Forest
- ▢ Mountain region
- ● Major conurbation

LAND USE

Cropland 24%
Pasture 50%
Other (including urban) 17%
Forest 9%

INDUSTRY

The United Kingdom's traditional industries, such as coal mining, iron and steel-making, and textiles, have declined in recent years. Today, newer industries make cars, chemicals, electronic and hi-tech goods. Service industries, especially banking and insurance, have grown in importance. The country's most valuable natural resource is its large North Sea oil and gas fields.

INDUSTRY

- ✈ Aerospace
- 🚗 Car manufacture
- 🧪 Chemicals
- ⚙ Engineering
- 👕 Textiles
- Ⓢ Finance
- 💻 Hi-tech industry
- 🎡 Tourism
- ▪ Major industrial centre / area
- — Major road

STRUCTURE OF INDUSTRY

Primary 2% | Services 67%
Manufacturing 31%

POPULATION

The United Kingdom is densely populated, with most of the people living in urban areas. The southeast is the most crowded part of the country. The Scottish Highlands are less populated today than they were 200 years ago. Ireland is still mainly rural, with many Irish people making their living from farming.

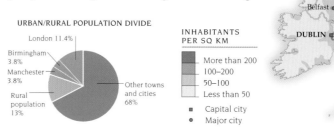

URBAN/RURAL POPULATION DIVIDE

London 11.4%
Birmingham 3.8%
Manchester 3.8%
Rural population 13%
Other towns and cities 68%

INHABITANTS PER SQ KM
- ▢ More than 200
- ▢ 100–200
- ▢ 50–100
- ▢ Less than 50
- ▪ Capital city
- ● Major city

EUROPE

British Isles

ENVIRONMENTAL ISSUES

Air pollution is becoming a serious problem in many British cities, as the number of vehicles using the roads increases. The seas around the British Isles have been polluted by sewage and industrial waste. In recent years, several major oil spills have occurred off the coast of the United Kingdom.

Shetland Islands 1993

Milford Haven 1996

ENVIRONMENTAL ISSUES

- Major oil spill
- Urban air pollution
- Sea pollution
- Polluted rivers
- Major industrial centre

CLIMATE

The British Isles' climate is moderated by the warm Atlantic ocean current called the Gulf Stream. The west is generally wetter than the east, and the south warmer than the north.

January

July

TEMPERATURE AND PRECIPITATION

- More than 15°C
- 10 to 15°C
- 5 to 10°C
- 2.5 to 5°C
- Less than 2.5°C

100 Precipitation (mm)

FRANCE

ANDORRA, MONACO, FRANCE

France has helped to shape the history and culture of Europe for centuries. Today, as a founder-member of the European Union, France is a keen supporter of the eventual political and economic integration of Europe's different countries. France is Western Europe's leading farming nation, and one of the world's top industrial powers. Its cultural attractions and scenery draw tourists from around the world.

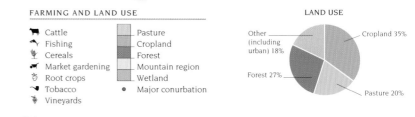

FARMING AND LAND USE

France is able to produce a variety of crops because of its rich soils and mild climate. Wheat is grown in many parts of the north, along with potatoes and other vegetables. Fields of maize and sunflowers and fruit orchards, are found in the south, while grapes for the famous wine industry are grown across the country. Beef and dairy cattle are grazed on low-lying pasture.

FARMING AND LAND USE

- 🐄 Cattle
- 🐟 Fishing
- 🌾 Cereals
- 🌱 Market gardening
- Root crops
- Tobacco
- 🍇 Vineyards
- Pasture
- Cropland
- Forest
- Mountain region
- Wetland
- Major conurbation

LAND USE

- Cropland 35%
- Pasture 20%
- Forest 27%
- Other (including urban) 18%

THE LANDSCAPE

The north and west of France is made up of mainly flat, grassy plains or low hills. Wooded mountains line the country's borders in the south and east, and much of central France is taken up by the Massif Central, an enormous plateau, cut by deep river valleys and scattered with extinct volcanoes. Three major rivers, the Loire, Seine and Garonne drain the lowland basins.

Paris Basin

The Paris Basin is a saucer-shaped hollow made up of layers of hard and soft rock, covered with very fertile soils. It runs across about 100,000 sq km of northern France.

Alps (E 5)

The western end of the European Alpine mountain chain stretches into southeast France. The French Alps can be crossed by several passes, which give access to Italy and Switzerland.

Normandy

The coast of Normandy is lined with high chalk cliffs.

Pyrenees (C 7)

These mountains form a natural barrier between France and Spain. Several of their peaks reach heights of over 3,000 m. The Pyrenees are difficult to cross, due to their height, and because they have few low passes.

Massif Central (D 5)

This vast granite plateau was formed over 200 million years ago. Volcanic activity here only stopped within the last 10,000 years and the region's rounded hills are the worn down remains of volcanic mountains.

Camargue (D 7)

The Camargue is an area of marshes, pastures, sand dunes and salt flats at the mouth of the River Rhône. Rare animal and plant species are found there.

Mont Blanc (E 5)

This mountain in the French Alps is the tallest in Western Europe. It is 4,807 m high.

INDUSTRY

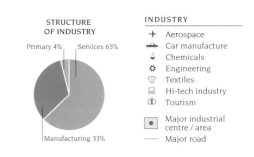

France is one of the world's top manufacturing nations, with a variety of both traditional and hi-tech industries. Cars, machinery and electronic products are exported worldwide, along with luxury goods such as perfumes, fashions and fine wines. Fossil fuels provide some energy, but France is currently the world's second-biggest producer of nuclear power.

STRUCTURE OF INDUSTRY

- Primary 4%
- Services 63%
- Manufacturing 33%

INDUSTRY

- ✈ Aerospace
- 🚗 Car manufacture
- ⚗ Chemicals
- ⚙ Engineering
- 👕 Textiles
- 💻 Hi-tech industry
- 🧳 Tourism
- ▪ Major industrial centre / area
- — Major road

POPULATION

In the past 50 years, most people have moved from the countryside into urban areas. Paris and its suburbs, the industrial cities, and the Côte d'Azur in the southeast are the most economically developed parts of France and now have the biggest populations.

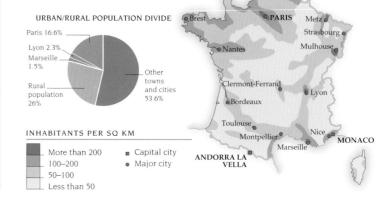

URBAN/RURAL POPULATION DIVIDE

- Paris 16.6%
- Lyon 2.3%
- Marseille 1.5%
- Rural population 26%
- Other towns and cities 53.6%

INHABITANTS PER SQ KM

- More than 200
- 100–200
- 50–100
- Less than 50
- ▪ Capital city
- ● Major city

ENVIRONMENTAL ISSUES

Many of France's coastal areas have been polluted by industry and tourism. The French government has recently introduced policies which aim to protect the country's environment. France's reliance on nuclear energy – 75% of its electricity is generated by nuclear power – means that it suffers less from the pollution caused by burning fossil fuels than many other countries in Europe.

ENVIRONMENTAL ISSUES

- Nuclear power station
- Sea pollution
- Polluted rivers
- Major industrial centre

CLIMATE

In winter, the coldest areas of France are the mountains of the Massif Central, and the Alps. Summers are hottest on the Mediterranean coast.

TEMPERATURE AND PRECIPITATION

- More than 20°C
- 15 to 20°C
- 10 to 15°C
- 5 to 10°C
- 0 to 5°C
- 0 to -5°C
- Less than -5°C

100 Precipitation (mm)

January

July

EUROPE

France

NORTH AMERICA
ASIA
AFRICA
SOUTH AMERICA
AUSTRALASIA AND OCEANIA
ANTARCTICA

LAND HEIGHT
- Above 4000 m
- 2000–4000 m
- 1000–2000 m
- 500–1000 m
- 250–500 m
- 100–250 m
- 0–100 m

SEA DEPTH
- 0–50 m
- 50–100 m
- 100–250 m
- 250–500 m
- 500–1000 m
- 1000–2000 m
- Below 2000 m

CITIES AND TOWNS
- Over 500,000 people
- 100,000–500,000
- 50,000–100,000
- Less than 50,000

SCALE BAR
0 km 50 100
0 miles 50 100

65

SPAIN AND PORTUGAL

PORTUGAL, SPAIN

Spain and Portugal occupy the Iberian Peninsula, which is cut off from the rest of Europe by the Pyrenees. Over the centuries, Iberia has been invaded and settled by many different peoples. The Moors, who arrived from North Africa in the 8th century, ruled much of Spain for almost 800 years and their influence can still be seen in Spanish culture. Portugal is one of the poorest countries in western Europe, but Spain's economy is rapidly expanding.

INDUSTRY

Madrid, Barcelona and the northern ports are Spain's industrial centres. Here, iron ore from Spanish mines is used to make steel, and factories produce cars, machinery and chemicals. Portugal exports textiles, clothing and footwear, along with fish such as sardines and tuna, caught off the Atlantic coast. In both countries, tourism is very important to the economy.

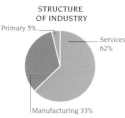

STRUCTURE
OF INDUSTRY

Primary 5%
Services 62%
Manufacturing 33%

INDUSTRY

- 🚗 Car manufacture
- 🧴 Chemicals
- ⚙ Engineering
- 🐟 Fish processing
- ⚓ Shipbuilding
- ⚒ Steel
- 👕 Textiles
- ⛏ Mining
- 📖 Publishing
- 🏛 Tourism
- ● Major industrial centre / area
- — Major road

POPULATION

In the first half of the 20th century, most Spaniards lived in villages or small towns, scattered around the country. Today, tourism and industry have drawn most of the population to the cities and coastal areas. Most Portuguese still live in rural areas along the coast or in the river valleys, but the cities are growing fast.

URBAN/RURAL POPULATION DIVIDE

Madrid 7.8%
Barcelona 6.8%
Lisbon 3.4%
Other towns and cities 52%
Rural population 30%

INHABITANTS PER SQ KM

- More than 200
- 100–200
- 50–100
- Less than 50
- ■ Capital city
- ● Major city

FARMING AND LAND USE

Cereals, especially wheat and barley, are Iberia's chief crops. In the dry south of Spain, the land is irrigated to grow citrus fruits, especially oranges, and vegetables. In both countries, olive trees and vineyards occupy large areas of land; olive oil and wine are important exports. Cork oak trees from Iberia's forests supply 80% of the world's cork.

FARMING AND LAND USE

- 🐟 Fishing
- 🐑 Sheep
- 🌾 Cereals
- 🍊 Citrus fruit
- 🫒 Olive oil
- 🍇 Vineyards
- ♠ Cork
- Pasture
- Cropland
- Forest
- Mountain region
- ● Major conurbation

LAND USE

Other 10%
Cropland 39%
Forest 33%
Pasture 18%

THE LANDSCAPE

Most of inland Spain is taken up by the Meseta, a dry, almost treeless plateau surrounded by steep mountain ranges. The only lowlands, apart from narrow strips along the Mediterranean coast, are the valleys of the Ebro, Tagus, Guadiana and Guadalquivir rivers. Portugal's coast is lined by wide plains. Inland, the River Tagus divides the country in two. To the north the land is hilly and wooded; to the south it is low-lying and drier.

Westward-flowing rivers
The Duero, Tagus and Guadalquivir rivers flow across the Meseta on their courses to the Atlantic Ocean.

River Ebro (E 2)
The River Ebro carries vital irrigation water to Spain's northeastern plains before flowing into the Mediterranean Sea.

Cordillera Cantábrica (C 1)
These rugged, forested mountains rise on Spain's Atlantic coast. They form the northern edge of the Meseta.

The Pyrenees (F 2)
These high mountains form a natural boundary with France.

River Duero (D 2)

River Tagus (B 4)

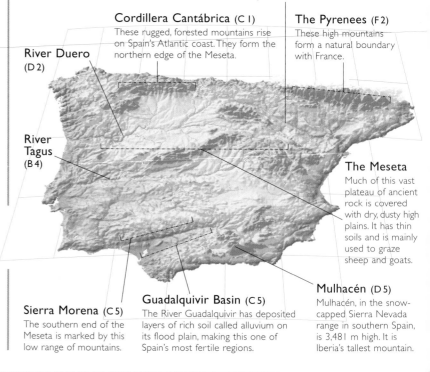

The Meseta
Much of this vast plateau of ancient rock is covered with dry, dusty high plains. It has thin soils and is mainly used to graze sheep and goats.

Sierra Morena (C 5)
The southern end of the Meseta is marked by this low range of mountains.

Guadalquivir Basin (C 5)
The River Guadalquivir has deposited layers of rich soil called alluvium on its flood plain, making this one of Spain's most fertile regions.

Mulhacén (D 5)
Mulhacén, in the snow-capped Sierra Nevada range in southern Spain, is 3,481 m high. It is Iberia's tallest mountain.

ENVIRONMENTAL ISSUES

Soil erosion – where the top layer of soil has been worn away by wind and rain – has affected much of the Iberian Peninsula. This is caused by farming, combined with drought and deforestation. In Spain, a national tree-planting scheme has been started to combat this problem. Industrial and tourist development along the Mediterranean coast of Spain, and in the Balearic Islands, has damaged natural habitats on both land and sea.

EUROPE
Spain and Portugal

CLIMATE

Northern Spain is wetter and cooler than the south. On the central plateau, summers are very hot and dry, and winters often freezing. The north of Portugal is cooled by winds blowing off the Atlantic Ocean. The south is warmer, with dry, mild winters.

January

July

ENVIRONMENTAL ISSUES
- Major oil spill
- Overbuilding
- Soil degradation
- Severe soil degradation
- Polluted rivers

Cabo Fisterra 2003
Douro
Ebro
Costa Brava
Guadiana
Majorca
Ibiza
Segura
Costa Blanca
Guadalquivir
Costa del Sol

TEMPERATURE AND PRECIPITATION
- More than 25°C
- 20 to 25°C
- 15 to 20°C
- 10 to 15°C
- 5 to 10°C
- 0 to 5°C
- 0 to -5°C
- -5 to -10°C
- Less than -10°C

100 Precipitation (mm)

LAND HEIGHT
- 2000–4000 m
- 1000–2000 m
- 500–1000 m
- 250–500 m
- 100–250 m
- 0–100 m

SEA DEPTH
- 0–250 m
- 250–500 m
- 500–1000 m
- 1000–2000 m
- 2000–3000 m
- 3000–4000 m
- Below 4000 m

CITIES AND TOWNS
- Over 500,000 people
- 100,000–500,000
- 50,000–100,000
- Less than 50,000

SCALE BAR

GERMANY AND THE ALPINE STATES

AUSTRIA, GERMANY, LIECHTENSTEIN, SLOVENIA, SWITZERLAND

Germany lies at the heart of Europe and is the biggest industrial power in the continent. In 1945, Germany was divided into two separate countries, East and West Germany, which were reunited in 1990. To the south, the snow-capped peaks of the Alps, Europe's highest mountains, tower over the Alpine states – Switzerland, Austria, Liechtenstein and the former Yugoslavian state of Slovenia.

INDUSTRY

Germany is a leading manufacturer of cars, chemicals, machinery and transport equipment. Switzerland and Liechtenstein, with few raw materials, make high-value products such as watches and pharmaceuticals, and provide services such as banking. The Alpine states are a popular tourist location all year round.

INDUSTRY

- 🚗 Car manufacture
- ⚗ Chemicals
- ⚙ Engineering
- 🏭 Iron & steel
- ⚓ Shipbuilding
- 💊 Pharmaceuticals
- $ Finance
- 💻 Hi-tech industry
- 🏛 Tourism

- ▪ Major industrial centre / area
- — Major road

STRUCTURE OF INDUSTRY

Primary 1%
Services 62%
Manufacturing 37%

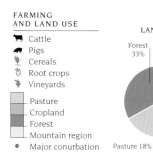

POPULATION

Western and central Germany are the most densely populated areas in this region – particularly in and around the Rhine and Ruhr valleys, where there are many industries. In the south, the steep slopes of the Alps and permanent snow cover on the higher peaks means that most large towns and cities are in scattered lowland areas.

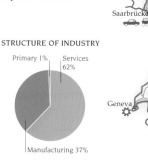

INHABITANTS PER SQ KM

- More than 200
- 100–200
- 50–100
- Less than 50

- ■ Capital city
- ● Major city

URBAN/RURAL POPULATION DIVIDE

Vienna 1.4% Berlin 3.6%
Munich 1%
Rural population 18%
Other towns and cities 76%

FARMING AND LAND USE

Germany produces three-quarters of its own food. Crop farming is widespread, with cereals and root crops grown in flat, fertile areas. Cattle and pig farming supplies meat and dairy products. Across the Alps, the mountains limit farming, although vines are grown on the warmer, south-facing slopes. The rich pastures of the lower slopes are used to graze beef and dairy cattle.

FARMING AND LAND USE

- 🐄 Cattle
- 🐖 Pigs
- 🌾 Cereals
- Root crops
- 🍇 Vineyards

- Pasture
- Cropland
- Forest
- Mountain region
- ● Major conurbation

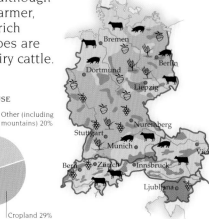

LAND USE

Forest 33%
Other (including mountains) 20%
Pasture 18%
Cropland 29%

THE LANDSCAPE

To the north, flat plains and heathlands surround the North Sea coast. Further south are Germany's central uplands, which are lower and older than the jagged peaks of the Alps, which began to form about 65 million years ago. From its source in the Black Forest, the River Danube flows eastward across Germany and Austria on its course to the Black Sea. The other major river, the Rhine, flows northward.

The River Rhine (B 5)
The Rhine is Germany's main waterway. It is an important transport route to and from northern ports. It twists and turns across 1,320 km of Europe, from its source in southeast Switzerland, to the North Sea.

The Danube (B 7)
The Danube is Europe's second longest river, flowing 2,840 km.

Lake Constance (B 7)
Lake Constance covers 540 sq km and is Germany's largest lake, although its waters are shared by Austria and Switzerland.

The Harz mountains (C 4)
These rugged, wooded mountains are much older than the Alps. They were formed over 300 million years ago.

Karst region (E 8)
Most of the water in this limestone region of Slovenia flows underground, through huge caves and caverns.

The Alps (C 8)
The Alps were formed when the African Plate collided with the Eurasian Plate, pushing up and crushing huge amounts of rock, to form mountains.

ENVIRONMENTAL ISSUES

The large number of industries in Germany, especially in the east of the country, has led to high levels of pollution in cities, and in rivers like the Rhine. Acid rain from car fumes and industrial pollution has poisoned many of Germany's forests. The popularity of the Alps as a year-round tourist destination puts great demands on the environment. The development of new resorts has destroyed the natural habitats of many plants and animals.

ENVIRONMENTAL ISSUES

- Urban air pollution
- Winter tourist resort
- Affected by acid rain
- Polluted rivers
- Major industrial centre

CLIMATE

Winter temperatures decrease eastwards, and the high Alpine region is coldest. Rainfall is higher in the summer. Climate variations in the Alps are common, due to turbulent air flows.

January

July

TEMPERATURE AND PRECIPITATION

- More than 20°C
- 15 to 20°C
- 10 to 15°C
- 5 to 10°C
- 0 to 5°C
- 0 to -5°C
- -5 to -10°C
- Less than -10°C
- 100 Precipitation (mm)

ITALY

ITALY, SAN MARINO, VATICAN CITY

Italy has played an important role in Europe since the Romans based their mighty empire here over 2,000 years ago. The famous boot shape divides into two very different halves. Northern Italy has a varied range of industries and agriculture. Beautiful cities like Venice, Florence, and Rome draw tourists from all over the world. Southern Italy is poorer and less developed than the north, with a hotter, drier climate and less productive land.

THE LANDSCAPE

Italy is a peninsula jutting south from mainland Europe into the Mediterranean Sea. In northern and central Italy the land is mainly mountainous. Most of the flat land is in the Po Valley and along the eastern coast. Italy lies within an earthquake zone, which makes the land unstable, and there are also a number of active volcanoes.

Italian lakes
Great lakes like Garda (B3) and Como (B2) fill several south-facing valleys once occupied by glaciers.

Po Valley (C 2)
The basin of the River Po has the best soils in Italy. Rich alluvium is washed from the mountains by the river to form a wide plain.

The Dolomites (D 2)
These high mountains are part of the same range as the Alps. They were formed 65 million years ago.

Earthquakes
The southern Apennines, as well as coastal areas of southwestern Italy, often experience earthquakes and mudslides.

The Apennines (C 4)
This mountain range forms the 'backbone' of Italy, dividing the rocky west coast from the flatter, sandy east coast.

Tyrrhenian Sea (C 6)
This sea, which divides the Italian mainland from Sardinia, is gradually filling with sediment from the rivers which flow into it.

Sardinia
The island of Sardinia is made from very old rocks which were thrust up to form mountains.

Sicily
Sicily is the largest island in the Mediterranean. It has a famous active volcano called Mount Etna, and often experiences earthquakes

Gulf of Taranto (F 7)
During earthquakes, great blocks of land have broken away and sunk into the sea, forming the Gulf's square shape.

FARMING AND LAND USE

The Po Valley is a broad, flat plain in the north of Italy. It contains the most fertile land in the country, and wheat and rice are the main cereal crops grown here. Grapes for wine are grown everywhere in Italy. In much of the south, the land must be irrigated to support crops. Where there is enough water, citrus fruits, olives, and many kinds of tomatoes are grown.

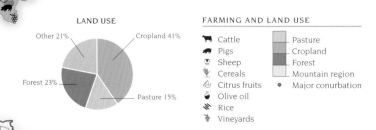

LAND USE

Other 21%
Cropland 41%
Forest 23%
Pasture 15%

FARMING AND LAND USE
- 🐂 Cattle
- 🐖 Pigs
- 🐑 Sheep
- Cereals
- Citrus fruits
- Olive oil
- Rice
- Vineyards
- Pasture
- Cropland
- Forest
- Mountain region
- Major conurbation

INDUSTRY

Italian industry is located mainly in the north. Design is extremely important to Italians and they are proud of the elegant designs of their furniture, clothes and shoes. Though many firms are small, they are very efficient. Italy has few mineral resources so it needs to import raw materials to make cars, engines and other hi-tech products.

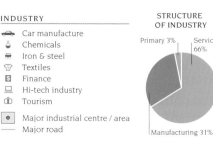

INDUSTRY
- 🚗 Car manufacture
- Chemicals
- Iron & steel
- Textiles
- Finance
- Hi-tech industry
- Tourism
- ⊙ Major industrial centre / area
- — Major road

STRUCTURE OF INDUSTRY
Primary 3%
Services 66%
Manufacturing 31%

POPULATION

Most of Italy's population lives in the north, mainly in and around the Po Valley, which is home to over 25 million people. Most people here have a high standard of living. Southern Italy is much more rural; towns are smaller and life is often much harder.

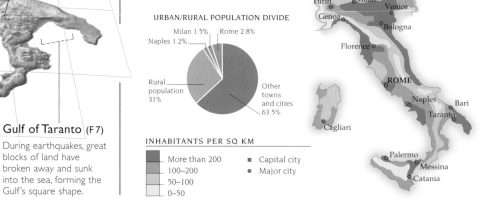

URBAN/RURAL POPULATION DIVIDE
Milan 1.5%
Rome 2.8%
Naples 1.2%
Rural population 31%
Other towns and cities 63.5%

INHABITANTS PER SQ KM
- More than 200
- 100–200
- 50–100
- 0–50
- ■ Capital city
- ● Major city

ITALY

EUROPE

ENVIRONMENTAL ISSUES

Sewage and chemical by-products from industry have polluted the Mediterranean and Adriatic seas. In many northern cities, severe air pollution is a health hazard. Southern Italy is subject to natural dangers like earthquakes and mudslides.

ENVIRONMENTAL ISSUES
- Catastrophic earthquakes
- Urban air pollution
- Acid rain
- Sea pollution
- Major industrial centre

CLIMATE

The Alpine north has cold winters, often with snow. Further south, temperatures are higher. Sicily has Italy's highest temperatures, due to warm African winds.

January

July

TEMPERATURE AND PRECIPITATION
- More than 25°C
- 20 to 25°C
- 15 to 20°C
- 10 to 15°C
- 5 to 10°C
- 0 to 5°C
- 0 to -5°C
- -5 to -10°C
- Less than -10°C

100 Precipitation (mm)

LAND HEIGHT
- Above 4000m
- 2000–4000 m
- 1000–2000 m
- 500–1000 m
- 250–500 m
- 100–250 m
- 0–100 m

SEA DEPTH
- 0–50 m
- 50–100 m
- 100–250 m
- 250–500 m
- 500–1000 m
- 1000–2000 m
- Below 2000m

SCALE BAR

CITIES AND TOWNS
- Over 500,000 people
- 100,000–500,000
- 50,000–100,000
- Less than 50,000

71

CENTRAL EUROPE

CZECH REPUBLIC, HUNGARY, POLAND, SLOVAKIA

Central Europe has been invaded many times throughout history. The countries have changed shape frequently as their borders have shifted backwards and forwards. From the end of the Second World War until 1989, they were ruled by communist governments, which were supported by the Soviet Union. In 1993, the state of Czechoslovakia voted to split into two separate nations, called the Czech Republic and Slovakia.

INDUSTRY

Brown coal, or lignite, is central Europe's main fuel, and one of Poland's major exports. A variety of minerals are mined in the mountains of the Czech Republic and Slovakia. Hungary has a wide range of industries producing vehicles, metals, and chemicals, as well as textiles and electrical goods. The Czech Republic is famous for its breweries and glass-making.

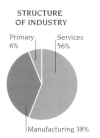

STRUCTURE OF INDUSTRY

Primary 6%
Services 56%
Manufacturing 38%

INDUSTRY
- Brewing
- Car manufacture
- Chemicals
- Engineering
- Food processing
- Iron & steel
- Coal mining
- Major industrial centre / area
- Major road

ENVIRONMENTAL ISSUES

The growth of heavy industries that took place under communist rule has caused terrible environmental pollution in some places. Hungary's oil and Poland's brown coal have a high sulphur content. Burning these fuels to produce electricity causes air pollution, and the sulphur dioxide produced combines with moisture in the air, leading to acid rain.

ENVIRONMENTAL ISSUES
- Severe industrial pollution
- Urban air pollution
- Affected by acid rain
- Polluted rivers
- Major industrial centre

FARMING AND LAND USE

Central Europe's main crops are cereals such as maize, wheat and rye, along with sugar beet and potatoes. In Hungary, sweet peppers grow, helped by the warm summers and mild winters. They are used to make paprika. Grapes are also grown, to make wine. Large areas of the plains of Hungary and Poland are used for rearing pigs and cattle. Trees for timber grow in the mountains of Slovakia and the Czech Republic.

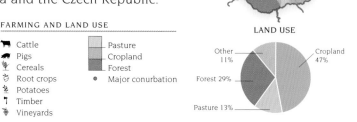

FARMING AND LAND USE
- Cattle
- Pigs
- Cereals
- Root crops
- Potatoes
- Timber
- Vineyards
- Pasture
- Cropland
- Forest
- Major conurbation

LAND USE

Other 11%
Cropland 47%
Forest 29%
Pasture 13%

THE LANDSCAPE

The high Carpathian Mountains sweep across northern Slovakia. The lower Sudeten Mountains lie on the border of the Czech Republic and Poland. Together, these mountains form a barrier which divides the Great Hungarian Plain and the River Danube basin in the south from Poland and the vast rolling lowlands of the North European Plain.

Pomerania (C2)
This is a sandy coastal area with lakes formed by glaciers. It stretches west from the River Vistula to just beyond the German border.

River Vistula (F4)
Poland's largest river is the Vistula. It flows northwards, passing through the capital, Warsaw, on its way to the Baltic Sea.

North European Plain

Hot springs
The Sudeten mountains (C5) are famous for their hot mineral springs. These occur where water heated deep within the Earth's crust finds its way to the surface along fractures in the rock.

River Danube (D7)
The River Danube forms the border between Slovakia and Hungary for over 162 km. It then turns south to flow across the Great Hungarian Plain.

Great Hungarian Plain (E8)
This huge plain covers almost half of Hungary's land area. It is a mixture of farmland and steppe.

Tatra Mountains (E6)
The Tatra Mountains are a small range at the northern end of the Carpathian Mountains. They include Gerlachovsky Stít, which is Central Europe's highest point at 2,655 m.

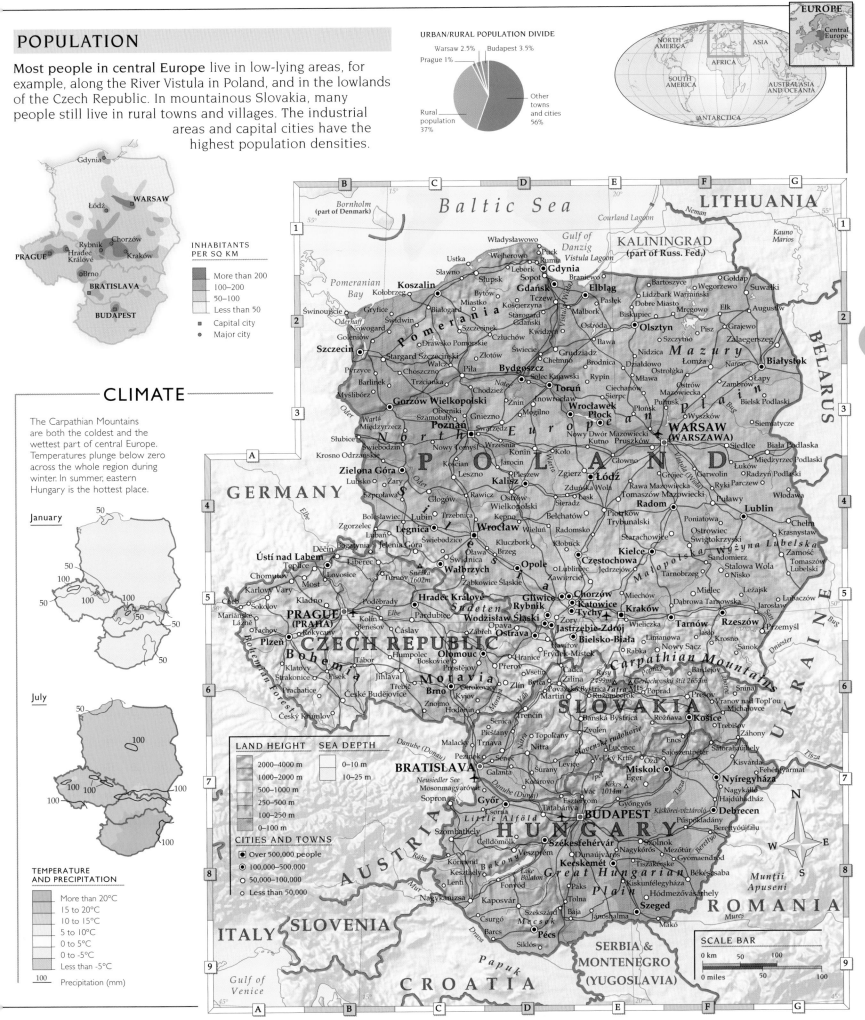

POPULATION

Most people in central Europe live in low-lying areas, for example, along the River Vistula in Poland, and in the lowlands of the Czech Republic. In mountainous Slovakia, many people still live in rural towns and villages. The industrial areas and capital cities have the highest population densities.

URBAN/RURAL POPULATION DIVIDE

Warsaw 2.5%
Budapest 3.5%
Prague 1%
Other towns and cities 56%
Rural population 37%

INHABITANTS PER SQ KM
More than 200
100–200
50–100
Less than 50
■ Capital city
● Major city

CLIMATE

The Carpathian Mountains are both the coldest and the wettest part of central Europe. Temperatures plunge below zero across the whole region during winter. In summer, eastern Hungary is the hottest place.

January

July

TEMPERATURE AND PRECIPITATION
More than 20°C
15 to 20°C
10 to 15°C
5 to 10°C
0 to 5°C
0 to -5°C
Less than -5°C
100 Precipitation (mm)

LAND HEIGHT
2000–4000 m
1000–2000 m
500–1000 m
250–500 m
100–250 m
0–100 m

SEA DEPTH
0–10 m
10–25 m

CITIES AND TOWNS
◉ Over 500,000 people
◉ 100,000–500,000
○ 50,000–100,000
○ Less than 50,000

SCALE BAR
0 km   50   100
0 miles   50   100

SOUTHEAST EUROPE

ALBANIA, BOSNIA AND HERZEGOVINA, BULGARIA, CROATIA, GREECE, MACEDONIA, SERBIA & MONTENEGRO (YUGOSLAVIA)

Southeast Europe extends inland from the coasts of the Aegean, Adriatic and Black seas. Ancient Greece was the birthplace of European civilization. Albania and Bulgaria were ruled by communists for over 50 years, until the early 1990s. The rest of the region was part of a communist union of states called Yugoslavia. The collapse of this union in 1991 led to a civil war, after which five separate countries emerged.

THE LANDSCAPE

Southeast Europe is largely mountainous, with ranges running from northwest to southeast. The Dinaric Alps run parallel to the Dalmatian coast, and the Pindus Mountains continue this line into Greece. In the Aegean Sea, the drowned peaks of an old mountain chain form thousands of islands.

Earthquakes
Bulgaria, Greece, and Macedonia lie in earthquake zones. Major earthquakes have hit the Ionian Islands in 1953, and Macedonia in 1963.

Dinaric Alps
(C 2)

Great Hungarian Plain (D 1)
The Vojvodina region of Serbia and Montenegro is the southern part of the Great Hungarian Plain. The plain is flat and fertile soils allow grain crops like corn and wheat to be grown.

Balkan Mountains (F 3)
The mountains form a spur running east to west through Bulgaria and separate the two main rivers, the Danube and the Maritsa.

Dalmatian coast (B 2)
The Dalmatian coast has many long, narrow islands near the shore. These were formed as the Adriatic Sea flooded the river valleys which ran parallel to the coast.

Greek Islands

The Peloponnese (E 6)
The Peloponnese is a mountainous peninsula linked to the Greek mainland only by a narrow strip of land called an isthmus. Here, it is the Isthmus of Corinth.

Greek Islands
There are two groups of Greek Islands, the Ionian Islands to the west of mainland Greece, and the more numerous islands to the east in the Aegean Sea.

FARMING AND LAND USE

Cereals like wheat, and fruits, vegetables and grapes are grown in the fertile north of the region. The band of mountains across southeast Europe is used mainly for grazing sheep and goats. Further south, and in coastal areas, the warm Mediterranean climate is ideal for growing grapes, olives and tobacco.

FARMING AND LAND USE
- Fishing
- Goats
- Pigs
- Sheep
- Fruit
- Olive oil
- Tobacco
- Vineyards
- Wheat
- Cropland
- Forest
- Mountains
- Pasture
- Major conurbation

LAND USE
- Pasture 27%
- Forest 34%
- Cropland 30%
- Other 9%

INDUSTRY

Mainland Greece and the many islands in the Aegean Sea are centres of a thriving tourist trade, while tourism on the Black Sea coast continues to grow. The Dalmatian coast had a small, but growing tourist industry, until the civil war in former Yugoslavia disrupted that, and other industries. Heavy industries like chemicals, engineering and shipbuilding remain an important source of income in Bulgaria.

STRUCTURE OF INDUSTRY
- Primary 16%
- Services 52%
- Manufacturing 32%

INDUSTRY
- Chemicals
- Engineering
- Food processing
- Metal refining
- Shipbuilding
- Textiles
- Mining
- Tourism
- Major industrial centre / area
- Major road

POPULATION

Greece's population is mostly urban; over 50% live in the capital, Athens and in Salonica. In Bulgaria, most people live in cities. About half of Albania's and Macedonia's people are still rural. Since the civil war, the different ethnic groups in Bosnia and Herzegovina, Serbia and Montenegro and Croatia have lived apart from one another.

URBAN/RURAL POPULATION DIVIDE
- Belgrade 3.5%
- Athens 8%
- Sofia 2.5%
- Other towns and cities 42%
- Rural population 44%

INHABITANTS PER SQ KM
- More than 200
- 100–200
- 50–100
- Less than 50
- Capital city
- Major city

CLIMATE

Southeastern Europe's climate varies from north to south. Continental climates are found in the north; winters are cold and dry, while towards the south, winters are milder and summers much hotter. Europe's wettest place is found in the mountains in Bosnia and Herzegovina.

January

July

TEMPERATURE AND PRECIPITATION

	More than 25°C
	20 to 25°C
	15 to 20°C
	10 to 15°C
	5 to 10°C
	0 to 5°C
	0 to -5°C
	Less than -5°C

100 —— Precipitation (mm)

EUROPE
Southeast Europe

CITIES AND TOWNS
- ⊙ Over 500,000 people
- ◉ 100,000–500,000
- ○ 50,000–100,000
- ○ Less than 50,000

SCALE BAR

0 km   50   100

0 miles   50   100

LAND HEIGHT
- 2000–4000 m
- 1000–2000 m
- 500–1000 m
- 250–500 m
- 100–250 m
- 0–100 m

SEA DEPTH
- 0–50 m
- 50–100 m
- 100–250 m
- 250–500 m
- 500–1000 m
- 1000–2000 m
- Below 2000 m

ENVIRONMENTAL ISSUES

Emissions from industry and traffic fumes have polluted the air in Athens and Zagreb. In Athens, smog caused by vehicle exhausts can become so severe on some days that the use of cars is banned. Earthquakes are common; Macedonia's capital city, Skopje, was badly hit in 1963, and Bulgaria's run-down Kozloduy nuclear power station lies within the earthquake zone.

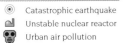

Zagreb

Kozloduy

Danube

Skopje 1963

Salonica 1978

Athens

ENVIRONMENTAL ISSUES
- ⊚ Catastrophic earthquake
- Unstable nuclear reactor
- Urban air pollution
- Sea pollution
- Polluted river
- • Major town

EASTERN EUROPE

BELARUS, MOLDOVA, ROMANIA, UKRAINE

Much of Eastern Europe, which extends north from the River Danube and the Black Sea, is covered by open grasslands called steppe. Ukraine's excellent farmland and large mineral reserves make it one of the strongest new countries to emerge from the former Soviet Union. Moldova and Belarus were also part of the USSR, until they became independent in 1991. Romania was a strict communist regime from 1945 until 1989.

POPULATION

Most Romanians live in Bucharest, the capital, or in other cities and towns. In Ukraine, two-thirds of the population lives in cities in the Donbass industrial area. Most of Belarus's people are city dwellers. Moldova is the most rural country in Eastern Europe; half its people live in the countryside and make their living from farming.

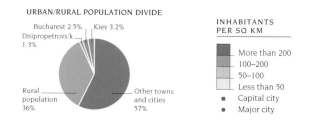

URBAN/RURAL POPULATION DIVIDE

Bucharest 2.5% Kiev 3.2%
Dnipropetrovs'k 1.3%
Rural population 36%
Other towns and cities 57%

INHABITANTS PER SQ KM
- More than 200
- 100–200
- 50–100
- Less than 50
- ■ Capital city
- ● Major city

INDUSTRY

In Ukraine, most industry is based around the country's mineral reserves. The Donbass region has Europe's largest coalfield and is an important centre for iron and steel production. Belarus's main industries are chemicals, machine building and food-processing. Romania's manufacturing industries are growing, with the help of foreign investment.

STRUCTURE OF INDUSTRY
Primary 20%
Manufacturing 47%
Services 33%

INDUSTRY
- 🚗 Car manufacture
- 🍶 Chemicals
- ⚙ Engineering
- 🗋 Food processing
- Iron & steel
- 👕 Textiles
- Coal
- Mining
- Oil and gas
- Tourism

■ Major industrial centre / area
— Major road

THE LANDSCAPE

Flat or rolling grasslands, marshes and river flood plains cover almost all of Ukraine and Belarus. The Carpathian Mountains cross the southwestern corner of Ukraine and continue in a large arc-shaped chain of high peaks at the heart of Romania. Along the southern part of this chain, the Carpathians are called the Transylvanian Alps.

Pripet Marshes (C 3)
The Pripet Marshes in Belarus and Ukraine form the largest area of marshland in Europe.

The steppes
The steppes are great, wide grasslands which are found across eastern Europe and central Asia. Over 70% of the Ukrainian landscape is steppe. Little rain falls throughout the steppes.

FARMING AND LAND USE

The black soils found across much of Ukraine are very fertile and the country is a big producer of cereals, sugar beet, and sunflowers, which are grown for their oil. In Moldova and southern Romania, the warm summers are ideal for growing grapes for wine, along with sunflowers and a variety of vegetables. Cattle and pigs are farmed throughout Eastern Europe.

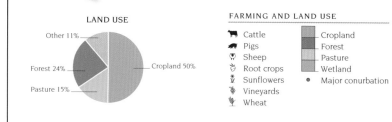

LAND USE
Other 11%
Forest 24%
Pasture 15%
Cropland 50%

FARMING AND LAND USE
- 🐄 Cattle
- 🐖 Pigs
- 🐑 Sheep
- Root crops
- Sunflowers
- Vineyards
- Wheat

- Cropland
- Forest
- Pasture
- Wetland
- ● Major conurbation

Carpathian Mountains (C 5)
The Carpathians are the largest mountain range in Eastern Europe. They are a rich source of timber and minerals.

Dnieper (E 5) **and Dniester** (D 5) **rivers**
The Dnieper and Dniester run south and east towards the Black Sea. They flow slowly across huge areas of low-lying land.

The Crimea (F 6)
This peninsula divides the Sea of Azov from the Black Sea. The steep mountains of Kryms'ki Hory run along the southeastern coast of the Crimea.

CLIMATE

January

July

The climate is continental, with warm, dry summers and very cold, dry winters. Temperatures are higher along the fringes of the Black Sea, while the Carpathian Mountains are colder and wetter all year round.

Less than 50

TEMPERATURE AND PRECIPITATION

- More than 20°C
- 15 to 20°C
- 10 to 15°C
- 5 to 10°C
- 0 to 5°C
- 0 to -5°C
- Less than -5°C

100 Precipitation (mm)

EUROPE

Eastern Europe

NORTH AMERICA

ASIA

AFRICA

SOUTH AMERICA

AUSTRALASIA AND OCEANIA

ANTARCTICA

ENVIRONMENTAL ISSUES

The worst nuclear accident in history happened at Chornobyl' nuclear power station in northern Ukraine in 1986. Around 70% of the nuclear fallout was received by Belarus, contaminating its farmland, forests and water supplies. Four million Ukrainians still live in dangerously radioactive areas.

ENVIRONMENTAL ISSUES

- Destroyed nuclear reactor
- Urban air pollution
- Levels of nuclear fallout
- Very high
- High
- Moderate
- Polluted river
- Major industrial centre

Minsk

Chornobyl' • Kiev

Kharkiv

Dnipropetrovs'k

Donets'k

Târgu Mureş

Arad

Dnieper

Bucharest

LAND HEIGHT

- 2000–4000 m
- 1000–2000 m
- 500–1000 m
- 250–500 m
- 100–250 m
- 0–100 m

SEA DEPTH

- 0–50 m
- 50–100 m
- 100–250 m
- 250–500 m
- 500–1000 m
- 1000–2000 m
- Below 2000 m

CITIES AND TOWNS

- Over 500,000 people
- 100,000–500,000
- 50,000–100,000
- Less than 50,000

LATVIA

RUSSIAN FEDERATION

LITHUANIA

Bihosava

Drysa

Haradok

Navapolatsk
Polatsk

Vitsyebsk

Western Dvina

Hlybokaye
Bacheykava
Bahushevsk

Myadzyel
Lyepyel'
Chashniki

Orsha

Dnieper

Maladzyechna **Barysaw**

Zhodzina

Horki

Lida
Minskaya
Vzvyshsha

MINSK

Mahilyow

Neris

Vilyia

Hrodna
Shchuchyn

Byarezina

Babruysk

Kastsyukovichy

BELARUS

Asipovichy

Vawkavysk
Neman

Byelaruskaya Hrada

Baranavichy
Slutsk

Zhlobin

Salihorsk

Svyetlahorsk

Bug

Yasyel'da

Drahichyn

Luninyets

Psich

Homyel'

Pina

Mazyr

Shostka

Hlukhiv

Brest
Kobryn

Pinsk

Pripet

Narowlya
Pripet

Chernihiv

Makrany

Pripet Marshes

Chornobyl'

Dnieper

Konotop

Sumy

POLAND

Kovel'

Stokhid

Sarny

Sluch

Olevs'k

Korosten'

Kiev Reservoir

Nizhyn

Romny

Psel

Okhtyrka

Volodymyr-Volyns'kyy

Dnieper Lowland

Lubny

Kharkiv

Kup"yans'k

Luts'k

Rivne

KIEV (KYYIV)

Fastiv

Pryluky

Dubno

Zhytomyr

Kaniv's'ke
Vodoskhovyshche

Poltava

Starobil's'k

Zhovkva

Bila Tserkva

Donets

Kreminna

Rubizhne

L'viv

UKRAINE

Khmel'nyts'kyy

Cherkasy

Zvenyhorodka

Kremenchuk

Kremenchuk
Reservoir

Dniprodzerzhyns'ke
Vodoskhovyshche

Slov"yans'k
Kramators'k

Syeverodonets'k
Lysychans'k
Stakhanov **Luhans'k**

Ternopil'

Sambir
Stryy

Vinnytsya

Uman'

Oleksandriya

Novomoskovs'k

Kostyantynivka

Donbass

Horlivka

Ivano-Frankivs'k

Haysyn

Podil's'ka Vysochyna

Dniprodzerzhyns'k

Pavlohrad

Yenakiyeve
Krasnyy Luch

SLOVAKIA

Uzhhorod

Mukacheve

Kamyanets'-Podil's'kyy

Dniester

Pervomays'k

Kirovohrad

Zhovti Vody

Dnipropetrovs'k

Torez

Donets'k
Makiyivka

Khust

Chernivtsi

Hora Hoverla
2061m

Botoşani

Bălţi

Kotovs'k

Kryvyy Rih

Novyy Buh

Zaporizhzhya

Nikopol'

Orikhiv

Volnovakha

Don

Novoazovs'k

HUNGARY

Satu Mare

Carpathian Mountains

Suceava

Prut

Iaşi

CHIŞINĂU

Black

Kakhovs'ke
Vodoskhovyshche

Dniprorudne

Mariupol'

Berdyans'k

Gulf of Taganrog

Yeya

Baia Mare

Bistriţa

Piatra-Neamţ

Roman

Tighina
Tiraspol

Mykolayiv

Melitopol'

RUSSIAN FEDERATION

Zalău

Cluj-Napoca

Oradea

Transylvania

Turda

Vaslui

Basarabeasca

Kherson

Heniches'k

Sea of Azov

Arad

Muntii Apuseni

Târgu Mureş

Bacău

Bârlad

Illichivs'k

Armyans'k

Zatoka
Syvash

Kerch

Great Hungarian Plain

Alba Iulia

Mediaş

Miercurea-Ciuc
Stântu Gheorghe

Focşani

Cahul

Artsyz

Dzhankoy

Kerch Strait

Kuban'

Timişoara

Deva
Hunedoara

Sibiu

Vârful Moldoveanu
2544m

Braşov

ROMANIA

Transylvanian Alps

Galaţi

Brăila

Buzău

Izmayil

Ozero Shahany

Tulcea

Ozero Sasyk

Yevpatoriya

Simferopol'

Crimea

Feodosiya

Kryms'ki Hory

Caucasus

Lugoj

Reşiţa

Târgu Jiu

Râmnicu Vâlcea

Ploieşti

Târgovişte

Sevastopol'

Yalta

Danube (Dunărea)

Drobeta-Turnu Severin

Pitesti

Ialomiţa

Lacul Razim

Lacul Sinoie

GEORGIA

SERB. & MON. (YUGO.)

Strehaia

Slatina

Wallachia

Craiova

Caracal

BUCHAREST (BUCUREŞTI)

Călăraşi

Olt

Giurgiu

Danube (Dunărea)

Constanţa

Black Sea

Velika Morava

BULGARIA

SCALE BAR

0 km 50 100

0 miles 50 100

EUROPEAN RUSSIA

RUSSIAN FEDERATION

European Russia is separated from the Asiatic part of the Russian Federation by the Ural Mountains. It is home to two-thirds of the country's population. Russia was the largest and most powerful republic of the communist Soviet Union, which collapsed in 1991. Though new businesses were set up when communism ended, many old state industries closed down, causing unemployment and further hardship for many people.

INDUSTRY

European Russia is rich in natural resources. Minerals are mined on the Kola Peninsula, and in the Urals, while dense forests are felled and processed in many of the larger northern cities. The Volga basin is one of Europe's largest sources of oil and gas. Moscow, and the cities near the Volga are centres of skilled labour for a wide range of manufacturing industries like cars, chemicals and heavy engineering and steel production.

INDUSTRY

🚗 Car manufacture		🛢 Oil & gas	
⚗ Chemicals		🌲 Timber processing	
⚙ Engineering		● Major industrial centre/area	
⛭ Iron & steel		— Major road	
⊤ Textiles			
⛏ Mining			

FARMING AND LAND USE

Russia's best farmland lies within this region. Big crops of wheat, barley and oats, potatoes and sunflowers are produced in the fertile black soil which forms a thick band across the country to the south of Moscow. The far north is cold and frozen, with bare mountains and tundra making cultivation impossible. Further south there are extensive forests, and rough pastures used for herding and hunting.

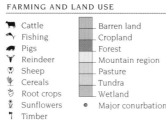

FARMING AND LAND USE

🐄 Cattle	▢ Barren land	
🐟 Fishing	▢ Cropland	
🐖 Pigs	▢ Forest	
🦌 Reindeer	▢ Mountain region	
🐑 Sheep	▢ Pasture	
🌾 Cereals	▢ Tundra	
🥔 Root crops	▢ Wetland	
🌻 Sunflowers	● Major conurbation	
🌲 Timber		

POPULATION

Three-quarters of European Russia's people live in towns and cities, most in a broad band stretching south from Saint Petersburg to Moscow, and eastwards to the Urals. The capital, Moscow, and Saint Petersburg are very crowded cities. Living conditions there are cramped, with two families often sharing one flat. The southeast is also heavily populated. Over 12 million people live in the cities and towns which line the banks of the River Volga.

INHABITANTS PER SQ KM

▓ More than 100	
▓ 50–100	
▒ 10–50	
░ Less than 10	
▪ Capital city	
● Major city	

THE LANDSCAPE

European Russia lies on the North European Plain, a huge, rolling lowland with wide river basins. The northern half of the plain, which was once covered by glaciers, has many lakes and swamps. The River Volga drains much of the plain as it flows south to the Caspian Sea. The Caucasus and Ural mountains form natural boundaries in the south and east.

Northern European Russia (C 3)
Northern European Russia reaches into the Arctic Circle. It is a region of pine and birch forests, marshes and tundra. There are also tens of thousands of lakes, including the biggest in Europe, Ladoga, which covers about 17,700 sq km.

Ural Mountains (E 5)
The Ural Mountains run from north to south, stretching almost 4,020 km.

Lake Ladoga (B 4)

Valdai Hills (A 5)
The Valdai Hills are a high, swampy region of the North European Plain. Two of Europe's biggest rivers, the Volga and the Western Dvina, have their sources here.

Caucasus (A 9)
This massive barrier of mountains stretches from the Black Sea to the Caspian Sea. It includes El'brus, the highest peak in Europe, at 5,642 m.

Caspian Sea (C 9)

River Volga (C 7)
The River Volga flows for 3,688 km, making it Europe's longest river and Russia's most important inland waterway. It is used for transport and to generate hydro-electric power.

The North European Plain (C 4)
The North European Plain sweeps west from the Ural Mountains, all the way to the River Rhine in Germany. In European Russia it includes a number of hill ranges, such as the Volga Uplands and the Central Russian Upland.

ENVIRONMENTAL ISSUES

The many factories in European Russia have caused widespread pollution, and in most industrial cities air quality is poor. Several of Russia's older nuclear power stations have been declared unsafe, but are yet to be shut down. Waste from these power stations, as well as from nuclear submarines, has for many years been dumped in the Barents Sea and off Novaya Zemlya.

ENVIRONMENTAL ISSUES

- Nuclear waste dump site
- Unstable nuclear reactor
- Urban air pollution
- Polluted rivers
- Major industrial centre

CLIMATE

Winters are extremely cold and dry; temperatures plunge well below zero in the north and east. Summer brings much warmer and wetter weather, especially in the south, while along the northern coast, it remains relatively cold. Rainfall is highest in the Caucasus.

January

July

TEMPERATURE AND PRECIPITATION

- More than 20°C
- 15 to 20°C
- 10 to 15°C
- 5 to 10°C
- 0 to 5°C
- 0 to -5°C
- -5 to -10°C
- -10 to -15°C
- Less than -15°C

Precipitation (mm)

CITIES AND TOWNS

- Over 500,000 people
- 100,000–500,000
- 50,000–100,000
- Less than 50,000

LAND HEIGHT	SEA DEPTH
Above 4000 m	0–50 m
2000–4000 m	50–100 m
1000–2000 m	100–250 m
500–1000 m	250–500 m
250–500 m	500–1000 m
100–250 m	1000–2000 m
0–100 m	Below 2000 m
Below sea level	

SCALE BAR

0 km 100 200
0 miles 100 200

THE MEDITERRANEAN

The Mediterranean Sea separates Europe from Africa. It stretches more than 4,000 km from east to west and is almost completely enclosed by land. Many great civilizations, including the Greek and Roman empires grew up around the Mediterranean. It has been a crossroads of international trade routes for many centuries. More than 100 million people live in the 28 countries which border the sea and their numbers are increased by the large crowds of tourists who regularly visit the area.

ENVIRONMENTAL ISSUES

Sea pollution is widespread in the Mediterranean, especially near the large coastal resorts where raw sewage and industrial effluent is pumped out to sea and often ends up on the beaches. Oil refining and oil spills have also furthered pollution.

ENVIRONMENTAL ISSUES

🐚 Oil spill

⬜ Mild sea pollution
🟥 Severe sea pollution

SCALE BAR

0 km 100 200

0 miles 100 200

MALTA

Victoria Nadur

Gozo Mgarr Comino

Mellieha

Mosta St Julian's

Sliema

Hamrun VALLETTA

Rabat Paola

Birzebbuga

0 km 10

0 miles 10

CYPRUS

Mediterranean Sea

Lápithos (Lapta) Kyrenia (Girne)

Mórfou (Güzelyurt) Kythrea (Değirmenlik)

TURKISH REPUBLIC OF NORTHERN CYPRUS (recognized only by Turkey)

Famagusta Bay

Pólis

NICOSIA

Famagusta (Ammochostos / Gazimağusa)

Larnaca (Larnaka)

Dhekelia Sovereign Base Area (to UK)

Troodos

Páfos

Akrotiri Sovereign Base Area (to UK)

Agialousa (Yenierenköy)

Limassol (Lemesós)

0 km 25

0 miles 25

LAND HEIGHT	SEA DEPTH
Above 4000 m	0–250 m
2000–4000 m	250–500 m
1000–2000 m	500–1000 m
500–1000 m	1000–2000 m
250–500 m	2000–3000 m
100–250 m	3000–4000 m
0–100 m	Below 4000 m
Below sea level	

CITIES AND TOWNS
- ■ Over 500,000 people
- ◉ 100,000–500,000
- ○ 50,000–100,000
- ○ Less than 50,000

THE LANDSCAPE

The Mediterranean Sea would be an enormous lake if it were not for the Strait of Gibraltar, a narrow opening only 13 km wide, which joins it to the Atlantic Ocean. The Mediterranean lies over the boundary of two continental plates. Where they meet, earthquakes and volcanoes are common.

Strait of Gibraltar

Sandy beaches
The Mediterranean coasts are bordered by several thousand miles of sandy beaches.

Shallow shelves
The area of sea off the coast of Tunisia and also the Adriatic sea, are shallower than the rest of the Mediterranean.

Greek islands
Greece has thousands of islands which lie both in the Mediterranean and in the smaller Aegean Sea. Some of them are the remains of old volcanoes which have left black sand on the beaches.

Suez Canal
The Suez Canal links the Mediterranean to the Gulf of Suez and the Red Sea. Before it was built, ships had to sail around the whole of Africa to reach Asia.

Atlas Mountains
The rugged Atlas Mountains run through most of Morocco and Algeria. They form a barrier between the Mediterranean coast and the Sahara which lies south of them.

TOURISM

The tourist industry in and around the Mediterranean is one of the most highly developed in the world. More than half the world's income from tourism is generated here. Resorts have grown up along the northwest coast of Africa, and in Egypt, in southern Spain, France, Italy, Greece and Turkey. Tourism brings huge economic benefits, but the ever-increasing number of visitors has also damaged the environment.

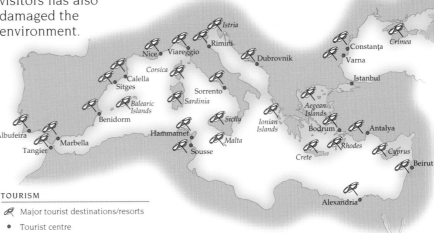

TOURISM

- Major tourist destinations/resorts
- Tourist centre

INDUSTRY

The Mediterranean has a large fishing industry, although most of the fishing is small-scale. Tuna and sardines are caught throughout the region and mussels are farmed off the coast of Italy. Fish canning and packing takes place at most of the larger ports. Small oil and gas reserves are extracted off the coast of North Africa and near Greece, Spain and Italy.

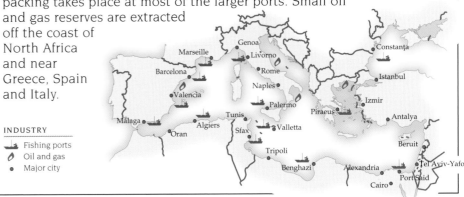

INDUSTRY

- Fishing ports
- Oil and gas
- Major city

81

CONTINENTAL ASIA

Asia is the world's largest continent, and has the greatest range of physical extremes. Some of the highest, lowest, and coldest places on Earth are found in Asia: Mount Everest in the Himalayas is the highest, the Dead Sea in the west is the lowest, and the frozen wastes of northern Siberia are among the coldest. More people live in Asia than on any other continent – 1.29 billion of them in China, and 1.04 billion in India.

6,500 km

9,700 km

CROSS-SECTION THROUGH ASIA

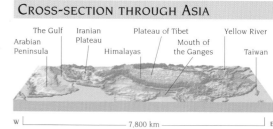

The Gulf | Iranian | Plateau of Tibet | Yellow River
Arabian | Plateau | |
Peninsula | | Himalayas | Mouth of | Taiwan
| | the Ganges

W ——— 7,800 km ——— E

The Arabian Peninsula and the mountainous Iranian Plateau are divided by the Persian Gulf, fed by the Tigris and Euphrates rivers. Further east, the land begins to rise, the mountains spreading north to the Plateau of Tibet, and south to the Himalayas. The plains to the south of the Himalayas are drained by the Indus and Ganges, and to the east of the Plateau of Tibet by the Yellow River.

PHYSICAL ASIA

Northern Asia is made up of old mountains and ancient, stable plateaus. The jagged Himalayan mountains dominate the central part of the continent, along with the Plateau of Tibet, which stretches north into China. In Southeast Asia, there are many islands. Volcanoes and earthquakes are common, and some of the islands are volcanically-formed.

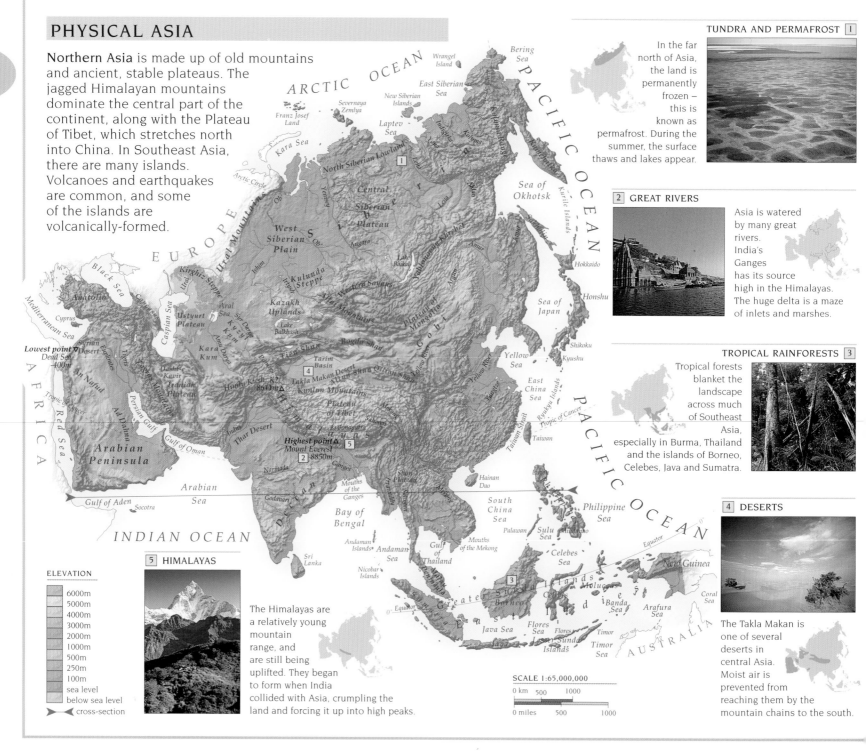

TUNDRA AND PERMAFROST 1

In the far north of Asia, the land is permanently frozen – this is known as permafrost. During the summer, the surface thaws and lakes appear.

2 GREAT RIVERS

Asia is watered by many great rivers. India's Ganges has its source high in the Himalayas. The huge delta is a maze of inlets and marshes.

TROPICAL RAINFORESTS 3

Tropical forests blanket the landscape across much of Southeast Asia, especially in Burma, Thailand and the islands of Borneo, Celebes, Java and Sumatra.

4 DESERTS

The Takla Makan is one of several deserts in central Asia. Moist air is prevented from reaching them by the mountain chains to the south.

5 HIMALAYAS

ELEVATION
- 6000m
- 5000m
- 4000m
- 3000m
- 2000m
- 1000m
- 500m
- 250m
- 100m
- sea level
- below sea level
- cross-section

The Himalayas are a relatively young mountain range, and are still being uplifted. They began to form when India collided with Asia, crumpling the land and forcing it up into high peaks.

SCALE 1:65,000,000

0 km 500   1000

0 miles   500   1000

POLITICAL ASIA

Asia is a continent of many contrasts: in its lands, its peoples and its traditions. The break up of the Soviet Union, which once stretched south from Russia to Iran, produced the new central Asian republics of Kazakhstan, Kyrgyzstan, Tajikistan, Turkmenistan and Uzbekistan. The countries in southwest Asia are mainly Muslim, but are divided by religious differences and conflicts. India is the world's largest democracy, while China is a communist power with restricted access to the rest of the world.

POPULATION

Capital cities
- ● 50,000 to 100,000
- ◉ Above 500,000
- ● Below 50,000
- ◉ 100,000 to 500,000

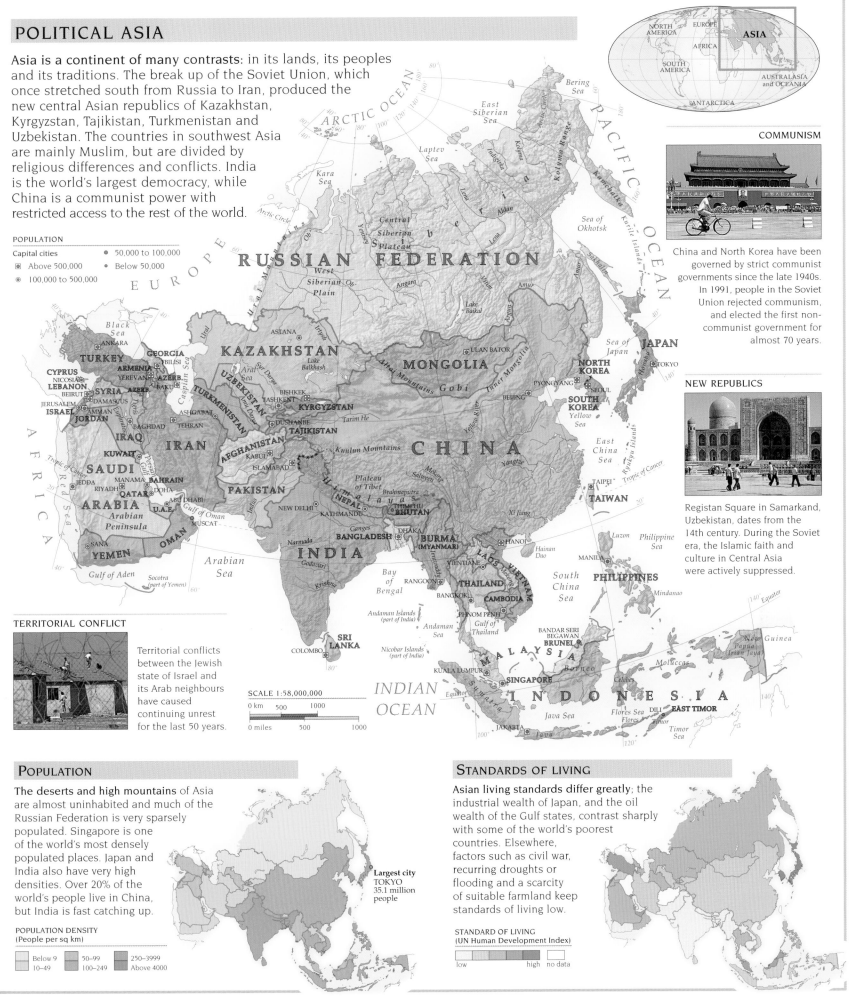

COMMUNISM

China and North Korea have been governed by strict communist governments since the late 1940s. In 1991, people in the Soviet Union rejected communism, and elected the first non-communist government for almost 70 years.

NEW REPUBLICS

Registan Square in Samarkand, Uzbekistan, dates from the 14th century. During the Soviet era, the Islamic faith and culture in Central Asia were actively suppressed.

TERRITORIAL CONFLICT

Territorial conflicts between the Jewish state of Israel and its Arab neighbours have caused continuing unrest for the last 50 years.

SCALE 1:58,000,000

0 km   500   1000

0 miles   500   1000

POPULATION

The deserts and high mountains of Asia are almost uninhabited and much of the Russian Federation is very sparsely populated. Singapore is one of the world's most densely populated places. Japan and India also have very high densities. Over 20% of the world's people live in China, but India is fast catching up.

Largest city
TOKYO
35.1 million
people

POPULATION DENSITY
(People per sq km)

- Below 9
- 10–49
- 50–99
- 100–249
- 250–3999
- Above 4000

STANDARDS OF LIVING

Asian living standards differ greatly; the industrial wealth of Japan, and the oil wealth of the Gulf states, contrast sharply with some of the world's poorest countries. Elsewhere, factors such as civil war, recurring droughts or flooding and a scarcity of suitable farmland keep standards of living low.

STANDARD OF LIVING
(UN Human Development Index)

low   high   no data

ASIAN GEOGRAPHY

Asia's forbidding mountain ranges, barren deserts and fertile plains have affected the way in which people settled the continent. Intensive agriculture is found in the more fertile areas, and the largest concentrations of people grew up near fertile land, and close to great rivers. Asia's mineral wealth has brought people to the more inhospitable parts of the continent; the deserts of southwest Asia for oil, and frozen Siberia for oil, gas, and minerals.

MINERAL RESOURCES

Over half of the world's oil and gas reserves are in Asia, most importantly around the Persian Gulf, and in western Siberia. Coal in Siberia and China has provided power for steel industries. Metallic minerals are also abundant: tin in Southeast Asia, and platinum and nickel in Siberia.

MINERAL RESOURCES

- Chromium
- Tin
- Nickel
- Iron
- Platinum
- Gold
- Lead
- Oil/gas field
- Coal field

INDUSTRY

Many people in Asia still rely on agriculture as a source of income, and some countries have very few industries. Heavy industry dominates eastern China and Russia, but Japan is the most industrially productive country. In recent years, booming 'tiger' economies have developed in countries such as Taiwan, which border the Pacific Ocean.

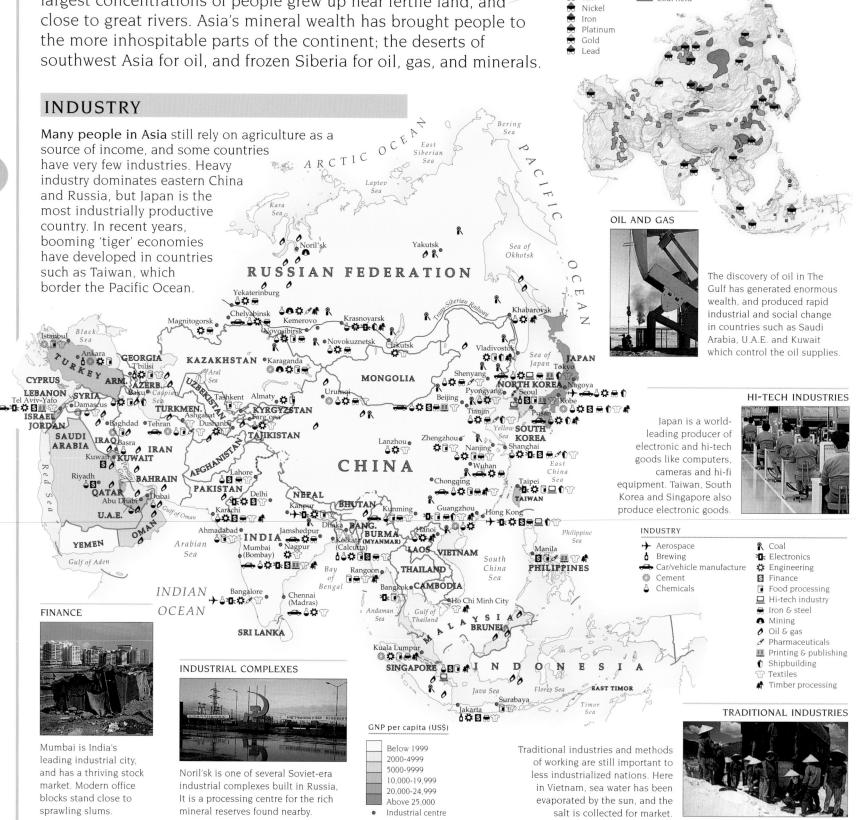

OIL AND GAS

The discovery of oil in The Gulf has generated enormous wealth, and produced rapid industrial and social change in countries such as Saudi Arabia, U.A.E. and Kuwait which control the oil supplies.

HI-TECH INDUSTRIES

Japan is a world-leading producer of electronic and hi-tech goods like computers, cameras and hi-fi equipment. Taiwan, South Korea and Singapore also produce electronic goods.

INDUSTRY

- ✈ Aerospace
- Brewing
- Car/vehicle manufacture
- Cement
- Chemicals
- Coal
- Electronics
- Engineering
- Finance
- Food processing
- Hi-tech industry
- Iron & steel
- Mining
- Oil & gas
- Pharmaceuticals
- Printing & publishing
- Shipbuilding
- Textiles
- Timber processing

FINANCE

Mumbai is India's leading industrial city, and has a thriving stock market. Modern office blocks stand close to sprawling slums.

INDUSTRIAL COMPLEXES

Noril'sk is one of several Soviet-era industrial complexes built in Russia, It is a processing centre for the rich mineral reserves found nearby.

GNP per capita (US$)

- Below 1999
- 2000-4999
- 5000-9999
- 10,000-19,999
- 20,000-24,999
- Above 25,000
- • Industrial centre

TRADITIONAL INDUSTRIES

Traditional industries and methods of working are still important to less industrialized nations. Here in Vietnam, sea water has been evaporated by the sun, and the salt is collected for market.

CLIMATE

Most of Asia has a continental climate, apart from coastal areas. Without the moderating effects of the ocean, temperatures can soar during the day, and plummet at night; while rainfall is generally low – producing several large deserts. Temperatures as low as –68°C have been recorded in the frozen wastes of Siberia, while the islands in Southeast Asia have tropical climates. Southern and eastern Asia are also affected by a seasonal wind called the monsoon. This originates in the Indian Ocean and brings heavy rainfall and high winds, often devastating small coastal and low-lying villages and towns.

EXTREME WEATHER EVENTS

Symbols indicate climatic extremes

CLIMATE
- Tundra
- Subarctic
- Cool continental
- Warm temperate
- Mediterranean
- Semi-arid
- Arid
- Humid equatorial
- Tropical
- Hot humid

Coldest place
VERKHOYANSK (Russ. Fed.)
Temperature –68°C

Hottest place
TIRAT TSVI (Israel)
Temperature 54°C

Driest place
ADEN (Yemen)
Annual rainfall 4.6 cm

Wettest place
CHERRAPUNJI (India)
Annual rainfall 1143cm

RAINFORESTS

The tropical climate across the islands of Southeast Asia produces warm, humid conditions in which rainforests flourish. Each island provides a slightly different habitat, so the animals and plants that have evolved on one island may be very different to those on the next.

LAND USE AND AGRICULTURE

Large expanses of Asia are uncultivated, because the soil is too poor, or the climate is too cold or dry for crops to grow. The Plateau of Tibet, much of Siberia, and the Arabian Peninsula have limited agriculture. Some of the most fertile land is found in eastern China and India, where rice is a staple. Elsewhere, cash crops are grown for profit, such as dates in southwest Asia, rubber in Southeast Asia, tea in India, China and Sri Lanka, and coconuts throughout the island archipelago of Southeast Asia.

RICE

China is the world's largest producer of rice, which is grown in muddy fields called paddy fields. Water buffaloes are used to plough the ground before planting.

COTTON

Uzbekistan is the world's fourth largest producer of cotton. Water has been diverted from nearby rivers to water the crops, which has led to the drying-up of the Aral Sea.

LAND USE AND AGRICULTURE
- Cattle
- Goats
- Pigs
- Sheep
- Cereals
- Coconuts
- Corn (maize)
- Cotton
- Dates
- Fishing
- Fruit
- Jute
- Peanuts
- Rice
- Root crops
- Rubber
- Shellfish
- Sugar cane
- Soya beans
- Tea
- Timber

- Mountains
- Cropland
- Desert
- Forest
- Pasture
- Wetland
- Major conurbation

DATES

Dates have been cultivated on the Arabian Peninsula since ancient times. They are an important cash crop, grown for export in dry sandy areas where few other crops can grow.

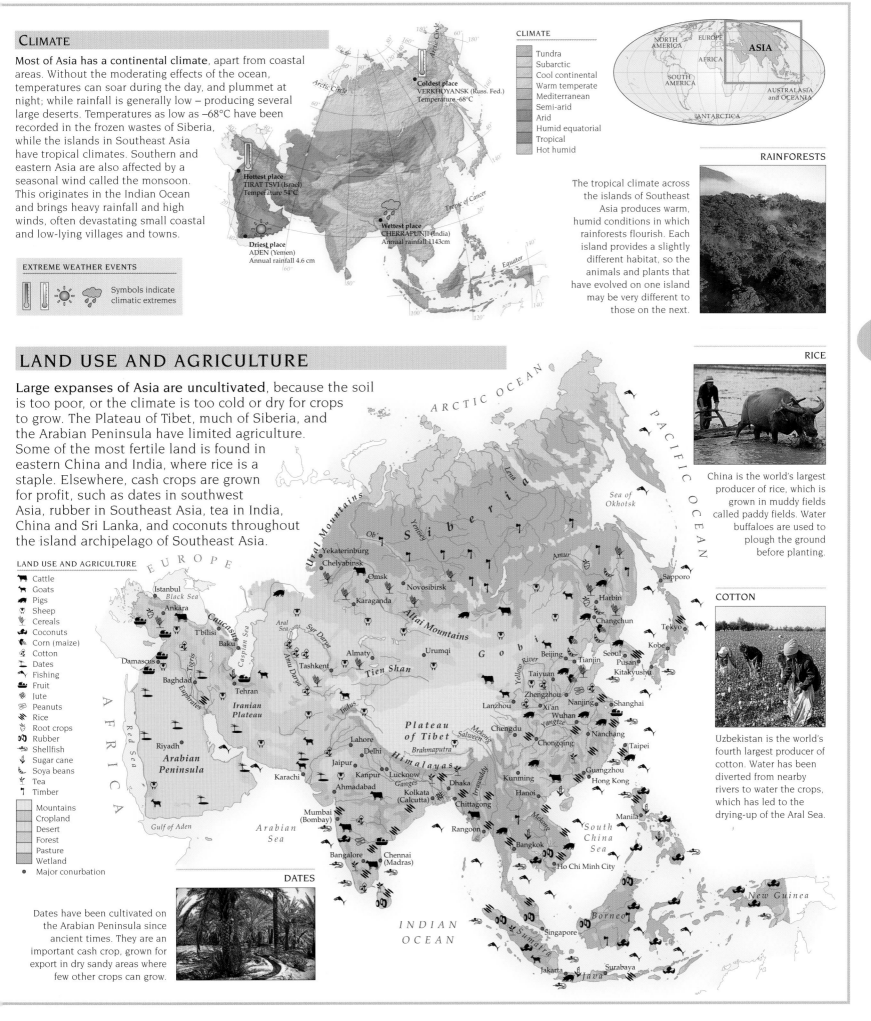

RUSSIA AND KAZAKHSTAN

Russia lies partly in Europe, but mostly in Asia. The land to the east of the Ural Mountains is called Siberia. This immense stretch of grasslands, thick, evergreen forest and tundra is crossed by giant rivers. Vast areas of Siberia are almost untouched by human activity, yet in the industrial regions set up under communism (1922–1991), air, water and soil are heavily polluted with harmful substances. Along with the former Soviet state of Kazakhstan, Siberia is rich in a huge variety of minerals.

INDUSTRY

The discovery of gold in the 19th century opened Siberia up to economic and industrial development. Later, vast reserves of oil, coal and gas were found, especially in the west, which is now the main centre for oil extraction. Gold and diamonds are mined in the east. In Kazakhstan, mining and other industries are growing, with the help of foreign investors.

STRUCTURE OF INDUSTRY

Primary 9%
Services 53%
Manufacturing 38%

INDUSTRY

Car manufacture	Textiles	Timber manufacturing
Chemicals	Diamonds	Major industrial centre / area
Engineering	Mining	Major road
Iron & steel	Oil and gas	

LAND HEIGHT

- above 4000 m
- 2000–4000 m
- 1000–2000 m
- 500–1000 m
- 250–500 m
- 100–250 m
- 0–100 m
- Below sea level

SEA DEPTH

- 0–250 m
- 250–500 m
- 500–1000 m
- 1000–2000 m
- 2000–3000 m
- 3000–4000 m
- Below 4000 m

SCALE BAR

0 km 200 400
0 miles 200 400

CITIES AND TOWNS

- Over 500,000 people
- 100,000–500,000
- 50,000–100,000
- Less than 50,000

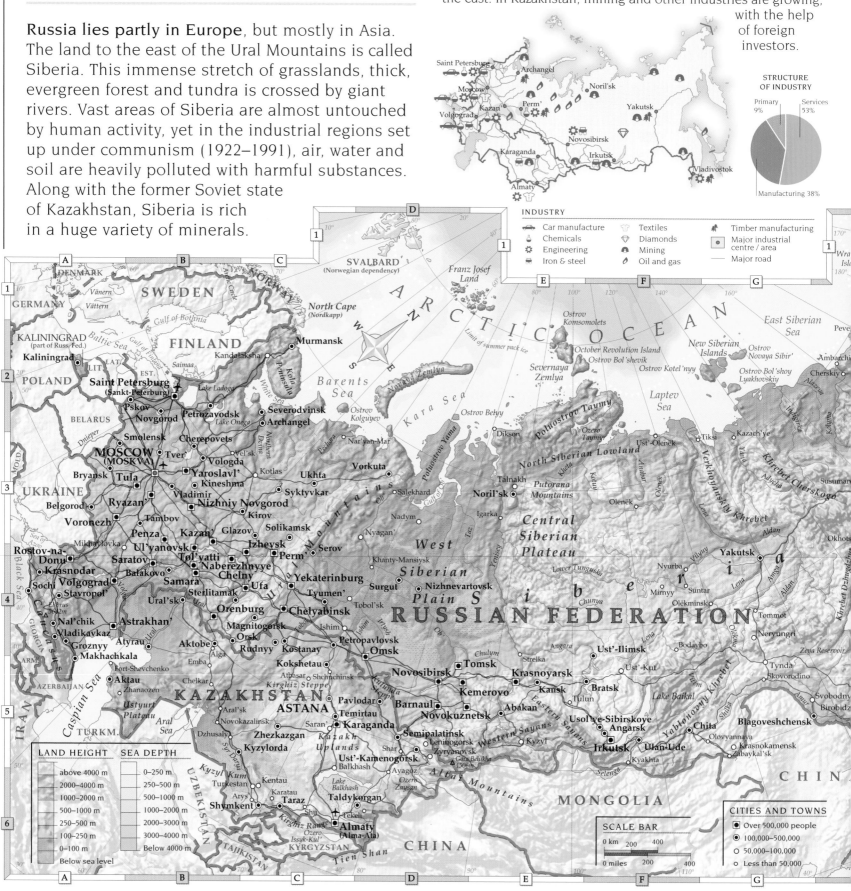

THE LANDSCAPE

East of the Ural Mountains lies the West Siberian Plain – the world's biggest area of flat ground. The plain gradually rises to the Central Siberian Plateau, and then again to highlands in the southeast. Great coniferous forests called *taiga* stretch across most of this land. The far north of Siberia extends into the Arctic Circle. There, the landscape is made up of frozen plains called tundra. Much of Kazakhstan is covered by huge rolling grasslands, or steppe; in the south are arid sandy deserts.

Tundra and *taiga*

Stubby birch trees, dwarf bushes, moss and lichen huddle close to the ground in the frozen tundra wastes of northern Russia. They lie between the permanent ice and snow of the Arctic, and the thick *taiga* forests which cover an area greater than the Amazon rainforest.

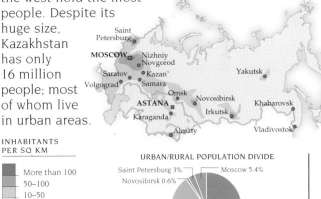

The Caspian Sea (A 5)

The Caspian Sea covers 371,000 sq km and is the world's largest expanse of inland water. It is fed by the Volga and Ural rivers, which flow in from the plains of the north.

West Siberian Plain (D 4)

This vast, flat expanse is covered with a network of marshes and streams. The Ob' river, which winds its way north across the plains, is frozen for up to half the year.

Lake Baikal (F 5)

Lake Baikal is the deepest lake in the world, and the largest freshwater one – it is more than 1.6 km deep, and covers 32,500 sq km. It is fed by 336 rivers and contains around 20% of all the fresh water in the world.

CLIMATE

Russia and Kazakhstan have strongly continental climates, and their distance away from seas and oceans means that temperatures fluctuate wildly, both daily and seasonally. Temperatures in eastern Siberia have been known to reach -68°C.

January

July

TEMPERATURE AND PRECIPITATION

- More than 30°C
- 25 to 30°C
- 20 to 25°C
- 15 to 20°C
- 10 to 15°C
- 5 to 10°C
- 0 to 5°C
- 0 to -5°C
- -5 to -10°C
- -10 to -15°C
- Less than -15°C

—100— Precipitation (mm)

FARMING AND LAND USE

Siberia's harsh climate has restricted farming to the south, where there are a few areas warm enough to grow cereal crops, such as wheat and oats, and to raise cattle on the small pockets of pasture. The rest of the region is used for hunting, herding reindeer, and forestry – the *taiga* forests contain the world's biggest timber reserves. In Kazakhstan, big herds of cattle, goats and sheep are raised for wool and meat, and wheat is cultivated in the fertile north.

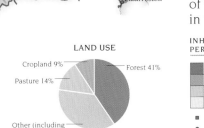

FARMING AND LAND USE

- 🐄 Cattle
- 🐟 Fishing
- 🐖 Pigs
- ⅄ Reindeer
- 🐑 Sheep
- Root crops
- Timber
- Tobacco
- Wheat

- Barren land
- Cropland
- Desert
- Forest
- Mountains
- Pasture
- Tundra
- Wetland
- ● Major conurbation

LAND USE

- Cropland 9%
- Pasture 14%
- Forest 41%
- Other (including mountains) 36%

POPULATION

Siberia has some of the world's largest areas of uninhabited land – the bitingly cold climate and harsh living conditions have kept the population small. The industrial cities in the west hold the most people. Despite its huge size, Kazakhstan has only 16 million people; most of whom live in urban areas.

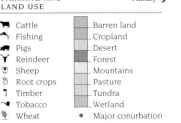

INHABITANTS PER SQ KM

- More than 100
- 50–100
- 10–50
- Less than 10
- ■ Capital city
- ● Major city

URBAN/RURAL POPULATION DIVIDE

- Saint Petersburg 3%
- Moscow 5.4%
- Novosibirsk 0.6%
- Rural population 28%
- Other towns and cities 63%

ENVIRONMENTAL ISSUES

Decades of industrial development during the communist regime brought new industries to undeveloped parts of the region, like Siberia. This industrial development has now led to environmental degradation on a massive scale and river, air and land pollution in Russia is among the worst in the world.

ENVIRONMENTAL ISSUES

- ☠ Urban air pollution
- Polluted rivers
- ● Major industrial centre

TURKEY AND THE CAUCASUS

ARMENIA, AZERBAIJAN, GEORGIA, TURKEY

Turkey and the Caucasus lie partly in Europe, partly in Asia. Turkey has a long Islamic tradition, and although the country is now a secular (non-religious) one, most Turks are Muslims. Turkey is becoming more industrialized, although half its workforce is still employed in agriculture. The ancient countries of the Caucasus were under Russian rule for 70 years, until 1991. They are home to more than 50 different ethnic groups.

INDUSTRY

Turkey has a wide range of industries, including tourism and growing trade links with Europe. Azerbaijan has large oil reserves and is able to export oil. The other states use imported fuel and hydro-electric power generated by their rushing rivers. Georgia produces industrial machinery and chemicals. Armenia's economy is recovering from civil war and earthquake damage.

FARMING AND LAND USE

With its warm climate and good soils, Turkey is able to produce all of its own food. Cattle and goats are kept on the central plateau. Along the Mediterranean coast, farmers grow olives, figs, grapes and peaches. Hazelnuts are cultivated along the shores of the Black Sea. Across the Caucasus, the limited fertile land is used to grow wine grapes, tobacco and cotton.

FARMING AND LAND USE

- 🐂 Livestock
- 🐟 Fishing
- Cotton
- 🐟 Fruit
- Hazelnuts
- Root crops
- Tobacco
- 🍇 Vineyards

- Pasture
- Cropland
- Forest
- • Major conurbation

LAND USE

Other 26%
Cropland 31%
Forest 25%
Pasture 18%

INDUSTRY

- Cement manufacturing
- ♨ Chemicals
- ✿ Engineering
- Food processing
- Textiles
- ⚓ Oil field
- Tourism
- Major industrial centre / area
- — Major road

STRUCTURE OF INDUSTRY

Primary 18%
Services 51%
Manufacturing 31%

THE LANDSCAPE

A huge semi-arid plateau called Anatolia runs across the centre of Turkey. It is rimmed by several mountain ranges along the Black Sea coast, and the steep Taurus Mountains in the south. A narrow strip of lowland separates the Caucasus and the Lesser Caucasus mountains in the northeast.

Anatolia
Anatolia has large areas of soft limestone rock. Over a long period of time, layers of rock have been worn away by water to produce strange landscapes with caves, and tall, isolated rock pinnacles.

Caucasus Mountains (H1)

Lesser Caucasus (H2)

Earthquakes
In 1988, 25,000 people were killed in an earthquake in the west of Armenia.

Between two continents
The city of Istanbul (B2) in Turkey is divided in two by a narrow channel of water called the Bosporus. One part of the city is in Europe, the other in Asia. The two parts are linked by bridges.

Taurus Mountains (D5)
The Taurus Mountains were formed around 60 to 65 million years ago. Weathering has formed caves and deep gorges.

Lake Van (H4)
Lake Van is one of the shallow salt lakes found in Anatolia. Salt lakes develop in hot, dry areas where large quantities of water evaporate, leaving behind salty deposits.

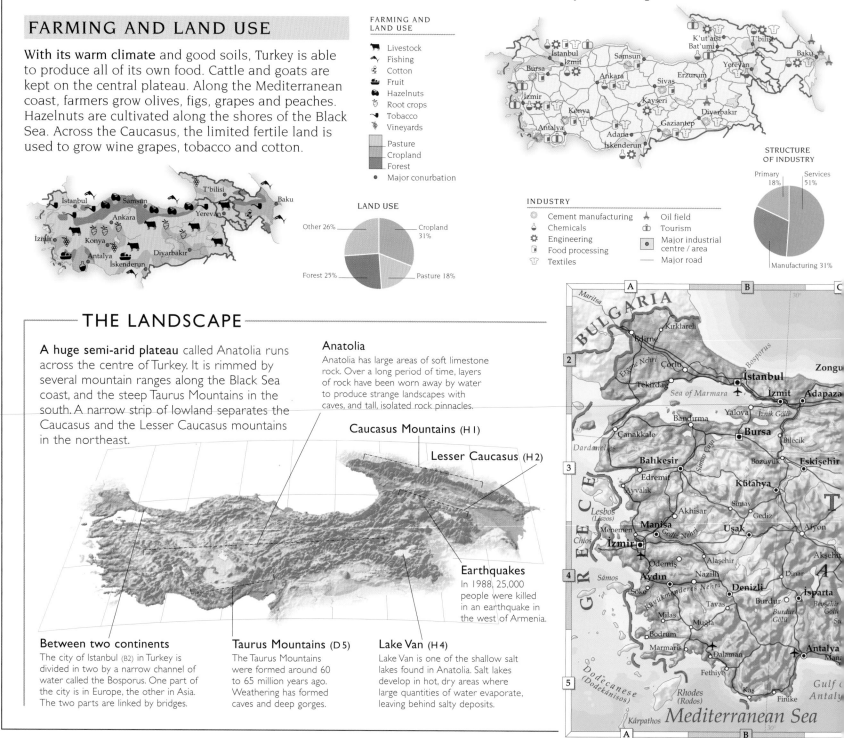

POPULATION

Over 65% of Turks live in large towns or cities, mostly in the western half of the country. The eastern and southeastern parts of Anatolia are home to the Kurdish people. The Caucasian republics became more industrialized under Russian rule, and today, over half of their people live in urban places.

ENVIRONMENTAL ISSUES

Turkey has built many large dams to use water from rivers – especially the Euphrates – to irrigate its farmland. Syria and Iraq, which lie downstream, have opposed the dams, because they will have less water flowing into their countries. The safety of old-style nuclear plants such as Metsamor in Armenia has caused concern.

ASIA
Turkey & the Caucasus

NORTH AMERICA
EUROPE
AFRICA
SOUTH AMERICA
AUSTRALASIA AND OCEANIA
ANTARCTICA

CLIMATE

Winters are coldest in the Caucasus Mountains and in Anatolia, while the shores of the Mediterranean and Black seas remain mild. Summers are hottest around the edge of the Mediterranean and near Turkey's border with Syria and Iraq.

January

July

TEMPERATURE AND PRECIPITATION

- More than 30°C
- 25 to 30°C
- 20 to 25°C
- 15 to 20°C
- 10 to 15°C
- 5 to 10°C
- 0 to 5°C
- 0 to -5°C
- -5 to -10°C
- Less than -10°C
- 100 Precipitation (mm)

Population map labels

İstanbul, Zonguldak, TBILISI, YEREVAN, BAKU, Bursa, Samsun, Trabzon, İzmir, ANKARA, Konya, Adana

URBAN/RURAL POPULATION DIVIDE

- Istanbul 10.3%
- Baku 2.4%
- Ankara 2.3%
- Other towns and cities 46%
- Rural population 39%

INHABITANTS PER SQ KM

- More than 200
- 100–200
- 50–100
- Less than 50
- ■ Capital city
- ● Major city

Environmental issues map labels

İstanbul, 1999, T'bilisi 1998, Metsamor, Yerevan, Atatürk Dam, Euphrates

ENVIRONMENTAL ISSUES

- ◉ Earthquake zone
- Major dam
- Unstable nuclear power station
- Urban air pollution
- ● Major industrial centre

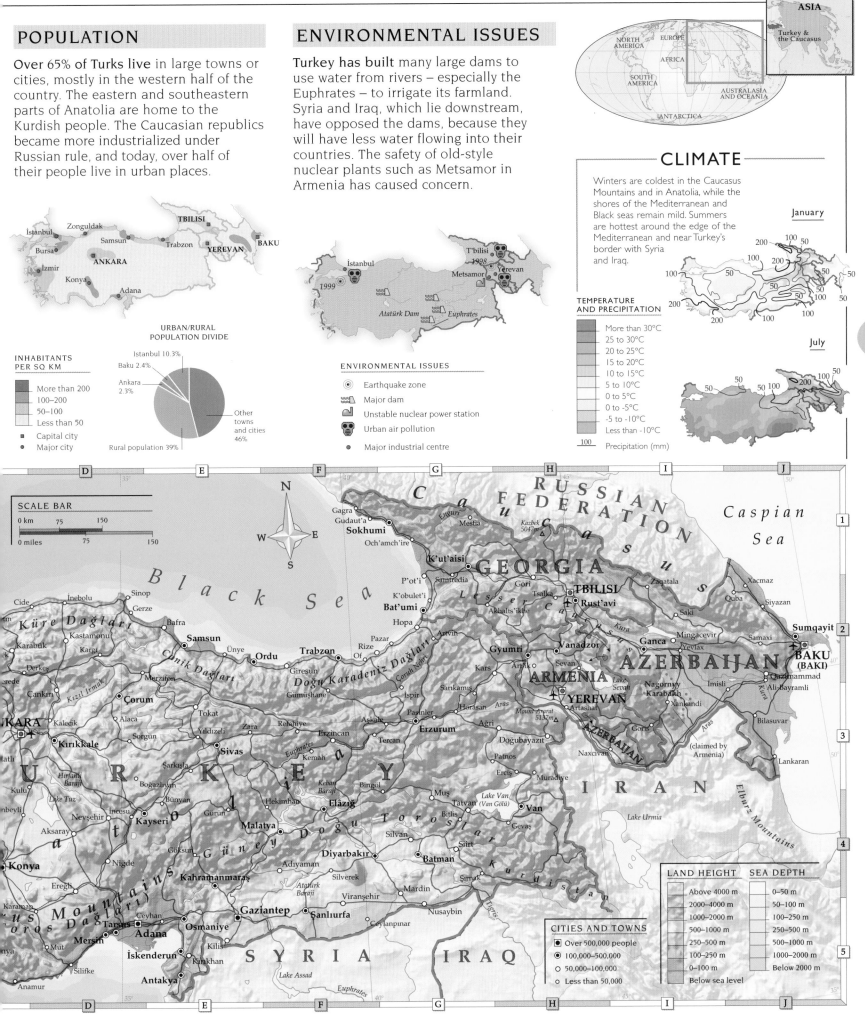

Main map

SCALE BAR
0 km 75 150
0 miles 75 150

N W E S

Black Sea

Caspian Sea

RUSSIAN FEDERATION

Caucasus

Gagra, Gudaut'a, Sokhumi, Och'amch'ire, Enguri, Mestia, Kazbek 5047m, K'ut'aisi, GEORGIA, P'ot'i, Samtredia, Gori, Tsalka, TBILISI, Rust'avi, Zaqatala, Xacmaz, K'obulet'i, Bat'umi, Akhalts'ikhe, Lesser Caucasus, Kura, Saki, Quba, Siyazan, Hopa, Artvin, Gyumri, Vanadzor, Sevan, Ganca, Mingacevir, Nevlax, Sumqayit, Pazar, Rize, Of, Kars, Arik, Lake Sevan, AZERBAIJAN, Samaxi, BAKU (BAKI), Giresun, Doğu Karadeniz Dağları, Çoruh Nehri, İspir, Sarıkamış, ARMENIA, Nagornyy Karabakh, İmisli, Qazimammad, Gümüşhane, Horasan, YEREVAN, Xankandi, Ali-Bayramli, Kure Dağları, Sinop, İnebolu, Gerze, Bafra, Samsun, Ünye, Ordu, Trabzon, Cide, Kastamonu, Karabük, Kargı, Çankırı, Kızıl Irmak, Çorum, Tokat, Aşkale, Paşinler, Erzurum, Aras, Artashat, Mount Ararat 5137m, Goris, Bilasuvar, Lankaran, Derbes, Kalecik, Alaca, Sorgun, Yıldızeli, Zara, Relahiye, Erzincan, Kemah, Tercan, Ağri, Doğubayazıt, Naxcivan, ANKARA, Kırıkkale, Sivas, Şarkışla, Bogazliyan, Keban Baraji, Bingöl, Muş, Patnos, Erciş, Muradiye, (claimed by Armenia), IRAN, Elburz Mountains, Kulu, Lake Tuz, Bünyan, Hekimhan, Lake Van (Van Gölü), Tatvan, Van, Hirfanli Baraji, TURKEY, Nevşehir, İncesu, Kayseri, Gürün, Malatya, Silvan, Bitlis, Gevaş, Lake Urmia, Aksaray, Göksun, Doğu Toroslar, Siirt, Niğde, Kahramanmaraş, Silverek, Diyarbakır, Batman, Şırnak, Kurdistan, Konya, Ereğli, Adıyaman, Atatürk Baraji, Viranşehir, Mardin, Nusaybin, Karaman, Toros Mountains, Gaziantep, Şanlıurfa, Ceylanpınar, Tarsus, Ceyhan, Osmaniye, Kilis, Adana, Mersin, İskenderun, Kırıkhan, SYRIA, IRAQ, Lake Assad, Tigris, Euphrates, Mut, Silifke, Antakya, Anamur

LAND HEIGHT
- Above 4000 m
- 2000–4000 m
- 1000–2000 m
- 500–1000 m
- 250–500 m
- 100–250 m
- 0–100 m
- Below sea level

SEA DEPTH
- 0–50 m
- 50–100 m
- 100–250 m
- 250–500 m
- 500–1000 m
- 1000–2000 m
- Below 2000 m

CITIES AND TOWNS
- ■ Over 500,000 people
- ◉ 100,000–500,000
- ○ 50,000–100,000
- ○ Less than 50,000

SOUTHWEST ASIA

BAHRAIN, IRAN, IRAQ, ISRAEL, JORDAN, KUWAIT, LEBANON, OMAN, QATAR, SAUDI ARABIA, SYRIA, UNITED ARAB EMIRATES, YEMEN

Most of southwest Asia is barren desert, yet the world's first cities developed here, over 5,000 years ago. It was also the birthplace of three major religions: Islam, Judaism and Christianity. In recent years, the discovery of oil has brought great wealth to much of the region, but it has been torn by civil wars, and conflict between neighbouring countries. Most people here are Muslims, although Israel is the world's only Jewish state.

INDUSTRY

Oil has made the previously poor Arab states very wealthy. Oil and natural gas continue to be the main source of income for many of the countries here, although other industries are being developed to support their economies when these resources run out. Iran is famous for its carpets, which are woven from wool or silk.

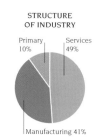

INDUSTRY

- ⊙ Cement manufacturing
- 🏭 Food processing
- 🚗 Iron and steel
- 🛢 Oil refining
- 👕 Textiles
- 🛢 Oil and gas
- Ⓢ Finance

- ▣ Major industrial centre / area
- — Major road

STRUCTURE OF INDUSTRY

Primary 10%
Services 49%
Manufacturing 41%

ENVIRONMENTAL ISSUES

Water shortages are common because of the hot, dry climate and the lack of rivers. Desalination plants convert sea water into fresh water, and are found along the Red Sea and Persian Gulf coasts. Lack of water also makes the risk of desertification greater. Iran has had many catastrophic earthquakes; in 1978 an earthquake killed 25,000 people.

ENVIRONMENTAL ISSUES

- 🚰 Area with many desalination plants
- ⊙ Catastrophic earthquake
- ☠ Urban air pollution

- Existing desert
- Risk of desertification
- • Major industrial centre

THE LANDSCAPE

Great desert plateaus, both sandy and rocky, cover much of southwest Asia. On the enormous Arabian Peninsula, which covers an area almost the size of India, narrow, sandy plains along the Red Sea and south coast rise to dry mountains. In the centre is a vast, high plateau that slopes gently down to the flat shores of the Persian Gulf. The mountainous areas of Iran experience frequent earthquakes.

Wadis
Valleys or riverbeds, called *wadis*, are found in the Saudi Arabian desert. Usually they are dry, but after heavy rains, they are briefly filled by fast flowing rivers.

Syrian Desert (B 2)
The Syrian Desert extends from the Jordan valley in the west, to the fertile plains of the Tigris and Euphrates rivers in the east. It is mainly a rocky desert, as the sand has been swept away by winds and occasional heavy rainstorms.

Oases
Oases are areas within a desert where water is available for plants, and human use. They are usually formed when a fault, or split, in the rock allows water to come to the surface. Oases can be no bigger than a few palm trees, or cover several hundred sq km.

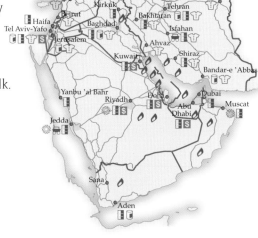

FARMING AND LAND USE

The best farmland is found along the Mediterranean coast, and in the fertile valleys of the Tigris, Euphrates and Jordan rivers. Wheat is the main cereal crop, and cotton, dates, citrus and orchard fruits are grown for export. Elsewhere, modern irrigation techniques have created patches of fertile land in the desert. Dates, wheat and coffee are cultivated in the oases and along the Persian Gulf coast.

LAND USE

Forest 5%
Pasture 36%
Cropland 7%
Other (including desert) 52%

FARMING AND LAND USE

- 🐐 Goats
- 🐟 Fishing
- 🐑 Sheep
- 🍊 Citrus fruits
- ☕ Coffee
- 🌿 Cotton
- 🌴 Dates
- 🍎 Fruit
- 🌿 Tobacco
- 🌾 Wheat

- Cropland
- Desert
- Forest
- Pasture
- Wetland
- • Major conurbation

Dead Sea (A 2)
This large lake on the border between Israel and Jordan is the lowest point on the Earth's surface – its shores lie 392 m below sea level. It is also the world's saltiest body of water, and can support no life forms.

Ar Rub' al Khali (D 5)
The Ar Rub' al Khali desert, also known as the 'Empty Quarter', is the largest uninterrupted stretch of sand on Earth. It covers some 650,000 sq km and is one of the world's driest and most hostile deserts.

Iranian Plateau (E 3)
Central Iran is taken up by a vast, semi-arid plateau, which rises steeply from the coastal lowlands bordering the Persian Gulf. It is ringed by the high Zagros and Elburz mountains.

ASIA
Southwest
Asia

POPULATION

Desert has kept much of the population clustered along the coastal areas and rivers, or around the oases. Most people live in the cities, some of which are the fastest growing in the world. Oman and Yemen have mainly rural populations, and in Saudi Arabia, small groups of Bedouin tribespeople roam the desert with their animals.

URBAN/RURAL POPULATION DIVIDE

Baghdad 3%   Tehran 5%
Riyadh 1%
Other towns and cities 52%
Rural population 39%

INHABITANTS PER SQ KM
More than 200
100–200
50–100
Less than 50
■ Capital city
● Major city

CLIMATE

Most of the region receives very little rain, apart from a few isolated pockets. During July, temperatures soar, but in January temperatures are much cooler, especially in the north.

TEMPERATURE AND PRECIPITATION
More than 30°C
25 to 30°C
20 to 25°C
15 to 20°C
10 to 15°C
5 to 10°C
0 to 5°C
Less than 0°C
100 Precipitation (mm)

January

July

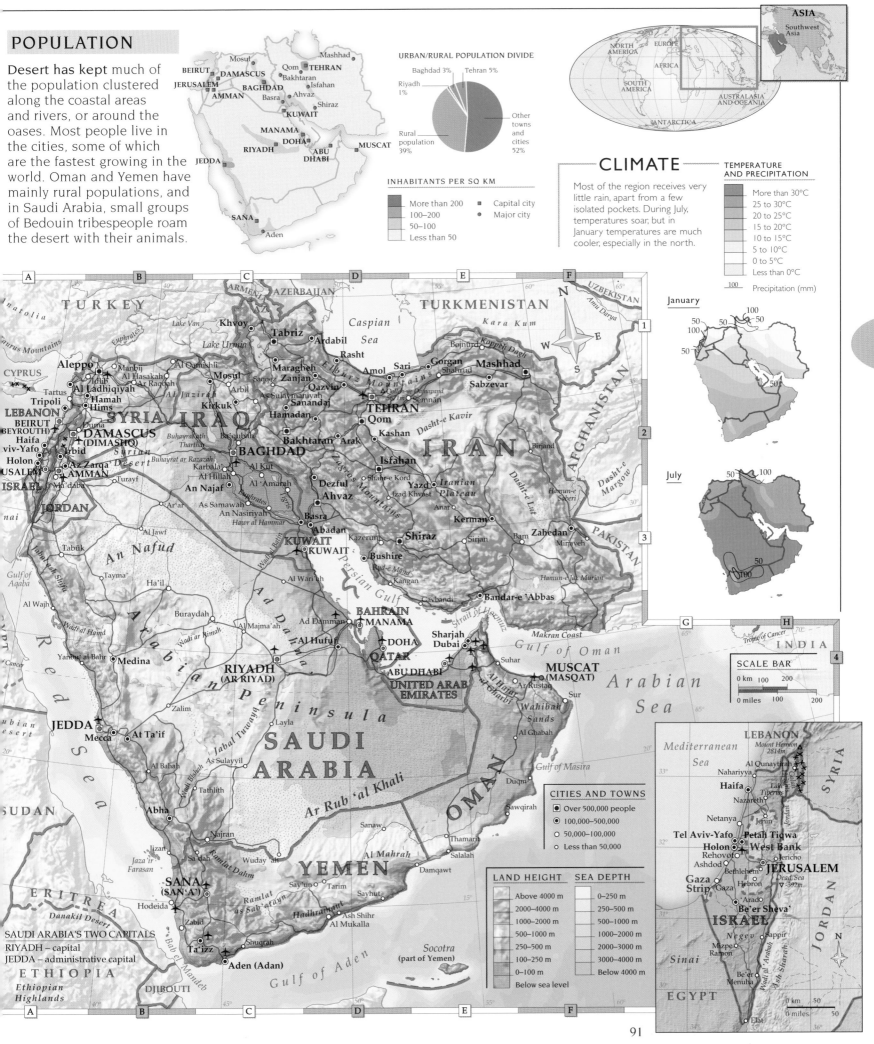

SCALE BAR
0 km 100 200
0 miles 100 200

CITIES AND TOWNS
◉ Over 500,000 people
◎ 100,000–500,000
○ 50,000–100,000
○ Less than 50,000

LAND HEIGHT
Above 4000 m
2000–4000 m
1000–2000 m
500–1000 m
250–500 m
100–250 m
0–100 m
Below sea level

SEA DEPTH
0–250 m
250–500 m
500–1000 m
1000–2000 m
2000–3000 m
3000–4000 m
Below 4000 m

SAUDI ARABIA'S TWO CAPITALS
RIYADH – capital
JEDDA – administrative capital

91

CENTRAL ASIA

AFGHANISTAN, KYRGYZSTAN, TAJIKISTAN, TURKMENISTAN, UZBEKISTAN

Central Asia is a land of hot, dry deserts and high, rugged mountains. It lies on the ancient Silk Road, an important trade route between China and Europe for over 400 years, until the 15th century. All of the countries here, apart from Afghanistan, were part of the Soviet Union from the 1920s, until 1991, when they gained independence. Since then, their people have re-established their local languages and Islamic faith, all of which were restricted under Russian rule.

INDUSTRY

Fossil fuels, especially coal, natural gas and oil, are extracted and processed throughout Central Asia. Agriculture supplies the raw materials for many industries, including food and textile processing, and the manufacture of leather goods and clothing. The region is famous for its colourful traditional carpets, hand-woven from the wool of the Karakul sheep. The Fergana Valley, southeast of Tashkent, is the main industrial area.

INDUSTRY

- ♨ Chemicals
- ⚙ Engineering
- ▣ Food processing
- 👕 Textiles
- ⛏ Mining
- ◊ Oil and gas
- ◉ Major industrial centre / area
- — Major road

STRUCTURE OF INDUSTRY

- Primary 16%
- Manufacturing 58%
- Services 26%

POPULATION

The peoples of Central Asia are mostly rural farmers, living in the river valleys and in oases. There are few large cities. A few still lead a traditional nomadic lifestyle, moving from place to place with their animals, in search of new pastures. Large areas of Afghanistan, the western deserts and the mountain regions in the east, are virtually uninhabited.

INHABITANTS PER SQ KM

- More than 100
- 50–100
- 10–50
- Less than 10
- ■ Capital city
- ● Major city

URBAN/RURAL POPULATION DIVIDE

- Kabul 2.9%
- Tashkent 3%
- Bishkek 1.1%
- Rural population 62%
- Other towns and cities 31%

FARMING AND LAND USE

Farming is concentrated around the fertile river valleys in the east, like the Fergana Valley. A variety of cereals, and fruits, including peaches, melons and apricots, are grown. In drier areas, animal breeding is important, with goats, sheep and cattle supplying wool, meat and hides. Big crops of cotton, which is a major export, are produced on land irrigated by the Amu Darya river.

FARMING AND LAND USE

- 🐂 Cattle
- 🐐 Goats
- 🐑 Sheep
- ⚕ Cotton
- 🍂 Fruit
- ⚘ Opium poppies
- 🌿 Tobacco
- 🌾 Wheat
- Cropland
- Desert
- Mountains
- Pasture
- Wetland
- ● Major conurbation

LAND USE

- Forest 4%
- Cropland 9%
- Pasture 41%
- Other (including mountains and deserts) 45%

THE LANDSCAPE

Two of the world's great deserts, the Garagum and the Kyzyl Kum, cover much of the western portion of Central Asia. In the east, a belt of high mountain ranges – the Hindu Kush, the Tien Shan and the Pamirs – tower above the land. Few rivers cross the deserts, apart from the Amu Darya, which flows from the Pamirs to the shrinking Aral Sea.

The Aral Sea (D 1)
The Aral Sea was once the fourth largest lake in the world, but it has shrunk by 40% since 1960. Diversion of its water for irrigation has made the lake shallower, so its waters evaporate faster.

Garagum (D 3)
The sandy desert of the Kara Kum occupies over 70% of Turkmenistan. Its surface consists of wind-sculpted dunes and depressions. Human settlement is limited to the desert's fringes.

Tien Shan (H 2)

Fergana Valley (G 3)
Stresses and strains in the Earth created the Fergana Valley, a deep depression encircled by high mountains. The valley's fertile soils are irrigated by water from the Syr Darya river, and underground sources.

Amu Darya river (E 3)

Hindu Kush (G 4)

Pamirs (G 4)
The Pamirs lie mainly in Tajikistan. Their highest point, at 7,495 m, is Communism Peak, so named because it was the highest peak in the former Soviet Union.

ENVIRONMENTAL ISSUES

The Aral Sea is rapidly drying up, as the rivers feeding it are being diverted to irrigate fields of cotton. Central Asia is a very dry area, and desertification is a constant threat, especially in Afghanistan. Severe urban and industrial air pollution is a legacy from the communist era, when heavy industries were established in the countries here.

CLIMATE

Central Asia's climate is strongly inflenced by its position deep within Asia, far from the moderating effects of the oceans. Winters are cold, summers are very hot everywhere. Rainfall is virtually non-existent all year round.

ASIA
NORTH AMERICA
EUROPE
ASIA
Central Asia
AFRICA
SOUTH AMERICA
AUSTRALASIA AND OCEANIA
ANTARCTICA

ENVIRONMENTAL ISSUES

- Urban air pollution
- Existing desert
- Risk of desertification
- Severe risk of desertification
- Polluted river
- Major industrial centre

Aral Sea
Amu Darya
Bishkek
Dushanbe
Fergana Valley

January
Less than 50mm precipitation

July
Less than 50mm precipitation

TEMPERATURE AND PRECIPITATION

- More than 30°C
- 25 to 30°C
- 5 to 10°C
- 0 to 5°C
- Less than 0°C

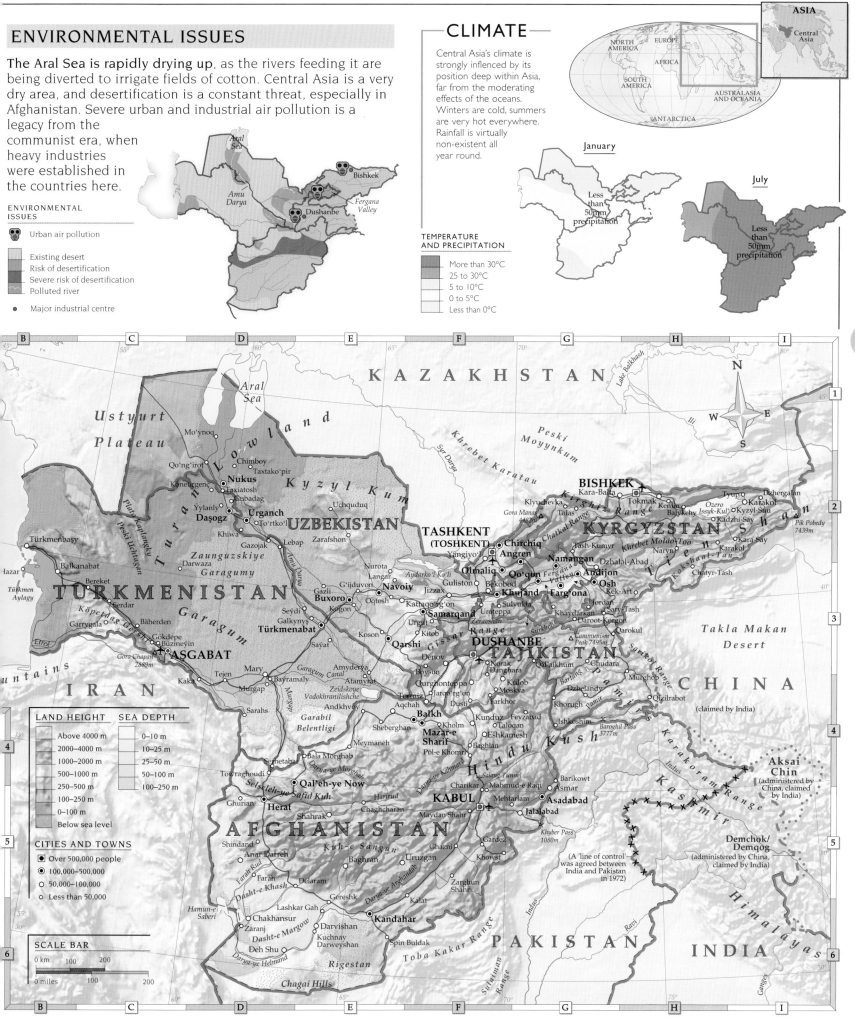

JAPAN AND KOREA

JAPAN, NORTH KOREA, SOUTH KOREA

Japan is a curved chain of over 4,000 islands in the Pacific Ocean. To the west, Korea juts out from northern China. Japan has few natural resources but it has become one of the world's most successful industrial nations due to investment in new technology and a highly efficient workforce. North Korea is a communist state with limited contact with the outside world, while South Korea is a democracy with major international trade links.

THE LANDSCAPE

Most of Japan is covered by forested mountains and hills, among which are many short, fast-flowing rivers and small lakes. Only about a quarter of the land is suitable for building and farming and new land has been created by cutting back hillsides and reclaiming land from the sea. North and South Korea are mostly mountainous, with some coastal plains.

Hokkaido, Honshu, Shikoku and Kyushu
Japan's four main islands were formed when two giant plates making up the Earth's crust collided, making their edges buckle upwards.

T'aebaek-sanmaek (C 5)
This wooded mountain range forms the 'backbone' of the Korean peninsula. It runs from north to south close to the east coast.

Tsunamis
Huge sea waves called tsunamis frequently threaten the east coast of Japan. They are set off by submarine earthquakes. The waves increase in size as they near the shore, and can flood coastal areas and sink ships.

Earthquakes
In Japan, earthquakes are part of everyday life. The islands lie on a fault line, and earthquake tremors occur, on average, 5,000 times a year. Most of these are mild, and may go unnoticed, but there is a constant threat of disaster.

Volcanoes
Japan's mountain ranges are studded with volcanoes, 60 of which are still active. Mount Fuji is a 3,776 m snow-capped volcano and the highest mountain in Japan. It last erupted in 1707.

FARMING AND LAND USE

Modern farming methods allow Japan to grow much of its own food, despite a shortage of farmland. Rice is the main crop grown throughout the region. Japan has a large fishing fleet; the Japanese eat more fish than any other nation. In North Korea, farming is controlled by the government.

Sapporo
Sendai
Pyongyang
Seoul
Tokyo
Yokohama
Nagoya
Pusan
Kobe
Kwangju
Hiroshima
Osaka
Fukuoka

FARMING AND LAND USE

- 🐄 Cattle
- 🎣 Fishing
- 🐷 Pigs
- 🍎 Fruit
- 🌾 Rice
- 🌱 Soya beans
- 🌿 Tea
- 🍃 Tobacco

Cropland
Forest
Pasture
● Major conurbation

LAND USE

- Pasture 1%
- Cropland 14%
- Other (including mountains) 30%
- Forest 55%

POPULATION

Most of Japan's 128 million people live in crowded cities on the coasts of the four main islands. The Kanto Plain around Tokyo is Japan's biggest area of flat land, and the most populous part of the country. In South Korea, a quarter of the population lives in the capital, Seoul. Most North Koreans live on the coastal plains.

Sapporo
Hamhung
PYONGYANG
Sendai
Nagaoka
SEOUL
TOKYO
Yokohama
Taejon
Taegu
Kobe
Nagoya
Pusan
Osaka
Kwangju
Hiroshima
Fukuoka
Kagoshima

URBAN/RURAL POPULATION DIVIDE

- Tokyo-Yokohama 7.5%
- Seoul 6%
- Kobe-Osaka 5.5%
- Other towns and cities 55%
- Rural population 26%

INHABITANTS PER SQ KM

- More than 200
- 100–200
- 50–100
- Less than 50
- ■ Capital city
- ● Major city

INDUSTRY

Japan is a world leader in hi-tech electronic goods like computers, televisions and cameras, as well as cars. South Korea also has a thriving economy. It produces ships, cars, hi-tech goods, shoes and clothes for worldwide export. Both countries have to import most of their raw materials and energy. North Korea has little trade with other countries, but it is rich in minerals such as coal and silver.

Kushiro
Sapporo
Hachinohe
Ch'ongjin
Sendai
Nagaoka
Hitachi
Pyongyang
Toyama
Tokyo
Seoul
Kyoto
Yokohama
Inch'on
Kobe
Nagoya
Pusan
Osaka
Kwangju
Hiroshima
Fukuoka
Kitakyushu

STRUCTURE OF INDUSTRY

- Primary 3%
- Services 57%
- Manufacturing 40%

INDUSTRY

- 🚗 Car manufacture
- ⚗️ Chemicals
- ⚙️ Engineering
- 🏭 Food processing
- ⚒️ Iron & steel
- ⚓ Shipbuilding
- 👕 Textiles
- ⛏️ Mining
- Ⓢ Finance
- 🖥️ Hi-tech
- ⚙️ Research & Development
- ■ Major industrial centre / area
- — Major road

ENVIRONMENTAL ISSUES

Industrial pollution from Korea and China has produced acid rain, and pollution in Japanese cities has led to people wearing masks to filter the air. Russia regularly dumps nuclear waste into the Sea of Japan. In 1995, an earthquake caused great destruction to the city of Kobe.

Sea of Japan

Seoul

Tokyo

Kobe 1995

Osaka

ENVIRONMENTAL ISSUES

- ⊚ Catastrophic earthquake
- ⬤ Nuclear waste dump site
- ☷ Urban air pollution
- Affected by acid rain
- • Major industrial area

CLIMATE

Korea has hot summers and dry, very cold winters, especially in the north, where snow is common. In Japan, winters are less cold than on the Asian mainland; summers are hot, wet and humid.

January
200
50
100
100
100
Less than 50

July
50
200
100
100

ASIA
Japan and Korea

TEMPERATURE AND PRECIPITATION

More than 20°C	0 to 5°C
15 to 20°C	0 to -5°C
10 to 15°C	Less than -5°C
5 to 10°C	

100 Precipitation (mm)

SCALE BAR
0 km   100   200
0 miles   100   200

0 km   200
0 miles   200

CHINA

RUSS. FED.

Hoeryong

Najin

Paektu-san 2750m

Ch'ongjin

Hyesan

Huch'ang

Kilchu

Kanggye

Kimch'aek

Ch'osan

Pukch'ong

Namsan-ni

Huich'on

Sinp'o

Sinuiju

Hamhung

NORTH KOREA

Chongju

Anju

Yenghung

East Korea Bay

Sinmi-do

Sunch'on

Wonsan

Yellow Sea

Namp'o

PYONGYANG

Kosong

Sariwon

Sokch'o

Changyon

Haeju Kaesong

Kangnung

(North and South Korea have been divided by a ceasefire agreement since 1953)

Ongjin

Ch'unch'on

Wonju

Tonghae

Sea of Japan

Inch'on

SEOUL (SŎUL)

Suwon

Ch'onan

Ch'ungju

Andong

P'ohang

SOUTH KOREA

Taejon

Liancourt Rocks (claimed by Japan and South Korea)

Oki-shoto

Dogo

Dozen

Kunsan

Taegu

Ulsan

Namwon

Masan

Pusan

Tottori

Matsue

Yonago

Kwangju

Sunch'on

Kyushu

Mokp'o

Roje-do

Namhae-do

Gotsu

Hamada

Okayama

Kurashiki

Takamatsu

Chugoku-sanchi

East China Sea

Osumi-shoto

Satsunan-shoto

Naze

Amami-gunto

Amami-o-shima

Ryukyu Islands (part of Japan)

Okinawa

Naha

Senkaku-shoto

Sakishima-shoto

Ishigaki-jima

Iriomote-jima

Tsushima

Nagato

Yamaguchi

Iwakuni

Hofu

Hiroshima

Kure

Niihama

Matsuyama

Iyo-nada

Philippine Sea

Cheju Strait

Chin-do

Ko-gum-do

Shimonoseki

Ube

Kitakyushu

Fukuoka

Kurume

Saga

Omuta

Sasebo

Nagasaki

Yatsushiro

Goto-retto

Kumamoto

Nobeoka

Amakusa-nada

Koshikijima-retto

Miyazaki

Miyakonojō

Kagoshima

Sendai

Cheju-do

Korea Strait

Oita

Kochi

Nakamura

Sukumo

Tosa-wan

Nakamura

Shikoku

Bungo-suido

Shibushi-wan

PACIFIC OCEAN

F   G   H

La Perouse Strait

Rebun-to

Wakkanai

Sea of Okhotsk

Rishiri-to

Monbetsu

Abashiri

Kurile Islands (administered by Russian Federation, claimed by Japan)

Nemuro

Hokkaido

Nayoro

Shibetsu

Kitami

Asahikawa

Asahi-dake 2290m

Takikawa

Akkeshi

Obihiro

Kushiro

Otaru

Ebetsu

Horoshiridake 2052m

Sapporo

Chitose

Ishikari-wan

Iwanai

Tomakomai

Noboribetsu

Muroran

Uchiura-wan

Okushiri-to

Hakodate

Tsugaru-kaikyo

Aomori

JAPAN

Goshogawara

Hachinohe

Hirosaki

Kuji

Odate

Iwate

Noshiro

Miyako

Gojome

Ou-sanmyaku

Morioka

Akita

Yokote

Kesennuma

Honjo

Shinjo

Shizugawa

Sakata

Tsuruoka

Furukawa

Ishinomaki

Sendai

Yamagata

Sendai-wan

Fukushima

Soma

Haramachi

Sado

Niigata

Koriyama

Nagaoka

Inawashiro-ko

Sukagawa

Iwaki

Joetsu

Itoigawa

Hitachi

Toyama-wan

Utsunomiya

Honshu

Takaoka

Nagano

Maebashi

Oyama

Mito

Kanazawa

Toyama

Kawagoe

Kanto Plain

Kasumiga-ura

Komatsu

Shinano

Matsumoto

Choshi

Hida-sanmyaku

Fukui

TOKYO

Chiba

Kofu

Kawasaki

Mount Fuji 3776m

Yokohama

Tsuruga

Gifu

Nakatsugawa

Boso-hanto

Wakasa-wan

Shizuoka

Izu-hanto

O-shima

Biwa-ko

Ogaki

Toyota

Okazaki

Suruga-wan

Sagami-nada

Nagoya

Hamamatsu

Nii-jima

Kyoto

Otsu

Tsu

Ise-wan

Kozu-shima

Miyako-jima

Mikura-jima

Himeji

Kobe

Ise

Owase

Hachijo-jima

Osaka

Wakayama

Gobo

Kii-suido

Tanabe

Shingu

Harima-nada

Awaji-shima

Kii-suido

LAND HEIGHT

2000–4000 m
1000–2000 m
500–1000 m
250–500 m
100–250 m
0–100 m

SEA DEPTH

0–250 m
250–500 m
500–1000 m
1000–2000 m
2000–3000 m
3000–4000 m
Below 4000 m

CITIES AND TOWNS

- ■ Over 500,000 people
- ◉ 100,000–500,000
- ○ 50,000–100,000
- ∘ Less than 50,000

EAST ASIA

CHINA, MONGOLIA, TAIWAN

China is the world's third largest country and its most populous – over one billion people live there. Under its communist government, which came to power in 1949, China has become a major industrial nation, but most of its people still live and work on the land, as they have for thousands of years. Taiwan also has a booming economy and exports its products around the world. Mongolia is a vast, remote country with a small population, many of whom are nomads.

INDUSTRY

Chemicals, iron and steel, engineering and textiles are the main industries in China's east coast cities, and in industrial centres like Shenyang. Shanghai, Hong Kong and Beijing are also important financial centres. In the interior, large deposits of coal support the heavy industries in major cities such as Chengdu and Wuhan. Taiwan specializes in textiles and shoe manufacture, along with electronic goods. Mongolia's economy is mainly agricultural.

INDUSTRY

- 🚗 Car manufacture
- ⚗ Chemicals
- ⚙ Electronics
- 💻 Electronic goods
- ⚙ Engineering
- 🍲 Food processing
- 🚢 Iron & steel
- ⚓ Shipbuilding
- 👕 Textiles
- ⚒ Coal
- ⛏ Mining
- Ⓢ Finance
- ⦿ Major industrial centre / area
- — Major road

STRUCTURE OF INDUSTRY

Services 21%
Manufacturing 47%
Primary 32%

POPULATION

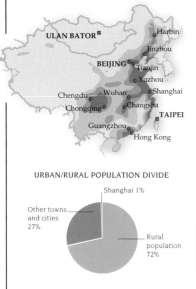

Most of China's people live in the eastern part of the country, where the climate, landscape and soils are most favourable. Urban areas there house over 250 million people, but almost 75% of the population lives in villages and farm the land. Taiwan's lowlands are very densely populated. In Mongolia, about 50% of the people live in the countryside.

URBAN/RURAL POPULATION DIVIDE

Shanghai 1%
Other towns and cities 27%
Rural population 72%

INHABITANTS PER SQ KM

- More than 200
- 100–200
- 50–100
- Less than 50
- ■ Capital city
- ● Major city

FARMING AND LAND USE

Despite its size, about 90% of China is unsuitable for farming. Either the soils and climate are poor, or the landscape is too mountainous. In the north and west, most farmers make their living by herding animals. On the fertile eastern plains, soya beans, wheat, corn and cotton are grown. Further south, rice becomes the main crop, and pigs are raised in large numbers.

FARMING AND LAND USE

- 🎣 Fishing
- 🐖 Pigs
- 🐑 Sheep
- 🌽 Corn (maize)
- 🌱 Cotton
- 🍎 Fruit
- 🌾 Rice
- 🌿 Soya beans
- ↓ Sugar cane
- 🌿 Tea
- 🌿 Tobacco
- 🌾 Wheat
- Cropland
- Desert
- Forest
- Mountain region
- Pasture
- ● Major conurbation

LAND USE

Cropland 7%
Pasture 42%
Other (including mountains) 24%
Forest 27%

THE LANDSCAPE

China's landscape divides into three areas. The vast Plateau of Tibet in the southwest is the highest and largest plateau on Earth. It contains both dry deserts and pockets of pasture surrounded by high mountains. Northwest China has dry highlands. The great plains of eastern China were formed from soils deposited by rivers like the Yellow River over thousands of years. Most of Mongolia is dry, grassland steppe and cold, arid desert.

Tien Shan mountains (B 2)
The Tien Shan, or 'Heavenly Mountains' reach heights of 7,435 m. They surround fields of permanent ice and spectacular glaciers.

Gobi (E2) and Takla Makan (B 3) deserts
The arid landscapes of the Gobi and Takla Makan deserts are made up of bare rock surfaces and huge areas of shifting sand dunes. They are hot in summer, but unlike most other deserts, are extremely cold in winter.

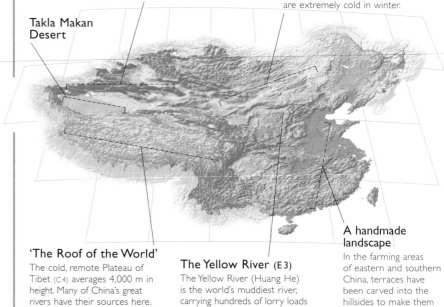

Takla Makan Desert

'The Roof of the World'
The cold, remote Plateau of Tibet (C4) averages 4,000 m in height. Many of China's great rivers have their sources here. The world's highest human settlement, a town called Wenquan, is found in the east of the plateau. It lies 5,099 m above sea level.

The Yellow River (E 3)
The Yellow River (Huang He) is the world's muddiest river, carrying hundreds of lorry loads of sediment to the sea every minute. The river has burst its banks many times throughout history, causing enormous damage and claiming millions of human lives.

A handmade landscape
In the farming areas of eastern and southern China, terraces have been carved into the hillsides to make them flat enough to grow rice and other crops. This method of farming has been used for over 7,000 years.

ENVIRONMENTAL ISSUES

The Three Gorges hydro-electric scheme on the Yangtze River will be the world's largest. Nearly 563 km of canyon will be flooded, and 1.3 million people forced to move. Earthquakes are common in the area and 100 million people downstream will be threatened if the dam breaks. In eastern China, many cities are affected by industrial pollution.

Shenyang
Beijing
Xi'an
Shanghai
Three Gorges Dam
Guangzhou
Hong Kong

ENVIRONMENTAL ISSUES

- Major dam
- Urban air pollution
- Industrial city

CLIMATE

Two air masses control climate; one cold and dry from Siberia, and one moist and warm from the Pacific. Winters are long and cold away from the coast – especially on the Plateau of Tibet.

ASIA
NORTH AMERICA   EUROPE
AFRICA
SOUTH AMERICA
AUSTRALASIA AND OCEANIA
ANTARCTICA
East Asia

TEMPERATURE AND PRECIPITATION

- More than 30°C
- 20 to 30°C
- 10 to 20°C
- 0 to 10°C
- 0° to -10°C
- -10°C to -20°C
- Less than -20°C

100 — Precipitation (mm)

January

July

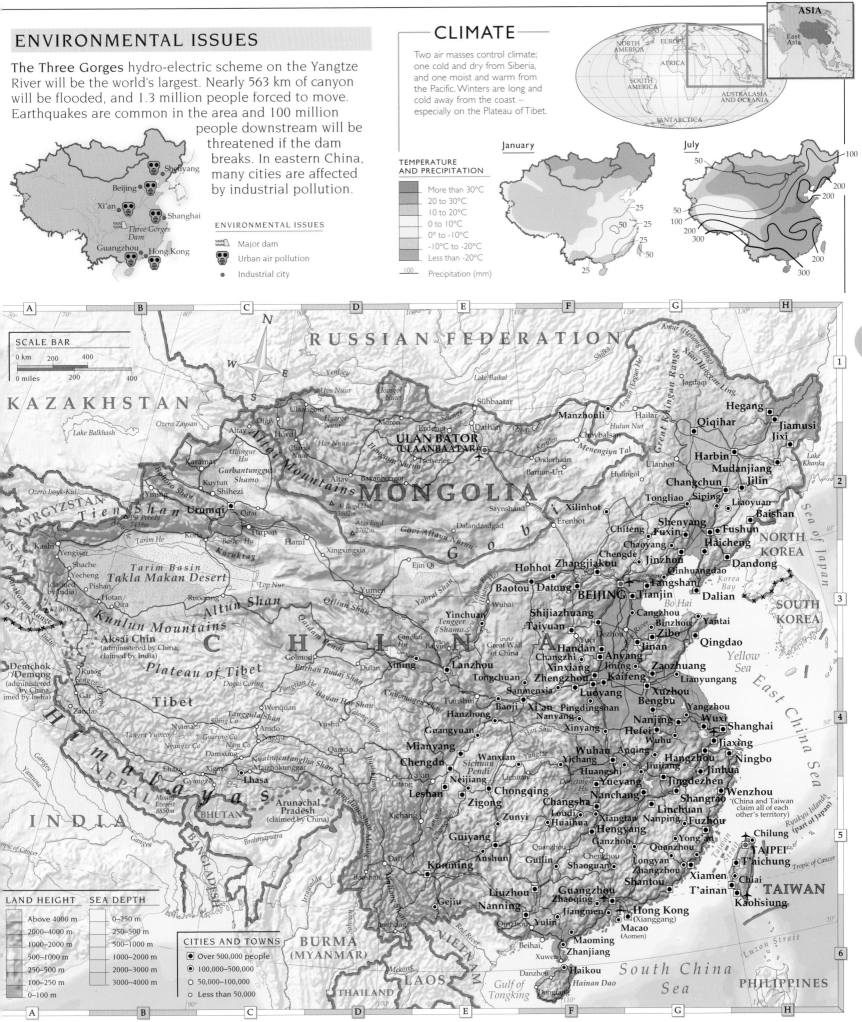

SOUTH ASIA

BANGLADESH, BHUTAN, INDIA, NEPAL, PAKISTAN, SRI LANKA

South Asia is a land of many contrasts. Its landscape ranges from the mighty peaks of the Himalayas in the north, through vast plains and arid desert, to tropical forests and palm-fringed beaches in the south. More than one-fifth of the world's people live here, and a long history of foreign invasions has left a mosaic of hugely different cultures, religions and traditions, and thousands of languages and dialects.

FARMING AND LAND USE

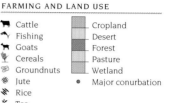

Over 60% of the population is involved in agriculture, but most farms are small, and produce only enough food to feed one family. Grains are the staple food crops – rice in the wetter parts of the east and west, corn and millet on the Deccan plateau, and wheat in the north. Groundnuts are widely grown as a source of cooking oil. Cash crops include tea, which is grown on plantations, and jute.

FARMING AND LAND USE

🐂	Cattle		Cropland
🦌	Fishing		Desert
🐐	Goats		Forest
🌿	Cereals		Pasture
🥜	Groundnuts		Wetland
❋	Jute	●	Major conurbation
🌾	Rice		
❧	Tea		

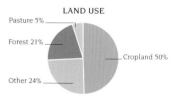

LAND USE

Pasture 5%
Forest 21%
Other 24%
Cropland 50%

INDUSTRY

Industry has expanded in India in recent years, and in the cities a variety of goods are produced and processed, including cars, aeroplanes, chemicals, food and drink. Service industries such as tourism and banking are also growing. Elsewhere, small-scale cottage industries serve the needs of local people, but many products, mainly silk and cotton textiles, clothing, leather and jewellery, are also exported.

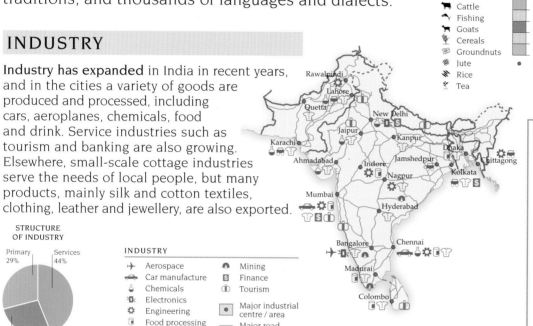

STRUCTURE OF INDUSTRY

Primary 29%
Services 44%
Manufacturing 27%

INDUSTRY

✈	Aerospace	⛏	Mining
🚗	Car manufacture	S	Finance
⚗	Chemicals	⊕	Tourism
▦	Electronics		
⚙	Engineering	▣	Major industrial centre / area
▤	Food processing		Major road
⛓	Iron and steel		
👕	Textiles		

THE LANDSCAPE

A massive, towering wall of snow-capped mountains stretches in an arc across the north, isolating South Asia from the rest of the continent. The huge floodplains and deltas of the Indus, Ganges and Brahmaputra rivers separate the mountains from the rest of the peninsula: a great rolling plateau, bordered on either side by coastal hills called the Eastern and Western Ghats.

Himalayas (E 2)

The Himalayas are the highest mountain system in the world. They were formed about 40 million years ago when two of the Earth's plates collided, thrusting up huge masses of land.

Mount Everest (F 3)

The northern ranges of the Himalayas average 7,000 m in height. They include the highest point on Earth, Mount Everest on the Nepal–China border, which soars to 8,850 m.

Thar Desert (C 3)

The border between India and Pakistan runs through the arid, sandy Thar Desert.

POPULATION

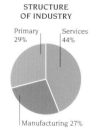

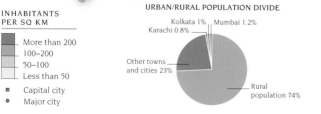

Most of South Asia's people live in villages scattered across the fertile river floodplains, in mountain valleys or along the coasts, but increasing numbers are migrating to the cities in search of work. Overcrowding is a serious problem in both rural and urban areas; in many cities, thousands of people are forced to live in slums, or on the streets.

INHABITANTS PER SQ KM

More than 200
100–200
50–100
Less than 50

■ Capital city
● Major city

URBAN/RURAL POPULATION DIVIDE

Kolkata 1%
Karachi 0.8%
Mumbai 1.2%
Other towns and cities 23%
Rural population 74%

Western Ghats (C 5)

The Western Ghats run continuously along the Arabian Sea coast, while the lower Eastern Ghats are interrupted by rivers that follow the gentle slope of the Deccan plateau and flow across broad lowlands into the Bay of Bengal. This is one of the wettest regions in the world.

Eastern Ghats (E 5)

Bangladesh (G 3)

Much of Bangladesh lies in an enormous delta formed by the Brahmaputra and Ganges rivers. During the summer monsoon, the rivers become swollen by the torrential rains – and meltwater from the Himalayas – and the delta floods. Over the years, millions of people have drowned or been made homeless by heavy flooding.

Deccan plateau (D 5)

This giant plateau makes up most of central and southern India. Its volcanic rock has been deeply cut by rivers such as the Krishna, creating stepped valleys called *traps*.

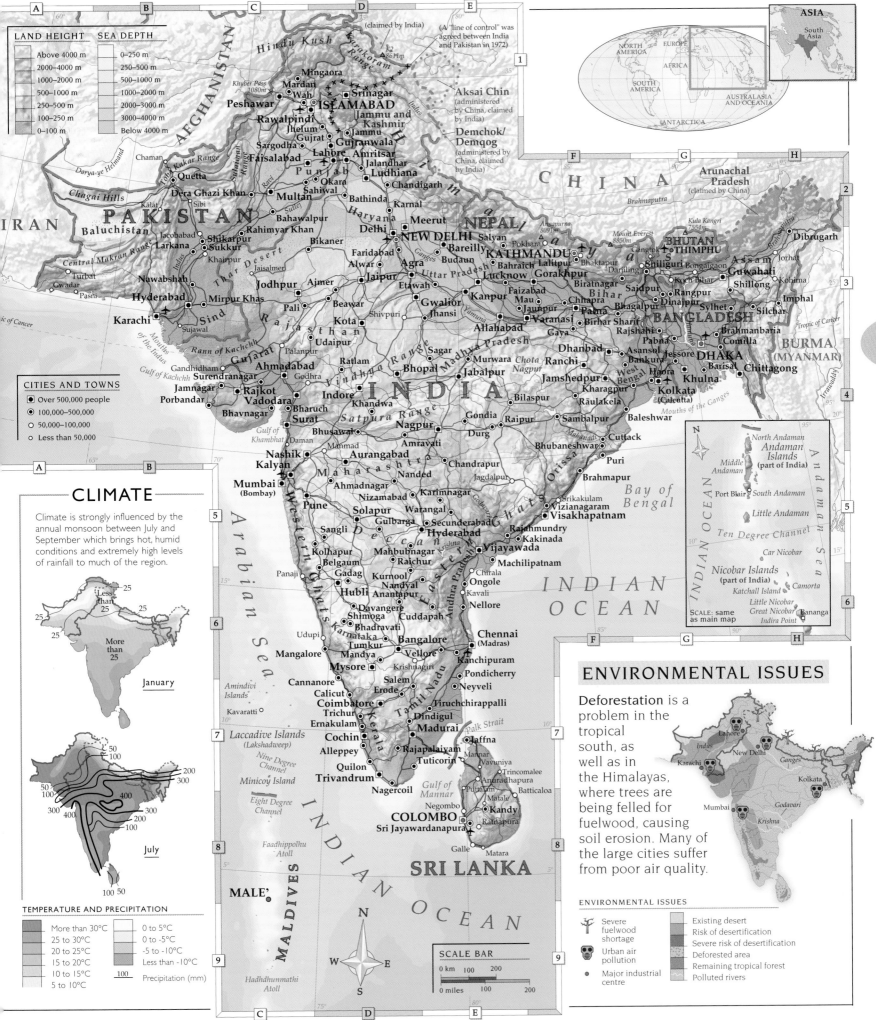

SOUTHEAST ASIA

BRUNEI, BURMA, CAMBODIA, EAST TIMOR, INDONESIA, LAOS, MALAYSIA, PHILIPPINES, SINGAPORE, THAILAND, VIETNAM

Southeast Asia is made up of a mainland area and many thousands of tropical islands. The region has great natural wealth – from precious stones to oil – and has recently experienced fast industrial growth. Some countries here, especially Singapore and Malaysia, have become prosperous, but Laos and Cambodia remain poor, and are still recovering from years of terrible warfare.

ENVIRONMENTAL ISSUES

In **Burma, Malaysia** and across Indonesia, ancient rainforests are being cut down faster than they can grow back. The fantastic biodiversity of the forests, with their thousands of unique species of plants and animals, is severely threatened. Forest burning has recently caused terrible smog in Indonesia.

ENVIRONMENTAL ISSUES
- Urban air pollution
- Deforested area
- Remaining tropical forest
- Major industrial centre

POPULATION

On the mainland, the population is concentrated in the river valleys, plateaus or plains. Upland areas are inhabited by small groups of hill peoples. Most people still live in rural areas, but the cities are growing fast. In Indonesia and the Philippines, the population is unevenly distributed. Some islands, such as Java, are densely settled; others are barely occupied.

INHABITANTS PER SQ KM
- More than 200
- 100–200
- 50–100
- Less than 50
- ■ Capital city
- ● Major city

URBAN/RURAL POPULATION DIVIDE
- Bangkok 1.8%
- Rural population 28.2%
- Other towns and cities 70%

INDUSTRY

Industries based on the processing of raw materials, like metallic minerals, timber, oil and gas and agricultural produce, are important here, but manufacturing has grown dramatically in recent years. Many foreign firms, attracted by low labour costs, have invested in the region. Malaysia and Singapore are major producers of electronic goods like disk drives for computers.

STRUCTURE OF INDUSTRY
- Primary 19%
- Services 45%
- Manufacturing 36%

INDUSTRY
- Chemicals
- Engineering
- Food processing
- Textiles
- Mining
- Oil and gas
- Timber
- Hi-tech
- Tourism
- ● Major industrial centre / area
- — Major road

THE LANDSCAPE

On the mainland, a belt of mountain ranges, cloaked in thick forest, runs north–south. The mountains are cut through by the wide valleys of five great rivers. On their route to the sea, these rivers have deposited sediment, forming immense, fertile flood plains and deltas. To the southeast of the mainland lies a huge arc of over 20,000 mountainous, volcanic islands.

Borneo (D7)

Borneo is the world's third-largest island, with a total area of 757,050 sq km. Lying on the Equator and in the path of two monsoons, the island is hot, and one of the wettest places on Earth. The landscape contains thickly-forested central highlands and swampy lowlands.

Mekong river (C4)

The mighty Mekong river flows through southern China and Burma and forms much of the border between Laos and Thailand. It then travels through Cambodia before ending in a vast delta on the southern coast of Vietnam, that is one of the world's most productive rice-growing areas.

Philippines (E4)

The Philippines' 7,000 islands are mountainous and volcanic with narrow coastal plains.

Papua (Irian Jaya) (I7)

Papua is a province of Indonesia. Its dense rainforests are some of the last unexplored areas on Earth and are inhabited by many rare plant and animal species.

Volcanoes

Indonesia is the most active volcanic region in the world; Java alone has over 50 active volcanoes out of the country's total of more than 220.

Indonesia (C7)

Indonesia is an archipelago of 13,677 islands, scattered over almost 5,000 km. The islands lie on the boundary between two of the Earth's tectonic plates and frequently experience earthquakes.

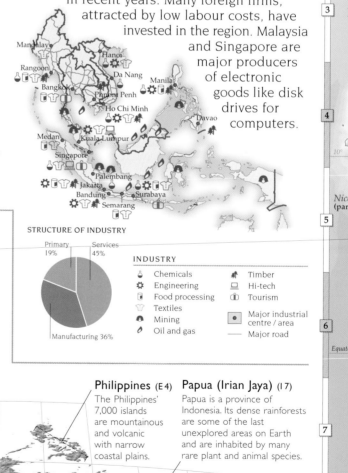

SCALE BAR
0 km 200 400
0 miles 200

FARMING AND LAND USE

The staple crop here is rice, which grows in low-lying flooded fields called paddies, or on terraces cut into the hillsides. Sugar cane, coconuts, bananas and pineapples are widely grown as cash crops, and Malaysia produces 25% of the world's rubber. Freshwater and marine fish are caught in large quantities; fish is one of the main foods in this region.

FARMING AND LAND USE

- Cattle
- Fishing
- Pigs
- Shellfish
- Coconuts
- Fruit
- Rice
- Rubber
- Sugar cane
- Timber
- Cropland
- Forest
- Pasture
- Wetland
- Major conurbation

LAND USE

- Pasture 4%
- Cropland 21%
- Forest 51%
- Other 24%

CLIMATE

Southeast Asia's climate is strongly affected by the monsoon, which brings warm, humid air and high rainfall to mainland Southeast Asia during July, and to maritime southeast Asia during January.

January

July

TEMPERATURE AND PRECIPITATION

- More than 30°C
- 20 to 30°C
- 10 to 20°C
- Less than 10°C
- 100 Precipitation (mm)

LAND HEIGHT

- Above 4000 m
- 2000–4000 m
- 1000–2000 m
- 500–1000 m
- 250–500 m
- 100–250 m
- 0–100 m

SEA DEPTH

- 0–250 m
- 250–500 m
- 500–1000 m
- 1000–2000 m
- 2000–3000 m
- 3000–4000 m
- Below 4000 m

CITIES AND TOWNS

- Over 500,000 people
- 100,000–500,000
- 50,000–100,000
- Less than 50,000

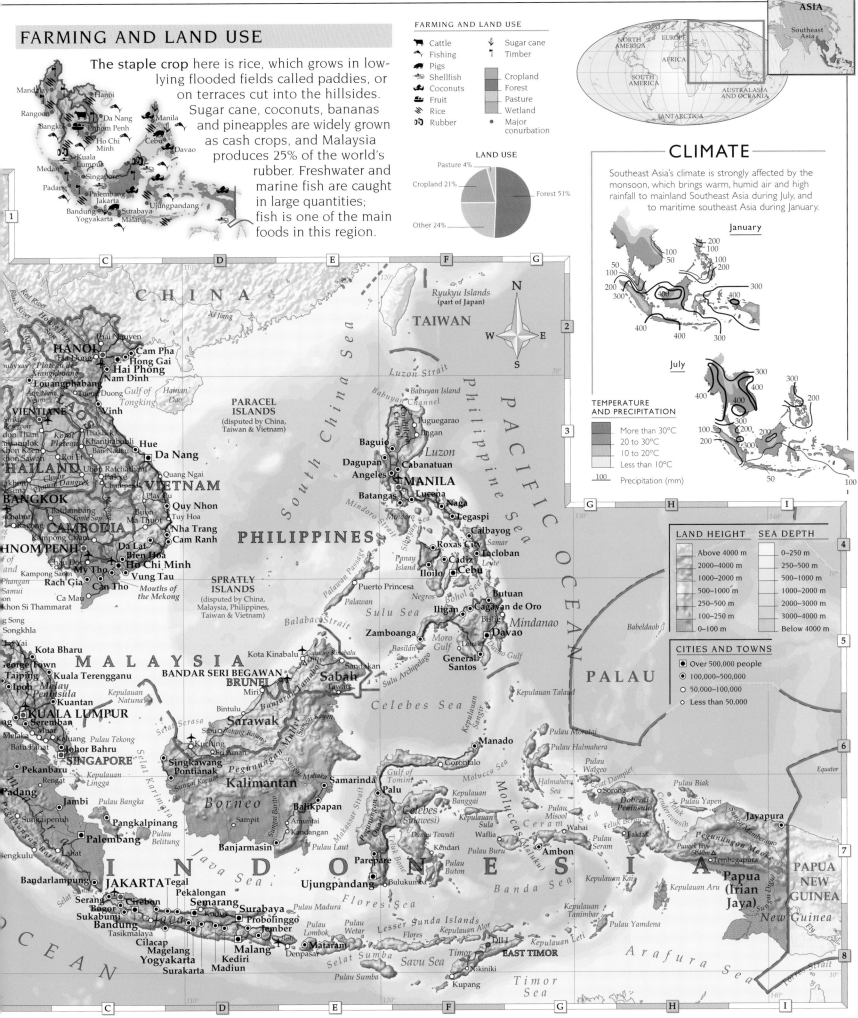

CONTINENTAL AFRICA

Africa is the second largest continent in the world. Its dramatic landscapes include arid deserts, humid rainforests, and the valleys of the east African rift – the place where humans first evolved. Today, there are 53 separate countries in Africa, and its people speak a rich variety of languages. The world's highest temperatures have been recorded in Africa's deserts.

7,260 km
7,623 km

CROSS-SECTION THROUGH AFRICA

Niger Delta
Congo Basin
Great Rift Valley
Lake Victoria
Ethiopian Highlands
Horn of Africa

W — 5,200 km — E

In the west, the Niger River flows into the Atlantic Ocean through the swampy Niger Delta. Further east is the immense Congo Basin, where the Congo River winds its way through thick rainforests. In the east is the Great Rift Valley, and the Ethiopian Highlands. The Horn of Africa is Africa's most easterly point.

1 DESERTS

The Sahara covers much of north Africa. One quarter of the desert is sandy dunes; the remainder consists of bare, rocky plains and mountainous outcrops. Other large deserts include the Namib and the Kalahari in the south.

2 GREAT RIFT VALLEY

Cracks beneath the Earth formed this valley, which runs from Lake Nyasa to the Red Sea. It is thought that east Africa – the Horn – will eventually split from the rest of Africa.

4 RAINFORESTS

Dense rainforests grow near the Equator, where rainfall is plentiful. Here, it is hot and humid enough for large areas of vegetation to flourish.

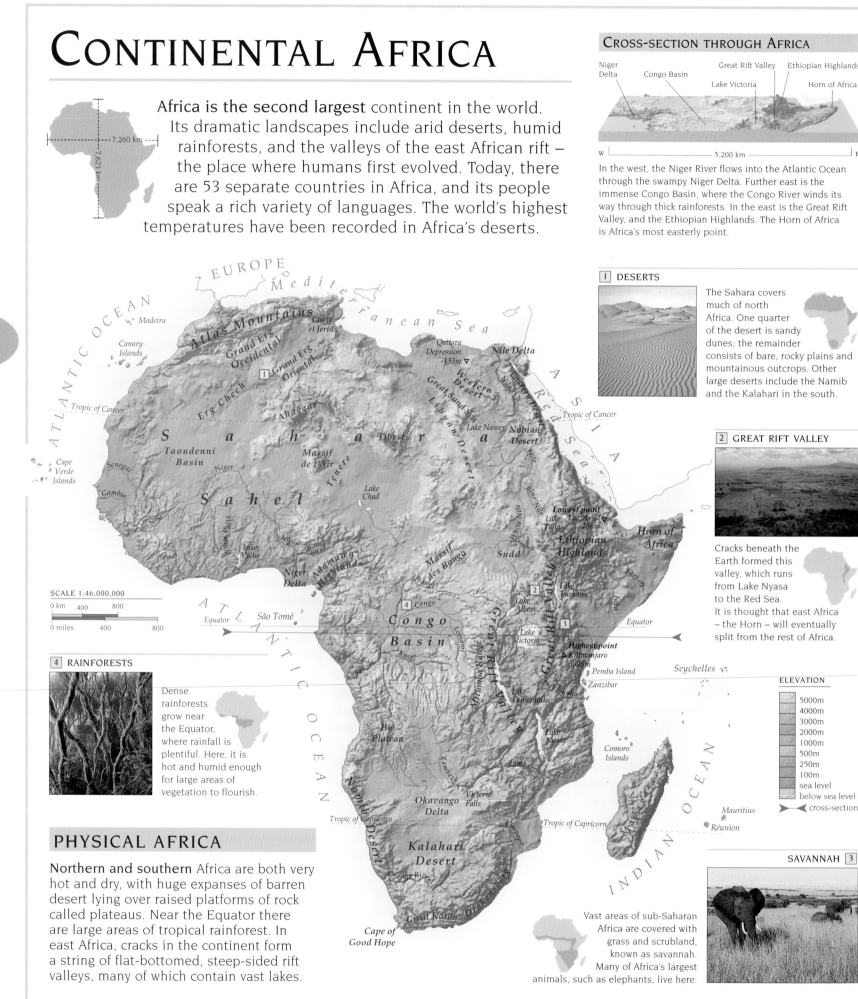

SCALE 1:46,000,000

0 km   400   800

0 miles   400   800

ELEVATION

5000m
4000m
3000m
2000m
1000m
500m
250m
100m
sea level
below sea level
◄ cross-section

SAVANNAH 3

Vast areas of sub-Saharan Africa are covered with grass and scrubland, known as savannah. Many of Africa's largest animals, such as elephants, live here.

PHYSICAL AFRICA

Northern and southern Africa are both very hot and dry, with huge expanses of barren desert lying over raised platforms of rock called plateaus. Near the Equator there are large areas of tropical rainforest. In east Africa, cracks in the continent form a string of flat-bottomed, steep-sided rift valleys, many of which contain vast lakes.

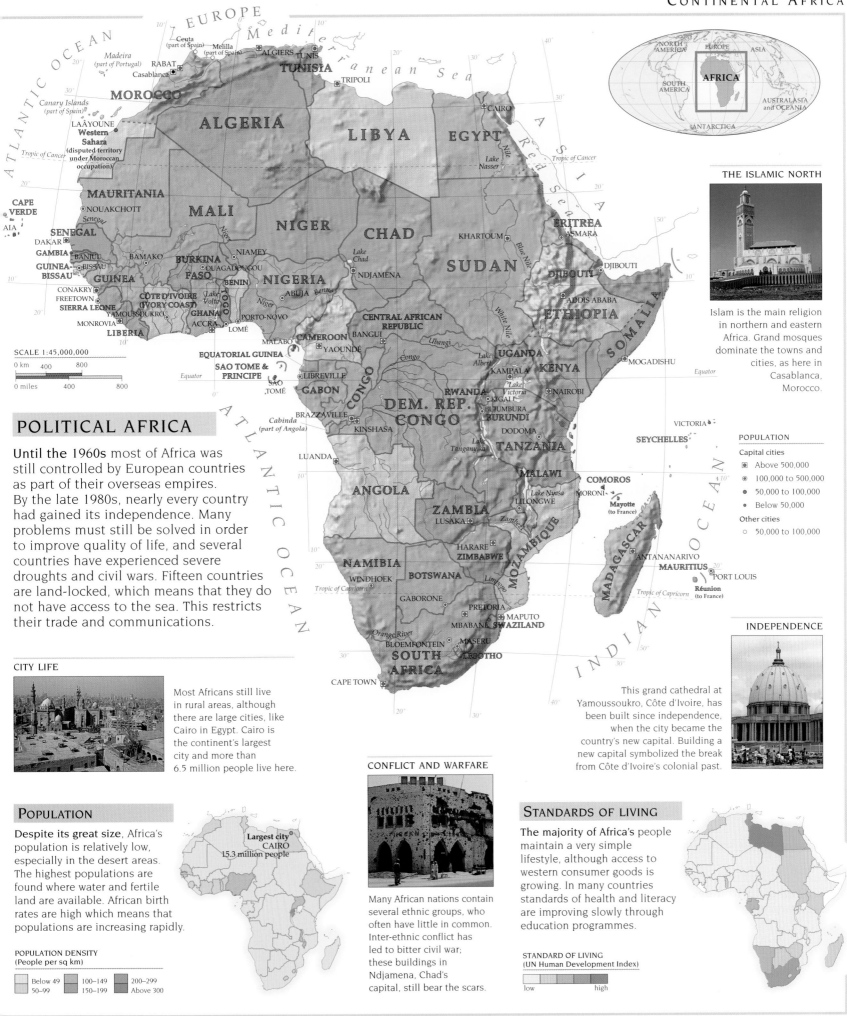

AFRICA

POLITICAL AFRICA

Until the 1960s most of Africa was still controlled by European countries as part of their overseas empires. By the late 1980s, nearly every country had gained its independence. Many problems must still be solved in order to improve quality of life, and several countries have experienced severe droughts and civil wars. Fifteen countries are land-locked, which means that they do not have access to the sea. This restricts their trade and communications.

THE ISLAMIC NORTH

Islam is the main religion in northern and eastern Africa. Grand mosques dominate the towns and cities, as here in Casablanca, Morocco.

POPULATION

Capital cities
- ⊚ Above 500,000
- ⊙ 100,000 to 500,000
- ● 50,000 to 100,000
- • Below 50,000

Other cities
- ○ 50,000 to 100,000

CITY LIFE

Most Africans still live in rural areas, although there are large cities, like Cairo in Egypt. Cairo is the continent's largest city and more than 6.5 million people live here.

INDEPENDENCE

This grand cathedral at Yamoussoukro, Côte d'Ivoire, has been built since independence, when the city became the country's new capital. Building a new capital symbolized the break from Côte d'Ivoire's colonial past.

CONFLICT AND WARFARE

Many African nations contain several ethnic groups, who often have little in common. Inter-ethnic conflict has led to bitter civil war; these buildings in Ndjamena, Chad's capital, still bear the scars.

POPULATION

Despite its great size, Africa's population is relatively low, especially in the desert areas. The highest populations are found where water and fertile land are available. African birth rates are high which means that populations are increasing rapidly.

Largest city
CAIRO
15.3 million people

POPULATION DENSITY
(People per sq km)

- Below 49
- 50–99
- 100–149
- 150–199
- 200–299
- Above 300

STANDARDS OF LIVING

The majority of Africa's people maintain a very simple lifestyle, although access to western consumer goods is growing. In many countries standards of health and literacy are improving slowly through education programmes.

STANDARD OF LIVING
(UN Human Development Index)

low   high

SCALE 1:45,000,000

0 km   400   800

0 miles   400   800

AFRICAN GEOGRAPHY

Africa's massive reserves of minerals, including oil, gold, copper and diamonds, are amongst the largest in the world. Mining is a very important industry for many countries, and has provided money for growth and development. Africa's wide range of environments means that many different types of crops can be grown. Rubber, bananas and oil palms are grown for export in the tropics, and east Africa is especially famous for its tea and coffee.

INDUSTRY

Most African industries are based on processing raw materials such as food crops or mineral ores. Some African countries depend on one product or crop for most of their income, but in many larger cities different industries are developing. Northern Africa, Nigeria, and South Africa have the widest range of industries.

MINERAL RESOURCES

The southern countries, in particular South Africa, have large reserves of diamonds, gold, uranium and copper. The large copper deposits in Dem. Rep. Congo and Zambia are known as the 'copper belt'. Oil and gas are extracted in Algeria, Angola, Egypt, Libya, and Nigeria.

MINING

The world's largest uranium mine is in Namibia. Uranium is used to fuel nuclear power stations, and is also mined in Niger and South Africa.

MINERAL RESOURCES

- ♠ Bauxite
- ♠ Copper
- ♠ Diamonds
- ♠ Iron
- ♠ Phosphates
- ♠ Gold
- ♠ Uranium
- Oil/gas field
- Coal field

OIL AND GAS

In the desert wastes of Algeria, a drilling rig searches for new sources of oil in the rich north African oilfields. There are several large oil fields in the Niger delta, and north Africa.

CHEMICALS

In Abidjan, Ivory Coast, petrochemicals are manufactured from oil. The chemical industry has expanded with the growth of Africa's oil and gas industry.

FOOD PROCESSING

Fruit and vegetables are sold in Africa's numerous local markets, as here in Dakar, Senegal. Many crops are grown specially for canning and export overseas and are known as 'cash crops.'

FINANCE AND TRADE

Johannesburg, in South Africa, is home to many international banks. Wealth has been generated from the country's large mineral resources, such as diamonds.

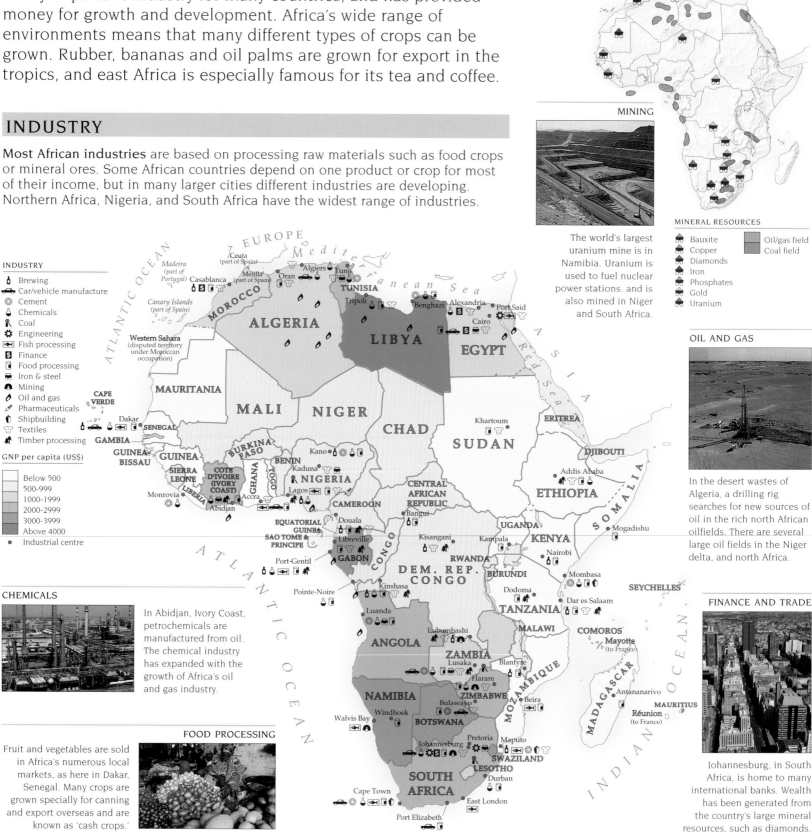

INDUSTRY

- ♨ Brewing
- 🚗 Car/vehicle manufacture
- Cement
- Chemicals
- Coal
- Engineering
- Fish processing
- S Finance
- Food processing
- Iron & steel
- Mining
- Oil and gas
- Pharmaceuticals
- Shipbuilding
- Textiles
- Timber processing

GNP per capita (US$)

- Below 500
- 500-999
- 1000-1999
- 2000-2999
- 3000-3999
- Above 4000
- • Industrial centre

CLIMATE

Africa is the world's hottest continent: temperatures of more than 50°C have been recorded in the Sahara. The northern coast has a hot, dry climate with little rainfall. Further inland, the Sahara is extremely arid, with strong, dry winds. South of the Sahara is the Sahel, where cutting down trees for fuel has turned farmland into desert. Close to the Equator there is more rainfall, and huge rainforests can grow in western and central Africa. In the south, the climate is much drier, and drought is a problem.

EXTREME WEATHER EVENTS

Symbols indicate climatic extremes

Coldest place
IFRANE (Morocco)
Temperature -24°C

Hottest place
AL 'AZIZIYAH (Libya)
Temperature 58°C

Driest place
WADI HALFA (Sudan)
Annual rainfall <2.5mm

Wettest place
CAPE DEBUNDSHA (Cameroon)
Annual rainfall 10290mm

Tropic of Cancer
Equator
Tropic of Capricorn

CLIMATE
- Warm tempe rate
- Mediterranean
- Semi-arid
- Arid
- Humid equatorial
- Tropical

NORTH AMERICA | EUROPE | ASIA
SOUTH AMERICA | AFRICA | AUSTRALASIA and OCEANIA
ANTARCTICA

THE ENCROACHING DESERT

Africa has three main desert areas: the Sahara in the north and the Namib and Kalahari deserts in the south. They are a mixture of sandy dunes and bare, rocky plateaus. At the desert's edges, low rainfall and land clearance is causing the deserts to expand into areas that were once grassland.

LAND USE AND AGRICULTURE

The quality of land and the amount of rainfall has a great impact on the type of farming. In the mountain regions of countries such as Rwanda, Uganda, and Kenya, tea and coffee are grown. In the north, there is not enough water to produce staple crops such as wheat for all the population, but 'cash crops' such as citrus fruits, dates and olives are grown for export. Sub-tropical west Africa grows peanuts, cocoa and coffee. In the southern part of the continent, South Africa grows many different crops: citrus fruits are grown for export, as well as grapes, which are used to make wine.

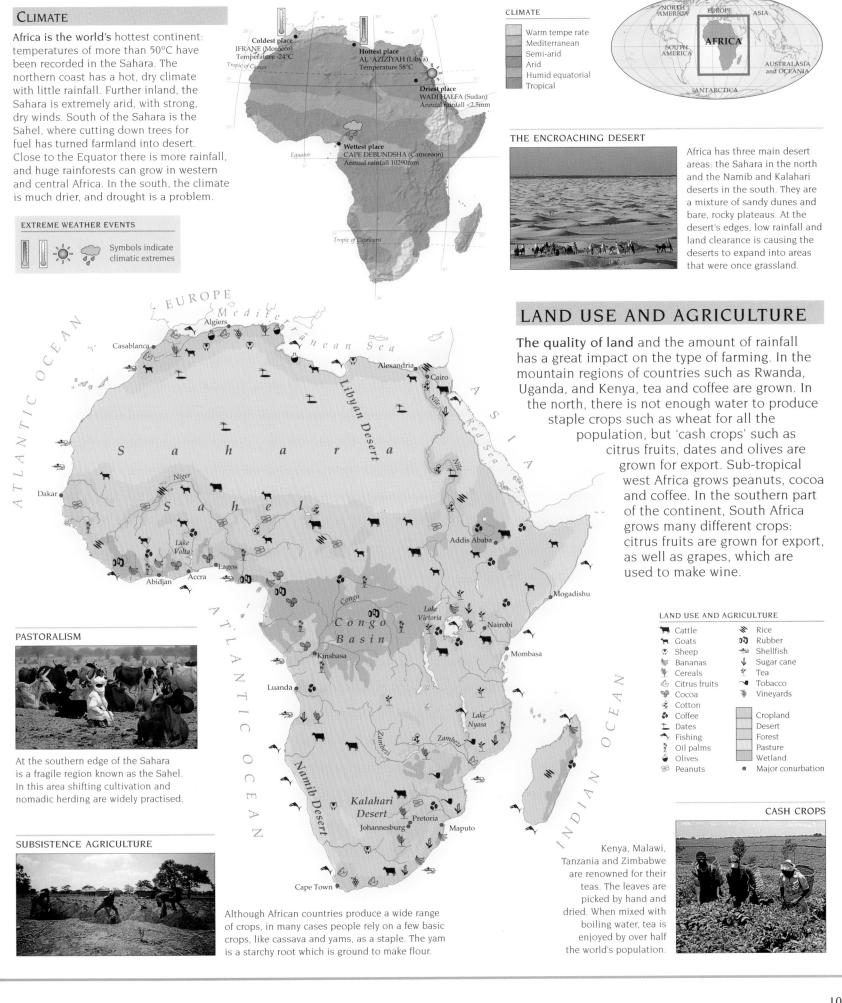

PASTORALISM

At the southern edge of the Sahara is a fragile region known as the Sahel. In this area shifting cultivation and nomadic herding are widely practised.

SUBSISTENCE AGRICULTURE

Although African countries produce a wide range of crops, in many cases people rely on a few basic crops, like cassava and yams, as a staple. The yam is a starchy root which is ground to make flour.

LAND USE AND AGRICULTURE
- Cattle
- Goats
- Sheep
- Bananas
- Cereals
- Citrus fruits
- Cocoa
- Cotton
- Coffee
- Dates
- Fishing
- Oil palms
- Olives
- Peanuts
- Rice
- Rubber
- Shellfish
- Sugar cane
- Tea
- Tobacco
- Vineyards
- Cropland
- Desert
- Forest
- Pasture
- Wetland
- Major conurbation

CASH CROPS

Kenya, Malawi, Tanzania and Zimbabwe are renowned for their teas. The leaves are picked by hand and dried. When mixed with boiling water, tea is enjoyed by over half the world's population.

NORTH AFRICA

ALGERIA, EGYPT, LIBYA, MOROCCO, TUNISIA.

Sandwiched between the Mediterranean and the Sahara, North Africa has a history dating back to the dawn of civilization. 6,000 years ago, settlements were established along the banks of the River Nile, and since that time, waves of settlers, including Romans, Arabs and Turks have brought a mix of different cultures to the area. In the 19th century, Spain, France and Britain claimed colonies in the region, but today North Africa is independent, although Western Sahara is occupied by Morocco.

FARMING AND LAND USE

Most farming in North Africa is restricted to the fertile Mediterranean coastal strip, and the banks of the Nile where it relies heavily on irrigation. In spite of these seemingly inhospitable conditions, the region is a major producer of dates, which grow in desert oases, and of cork, made from the bark of the cork oak tree. A wide variety of other crops is also grown, including grapes, olives and cotton.

FARMING AND LAND USE

- Fishing
- Goats
- Sheep
- Citrus Fruits
- Cork
- Cotton
- Dates
- Olives
- Vineyards
- Cropland
- Desert
- Forest
- Pasture
- Major conurbation

CLIMATE

Most of north Africa is desert, and the climate is harsh. Rainfall is scarce, and drought is common. Temperatures are freezing at night, scorching by day and have been known to climb to over 50°C.

January

July

whole area has below 25mm rainfall

LAND USE

Forest 3%
Pasture 9%
Cropland 12%
Other (including desert) 76%

TEMPERATURE AND PRECIPITATION

- More than 35°C
- 30 to 35°C
- 25 to 30°C
- 20 to 25°C
- 15 to 20°C
- 10 to 15°C
- 5 to 10°C
- Less than 5°C

100 Precipitation (mm)

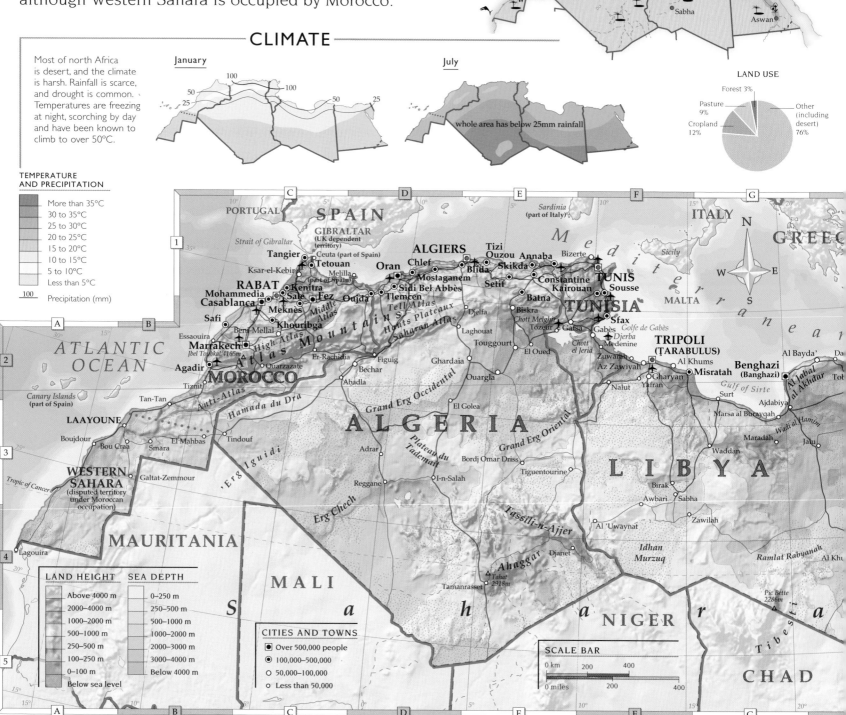

LAND HEIGHT
- Above 4000 m
- 2000–4000 m
- 1000–2000 m
- 500–1000 m
- 250–500 m
- 100–250 m
- 0–100 m
- Below sea level

SEA DEPTH
- 0–250 m
- 250–500 m
- 500–1000 m
- 1000–2000 m
- 2000–3000 m
- 3000–4000 m
- Below 4000 m

CITIES AND TOWNS
- Over 500,000 people
- 100,000–500,000
- 50,000–100,000
- Less than 50,000

SCALE BAR
0 km 200 400
0 miles 200 400

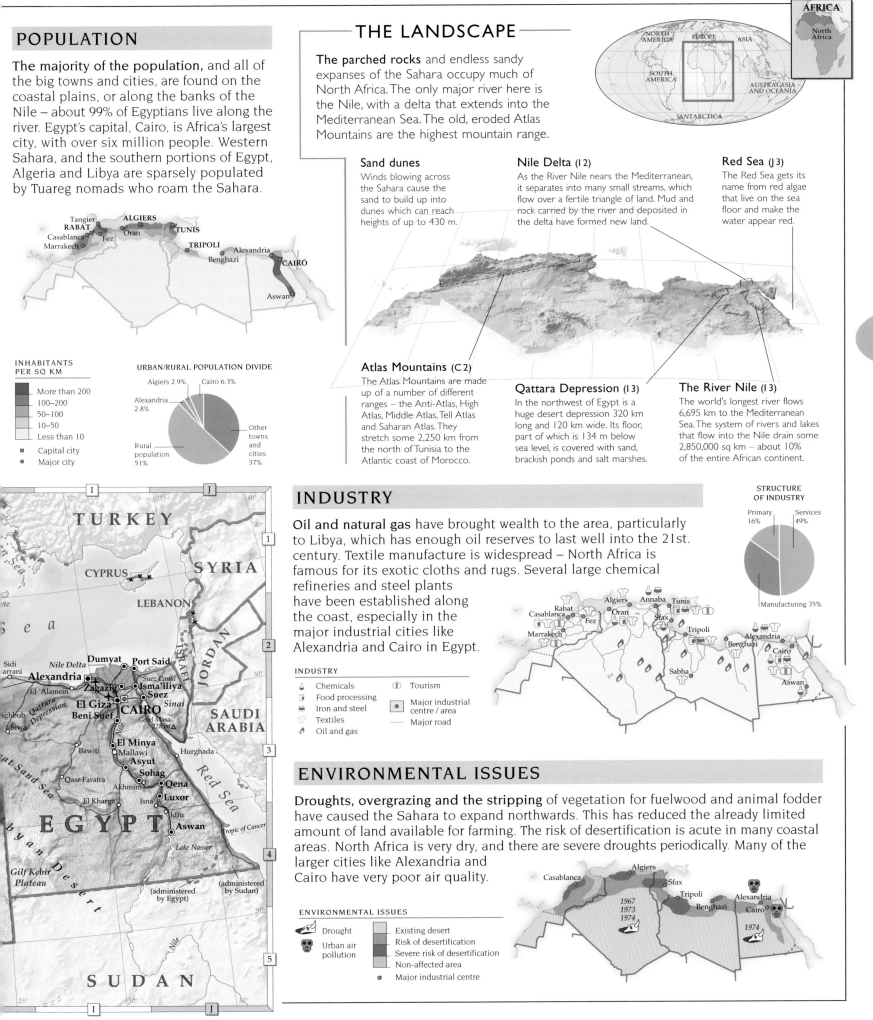

POPULATION

The majority of the population, and all of the big towns and cities, are found on the coastal plains, or along the banks of the Nile – about 99% of Egyptians live along the river. Egypt's capital, Cairo, is Africa's largest city, with over six million people. Western Sahara, and the southern portions of Egypt, Algeria and Libya are sparsely populated by Tuareg nomads who roam the Sahara.

INHABITANTS PER SQ KM

More than 200
100–200
50–100
10–50
Less than 10
■ Capital city
● Major city

Tangier
RABAT
Casablanca
Marrakech
Fez
Oran
ALGIERS
TUNIS
TRIPOLI
Benghazi
Alexandria
CAIRO
Aswan

URBAN/RURAL POPULATION DIVIDE

Algiers 2.9%
Cairo 6.3%
Alexandria 2.8%
Rural population 51%
Other towns and cities 37%

THE LANDSCAPE

The parched rocks and endless sandy expanses of the Sahara occupy much of North Africa. The only major river here is the Nile, with a delta that extends into the Mediterranean Sea. The old, eroded Atlas Mountains are the highest mountain range.

AFRICA
North Africa

Sand dunes
Winds blowing across the Sahara cause the sand to build up into dunes which can reach heights of up to 430 m.

Nile Delta (I2)
As the River Nile nears the Mediterranean, it separates into many small streams, which flow over a fertile triangle of land. Mud and rock carried by the river and deposited in the delta have formed new land.

Red Sea (J3)
The Red Sea gets its name from red algae that live on the sea floor and make the water appear red.

Atlas Mountains (C2)
The Atlas Mountains are made up of a number of different ranges – the Anti-Atlas, High Atlas, Middle Atlas, Tell Atlas and Saharan Atlas. They stretch some 2,250 km from the north of Tunisia to the Atlantic coast of Morocco.

Qattara Depression (I3)
In the northwest of Egypt is a huge desert depression 320 km long and 120 km wide. Its floor, part of which is 134 m below sea level, is covered with sand, brackish ponds and salt marshes.

The River Nile (I3)
The world's longest river flows 6,695 km to the Mediterranean Sea. The system of rivers and lakes that flow into the Nile drain some 2,850,000 sq km – about 10% of the entire African continent.

INDUSTRY

Oil and natural gas have brought wealth to the area, particularly to Libya, which has enough oil reserves to last well into the 21st. century. Textile manufacture is widespread – North Africa is famous for its exotic cloths and rugs. Several large chemical refineries and steel plants have been established along the coast, especially in the major industrial cities like Alexandria and Cairo in Egypt.

STRUCTURE OF INDUSTRY
Primary 16%
Services 49%
Manufacturing 35%

INDUSTRY
🝊 Chemicals
▣ Food processing
🚂 Iron and steel
🜊 Textiles
🝆 Oil and gas
🎫 Tourism
◉ Major industrial centre / area
— Major road

Rabat
Casablanca
Marrakech
Fez
Oran
Algiers
Annaba
Tunis
Sfax
Tripoli
Sabha
Alexandria
Benghazi
Cairo
Aswan

ENVIRONMENTAL ISSUES

Droughts, overgrazing and the stripping of vegetation for fuelwood and animal fodder have caused the Sahara to expand northwards. This has reduced the already limited amount of land available for farming. The risk of desertification is acute in many coastal areas. North Africa is very dry, and there are severe droughts periodically. Many of the larger cities like Alexandria and Cairo have very poor air quality.

ENVIRONMENTAL ISSUES
🖦 Drought
👥 Urban air pollution
Existing desert
Risk of desertification
Severe risk of desertification
Non-affected area
● Major industrial centre

Casablanca
Algiers
Sfax
Tripoli
Benghazi
Alexandria
Cairo
1967
1973
1974
1974

Map (Egypt region)

TURKEY
CYPRUS
SYRIA
LEBANON
ISRAEL
JORDAN
SAUDI ARABIA
Sidi Barrani
Nile Delta
Dumyat
Port Said
Alexandria
Suez Canal
El 'Alamein
Zagazig
Isma'iliya
Suez
Qattara Depression
El Giza
Beni Suef
CAIRO
Sinai
Gebel Musa 2285m △
Siwa
Bawiti
El Minya
Mallawi
Asyut
Hurghada
Qasr Farafra
Sohag
Akhmim
Qena
Luxor
El Kharga
Isna
Idfu
Great Sand Sea
Aswan
Tropic of Cancer
Red Sea
E G Y P T
Lake Nasser
Gilf Kebir Plateau
Libyan Desert
(administered by Egypt)
(administered by Sudan)
Nile
S U D A N

WEST AFRICA

BENIN, BURKINA FASO, CAMEROON, CENTRAL AFRICAN REPUBLIC, CHAD, EQUATORIAL GUINEA, GAMBIA, GHANA, GUINEA, GUINEA-BISSAU, CÔTE D'IVOIRE, LIBERIA, MALI, MAURITANIA, NIGER, NIGERIA, SAO TOME & PRINCIPE, SENEGAL, SIERRA LEONE, TOGO

West Africa's varied climate and agricultural and mineral wealth have provided the foundation for some of Africa's greatest civilizations, like those of the Malinke and Asante people. The area remains ethnically and culturally diverse today, as well as densely populated; Nigeria is by far the most populous country in Africa. Since independence from European colonial powers in the 1960s, political instability has been a feature of many countries here.

INDUSTRY

Agricultural products still form the basis of most economies in West Africa. Food processing is widespread – oil palms and groundnuts are processed for their valuable vegetable oils. Oil and gas are found off the coast of Côte d'Ivoire and around the Niger delta, where a large chemical industry has developed.

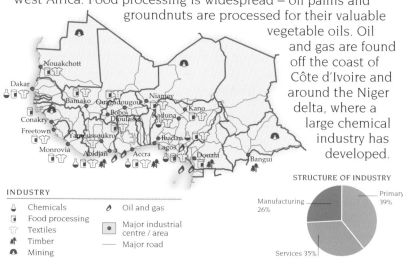

INDUSTRY

- 🜹 Chemicals
- 🏭 Food processing
- 👕 Textiles
- 🌲 Timber
- ⛏ Mining
- 🛢 Oil and gas
- ▣ Major industrial centre / area
- — Major road

STRUCTURE OF INDUSTRY

- Primary 39%
- Manufacturing 26%
- Services 35%

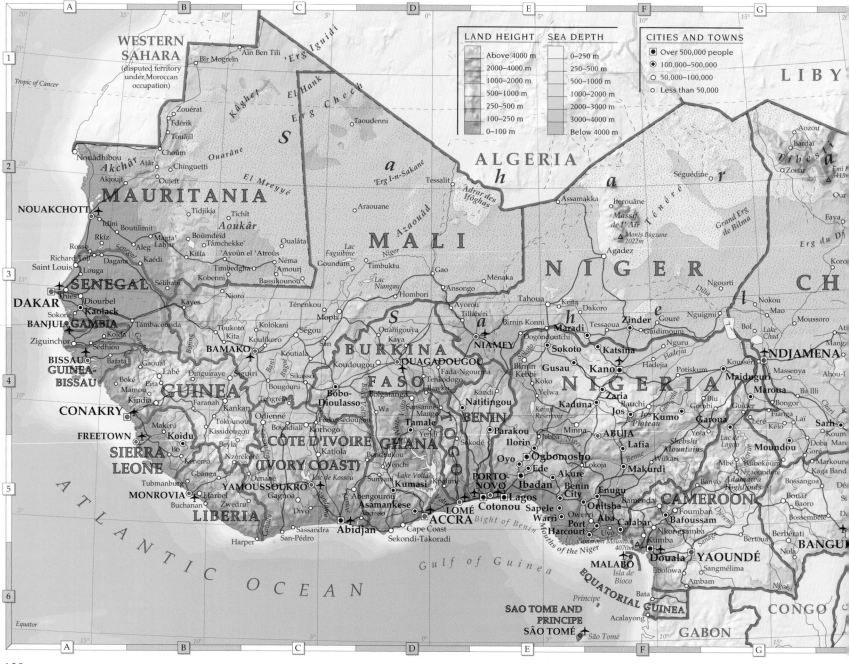

AFRICA

West
Africa

FARMING AND LAND USE

Well-watered land along the coast allows a wide variety of crops to be grown, including cocoa and oil palms, both of which provide important cash crops. In the drier north, goats and sheep are grazed, and subsistence crops such as yams, millet and cassava are grown.

Dakar
Conakry
Monrovia
Abidjan
Accra
Cotonou
Ibadan
Lagos
Yaoundé
Bangui
Ndjamena

FARMING AND LAND USE

- 🐐 Goats
- 🐑 Sheep
- 🦪 Shellfish
- 🌿 Cassava
- 🌿 Cocoa
- 🌿 Cotton
- 🌾 Millet
- 🌴 Oil palms
- 🥜 Peanuts
- Cropland
- Desert
- Forest
- Pasture
- Wetland
- • Major conurbation

LAND USE

Cropland 10%
Other (including desert) 40%
Pasture 23%
Forest 27 %

CLIMATE

The climate differs immensely from the hot desert north, through to the tropical rainforest south. July is the wet season, and rainfall is heavy in the south, while the desert areas remain dry throughout the year.

January

July

TEMPERATURE AND PRECIPITATION

- More than 35°C
- 30 to 35°C
- 25 to 30°C
- 20 to 25°C
- Less than 20°C

100 Precipitation (mm)

ENVIRONMENTAL ISSUES

Persistent droughts are the main concerns in the north of the region. The problem is made worse by a shortage of wood needed for fuel, which leads to the cutting down of any available trees for fuelwood. In the tropical south, the timber industry is destroying much of the ancient forest.

1968–1977
1982–1985
2003
1968–1977
1982–1985
1973–1974
1971–1974
1967–1974
1971–1974

ENVIRONMENTAL ISSUES

- 🐟 Drought
- 🌳 Severe fuelwood shortage
- Existing desert
- Risk of desertification
- Severe risk of desertification
- Deforested area

POPULATION

Most of the population lives in the southern coastal regions. In the drier north, settlement becomes more sporadic, and nomadic tribespeople are best suited to live in the desert north. Nigeria is the most populated country in Africa and Lagos is one of the continent's larger cities, although West Africa's population remains mainly rural.

INHABITANTS PER SQ KM

- More than 200
- 100–200
- 50–100
- 10–50
- Less than 10
- ■ Capital city
- • Major city

NOUAKCHOTT
DAKAR
BANJUL
BISSAU
BAMAKO
CONAKRY
FREETOWN
MONROVIA
NIAMEY
OUAGADOUGOU
ABUJA
Kano
Kaduna
PORTO-NOVO
Abidjan
ACCRA
Lagos
Port Harcourt
YAOUNDÉ
NDJAMENA
BANGUI

URBAN/RURAL POPULATION DIVIDE

Abidjan 1%
Dakar 1%
Lagos 2%
Other towns and cities 31%
Rural population 65%

THE LANDSCAPE

Large differences in rainfall from north to south have led to a varied landscape. The wet coastal regions contain tropical rainforest. To the north, savannah grasslands, arid Sahel scrubland and barren desert lie in successive bands. The Niger is one of the larger rivers and is unusual because it has two deltas; one at the sea, and one inland.

Sahel (E 3)
The band of semi-desert stretching from Senegal to Sudan along the southern boundary of the Sahara is called the Sahel. Frequent droughts in recent years, and excessive cutting of trees have meant that much of the Sahel is turning to desert.

Tibesti mountains (G 2)
These mountains in north-western Chad are a chain of extinct volcanoes which now form solitary peaks in the midst of the Sahara.

River Niger (D 3)
The River Niger is West Africa's longest river. When it reaches the sea, it flows through a vast delta of mud flats and mangrove swamps. Great oil deposits have been found here.

Adamawa Highlands (G 5)
This mountainous spine separates West Africa from the vast Congo Basin to the southeast.

EGYPT
Tropic of Cancer
Erdi
Ennedi
SUDAN
Beïda
El Azoui
Birao
Ouanda Djallé
Massif des Bongo
CENTRAL AFRICAN REPUBLIC
Bria
Djéma
Obo
Dembia
Bangassou
Alindao
Mobaye
DEM. REP. CONGO
Equator

SCALE BAR
km 200 400
miles 200 400

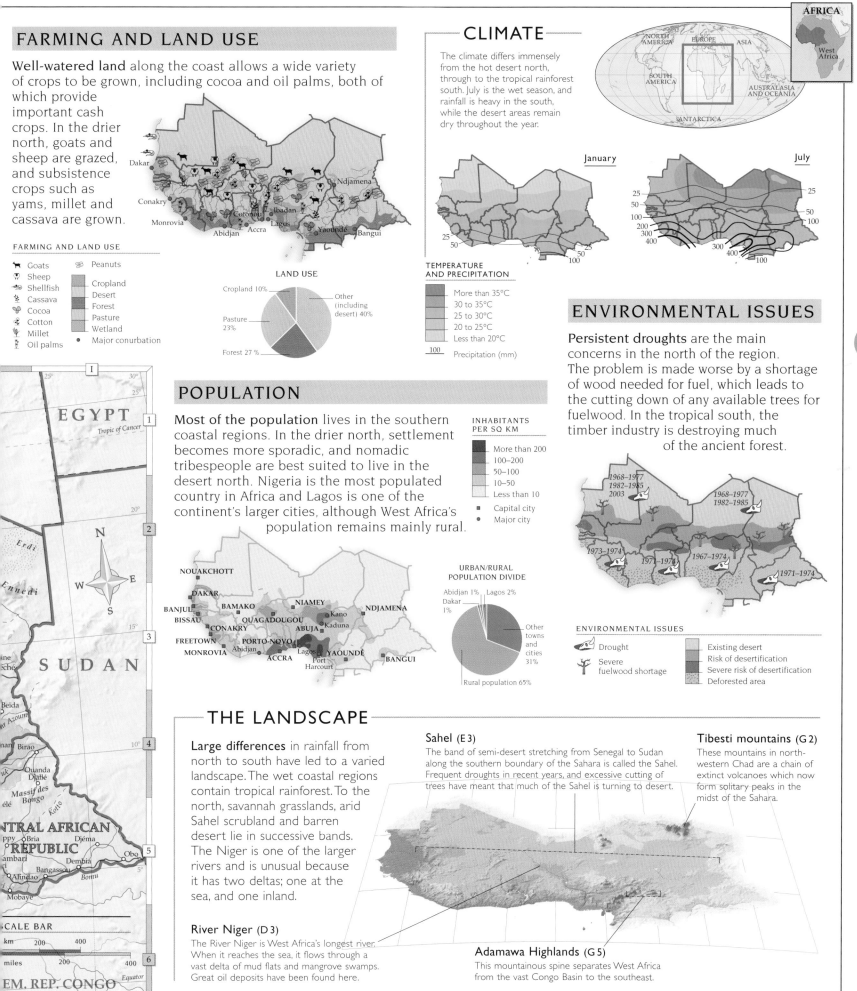

EAST AFRICA

BURUNDI, DJIBOUTI, ERITREA, ETHIOPIA, KENYA, RWANDA, SOMALIA, SUDAN, TANZANIA, UGANDA

Much of East Africa is covered by long grass, scrub and scattered trees, called savannah. This land is grazed by both domestic animals and a great variety of wild animals including lions, giraffes and elephants. The east of the region is known as the Horn of Africa, because it is shaped like an animal horn. Along with Sudan, the countries there have recently been devastated by civil wars, and periods of drought and famine. In contrast, Kenya in the south is one of Africa's more stable and wealthy countries.

FARMING AND LAND USE

Much of the north and east is too dry for farming, but in Sudan, cotton is grown on land irrigated by the River Nile. The Lake Victoria basin and rich volcanic soils of the highlands in Kenya, Uganda and Tanzania support staple food crops, and those grown for export, such as tea and coffee. Kenya also grows high-quality vegetables, like mangetout, and exports them by air to supermarkets abroad. Sheep, goats and cattle are herded on the savannah.

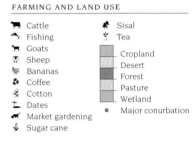

LAND USE

- Cropland 9%
- Pasture 40%
- Other 26%
- Forest 25%

FARMING AND LAND USE

- Cattle
- Fishing
- Goats
- Sheep
- Bananas
- Coffee
- Cotton
- Dates
- Market gardening
- Sugar cane
- Sisal
- Tea

- Cropland
- Desert
- Forest
- Pasture
- Wetland
- Major conurbation

INDUSTRY

East Africa has few mineral resources, and industry is mainly based on processing raw materials. Coffee, tea, sugar cane and sisal, are harvested and processed before being exported. Textile production is widespread, but is only on a small scale. Tourism is increasingly important in Kenya and Tanzania; each year, many thousands of people visit the wildlife reserves there.

INDUSTRY

- Cement manufacturing
- Chemicals
- Food processing
- Textiles
- Tourism
- Major industrial centre / area
- Major road

STRUCTURE OF INDUSTRY

- Primary 15%
- Services 46%
- Manufacturing 39%

THE LANDSCAPE

The south of East Africa is savannah grassland, broken by the rugged mountains — some of them active volcanoes — and large fresh and saltwater lakes that make up part of the Great Rift Valley. The River Nile has its source here, flowing through lakes Victoria, Kyoga and Albert as it takes much-needed water to the arid desert areas in the north.

Great Rift Valley (D 6) (D 4)
The Great Rift Valley is like a deep scar running 7,000 km from north to south through East Africa. It has been formed by the movements of two of the Earth's plates over millions of years. If these movements continue, East Africa may eventually become an island, separated by the ocean from the rest of the continent.

Sudd (B 4)
The north of Sudan is rocky desert, but in the south, the waters of the White Nile run into a swampy area called the Sudd where much of its water disperses and evaporates.

River Juba (E 5)
This river rises in the highlands of Ethiopia and flows some 1,200 km southwards to the Indian Ocean. It, and the River Shebeli, which joins it about 30 km from the coast, are the only permanent rivers in Somalia.

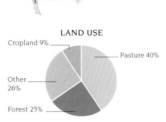

ENVIRONMENTAL ISSUES

Rapid population growth has created a need for increasing amounts of land for farming. This, as well as the need for fuelwood, has led to tree cover being stripped, allowing the soil to be washed or blown away. Over the past 30 years, eastern Africa has been stricken by many catastrophic droughts which have made desertification worse, and brought much human suffering.

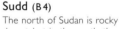

Lake Victoria (C 5)
Lake Victoria is Africa's largest lake and the second largest freshwater lake in the world. It lies on the Equator, between Kenya, Tanzania and Uganda, and covers 69,500 sq km. Its only outlet is the River Nile in the north.

Kilimanjaro (D 6)
This old volcano, made up of alternating layers of lava and ash, is Africa's highest mountain, rising to 5,895 m. Although it lies only three degrees from the Equator, its peak is permanently covered with snow.

ENVIRONMENTAL ISSUES

- Drought
- Severe fuelwood shortage
- Existing desert
- Risk of desertification
- Severe risk of desertification

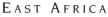

EAST AFRICA

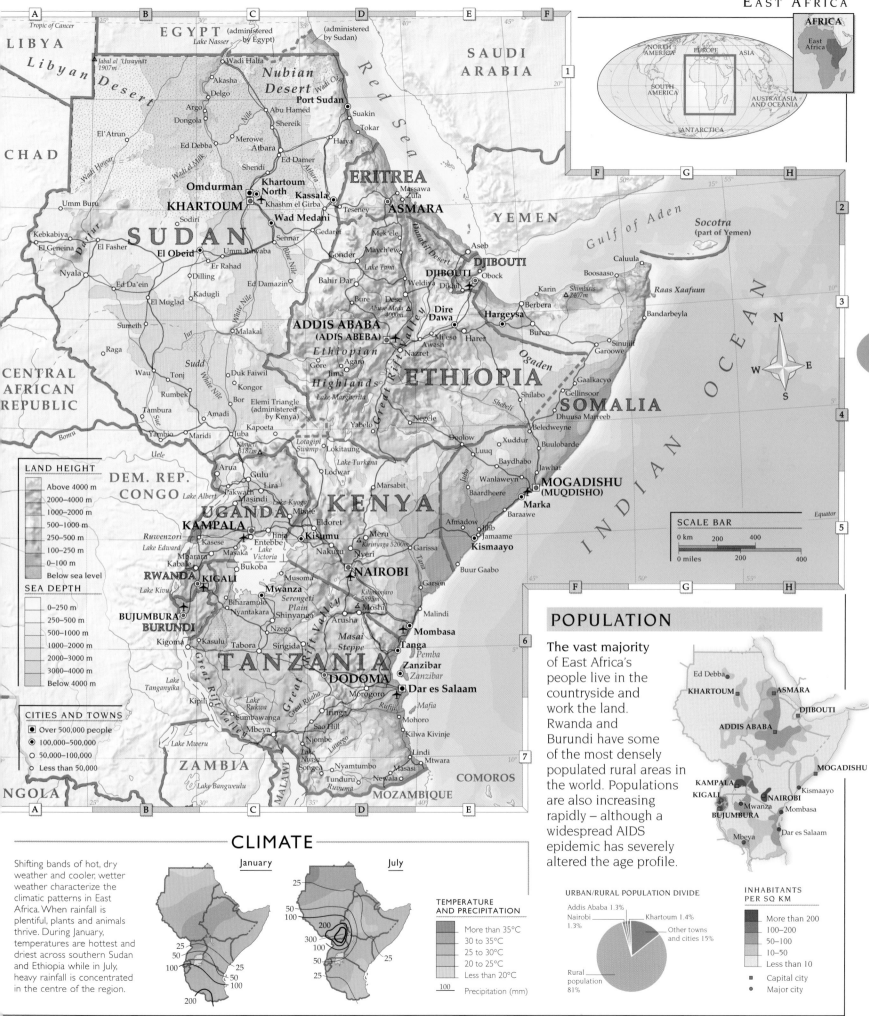

POPULATION

The vast majority of East Africa's people live in the countryside and work the land. Rwanda and Burundi have some of the most densely populated rural areas in the world. Populations are also increasing rapidly – although a widespread AIDS epidemic has severely altered the age profile.

URBAN/RURAL POPULATION DIVIDE

Addis Ababa 1.3%
Nairobi 1.3%
Khartoum 1.4%
Other towns and cities 15%
Rural population 81%

INHABITANTS PER SQ KM
- More than 200
- 100–200
- 50–100
- 10–50
- Less than 10
- ■ Capital city
- ● Major city

CLIMATE

Shifting bands of hot, dry weather and cooler, wetter weather characterize the climatic patterns in East Africa. When rainfall is plentiful, plants and animals thrive. During January, temperatures are hottest and driest across southern Sudan and Ethiopia while in July, heavy rainfall is concentrated in the centre of the region.

January

July

TEMPERATURE AND PRECIPITATION
- More than 35°C
- 30 to 35°C
- 25 to 30°C
- 20 to 25°C
- Less than 20°C

100 Precipitation (mm)

SOUTHERN AFRICA

ANGOLA, BOTSWANA, COMOROS, CONGO, DEM. REP. CONGO, GABON, LESOTHO, MADAGASCAR, MALAWI, MOZAMBIQUE, NAMIBIA, SOUTH AFRICA, SWAZILAND, ZAMBIA, ZIMBABWE

Southern Africa contains the richest deposits of valuable minerals on the continent. South Africa is the wealthiest and most industrialized country in the region. Most of the surrounding countries rely on it for trade and work. Racial segregation under apartheid operated from 1948 until 1994, when South Africa held its first multiracial elections.

FARMING AND LAND USE

Most of southern Africa's farmers grow just enough food to feed their families, though much of the farmland is in the hands of a few wealthy landowners. In the tropical north, oil palms and rubber are grown on large commercial plantations. Fruits are cultivated in the south, and tea and coffee are important in the east. Cattle farming is widespread across the dry grasslands.

FARMING AND LAND USE

- Cattle
- Fishing
- Cocoa
- Coffee
- Cotton
- Fruit
- Maize
- Oil palms
- Rubber
- Tea
- Timber
- Vineyard

LAND USE

- Cropland
- Desert
- Forest
- Pasture
- Wetland
- ● Major conurbation

Cropland 5%
Other 20%
Pasture 42%
Forest 33%

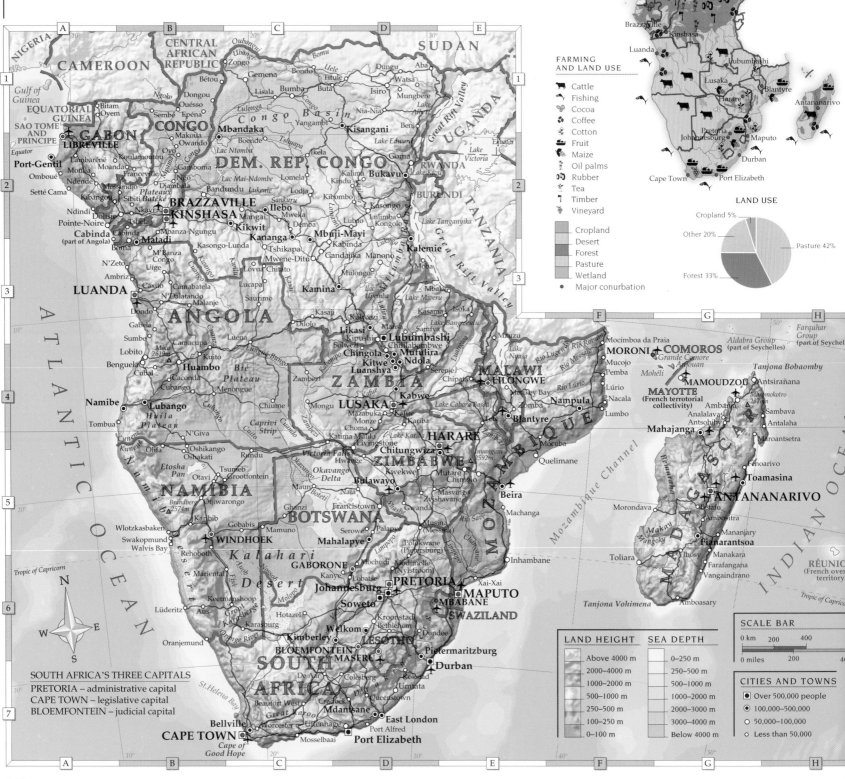

SOUTH AFRICA'S THREE CAPITALS
PRETORIA – administrative capital
CAPE TOWN – legislative capital
BLOEMFONTEIN – judicial capital

SCALE BAR
0 km 200 400
0 miles 200 400

LAND HEIGHT
- Above 4000 m
- 2000–4000 m
- 1000–2000 m
- 500–1000 m
- 250–500 m
- 100–250 m
- 0–100 m

SEA DEPTH
- 0–250 m
- 250–500 m
- 500–1000 m
- 1000–2000 m
- 2000–3000 m
- 3000–4000 m
- Below 4000 m

CITIES AND TOWNS
- ● Over 500,000 people
- ● 100,000–500,000
- ○ 50,000–100,000
- ○ Less than 50,000

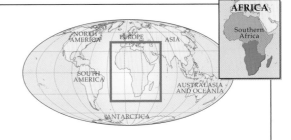

CLIMATE

During January, temperatures are highest in the Kalahari Desert and rainfall is plentiful in the center of southern Africa. July is cooler and drier with rainfall concentrated in north Dem. Rep. Congo. The Atlantic coast of Namibia receives little rain all year round.

January

July

TEMPERATURE AND PRECIPITATION

- More than 35°C
- 30 to 35°C
- 25 to 30°C
- 20 to 25°C
- 15 to 20°C
- Less than 15°C
- 100 Precipitation (mm)

ENVIRONMENTAL ISSUES

The immense rain forests of the Congo Basin in the north remain relatively untouched, but deforestation is beginning to occur at their edges, with more forest due to be cleared in the future. Large parts of Madagascar have also been deforested. Further south, occasional drought and the clearing of bushlands for fuelwood can cause soil loss.

1971–1974
1979–1983
1991–1992
1982–1984
1983–1985
1983 1985

ENVIRONMENTAL ISSUES

- Drought
- Severe fuelwood shortage
- Existing desert
- Risk of desertification
- Severe risk of desertification
- Deforested area
- Remaining tropical forest

INDUSTRY

Southern Africa has extraordinary mineral resources. Angola has large deposits of oil, and diamonds are found in Angola, Botswana, Namibia, and South Africa. Copper is mined in the region known as the "copper belt," that runs from Dem. Rep. Congo into Zambia and South Africa produces 40% of the world's gold. Manufacturing, such as fruit canning and steel production, is most developed in South Africa.

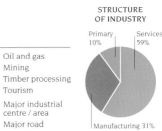

INDUSTRY

- Car manufacture
- Chemicals
- Engineering
- Food processing
- Iron & steel
- Metal refining
- Textiles
- Oil and gas
- Mining
- Timber processing
- Tourism
- Major industrial centre / area
- Major road

STRUCTURE OF INDUSTRY

Primary 10%
Services 59%
Manufacturing 31%

THE LANDSCAPE

Southern Africa stretches from just north of the equator down to the southern tip of the continent. It is an area with an extremely varied climate and geography. In the north are the tropical rain forests of the Congo Basin, while arid desert covers much of the southwest. The eastern regions are mostly grasslands, with lush vegetation found on the tropical coast of Mozambique.

Victoria Falls (D 5)

On its way to the Indian Ocean, the Zambezi River plunges over a 128 m cliff into a narrow chasm. The resultant spray rises up to 488 m, and the thunder of the water can be heard up to 40 km away.

Madagascar (G 5)

The world's fourth largest island lies in isolation 249 km off the east coast of southern Africa. It became separated from the African continent 135 million years ago, and its plant and animal life are unique. The rich biodiversity of the rain forests is being threatened by lumbering for wood and timber.

Congo Basin (C 1)

The Congo River is Africa's second longest river, flowing in an arc through the dense tropical forests of the Congo Basin before emptying into the Atlantic Ocean.

Namib Desert (B 5)

The Namib is one of the world's driest deserts. The only water it receives is from mists that roll in from the sea. Where the desert meets the coast is known as the Skeleton Coast because of sailors who were shipwrecked and died there.

Okavango Delta (C 5)

The Okavango River terminates in the Kalahari Desert, forming a vast, swampy inland delta.

Drakensberg (D 4)

The Drakensberg are a chain of mountains that lie at the edge of a broad plateau that has tilted because of the movement of the Earth's plates. Rivers have carved through the high mountains, creating dramatic gorges and waterfalls.

POPULATION

Although the population is still mostly rural, southern Africa has some of the continent's most urbanized nations. Dense tropical rain forest in the north and arid desert in the southwest have kept habitation to a bare minimum. Malawi is the most densely populated country in the region.

Cape Town 2%
Kinshasa 2.5%
Maputo 1.5%
Other towns and cities 28%
Rural population 66%

INHABITANTS PER SQ KM

- More than 100
- 50–100
- 10–50
- Less than 10
- Capital city
- Major city

AUSTRALASIA & OCEANIA

Australasia and Oceania encompasses the ancient land mass of Australia, the islands of New Zealand, and the scattering of thousands of small islands that stretch out into the Pacific Ocean. Indigenous peoples of the South Pacific, such as the Aborigines, Maoris, Polynesians, Micronesians and Melanesians, inhabit the region. In Australia and New Zealand, they live alongside people of European origin who settled in the 18th century, and more recent arrivals from East and Southeast Asia.

7,300 km

9,800 km

PACIFIC ISLANDS

Micronesia is one of the Pacific's island nations, consisting of a group of volcanic islands, low-lying coral reefs and lagoons. Many of the smaller Pacific islands are only a few metres above sea level.

LAND USE AND AGRICULTURE

Much of the centre of Australia is a dry, barren desert and unsuitable for agriculture. At its fringes, sheep farming is practised, and Australia and New Zealand alike are massive producers of wool and lamb. The Pacific islands export many exotic fruits and crops – especially oil palms and coconut palms. Oil from the palms is processed and sold, as well as the fruits themselves. Small-scale fishing is common, but larger scale operations are run by foreign fishing fleets, especially the Japanese, who fish tuna from the deeper waters of the Pacific.

SHEEP FARMING

New Zealand and Australia are the world's biggest producers of wool. In New Zealand, sheep outnumber people by 20 – 1.

POPULATION

Capital cities
- Above 500,000
- 100,000 to 500,000
- 50,000 to 100,000
- Below 50,000

State capitals
- Above 500,000
- 100,000 to 500,000
- 50,000 to 100,000

BORDERS

- full international border
- indication of maritime country extent
- indication of maritime dependent territory extent
- state border

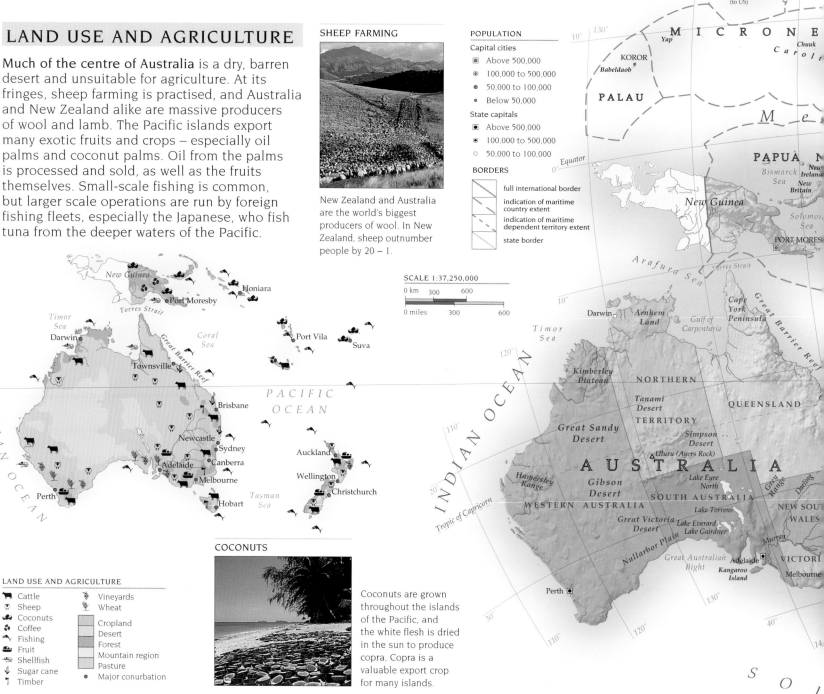

LAND USE AND AGRICULTURE

- Cattle
- Sheep
- Coconuts
- Coffee
- Fishing
- Fruit
- Shellfish
- Sugar cane
- Timber
- Vineyards
- Wheat
- Cropland
- Desert
- Forest
- Mountain region
- Pasture
- • Major conurbation

COCONUTS

Coconuts are grown throughout the islands of the Pacific, and the white flesh is dried in the sun to produce copra. Copra is a valuable export crop for many islands.

SCALE 1:37,250,000

0 km   300   600

0 miles   300   600

MINERAL RESOURCES

Mineral resources are not widespread, but where they are found, it is in great abundance. Most of the small Pacific islands have no mineral resources, but Australia has enormous reserves of bauxite and iron ore, and also sizeable reserves of gold and zinc. Copper is found in Papua New Guinea, and New Caledonia has large nickel reserves. There are ample supplies of fossil fuels and although coal is plentiful in eastern Australia, oil and gas are found only in isolated pockets around Australia's coast.

AUSTRALASIA
and OCEANIA

MINERAL RESOURCES

Bauxite		Iron			Oil/gas field	
Copper		Nickel			Coal field	
Gold		Zinc				

TOURISM

Tourism forms a valuable and growing boost to the economies of many countries and territories in Australasia and Oceania. Australia, New Zealand, Fiji, Guam and the Cook Islands are the most popular destinations.

ULURU (AYERS ROCK)

The large isolated rock called Uluru is a sacred place to Australia's aboriginal peoples. It attracts many tourists, who come to marvel as its colour changes during the course of the day.

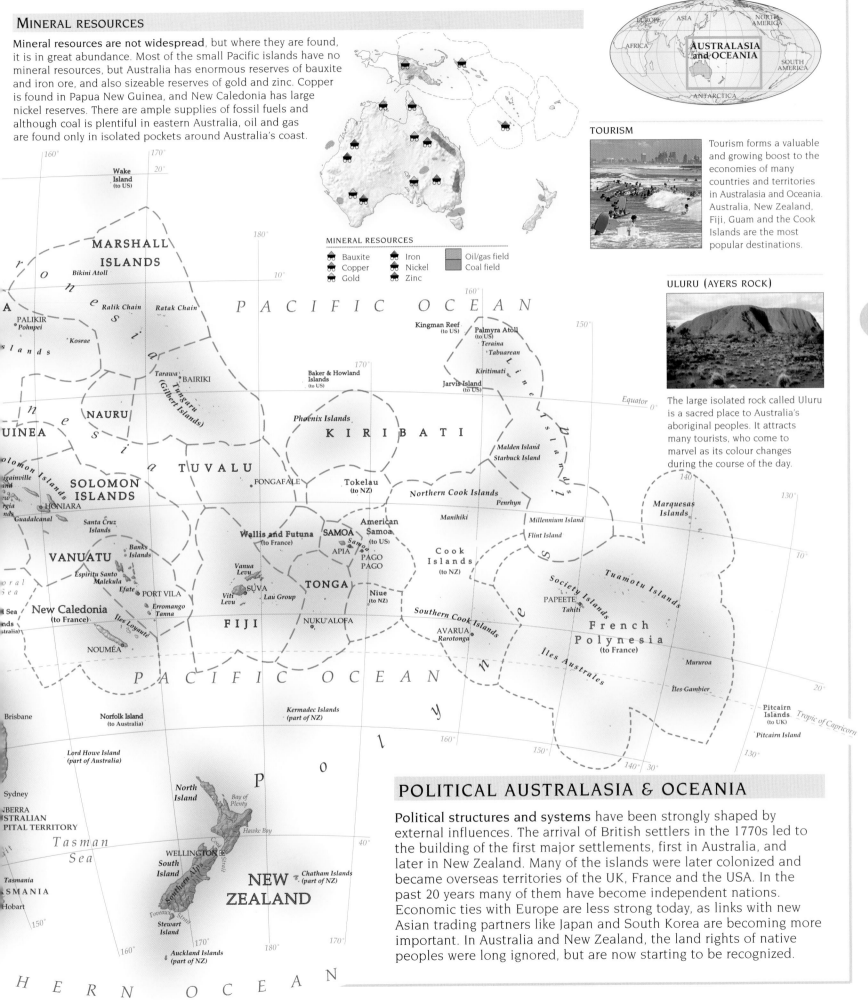

POLITICAL AUSTRALASIA & OCEANIA

Political structures and systems have been strongly shaped by external influences. The arrival of British settlers in the 1770s led to the building of the first major settlements, first in Australia, and later in New Zealand. Many of the islands were later colonized and became overseas territories of the UK, France and the USA. In the past 20 years many of them have become independent nations. Economic ties with Europe are less strong today, as links with new Asian trading partners like Japan and South Korea are becoming more important. In Australia and New Zealand, the land rights of native peoples were long ignored, but are now starting to be recognized.

AUSTRALIA

Australia is the world's sixth-largest country, and also the smallest, flattest continent, with the lowest rainfall. Most Australians are of European, mainly British, origin but in the past 50 years almost five million settlers from more than 200 countries have made Australia their home. The Aboriginal peoples, now only a tiny minority, were the first inhabitants. Recently, there have been several moves to restore their ancient lands.

FARMING AND LAND USE

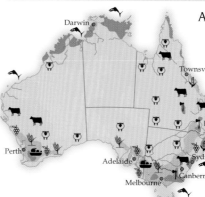

Away from the coasts, much of the land is too dry for agriculture. Fields of sugar cane grow close to the east coast, and grapes for the thriving wine industry are cultivated in the south and west, along with wheat. Vast numbers of cattle and sheep are raised for their meat and wool – both of which are major exports. They are grazed in the desert, on huge farms called 'stations', and in more fertile areas.

FARMING AND LAND USE

- Cattle
- Fishing
- Sheep
- Wheat
- Sugar cane
- Timber
- Vineyards

- Cropland
- Desert
- Forest
- Pasture
- Major conurbation

LAND USE

- Cropland 6%
- Other (including desert) 21%
- Forest 19%
- Pasture 54%

INDUSTRY

Australia has one of the world's biggest mining industries. Bauxite, coal, copper, gold and iron ore are mined and exported, especially to Japan. In the cities, service industries, particularly tourism, are growing fast; Australia's sunshine and dramatic scenery are attracting an increasing number of overseas visitors.

STRUCTURE OF INDUSTRY

- Primary 3%
- Services 67%
- Manufacturing 30%

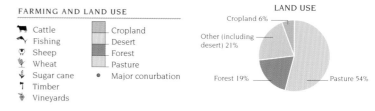

INDUSTRY

- Brewing
- Car manufacture
- Chemicals
- Electronics
- Engineering
- Food processing
- Coal

- Mining
- Oil and gas
- Tourism
- Major industrial centre / area
- Major road

THE LANDSCAPE

Most of Australia is dry, flat and barren; all of the wetter, fertile land is found along its coastline. Huge sun-baked deserts, fringed by semi-arid plains of scrub and grassland cover most of the west and centre of the country. In the east, the land rises to the highlands of the Great Dividing Range, which run the whole length of the east coast. The tropical north coast has rainforests and mangrove swamps.

Blue Mountains (G6)
The Blue Mountains lie towards the southern end of the Great Dividing Range. They get their name from the blue haze of oil droplets given off by the eucalyptus trees covering their slopes.

Great Barrier Reef (G2)
This spectacular coral reef, which stretches for over 2,000 km off the coast of Queensland, is the largest living structure on Earth. The reef has built up over millions of years and its waters are home to thousands of different species of coral and marine animals.

Uluru (Ayers Rock) (D4)
Uluru is an enormous block of red sandstone, standing almost in the middle of Australia. It is the world's biggest free-standing rock – 9.4 km around the base, and 867 m high. It is the summit of a sandstone hill that is buried beneath the sands of the desert.

POPULATION

Despite its vast size, Australia is sparsely populated. The desert 'outback', which covers most of the interior, is too dry and barren to support many people. About 70% of the population live in the cities and towns on the east and southeast coasts, and around Perth in the west.

INHABITANTS PER SQ KM

- More than 50
- 10–50
- 1–10
- Less than 1
- ■ Capital city
- ● Major city

URBAN/RURAL POPULATION DIVIDE

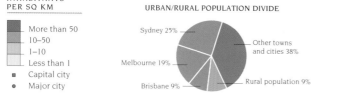

- Sydney 25%
- Melbourne 19%
- Brisbane 9%
- Other towns and cities 38%
- Rural population 9%

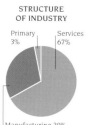

Simpson Desert (E4)
The Simpson Desert covers around 130,000 sq km. It contains long, parallel lines of sand dunes and is scattered with large salt pans and salt lakes, which were created when old rivers evaporated. They are now fed by the seasonal rains.

Murray River (F5)
Together with its tributaries, the Murray River is Australia's main river system. It winds slowly westwards for more than 2,500 km from the Great Dividing Range to the Indian Ocean. It is fed by snow from mountains in the far southeast.

Great Dividing Range (H5)
These highlands separate the desert regions from the fertile eastern plains. Rivers and streams have eroded them, creating deep valleys and gorges.

ENVIRONMENTAL ISSUES

Australia's dry climate and low rainfall make it susceptible to desertification. Around the fringes of the large deserts – especially in the north and southeast – cattle grazing and the removal of natural vegetation are destroying the natural habitat, allowing the desert areas to spread. During the dry season, vegetation becomes tinder-dry, and bush fires are common, burning huge tracts of land.

CLIMATE

Much of Australia's climate is continental, and temperatures soar during the day and fall rapidly at night. The climate is also arid and very little rain falls, apart from in the summer months when the north is affected by tropical storms.

January

July

AUSTRALASIA AND OCEANIA

TEMPERATURE AND PRECIPITATION

More than 35°C
30 to 35°C
25 to 30°C
20 to 25°C
15 to 20°C
10 to 15°C
5 to 10°C
Less than 5°C

Precipitation (mm)

ENVIRONMENTAL ISSUES

Area at risk from bushfires

Existing desert
Risk of desertification
Severe risk of desertification

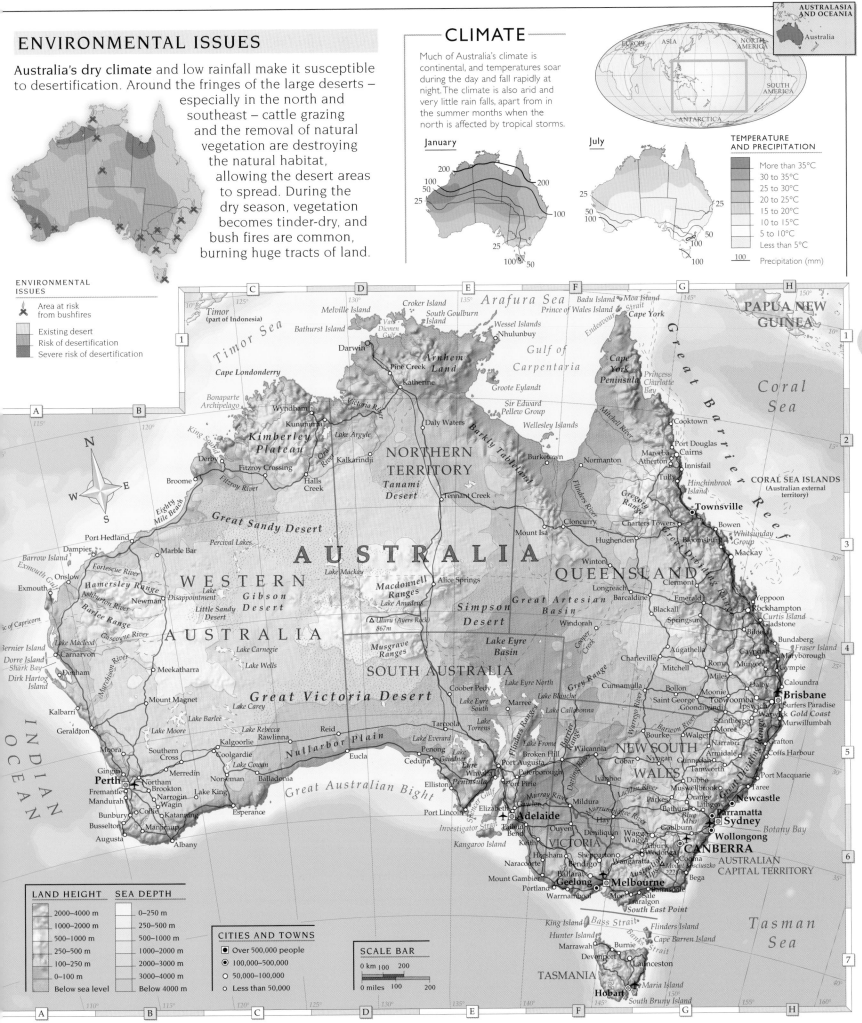

LAND HEIGHT
2000–4000 m
1000–2000 m
500–1000 m
250–500 m
100–250 m
0–100 m
Below sea level

SEA DEPTH
0–250 m
250–500 m
500–1000 m
1000–2000 m
2000–3000 m
3000–4000 m
Below 4000 m

CITIES AND TOWNS
Over 500,000 people
100,000–500,000
50,000–100,000
Less than 50,000

SCALE BAR
0 km 100 200
0 miles 100 200

117

NEW ZEALAND

New Zealand is one of the most remote populated places in the world. The first people to settle on the islands were the Maori, a Polynesian people. When European settlers arrived during the 19th century, the Maori became a minority, and now only make up about 9% of the population. With a small population and rich natural resources, New Zealand's people have high living standards. The country's magnificent rugged scenery is popular with tourists.

INDUSTRY

Hi-tech industries such as electronics and computing are growing in the major cities of Auckland and Wellington, although agricultural products such as meat, wool and milk are still among New Zealand's major exports, and large pine forests supply wood for paper pulp and timber. The exciting scenery and varied climate draw tourists from all over the world, especially for walking and adventure holidays.

STRUCTURE OF INDUSTRY

Primary 5%
Services 68%
Manufacturing 27%

INDUSTRY

- Chemicals
- Electronics
- Engineering
- Fish processing
- Food processing
- Iron and steel
- Textiles
- Timber
- Tourism
- Major industrial centre / area
- Major road

POPULATION

Most of the population is descended from European settlers, although immigrants from Asia and from the Pacific islands are increasing. More than one-third of New Zealand's 4 million people live in Auckland on North Island, which also has the largest Polynesian population of any city in the Pacific. Elsewhere, the population is clustered along the coasts, where the land is lower.

URBAN/RURAL POPULATION DIVIDE

Auckland 27.2%
Other towns and cities 38%
Wellington 9.5%
Christchurch 9.3%
Rural population 16%

INHABITANTS PER SQ KM

- More than 50
- 10–50
- 1–10
- Less than 1
- Capital city
- Major city

ENVIRONMENTAL ISSUES

New Zealand is one of the world's least polluted countries – largely due to its low population and lack of heavy industries, although air quality is occasionally poor in Auckland and Christchurch. Environment-friendly geothermal energy is tapped to make electricity in the volcanic region of North Island. Recently, logging companies have begun to exploit the rich forest reserves, although this has been widely opposed.

ENVIRONMENTAL ISSUES

- Geothermal power generation
- Logging activity
- Urban air pollution
- Major industrial centre

THE LANDSCAPE

Two large, mountainous islands form New Zealand's main land areas. A large crack or fault – the Alpine Fault, in the west of South Island – is the boundary between two plates in the Earth's crust. Land either side of the fault tends to move, causing earthquakes. Volcanoes, many of them still active, are also found, on both islands. South Island has many high peaks, several more than 3,000 m high.

Geysers and boiling mud

Geysers occur when hot volcanic rocks come into contact with underground water. The water boils and turns to steam forcing the water above it to burst through the Earth's surface into the air. There are many geysers and boiling mud pools in the areas around Rotorua and Taupo.

Northland (C 1)

This is a tropical region in the far northwest. Many of the inlets are fringed by mangrove swamps.

Mount Taranaki (C 4)

The dormant volcano of Mount Taranaki lies on New Zealand's North Island. It rises to a height of 2,518 m.

Probable location of Alpine Fault

Lake Taupo (D 3)

New Zealand's largest lake, Lake Taupo, covers 606 sq km of North Island. It lies in the crater of an extinct volcano

Southern Alps

New Zealand's Southern Alps stretch more than 483 km down the backbone of South Island. They were formed by the collision of the Indo-Australian and Pacific plates. Heavy snowfalls here, brought by westerly winds, feed the Fox Glacier which moves at a speed of 0.5–4.5 m a day.

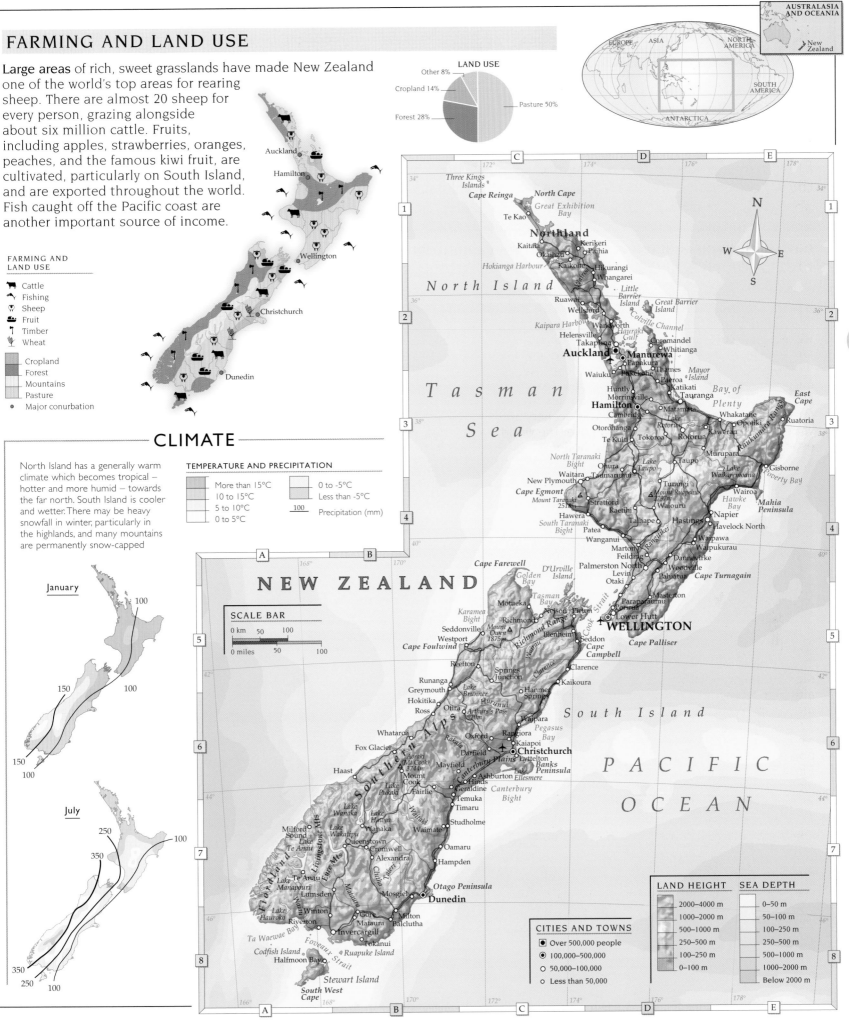

FARMING AND LAND USE

Large areas of rich, sweet grasslands have made New Zealand one of the world's top areas for rearing sheep. There are almost 20 sheep for every person, grazing alongside about six million cattle. Fruits, including apples, strawberries, oranges, peaches, and the famous kiwi fruit, are cultivated, particularly on South Island, and are exported throughout the world. Fish caught off the Pacific coast are another important source of income.

AUSTRALASIA AND OCEANIA
EUROPE ASIA NORTH AMERICA
New Zealand
SOUTH AMERICA
ANTARCTICA

LAND USE
Other 8%
Cropland 14%
Forest 28%
Pasture 50%

FARMING AND LAND USE

- 🐄 Cattle
- Fishing
- 🐑 Sheep
- Fruit
- 🌲 Timber
- Wheat

- Cropland
- Forest
- Mountains
- Pasture
- ● Major conurbation

Auckland
Hamilton
Wellington
Christchurch
Dunedin

CLIMATE

North Island has a generally warm climate which becomes tropical – hotter and more humid – towards the far north. South Island is cooler and wetter. There may be heavy snowfall in winter, particularly in the highlands, and many mountains are permanently snow-capped

TEMPERATURE AND PRECIPITATION

- More than 15°C
- 10 to 15°C
- 5 to 10°C
- 0 to 5°C
- 0 to -5°C
- Less than -5°C
- 100 Precipitation (mm)

January
100
150
100
150
100

July
250
350
100
350
250
100

NEW ZEALAND

SCALE BAR
0 km 50 100
0 miles 50 100

CITIES AND TOWNS
- ■ Over 500,000 people
- ◉ 100,000–500,000
- ◎ 50,000–100,000
- ○ Less than 50,000

LAND HEIGHT	SEA DEPTH
2000–4000 m	0–50 m
1000–2000 m	50–100 m
500–1000 m	100–250 m
250–500 m	250–500 m
100–250 m	500–1000 m
0–100 m	1000–2000 m
	Below 2000 m

SOUTHWEST PACIFIC

The many thousands of islands in the Pacific Ocean are scattered across an enormous area. The original inhabitants, the Polynesians, Melanesians and Micronesians, settled the islands following the last Ice Age. In the 1700s Europeans arrived. They colonized all of the Pacific islands, introducing their culture, languages and religion. Today, many, though not all, of the islands have become independent. Their economies are simple, based largely on fishing and agriculture. Many are increasingly relying on their beautiful scenery and tropical climates to attract tourists and give a valuable boost to their economies.

LANDSCAPE

Most of the Pacific islands are extremely small, the largest land mass is the half of the island of New Guinea occupied by Papua New Guinea. The edges of the Indo-Australian and Pacific plates meet on the western edge of the area, leading to much volcanic and earthquake activity. Many of the islands are coral atolls, originally formed by volcanic activity, and some are no more than a few metres above sea level.

New Guinea (A 2)
A mountainous spine runs through the centre of the island, separating the northern coast from the dense forests and mangroves found in the south.

Pacific Ocean
The Pacific Ocean is the Earth's oldest and deepest ocean. Its name means peaceful, though it is far from being so; the highest wave ever recorded on open ocean – 34 m – occurred during a hurricane in the Pacific.

Kavachi
Kavachi is a submarine volcano lying off the coast of New Georgia, in the Solomon Islands. It still erupts every few years.

Ring of Fire
The 'Ring of Fire' is the term used to describe the string of volcanoes which surround the entire Pacific Ocean and erupt frequently because of intense stress and movement from within the Earth. The ring crosses the south Pacific, running between Vanuatu and New Caledonia, along the edge of the Solomon Islands, and between New Britain and New Guinea.

Sea trenches
Deep trenches mark the sea floor boundary where the Indo-Australian plate 'dives' under the Pacific plate.

Coral atolls
Volcanic activity in the Pacific has led to the creation of many islands. These islands become fringed with a ring of coral. When the islands subside beneath the sea once again, only the circle of coral is left, forming an atoll.

INDUSTRY

Today, the main industry for many of the Pacific islands is tourism. Food processing and small-scale textile industries are also common on many islands.

INDUSTRY
- Brewing
- Food processing
- Textiles
- Timber processing
- Mining
- Tourism
- ● Major industrial centre
- — Major road

FARMING AND LAND USE

Most farming that takes place on the Pacific islands is at a subsistence level, and many people keep pigs and chickens. A few crops are grown for export, especially oil palms, and coconuts, which are dried in the sun to produce copra. Many islanders make their living from the rich fishing grounds of the Pacific. The thick forests of Papua New Guinea are increasingly cut down for timber.

AUSTRALASIA AND OCEANIA

LAND USE

- Fishing
- Bananas
- Cocoa
- Coconuts
- Coffee
- Oil palms
- Rubber
- Timber
- Cropland
- Forest
- Wetland
- Major conurbation

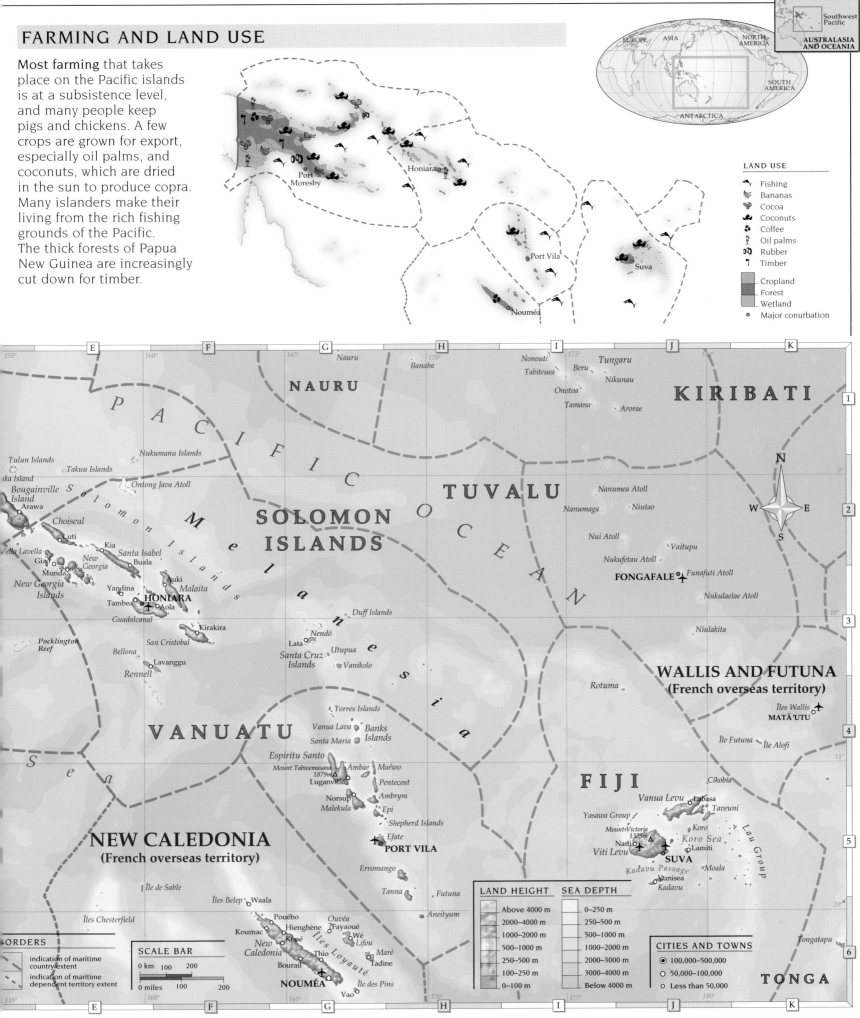

LAND HEIGHT
- Above 4000 m
- 2000–4000 m
- 1000–2000 m
- 500–1000 m
- 250–500 m
- 100–250 m
- 0–100 m

SEA DEPTH
- 0–250 m
- 250–500 m
- 500–1000 m
- 1000–2000 m
- 2000–3000 m
- 3000–4000 m
- Below 4000 m

CITIES AND TOWNS
- ◉ 100,000–500,000
- ○ 50,000–100,000
- ○ Less than 50,000

BORDERS
- indication of maritime country extent
- indication of maritime dependent territory extent

SCALE BAR
0 km 100 200
0 miles 100 200

121

ANTARCTICA

The continent of **Antarctica** has no permanent human population and very few animals can survive on the frozen land, although the surrounding seas teem with fish and mammals. Even in the summer the temperature is rarely above freezing and the sea-ice only partly melts; in winter, temperatures plummet to −80°C. The only people who live in Antarctica are teams of scientists who study the wildlife and monitor the ice for changes in the Earth's atmosphere.

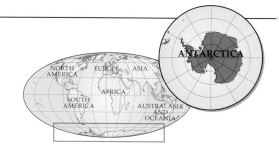

THE LANDSCAPE

Frozen seas
During the cold winter months, the seas surrounding Antarctica freeze, almost doubling the size of the continent.

Antarctica is the world's most southerly continent. It is also the world's coldest continent and its highest, mainly due to the great ice sheet – up to 2 km thick in parts – which lies over the mountains of the Antarctic Peninsula and the plateau of Greater Antarctica.

Lambert Glacier (E 4)
The Lambert Glacier is the world's largest series of glaciers. It is 80 km wide at the coast and reaches more than 300 km inland.

Transantarctic Mountains (C 5)
The Transantarctic Mountains run across the continent, splitting it into Greater and Lesser Antarctica.

Ice sheet
A massive sheet of ice, about 4,800 m thick at its deepest point, covers almost the entire area of Antarctica. It contains most of the fresh water on Earth. The weight of the ice pushes the land down below sea level.

The Ross Ice Shelf (C 5)
The Ross Sea is part of the Southern Ocean. This deep bay is covered by a thick sheet of ice which floats on the ocean.

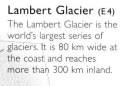

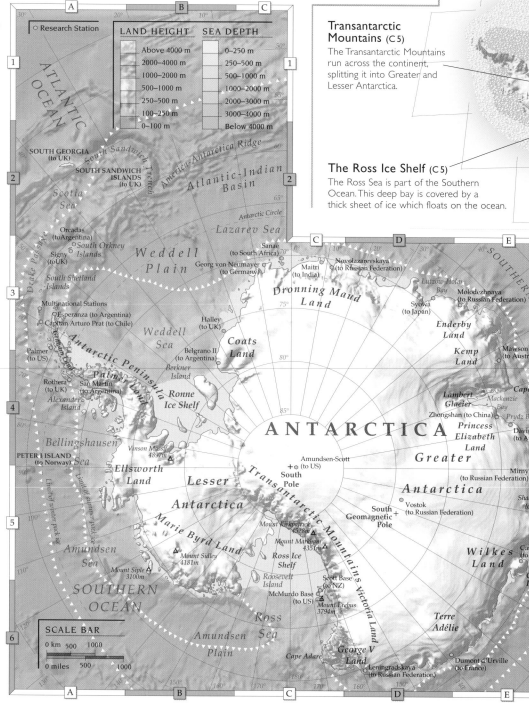

Research Station

LAND HEIGHT	SEA DEPTH
Above 4000 m	0–250 m
2000–4000 m	250–500 m
1000–2000 m	500–1000 m
500–1000 m	1000–2000 m
250–500 m	2000–3000 m
100–250 m	3000–4000 m
0–100 m	Below 4000 m

RESOURCES

The mountains of Antarctica have rich mineral reserves. Gold, iron and coal are found, and there is natural gas in the surrounding seas. The unique and abundant marine wildlife is Antarctica's greatest resource. Colonies of penguins breed on the ice sheet, and whales, seals and many bird and fish species thrive in the icy waters.

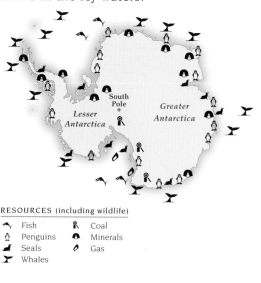

RESOURCES (including wildlife)
- Fish
- Penguins
- Seals
- Whales
- Coal
- Minerals
- Gas

THE ARCTIC

The ice-covered Arctic Ocean is encircled by the most northerly parts of Europe, North America and Asia. Very few people live in the often freezing conditions. Those who do, including the Sami of northern Scandinavia, the Siberian Yugyt and Nenet people and the Canadian Inuit, were nomads who lived by hunting and herding. Some live like this today, but many have now settled in small towns.

THE LANDSCAPE

The Arctic Ocean is the smallest ocean in the world, covering a total area of 15,100,000 sq km. The ocean is divided into two large basins, divided by three great underwater mountain ranges including the Lomonosov Ridge which is more than 3,000 m high on average.

Lomonosov Ridge (C 4)

Arctic islands (A 4)

In the far north of Canada, there are many thousands of islands including Baffin Island and Victoria Island. Many of them are almost entirely surrounded by pack-ice.

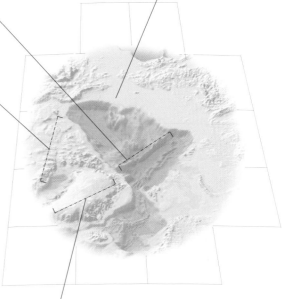

Pack-ice

Much of the Arctic Ocean is permanently covered by pack-ice. When the ice breaks up, it forms enormous floating ice-masses called icebergs.

Greenland (A 3)

Greenland is the world's largest island. It is covered by a huge ice sheet, more than 1,683,400 sq km across. The weight of the ice has pushed most of the land below sea level.

Sastrugi

Snow, blown by strong winds can scratch deep patterns in the snow. These patterns are known as sastrugi and line up with the direction of the wind.

RESOURCES

Coal, oil and gas are found beneath the Arctic Ocean and in Canada, Alaska and Russia. Fears about damage to the environment and the cost of extracting these resources have restricted the quantities removed. Overfishing has reduced fish stocks to very low levels. Quotas have been put in place to allow them to revive.

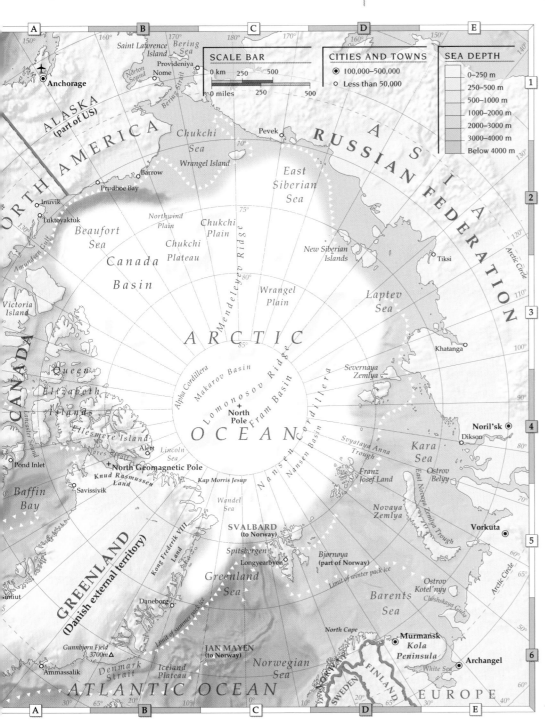

SCALE BAR
0 km   250   500
0 miles   250   500

CITIES AND TOWNS
◉ 100,000–500,000
○ Less than 50,000

SEA DEPTH
- 0–250 m
- 250–500 m
- 500–1000 m
- 1000–2000 m
- 2000–3000 m
- 3000–4000 m
- Below 4000 m

RESOURCES
- ⚓ Fish
- ⚒ Coal
- ⬡ Minerals
- ◊ Oil and gas
- ● Major town/city

GLOSSARY

This glossary defines certain geographical and technical terms used in this Atlas.

Acid rain Rain, sleet, snow or mist which has absorbed waste gases from fossil-fuelled power stations and vehicle exhausts, becoming acidic and poisonous.

Alluvium Material deposited by a river, such as silt, sand and mud.

Archipelago A group, or chain, of islands.

Atoll A circular or horseshoe-shaped coral reef enclosing a shallow area of water (lagoon).

Aquifer A body of rock that can absorb water. It may be a source of water for wells or springs.

Bar, coastal An offshore strip of sand or shingle, either above or below the water.

Biodiversity The quantity of different animal or plant species in a given area.

Birth rate The number of live births per 1000 individuals annually within a population.

Cash crop Agricultural produce grown for sale, often for foreign export, rather than to be consumed by the country or area where it was grown.

Climate The long term trends in weather conditions for an area.

Coniferous forest A type of forest containing trees or shrubs, like pines and firs, which have needles instead of leaves. They are found in temperate zones.

Continental plates The huge interlocking plates which make up the Earth's surface. A plate boundary is an area where two plates meet, and is the point at which earthquakes occur most frequently.

Conurbation A large urban area created by the merging of several towns.

Coral reef An underwater barrier created by colonies of coral polyps. The polyps secrete a protective skeleton of calcium carbonate, and reefs develop as live polyps build on the skeletons of dead generations.

Core The layers of liquid rock and solid iron at the centre of the Earth.

Crust The hard, thin outer shell of the Earth. The crust floats on the mantle, which is softer, but more dense.

Deciduous forest A type of broadleaf forest found in temperate regions.

Deforestation Cutting down trees or forest for timber or farmland. It can lead to soil erosion, flooding and landslides.

Delta A low-lying, fan-shaped area at a river mouth, formed by the deposition of successive layers of sediment. Slowing as it enters the sea, a river deposits sediment and may, as a result, split into many smaller channels called distributaries.

Deposition The laying down of material broken down by erosion or weathering and transported by the wind, water or gravity.

Desertification The spread of desert conditions into a region which was not previously a desert.

Drainage basin The land drained by a river and its tributaries.

Drought A long period of continuously low rainfall.

Earthquake A trembling or shaking of the ground caused by the sudden movement of rocks in the Earth's crust – and sometimes deeper than the crust. Earthquakes occur most frequently along continental plate boundaries.

Economy The organization of a country's finances, exports, imports, industry, agriculture and services.

Ecosytem A community of species dependent on each other and on the habitat in which they live.

Equator The 0° line of latitude. Equatorial climates are hot and there is plenty of rain.

Erosion The wearing down of the land surface by running water, waves, moving ice, wind and weather.

Estuary The mouth of a river, where the salt water from the sea meets the fresh water of the river.

Fault A crack or fracture in the Earth along which there has been movement of the rock masses relative to one another.

Fjord A coastal valley which was sculpted by glacial action.

Flood plain The broad, flat part of a river valley, next to the river itself, formed by sediment deposited during flooding.

Geyser A fountain of hot water or steam that erupts periodically as a result of underground streams coming into contact with hot rocks.

GDP Gross Domestic Product. The total value of goods and services produced by a country, excluding income from foreign countries.

GIS Geographical Information System. A computerized system for the collection, storage and retrieval of geographical data.

Glacier A huge mass of ice made up of compacted and frozen snow which moves slowly, eroding and depositing rock.

Glaciation The moulding of the land by a glacier or ice sheet.

GNP Gross National Product. The total value of goods and services produced by a country.

Groundwater Water that has seeped into the pores, cavities and cracks of rocks or into soil and water held in an aquifer or permeable rock.

Gully A deep, narrow chasm eroded in the landscape by a fast-flowing stream.

Heavy industry Industry that uses large amounts of energy and raw materials to produce heavy goods, such as machinery, ships, or locomotives.

Humidity The moisture content of the air.

Hurricane Violent tropical storms, also known as cyclones in the Indian Ocean and typhoons in the Pacific Ocean.

Hydroelectric power Energy produced by harnessing the rapid movement of water down steep mountain slopes to drive turbines to generate electricity.

Ice Age Periods of time in the past when much of the Earth's surface was covered by massive ice sheets. The most recent Ice Age began two million years ago and ended 10,000 years ago.

Iceberg A floating mass of ice that has broken off from a glacier or ice sheet.

Ice sheet A massive area of ice, thousands of metres thick.

Irrigation The artificial supply of water to dry areas – mainly for agricultural use. Water is carried or pumped to the area through pipes or ditches.

Lagoon A shallow stretch of coastal saltwater behind a partial barrier such as a sandbank or coral reef.

Latitude The distance north or south of the Equator, measured in degrees, and shown on a globe as imaginary circles running around the Earth parallel to the Equator.

Lava The molten rock, magma, which erupts onto the Earth's surface through a volcano, or through a fault or crack in the Earth's crust. Lava refers to the rock both in its liquid and its later, solidified form.

Load The material that is carried by a river or stream.

Longitude The distance, measured in degrees, east or west of the Prime Meridian.

Limestone A type of rock, formed by sediment, through which water can pass.

Magma Underground, molten rock, which is very hot and highly charged with gas. It originates in the Earth's lower crust or mantle.

Mantle The layer of the Earth's interior between the crust and the core. It is about 2,900 km thick.

Map projection A mathematical formula that is used to show the curved surface of the Earth on a flat map.

Market gardening The intensive growing of fruit and vegetables close to large local markets.

Meander A loop-like bend in a river. As a river nears the sea, it tends to wind more and more. The bigger the river and the shallower its slope, the more likely it is that meanders will form.

Mediterranean climate A temperate climate of hot, dry summers and warm, damp winters.

Meltwater Water which has melted from glaciers or ice sheets.

Mestizo A person of mixed native American and European origin.

Mineral A chemical compound that occurs naturally in the Earth.

Monsoon Winds that change direction according to the seasons. They are most common in South and East Asia, where they blow from the southwest in summer, bringing heavy rainfall, and the northeast in winter.

Moraine Sand and gravel that have been deposited by a glacier or ice sheet.

Nomads (nomadic) Wandering communities who move around in search of suitable pasture for their herds of animals.

Oasis A fertile area in a desert, usually watered by an underground aquifer.

Pack ice Ice masses more than three metres thick which form on the sea surface and are not attached to a landmass.

Pacific Rim The name given to the economically dynamic countries bordering the Pacific Ocean.

Peat Decomposed vegetation found in bogs. It can be dried and used as fuel.

Per capita A latin term meaning 'for each person'.

Plantation A large farm on which only one crop is usually grown, e.g, bananas or coffee.

Plain A flat, level region of land, often relatively low-lying.

Plateau A large area of high, flat land. When surrounded by steep slopes it is called a tableland.

Peninsula A thin strip of land surrounded on three of its sides by water. Large examples include Italy, Florida and Korea.

Permafrost Permanently frozen ground, in which temperatures have remained below 0°C for more than two years.

Precipitation The fall of moisture from the atmosphere onto the surface of the Earth, as dew, hail, rain, sleet or snow.

Prairie A Spanish-American term for grassy plains, with few or no trees.

Prime Meridian 0° longitude. Also known as the Greenwich Meridian because it runs through Greenwich in England.

Rainforest Dense forests in tropical zones with high rainfall, temperature and humidity.

Rainshadow An area downwind from high terrain which has little or no rainfall because it has fallen upon the high relief.

Remote-sensing A way of obtaining information about the environment by using unmanned equipment, such as a satellite, which relays the information to a point where it is collected.

Ria A flooded V-shaped river valley or estuary flooded by a rise in sea level or sinking land.

Rift valley A long, narrow depression in the Earth's crust, formed by the sinking of rocks between two faults.

Savannah Open grassland, where an annual dry season prevents the growth of most trees. They lie between the tropical rainforest and hot desert regions.

Scale The relationship between distance on a map and on the Earth's surface

Sediment Grains of rock transported and deposited by rivers, sea, ice or wind.

Semi-arid Areas between deserts and better-watered areas, where there is sufficient moisture to support a little more vegetation than in a true desert.

Service industry An industry that supplies services, such as banking, rather than producing manufactured goods.

Shanty town An area in or around a city where people live in temporary shacks, usually without basic facilities such as running water.

Silt Small particles, finer than sand, often carried by water and deposited on riverbanks, at river mouths and harbours.

Soil A thin layer of rock particles mixed with the remains of dead plants and animals. Soil occurs naturally on the surface of the Earth and provides a medium for plants to grow.

Soil erosion The wearing away of soil more quickly than it is replaced by natural processes. Over-grazing and the clearing of land for farming speeds up the process.

Sorghum A type of grass found in South America, similar to sugar cane.

Spit A narrow bank of shingle or sand extending out from the sea shore. Spits are made out of material transported along the coast by currents, wind and waves.

Staple crop The main food crop grown in a region, for example rice in Southeast Asia.

Steppe Large areas of dry grassland in the northern hemisphere – particularly found in southeast Europe and central Asia.

Subsistence farming A method of farming where enough food is produced to feed farmers and their families but not providing any extra to generate an income.

Taiga A Russian name given to the belt of coniferous forest found in Russia, which borders tundra in the north and mixed forests and grasslands in the south.

Temperate The mild, variable climate found in areas between the tropics and cold polar regions.

Terrace Steps cut into steep slopes to create flat surfaces for cultivating crops.

Tropics An area between the Equator and the Tropic of Cancer and Tropic of Capricorn that has heavy rainfall, high temperatures, and lacks any clear seasonal variation.

Tundra The land area lying in the very cold northern regions of Europe, Asia and Canada, where winters are long and cold and the ground beneath the surface is permanently frozen.

U-shaped valley A river valley that has been deepened and widened by a glacier. They are flat-bottomed and steep-sided, and usually much deeper than river valleys.

V-shaped valley A typical valley eroded by a river in its upper course.

Volcano An opening or vent in the Earth's crust where magma erupts. Volcanos are caused by the movement of the Earth's plates. When the plates collide or spread apart, magma is forced to the surface, at or near the place where the plates meet.

Watershed The dividing line between one drainage basin and another.

INDEX

ARLINGTON

Arlington 39 G4 Texas, USA
Arlon 60 E9 SE Belgium
Armagh 63 B5 S Northern Ireland, UK
Armagnac 65 C6 *Cultural region,* S France
Armenia 89 H2 ◆ *Republic,* SW Asia
Armenia 51 B2 W Colombia
Armidale 117 H5 NSW, SE Australia
Armstrong 33 B4 Ontario, S Canada
Armyans'k 77 F6 S Ukraine
Arnedo 67 E2 N Spain
Arnhem 60 E4 SE Netherlands
Arnhem Land 117 E1 *Physical region,* Northern Territory, N Australia
Arno 71 C3 〰 C Italy
Arorae 121 J1 *Atoll,* Tungaru, W Kiribati
Arran, Isle of 63 C5 *Island,* SW Scotland, UK
Ar Raqqah 91 B2 N Syria
Arras 65 D1 N France
Arriaga 41 G5 SE Mexico
Ar Riyad *see* Riyadh
Ar Rub 'al Khali 91 D6 *Desert,* SW Asia
Ar Rustaq 91 F4 N Oman
Árta 75 D5 W Greece
Artashat 89 H3 S Armenia
Artemisa 45 B2 W Cuba
Arthurs's Pass 119 C6 *Pass,* South Island, NZ
Artigas 53 C5 N Uruguay
Art'ik 89 H2 W Armenia
Artois 65 D1 *Cultural region,* N France
Artsyz 77 D6 SW Ukraine
Artvin 89 G2 NE Turkey
Arua 111 C5 NW Uganda
Aruba 45 G7 *Dutch* ◇, S West Indies
Aru, Kepulauan 101 H7 *Island group,* E Indonesia
Arunachal Pradesh 99 F2 *Cultural region,* NE India
Arusha 111 D6 N Tanzania
Arviat 35 H5 Nunavut, C Canada
Arvidsjaur 59 D3 N Sweden
Arys' 86 C6 S Kazakhstan
Asadabad 93 G5 E Afghanistan
Asahi-dake 95 G1 ▲ N Japan
Asahikawa 95 F1 N Japan
Asamankese 108 D5 SE Ghana
Asansol 99 F4 NE India
Ascoli Piceno 71 D4 C Italy
Aseb 111 E3 SE Eritrea
A Serra de Outes 67 B1 NW Spain
Aşgabat 93 C3 ● C Turkmenistan
Ashburton 119 C6 South Island, NZ
Ashburton River 117 B4 〰 Western Australia
Ashdod 91 G6 W Israel
Asheville 37 E4 North Carolina, USA
Ashgabat 93 C3 ✈ C Turkmenistan
Ash Sharah 91 H7 ⛰ W Jordan
Ash Shihr 91 D7 SE Yemen
Asia 82 *Continent,*
Asinara 71 A5 *Island,* W Italy
Asipovichy 77 D2 C Belarus
Aşkale 89 F3 NE Turkey
Askersund 59 C6 C Sweden
Asmar 93 G5 E Afghanistan
Asmara 111 D2 ● C Eritrea
Assad, Lake 89 E5 ▧ N Syria
Assam 99 G3 *Cultural region,* NE India
Assamakka 108 E2 NW Niger
As Samawah 91 C3 S Iraq
Assen 60 F2 NE Netherlands
Assenede 60 B6 NW Belgium
As Sulaymaniyah 91 C2 NE Iraq
As Sulayyil 91 C5 S Saudi Arabia
Astana 86 C5 ● E Kazakhstan
Asti 71 B2 NW Italy
Astorga 67 C2 N Spain
Astoria 39 B1 Oregon, USA
Astrakhan' 79 B8 SW Russ. Fed.
Asturias 67 C1 *Autonomous community,* NW Spain
Astypálaia 75 F6 *Island,* Cyclades, Greece
Asunción 53 C4 ● S Paraguay
Aswân 106 J4 SE Egypt
Asyût 106 I3 C Egypt
Atacama Desert 53 A3 *Desert,* N Chile
Atamyrat 93 E4 E Turkmenistan
Atâr 108 B2 W Mauritania
Atas Bogd 97 D2 ▲ SW Mongolia
Atatürk Baraji 89 F4 ▧ S Turkey
Atbara 111 D2 〰 Eritrea/Sudan
Atbara 111 C2 NE Sudan
Atbasar 86 C5 N Kazakhstan
Ath 60 B7 SW Belgium
Athabasca 35 F6 〰 Alberta, SW Canada
Athabasca 35 G6 Alberta, SW Canada
Athabasca, Lake 35 G5 ◎ Alberta/Saskatchewan, SW Canada
Athens 75 E5 ● C Greece
Atherton 117 G2 Queensland, NE Australia
Athina *see* Athens
Athlone 63 B6 C Ireland
Ati 108 H3 C Chad
Atikokan 33 A4 Ontario, S Canada
Atka 35 A3 Atka Island, Alaska, USA
Atka 86 H3 E Russ. Fed.
Atlanta 37 E5 Georgia, USA
Atlantic Ocean 14 *Ocean*
Atlas Mountains 106 C2 ⛰ NW Africa
Atlasovo 86 I3 E Russ. Fed.
Atlin 35 E5 British Columbia, W Canada
At Ta'if 91 B5 W Saudi Arabia
Attawapiskat 33 C3 〰 Ontario, S Canada
Attawapiskat 33 C3 Ontario, C Canada
Attu Island 35 A2 *Island,* Aleutian Islands, Alaska, USA
Atyrau 86 B4 W Kazakhstan
Aubagne 65 E7 SE France
Aubange 60 E9 SE Belgium
Auch 65 C6 S France
Auckland 119 D2 North Island, NZ
Audincourt 65 F3 E France
Augathella 117 G4 Queensland, E Australia
Augsburg 69 C7 S Germany
Augusta 37 H2 Maine, USA
Augusta 117 B6 Western Australia
Augustów 73 G2 NE Poland
Auki 121 F3 Malaita, N Solomon Islands
Auob 112 C6 〰 Namibia/South Africa
Aurangabad 99 D5 C India
Auray 65 B3 NW France
Aurès, Massif de l' 80 D4 ⛰ NE Algeria
Aurillac 65 D5 C France
Aurora 37 D3 Illinois, USA
Aurora 39 E3 Colorado, USA
Aus 112 B6 SW Namibia
Austin 39 F5 Texas, USA
Australes, Îles 115 *Island group,* SW French Polynesia
Australia 117 D3 ◆ *Commonwealth Republic*
Australian Alps 117 G6 ⛰ SE Australia
Australian Capital Territory 117 G6 *Territory,* SE Australia
Austria 69 E8 ◆ *Republic,* C Europe
Auvergne 65 D5 *Region,* C France
Auxerre 65 D3 C France
Avarua 115 ○ Rarotonga, S Cook Islands
Aveiro 67 B3 W Portugal
Avellino 71 D6 S Italy
Avesta 59 C5 C Sweden
Aveyron 65 C6 〰 S France
Avezzano 71 D5 C Italy
Aviemore 63 D3 N Scotland, UK
Avignon 65 E6 SE France
Ávila 67 D3 C Spain
Avilés 67 C1 NW Spain
Avranches 65 B2 N France
Awaji-shima 95 E6 *Island,* SW Japan
Awash 111 E3 C Ethiopia
Awbari 106 F3 SW Libya
Axel 60 B6 SW Netherlands
Axel Heiberg Island 35 G1 *Island,* Nunavut, N Canada
Ayacucho 51 C6 S Peru
Ayagoz 86 D6 E Kazakhstan
Ayamonte 67 B5 S Spain
Aydarko'l Ko'li 93 F3 ◎ C Uzbekistan
Aydın 89 A4 SW Turkey
Ayers Rock *see* Uluru
Ayorou 108 D3 W Niger
'Ayoûn el 'Atroûs 108 B3 SE Mauritania
Ayr 63 C5 W Scotland, UK
Aytos 75 F3 E Bulgaria
Ayvalık 89 A3 W Turkey
Azahar, Costa del 67 F4 *Coastal region,* E Spain
Azaouâd 108 D2 *Desert,* C Mali
Azerbaijan 89 I2 ◆ *Republic,* SW Asia
Azoum, Bahr 108 H4 *Seasonal river,* SE Chad
Azov 86 A4 SW Russ. Fed.
Azov, Sea of 77 F6 *Sea,* NE Black Sea
Azuaga 67 C5 W Spain
Azuero, Península de 43 G7 *Peninsula,* S Panama
Azul 53 C6 E Argentina
Az Zarqa' 91 A2 NW Jordan
Az Zawiyah 106 F2 NW Libya

B

Baardheere 111 E5 SW Somalia
Baarle-Hertog 60 D5 N Belgium
Baarn 60 D4 C Netherlands
Babayevo 79 B4 NW Russ. Fed.
Babeldaob 101 H5 *Island,* N Palau
Bab el Mandeb 91 B7 *Strait,* Gulf of Aden/Red Sea
Babruysk 77 D3 E Belarus
Babuyan Channel 101 F3 *Channel,* N Philippines
Babuyan Island 101 F3 *Island,* N Philippines
Bacabal 51 G4 E Brazil
Bacău 77 C6 NE Romania
Bacheykava 77 D2 N Belarus
Back 35 G4 〰 Nunavut, N Canada
Badajoz 67 B4 W Spain
Baden-Baden 69 B6 SW Germany
Bad Freienwalde 69 E3 NE Germany
Badgastein 69 D8 NW Austria
Bad Hersfeld 69 C5 C Germany
Bad Homburg vor der Höhe 69 B5 W Germany
Bad Ischl 69 E7 N Austria
Bad Krozingen 69 B7 SW Germany
Badlands 39 E2 *Physical region,* North Dakota, USA
Badu Island 117 F1 *Island,* Queensland, NE Australia
Bad Vöslau 69 F7 NE Austria
Bafatá 108 A4 C Guinea-Bissau
Baffin Bay 35 I2 *Bay,* Canada/Greenland
Baffin Island 35 I3 *Island,* Nunavut, NE Canada
Bafing 108 B4 *Headstream,* W Africa
Bafoussam 108 F5 W Cameroon
Bafra 89 D2 N Turkey
Bagaces 43 E5 NW Costa Rica
Bagé 51 F9 S Brazil
Baghdad 91 C2 ● C Iraq
Baghlan 93 F4 NE Afghanistan
Baghran 93 E5 S Afghanistan
Bagoé 108 C4 〰 Ivory Coast/Mali
Baguio 101 F3 N Philippines
Bagzane, Monts 108 F3 ▲ N Niger
Bahamas 45 D2 ◆ *Commonwealth Republic,* N West Indies
Bahawalpur 99 C2 E Pakistan
Bahia 51 G5 *State,* E Brazil
Bahía Blanca 53 B6 E Argentina
Bahir Dar 111 D3 NW Ethiopia
Bahraich 99 E3 N India
Bahrain 91 D4 ◆ *Monarchy,* SW Asia
Bahr el Azraq *see* Blue Nile
Bahret Lut *see* Dead Sea
Bahushewsk 77 D2 NE Belarus
Baia Mare 77 B5 NW Romania
Baïbokoum 108 G5 SW Chad
Baie-Comeau 33 F4 Québec, SE Canada
Baikal, Lake 86 F5 ◎ S Russ. Fed.
Baile Átha Cliath *see* Dublin
Bailén 67 D5 S Spain
Ba Illi 108 G4 SW Chad
Bairiki 115 ● Tarawa, NW Kiribati
Bairnsdale 117 G6 Victoria, SE Australia
Baishan 97 H2 NE China
Baiyin 97 E3 N China
Baja 73 E8 S Hungary
Baja California *see* Lower California
Baja, Punta 121 C6 *Headland,* Easter Island, Chile
Bajram Curri 75 D3 N Albania
Bakala 108 H5 C CAR
Baker & Howland Islands 115 *US* ◇, C Pacific Ocean
Baker Lake 35 H4 Nunavut, N Canada
Bakersfield 39 B4 California, USA
Bäherden 93 C3 C Turkmenistan
Bakhtaran 91 C2 W Iran
Baki *see* Baku
Bakony 73 D8 ⛰ W Hungary
Baku 89 J2 ● E Azerbaijan
Balabac Strait 101 E5 *Strait,* Malaysia/Philippines
Balaguer 67 G2 NE Spain
Balaitous 65 B7 ▲ France/Spain
Balakovo 79 C7 W Russ. Fed.
Bala Morghab 93 E4 NW Afghanistan
Balashov 79 B6 W Russ. Fed.
Balaton, Lake 73 D8 ◎ Hungary
Balbina, Represa 51 E3 ▧ NW Brazil
Balboa 43 H6 C Panama
Balcarce 53 C6 E Argentina
Balclutha 119 B8 South Island, NZ
Baleares, Islas *see* Balearic Islands
Balearic Islands 67 G4 *Island group,* Spain
Baleine, Rivière à la 33 E2 〰 Québec, E Canada
Balen 60 D6 N Belgium
Baleshwar 99 F4 E India
Bali 101 E8 *Island,* C Indonesia
Balıkesir 89 A3 W Turkey
Balikpapan 101 E7 C Indonesia
Balkanabat 93 B3 W Turkmenistan
Balkan Mountains 75 E3 ⛰ Bulgaria/Serbia and Montenegro (Yugoslavia)
Balkh 93 F4 N Afghanistan
Balkhash 86 C6 SE Kazakhstan
Balkhash, Lake 86 C6 ◎ SE Kazakhstan
Balladonia 117 C5 Western Australia
Ballarat 117 F6 Victoria, SE Australia
Balsas 51 G4 E Brazil
Balsas, Río 41 E5 〰 S Mexico
Bălţi 77 D5 N Moldova
Baltic Sea 59 D7 *Sea,* N Europe
Baltimore 37 F4 Maryland, USA
Baluchistan 99 B3 *Province,* SW Pakistan
Balykchy 93 H2 NE Kyrgyzstan
Bam 91 F3 SE Iran
Bamako 108 C4 ● SW Mali
Bambari 108 H5 C CAR
Bamberg 69 C5 SE Germany
Bamenda 108 F5 W Cameroon
Banaba 121 H1 *Island,* W Kiribati
Bananga 99 H6 Andaman and Nicobar Islands, India
Bandaaceh 101 A5 Sumatra, W Indonesia
Bandama 108 C5 〰 S Ivory Coast
Bandarbeyla 111 G3 NE Somalia
Bandar-e 'Abbas 91 E4 S Iran
Bandarlampung 101 B7 Sumatra, W Indonesia
Bandar Seri Begawan 101 D5 ● N Brunei
Banda Sea 101 G7 *Sea,* E Indonesia
Bandırma 89 A2 NW Turkey
Bandundu 112 B2 W Dem. Rep. Congo
Bandung 101 C8 Java, C Indonesia
Bangalore 99 D6 S India
Bangassou 108 I5 SE CAR
Banggai, Kepulauan 101 F6 *Island group,* C Indonesia
Benghazi 106 G2 NE Libya
Banghazi *see* Benghazi
Bangka, Pulau 101 C7 *Island,* W Indonesia
Bangkok 101 B4 ● C Thailand
Bangladesh 99 G3 ◆ *Republic,* S Asia
Bangor 37 H2 Maine, USA
Bangor 63 C5 E Northern Ireland, UK
Bangor 63 D6 NW Wales, UK
Bangui 108 H5 ● SW CAR
Bangweulu, Lake 112 D3 ◎ N Zambia
Bani 108 C4 〰 S Mali
Banja Luka 75 C2 NW Bosnia and Herzegovina
Banjarmasin 101 E7 C Indonesia
Banjul 108 A3 ● W Gambia
Banks Island 35 F3 *Island,* Banks Island, NW Terr., NW Canada
Banks Islands 121 G4 *Island group,* N Vanuatu
Banks Peninsula 119 C6 *Peninsula,* South Island, NZ
Banks Strait 117 G7 *Strait,* SW Tasman Sea
Bankura 99 F4 NE India
Banmauk 101 A2 N Burma
Ban Nadou 101 C3 S Laos
Banská Bystrica 73 E6 C Slovakia
Bantry Bay 63 A7 *Bay,* SW Ireland
Banyak, Kepulauan 101 A6 *Island group,* NW Indonesia
Banyo 108 F5 NW Cameroon
Banyoles 67 H2 NE Spain
Baoji 97 E4 C China
Baoro 108 G5 W CAR
Baoshan 97 D5 SW China
Baotou 97 F3 N China
Ba'qubah 91 C2 C Iraq
Baraawe 111 E5 S Somalia
Baranavichy 77 C3 SW Belarus
Barbados 45 K6 ◆ *Commonwealth Republic,* SE West Indies
Barbastro 67 F2 NE Spain
Barbate de Franco 67 C6 S Spain
Barbuda 45 J4 *Island,* N Antigua and Barbuda
Barcaldine 117 G3 Queensland, E Australia
Barcelona 67 G2 E Spain
Barcelona 51 D1 NE Venezuela
Barcs 73 D9 SW Hungary
Bardaï 108 G2 N Chad
Bardejov 73 F6 NE Slovakia
Bareilly 99 E3 N India
Barendrecht 60 C4 SW Netherlands
Barentin 65 C2 N France
Barents Sea 79 C2 *Sea,* Arctic Ocean
Bari 71 E6 SE Italy
Barikowt 93 G4 NE Afghanistan
Barillas 43 A2 NW Guatemala
Barinas 51 C2 W Venezuela
Barisal 99 G4 S Bangladesh
Barisan, Pegunungan 101 B7 ⛰ Sumatra, W Indonesia
Barito, Sungai 101 E7 〰 C Indonesia
Barkly Tableland 117 E2 *Plateau,* Northern Territory/Queensland, N Australia
Bârlad 77 C6 E Romania
Bar-le-Duc 65 E2 NE France
Barlee, Lake 117 B5 ◎ Western Australia
Barlee Range 117 B4 ⛰ Western Australia
Barletta 71 E5 SE Italy
Barlinek 73 C3 W Poland
Barmouth 63 D7 NW Wales, UK
Barnaul 86 D5 C Russ. Fed.
Barnstaple 63 D8 SW England, UK
Baroda *see* Vadodara
Baroghil Pass 93 G4 *Pass,* Afghanistan/Pakistan
Barquisimeto 51 C1 NW Venezuela
Barra de Río Grande 43 E4 E Nicaragua
Barranca 51 B5 W Peru
Barrancabermeja 51 B2 N Colombia
Barranquilla 51 B1 N Colombia
Barreiro 67 A4 W Portugal
Barrier Range 117 F5 *Hill range,* NSW, SE Australia
Barrier Reef 43 C1 *Reef,* E Belize
Barrow 63 B7 〰 SE Ireland
Barrow 35 E2 Alaska, USA
Barrow-in-Furness 63 D6 NW England, UK
Barrow Island 117 A3 *Island,* Western Australia
Bartang 93 G4 〰 SE Tajikistan
Bartın 89 C2 N Turkey
Bartoszyce 73 F2 N Poland
Baruun-Urt 97 F2 E Mongolia
Barú, Volcán 43 F6 🌋 W Panama
Barva, Volcán 43 E6 🌋 NW Costa Rica
Barwon River 117 G5 〰 NSW, SE Australia
Barysaw 77 D2 NE Belarus
Basarabeasca 77 D6 SE Moldova
Basel 69 B7 NW Switzerland
Basilan 101 F5 *Island,* SW Philippines
Basingstoke 63 E8 S England, UK
Basle *see* Basel
Basque Country, The 67 E1 *Cultural region,* N Spain
Basra 91 D3 SE Iraq
Bassano del Grappa 71 C2 NE Italy
Bassein 101 A3 SW Burma
Basse-Terre 45 J5 ○ Basse Terre, SW Guadeloupe
Basseterre 45 J4 ● Saint Kitts, Saint Kitts and Nevis
Bassikounou 108 C3 SE Mauritania
Bass Strait 117 F7 *Strait,* SE Australia
Bassum 69 B3 NW Germany
Bastia 65 G5 Corsica, France
Bastogne 60 E8 SE Belgium
Basutoland *see* Lesotho
Bata 108 F6 NW Equatorial Guinea
Batangas 101 F4 N Philippines
Batavia *see* Jakarta
Batdambang 101 C4 NW Cambodia
Batéké, Plateaux 112 B2 *Plateau,* S Congo
Bath 63 D8 SW England, UK
Bathinda 99 D2 NW India
Bathurst 33 F4 New Brunswick, SE Canada
Bathurst 117 G6 NSW, SE Australia
Bathurst Island 35 G2 *Island,* Parry Islands, Nunavut, N Canada
Bathurst Island 117 C1 *Island,* Northern Territory, N Australia
Batin, Wadi al 91 C3 *Dry watercourse,* SW Asia
Batman 89 G4 SE Turkey
Batna 106 E1 NE Algeria
Baton Rouge 39 H5 Louisiana, USA
Batticaloa 99 E8 E Sri Lanka
Battipaglia 71 D6 S Italy
Bat'umi 89 G2 W Georgia
Batu Pahat 101 C6 Peninsular Malaysia
Bauchi 108 F4 NE Nigeria
Bautzen 69 E4 E Germany
Bavaria 69 C7 *Cultural region,* SE Germany
Bavarian Alps 69 C7 ⛰ Austria/Germany
Bavispe, Río 41 C2 〰 NW Mexico
Bawiti 106 I3 N Egypt
Bawku 108 D4 N Ghana
Bayamo 45 D3 E Cuba
Bayan Har Shan 97 D4 ⛰ C China
Bayanhongor 97 D2 C Mongolia
Bayano, Lago 43 H6 ◎ E Panama
Baydhabo 111 E5 SW Somalia
Bayern *see* Bavaria
Bayeux 65 C2 N France
Bay Islands 43 D2 *Island group,* N Honduras
Baykal, Ozero *see* Baikal, Lake
Baymak 79 D7 W Russ. Fed.
Bayonne 65 B6 SW France
Baýramaly 93 D4 S Turkmenistan
Bayreuth 69 C5 SE Germany
Bayrût *see* Beirut
Baza 67 E5 S Spain
Beagle Channel 53 B9 *Channel,* Argentina/Chile
Bear Lake 39 D2 ◎ NW USA
Beas de Segura 67 E5 S Spain
Beata, Isla 45 F5 *Island,* SW Dominican Republic
Beaufort Sea 35 F2 *Sea,* Arctic Ocean
Beaufort West 112 C7 SW South Africa
Beaumont 39 G5 Texas, USA
Beaune 65 E4 C France
Beauvais 65 D2 N France
Beaver River 39 F4 〰 Oklahoma, USA
Beawar 99 D3 N India
Béchar 106 D2 W Algeria
Bedford 63 E7 E England, UK
Bedum 60 F2 NE Netherlands
Be'er Menuha 91 H7 S Israel
Beernem 60 B6 NW Belgium
Be'ér Sheva' 91 G6 S Israel
Beesel 60 E6 SE Netherlands
Bega 117 G6 NSW, SE Australia
Beihai 97 F6 S China
Beijing 97 F3 ● E China
Beilen 60 E3 NE Netherlands
Beira 112 E5 C Mozambique
Beirut 91 A2 ● W Lebanon
Beja 67 B5 SE Portugal
Béjar 67 C3 N Spain
Békéscsaba 73 F8 SE Hungary
Bekobod 93 F3 E Uzbekistan
Belarus 77 C2 ◆ *Republic,* E Europe
Bełchatów 73 E4 C Poland
Belcher Islands 33 C2 *Island group,* Nunavut, SE Canada
Beledweyne 111 F4 C Somalia
Belém 51 G3 N Brazil
Belén 43 D5 SW Nicaragua
Belep, Îles 121 F6 *Island group,* W New Caledonia
Belfast 63 C5 *Political division capital,* E Northern Ireland, UK
Belfort 65 F3 E France
Belgaum 99 D6 W India
Belgium 60 B7 ◆ *Monarchy,* NW Europe
Belgorod 79 A6 W Russ. Fed.
Belgrade 75 D2 ● N Serbia and Montenegro (Yugoslavia)
Belgrano II 122 B4 *Argentinian research station,* Antarctica
Belitung, Pulau 101 C7 *Island,* W Indonesia
Belize 43 B2 ◆ *Commonwealth Republic,* Central America
Belize 43 B1 〰 Belize/Guatemala
Belize City 43 C1 NE Belize
Belkofski 35 B4 Alaska, USA
Belle Île 65 A3 *Island,* NW France
Belle Isle, Strait of 33 G3 *Strait,* Newfoundland, E Canada
Bellingham 39 B1 Washington, USA
Bellingshausen Sea 122 A4 *Sea,* Antarctica
Bellinzona 69 B8 S Switzerland
Bello 51 B2 W Colombia
Bellona 121 E3 *Island,* S Solomon Islands
Bellville 112 C7 SW South Africa
Belmopan 43 B2 ● C Belize
Belo Horizonte 51 G7 SE Brazil
Belomorsk 79 B3 NW Russ. Fed.
Beloretsk 79 D6 W Russ. Fed.
Belorussia *see* Belarus
Belozersk 79 B4 NW Russ. Fed.
Belukha, Gora 86 D5 ▲ Kazakhstan/Russ. Fed.
Belyy, Ostrov 86 D2 *Island,* N Russ. Fed.
Bemaraha 112 G5 ⛰ W Madagascar
Bemmel 60 E4 SE Netherlands
Benavente 67 C2 N Spain
Bend 39 B2 Oregon, USA
Bendigo 117 F6 Victoria, SE Australia
Benešov 73 B5 W Czech Republic
Benevento 71 D6 S Italy
Bengbu 97 G4 E China
Bengkulu 101 B7 Sumatra, W Indonesia
Benguela 112 B4 W Angola
Ben Hope 63 C3 ▲ N Scotland, UK
Beni 112 D1 NE Dem. Rep. Congo
Benidorm 67 F4 SE Spain
Beni-Mellal 106 C2 C Morocco
Benin 108 D4 ◆ *Republic,* W Africa
Benin, Bight of 108 E5 *Gulf,* W Africa
Benin City 108 E5 SW Nigeria
Beni, Río 53 A2 〰 N Bolivia
Beni Suef 106 I3 N Egypt
Ben Nevis 63 C4 ▲ N Scotland, UK
Benue 108 F5 〰 Cameroon/Nigeria
Beograd *see* Belgrade
Berat 75 D4 C Albania
Berau, Teluk 101 H7 *Bay,* E Indonesia
Berbera 111 F3 NW Somalia
Berbérati 108 G5 SW CAR

◆ Country ● Country capital ◇ Dependent territory ○ Dependent territory capital ⛰ Mountain range ▲ Mountain 🌋 Volcano 〰 River ◎ Lake ▧ Reservoir

CANARY ISLANDS

Berck-Plage 65 D1 N France
Berdyans'k 77 G6 SE Ukraine
Bereket 93 C3 W Turkmenistan
Berettyó 73 F8 ≈ Hungary/Romania
Berettyóújfalu 73 F7 E Hungary
Berezniki 79 D5 NW Russ. Fed.
Berga 67 G2 NE Spain
Bergamo 71 B2 N Italy
Bergen 60 C3 NW Netherlands
Bergen 69 D2 NE Germany
Bergen 59 A5 S Norway
Bergen see Mons
Bergerac 65 C5 SW France
Bergeyk 60 D6 S Netherlands
Bergse Maas 60 D5 ≈ S Netherlands
Beringen 60 D6 NE Belgium
Bering Sea 35 A2 *Sea,* N Pacific Ocean
Bering Strait 35 C2 *Strait,* Bering Sea/Chukchi Sea
Berja 67 E6 S Spain
Berkeley 39 B3 California, USA
Berkner Island 122 B4 *Island,* Antarctica
Berlin 37 G2 New Hampshire, USA
Berlin 69 D3 ● NE Germany
Bermejo, Río 53 B3 ≈ N Argentina
Bermeo 67 E1 N Spain
Bern 69 A8 ● W Switzerland
Bernau 69 D3 NE Germany
Bernburg 69 D4 C Germany
Berne see Bern
Berner Alpen 69 A8 ▲▲ SW Switzerland
Bernier Island 117 A4 *Island,* Western Australia
Berry 65 D3 *Cultural region,* C France
Berry Islands 45 C1 *Island group,* N Bahamas
Bertoua 108 G5 E Cameroon
Berwick-upon-Tweed 63 D4 N England, UK
Besançon 65 E4 E France
Betafo 112 G5 C Madagascar
Betanzos 67 B1 NW Spain
Bethlehem 112 D6 C South Africa
Bethlehem 91 H6 C West Bank
Béticos, Sistemas 67 D5 ▲▲ S Spain
Bétou 112 C1 N Congo
Bette, Pic 106 G4 ▲ S Libya
Beveren 60 C6 N Belgium
Beverley 63 E6 E England, UK
Beyla 108 C4 SE Guinea
Beyrouth see Beirut
Beyşehir Gölü 89 B4 ◎ C Turkey
Béziers 65 D6 S France
Bhadravati 99 D6 SW India
Bhagalpur 99 F3 NE India
Bhaktapur 99 F3 C Nepal
Bharuch 99 C4 W India
Bhavnagar 99 C4 W India
Bhopal 99 D4 C India
Bhubaneshwar 99 F4 E India
Bhusawal 99 D4 C India
Bhutan 99 G3 ◆ *Monarchy,* S Asia
Biak, Pulau 101 H6 *Island,* E Indonesia
Biała Podlaska 73 G3 E Poland
Białogard 73 C2 NW Poland
Białystok 73 G2 E Poland
Biarritz 65 B6 SW France
Bideford 63 D8 SW England, UK
Biel 69 A8 W Switzerland
Bielefeld 69 B4 NW Germany
Bielsko-Biała 73 E5 *Province,* S Poland
Bielsk Podlaski 73 G3 E Poland
Biên Hoa 101 C4 S Vietnam
Bienville, Lac 33 D3 ◎ Québec, C Canada
Bié Plateau 112 C4 *Plateau,* C Angola
Big Cypress Swamp 37 E7 *Wetland,* SE USA
Bihać 75 B2 NW Bosnia and Herzegovina
Bihar 99 F3 *State,* N India
Biharamulo 111 C6 NW Tanzania
Bihosava 77 C1 NW Belarus
Bijelo Polje 75 D3 SW Serbia and Montenegro (Yugoslavia)
Bikaner 99 D3 NW India
Bikin 86 H5 SE Russ. Fed.
Bilaspur 99 E4 C India
Biläsuvar 89 I3 SE Azerbaijan
Bila Tserkva 77 D4 N Ukraine
Bilauktaung Range 101 B4 ▲▲ Burma/Thailand
Bilbao 67 E1 N Spain
Bilecik 89 B3 NW Turkey
Billings 39 D2 Montana, USA
Bilma, Grand Erg de 108 G2 *Desert,* NE Niger
Biloela 117 H4 Queensland, E Australia
Biltine 108 H3 E Chad
Bilzen 60 D6 NE Belgium
Bimini Islands 45 C1 *Island group,* W Bahamas
Binche 60 C7 S Belgium
Binghamton 37 G3 New York, USA
Bingöl 89 F3 E Turkey
Bintulu 101 D6 East Malaysia
Binzhou 97 G3 E China
Bío Bío, Río 53 A6 ≈ C Chile
Bioco, Isla de 108 F6 *Island,* NW Equatorial Guinea
Birak 106 F3 C Libya
Birao 108 I4 NE CAR
Biratnagar 99 F3 SE Nepal
Birhar Sharif 99 F3 N India
Birjand 91 F2 E Iran
Birkenfeld 69 A6 SW Germany
Birkenhead 63 D6 NW England, UK
Birmingham 37 D5 Alabama, USA
Birmingham 63 E7 C England, UK
Bîr Mogreïn 108 B1 N Mauritania
Birnin Kebbi 108 E4 NW Nigeria
Birnin Konni 108 E3 SW Niger
Birobidzhan 86 H5 SE Russ. Fed.
Birsk 79 D6 W Russ. Fed.
Birżebbuġa 80 B6 SE Malta
Biscay, Bay of 65 B4 *Bay,* France/Spain
Bishah, Wadi 91 B5 *Dry watercourse,* C Saudi Arabia
Bishkek 93 H2 ✕ N Kyrgyzstan
Bishkek 93 H2 ● N Kyrgyzstan
Biskra 106 E1 NE Algeria
Biskupiec 73 F2 N Poland
Bislig 101 G5 S Philippines
Bismarck 39 F1 North Dakota, USA
Bismarck Archipelago 121 B1 *Island group,* NE PNG
Bismarck Sea 121 B1 *Sea,* W Pacific Ocean
Bissau 108 A4 ● W Guinea-Bissau
Bistriţa 77 B6 N Romania
Bitam 112 A1 N Gabon
Bitburg 69 A5 SW Germany
Bitlis 89 G4 SE Turkey
Bitola 75 D4 S FYR Macedonia
Bitonto 71 E6 SE Italy
Bitterfeld 69 D4 E Germany
Bitterroot Range 39 C1 ▲▲ NW USA
Biu 108 G4 E Nigeria
Biwa-ko 95 E6 ◎ Honshū, SW Japan
Bizerte 106 F1 N Tunisia
Bjørnøya 123 D5 *Island,* N Norway
Blackall 117 G4 Queensland, E Australia
Black Drin 75 D3 ≈ Albania/FYR Macedonia
Black Forest 69 B7 ▲▲ SW Germany
Blackpool 63 D6 NW England, UK
Black River 101 B2 ≈ China/Vietnam
Black Sea 54 *Sea,* Asia/Europe
Black Sea Lowland 77 E6 *Depression,* SE Europe
Black Volta 108 D4 ≈ W Africa
Blackwater 63 B7 ≈ S Ireland
Blagoevgrad 75 E3 W Bulgaria
Blagoveshchensk 86 H5 SE Russ. Fed.
Blanca, Bahía 53 B6 *Bay,* E Argentina
Blanca, Costa 67 F5 *Physical region,* SE Spain
Blanche, Lake 117 F4 ◎ South Australia
Blanc, Mont 65 F5 ▲ France/Italy
Blanco, Cape 39 A2 *Headland,* Oregon, USA
Blanes 67 H2 NE Spain
Blankenberge 60 B5 NW Belgium
Blankenheim 69 A5 W Germany
Blanquilla, Isla 45 I7 *Island,* N Venezuela
Blantyre 112 E4 S Malawi
Blaricum 60 D4 C Netherlands
Blenheim 119 C5 South Island, NZ
Blida 106 D1 N Algeria
Bloemfontein 112 D6 ● C South Africa
Blois 65 C3 C France
Bloomington 37 D4 Indiana, USA
Bloomsbury 117 G3 Queensland, NE Australia
Bluefields 43 E4 SE Nicaragua
Blue Mountains 117 G6 ▲▲ NSW, SE Australia
Blue Nile 111 C3 ≈ Ethiopia/Sudan
Blumenau 51 F8 S Brazil
Bo 108 B5 S Sierra Leone
Boaco 43 D4 S Nicaragua
Boa Vista 51 E3 NW Brazil
Bobaomby, Tanjona 112 G4 *Headland,* N Madagascar
Bobo-Dioulasso 108 C4 SW Burkina
Bocay 43 D3 N Nicaragua
Bocholt 69 A4 W Germany
Bochum 69 A4 W Germany
Bodaybo 86 F4 E Russ. Fed.
Boden 59 D3 N Sweden
Bodensee see Constance, Lake
Bodmin 63 C8 SW England, UK
Bodø 59 C2 C Norway
Bodrum 89 A4 SW Turkey
Boende 112 C2 C Dem. Rep. Congo
Bogatynia 73 B4 SW Poland
Boğazlıyan 89 D3 C Turkey
Bogia 121 B1 N PNG
Bogor 101 C8 Java, C Indonesia
Bogotá 51 B2 ● C Colombia
Bo Hai 97 G3 *Gulf,* NE China
Bohemia 73 B6 *Cultural and historical region,* W Czech Republic
Bohemian Forest 69 D6 ▲▲ C Europe
Böhmerwald see Bohemian Forest
Bohol Sea 101 F5 *Sea,* S Philippines
Bohoro Shan 97 B2 ▲▲ NW China
Boise 39 C2 Idaho, USA
Boizenburg 69 C3 N Germany
Bojnūrd 91 E1 N Iran
Boké 108 A4 W Guinea
Boknafjorden 59 A5 *Fjord,* S Norway
Bol 108 G3 W Chad
Bolesławiec 73 C4 SW Poland
Bolgatanga 108 D4 N Ghana
Bolivia 53 A2 ◆ *Republic,* W South America
Bollene 65 E6 SE France
Bollnäs 59 C5 C Sweden
Bollon 117 G4 Queensland, C Australia
Bologna 71 C3 N Italy
Bol'shevik, Ostrov 86 F2 *Island,* Severnaya Zemlya, N Russ. Fed.
Bol'shezemel'skaya Tundra 79 E3 *Physical region,* NW Russ. Fed.
Bol'shoy Lyakhovskiy, Ostrov 86 G2 *Island,* NE Russ. Fed.
Bolton 63 D6 NW England, UK
Bolu 89 C2 NW Turkey
Bolungarvík 59 A1 NW Iceland
Bolzano 71 C1 N Italy
Boma 112 B3 W Dem. Rep. Congo
Bombay see Mumbai
Bomu 112 C1 ≈ CAR/Dem. Rep. Congo
Bonaire 45 H7 *Island,* E Netherlands Antilles
Bonanza 43 E3 NE Nicaragua
Bonaparte Archipelago 117 B2 *Island group,* Western Australia
Bon, Cap 80 E4 *Headland,* N Tunisia
Bondo 112 C1 N Dem. Rep. Congo
Bondoukou 108 D5 E Ivory Coast
Bone, Teluk 101 F7 *Bay,* Celebes, C Indonesia
Bongaigaon 99 G3 NE India
Bongo, Massif des 108 H4 ▲▲ NE CAR
Bongor 108 G4 SW Chad
Bonifacio 65 G6 Corsica, France
Bonifacio, Strait of 71 A5 *Strait,* C Mediterranean Sea
Bonin Trench 15 *Undersea feature,* NW Pacific Ocean
Bonn 69 A5 W Germany
Boosaaso 111 F3 N Somalia
Boothia, Gulf of 35 H3 *Gulf,* Nunavut, NE Canada
Boothia Peninsula 35 H3 *Peninsula,* Nunavut, NE Canada
Boppard 69 B5 W Germany
Boquete 43 F6 W Panama
Boquillas 41 D2 NE Mexico
Bor 111 C4 S Sudan
Bor 75 D2 E Serbia and Montenegro (Yugoslavia)
Borah Peak 39 C2 ▲ Idaho, USA
Borås 59 C6 S Sweden
Bordeaux 65 B5 SW France
Bordj Omer Driss 106 E3 E Algeria
Børgefjelt 59 C3 ▲ C Norway
Borger 60 F2 NE Netherlands
Borgholm 59 C6 S Sweden
Borisoglebsk 79 B6 W Russ. Fed.
Borlänge 59 C5 C Sweden
Borne 60 E4 E Netherlands
Borneo 101 D7 *Island,* Brunei/Indonesia/Malaysia
Bornholm 59 C7 *Island,* E Denmark
Borovichi 79 A4 W Russ. Fed.
Bosanski Novi 75 B1 NW Bosnia and Herzegovina
Boskovice 73 C6 SE Czech Republic
Bosna 75 C2 ≈ N Bosnia and Herzegovina
Bosna I Herzegovina, Federacija 75 C2 ◆ *Republic,* SE Europe
Bosnia and Herzegovina 75 ◆ *Republic,* SE Europe
Boso-hanto 95 G6 *Peninsula,* Honshū, S Japan
Bosporus 88 B2 *Strait,* NW Turkey
Bossangoa 108 H5 C CAR
Bossembélé 108 H5 C CAR
Bosten Hu 97 C3 ◎ NW China
Boston 37 H3 Massachusetts, USA
Boston 63 E6 E England, UK
Botany Bay 117 H6 *Inlet,* NSW, SE Australia
Boteti 112 C5 ≈ N Botswana
Bothnia, Gulf of 59 D4 *Gulf,* N Baltic Sea
Botoşani 77 C5 NE Romania
Botrange 60 E7 ▲ E Belgium
Botswana 112 C5 ◆ *Republic,* S Africa
Bouar 108 G5 W CAR
Bou Craa 106 B3 NW Western Sahara
Bougainville Island 121 D2 *Island,* NE PNG
Bougaroun, Cap 80 D4 *Headland,* NE Algeria
Bougouni 108 C4 SW Mali
Boujdour 106 A3 W Western Sahara
Boulder 39 E3 Colorado, USA
Boulogne-sur-Mer 65 D1 N France
Boûmdeïd 108 B3 S Mauritania
Boundiali 108 C4 N Ivory Coast
Bourail 121 G6 C New Caledonia
Bourbonnais 65 D4 *Cultural region,* C France
Bourg-en-Bresse 65 E4 E France
Bourges 65 D4 C France
Bourgogne 65 E4 *Region,* E France
Bourke 117 G5 NSW, SE Australia
Bournemouth 63 E8 S England, UK
Boutilimit 108 A3 SW Mauritania
Bowen 117 G3 Queensland, NE Australia
Boxmeer 60 E5 SE Netherlands
Boysun 93 F3 S Uzbekistan
Bozen see Bolzano
Bozüyük 89 B3 NW Turkey
Brač 75 B3 *Island,* S Croatia
Bradford 63 E6 N England, UK
Braga 67 B2 NW Portugal
Bragança 67 C2 NE Portugal
Brahmanbaria 99 G3 E Bangladesh
Brahmapur 99 F5 E India
Brahmaputra 99 H3 ≈ S Asia
Brăila 77 D7 E Romania
Braine-le-Comte 60 C7 SW Belgium
Brampton 33 D6 Ontario, S Canada
Brandberg 112 B5 ▲ NW Namibia
Brandenburg 69 D3 NE Germany
Brandon 35 H7 Manitoba, S Canada
Braniewo 73 E2 N Poland
Brasília 51 G6 ● C Brazil
Braşov 77 C6 C Romania
Brasstown Bald 37 E5 ▲ Georgia, USA
Bratislava 73 D7 ● SW Slovakia
Bratsk 86 F5 C Russ. Fed.
Braunschweig 69 C4 N Germany
Brava, Costa 67 H2 *Coastal region,* NE Spain
Bravo, Río 41 D2 ≈ Mexico/USA
Brazil 51 C4 ◆ *Federal Republic,* South America
Brazil Basin 14 *Undersea feature,* W Atlantic Ocean
Brazilian Highlands 51 G6 ▲▲ E Brazil
Brazzaville 112 B2 ● S Congo
Brecht 60 C5 N Belgium
Breda 60 D5 S Netherlands
Bree 60 D6 NE Belgium
Bregalnica 75 E3 ≈ E FYR Macedonia
Bremen 69 B3 NW Germany
Bremerhaven 69 B3 NW Germany
Brenner Pass 69 C8 *Pass,* Austria/Italy
Brescia 71 C2 N Italy
Breslau see Wrocíaw
Bressanone 71 C1 N Italy
Brest 77 B3 SW Belarus
Brest 65 A2 NW France
Bretagne 65 B2 *Region,* NW France
Bria 108 H5 C CAR
Briançon 65 F5 SE France
Bridgeport 37 G3 Connecticut, USA
Bridgetown 45 K6 ● SW Barbados
Bridlington 63 E6 E England, UK
Bridport 63 D8 S England, UK
Brig 69 B8 SW Switzerland
Brighton 63 E8 SE England, UK
Brindisi 71 F6 SE Italy
Brisbane 117 H4 Queensland, E Australia
Bristol 63 D7 SW England, UK
Bristol Bay 35 C4 *Bay,* Alaska, USA
Bristol Channel 63 D8 *Inlet,* England/Wales, UK
British Columbia 35 E5 *Province,* SW Canada
British Guiana see Guyana
British Isles 54 *Island,* Ireland/United Kingdom
British Virgin Islands 45 I4 *UK* ◇, E West Indies
Brittany see Bretagne
Brive-la-Gaillarde 65 C5 C France
Brno 73 C6 SE Czech Republic
Brodeur Peninsula 35 H3 *Peninsula,* Baffin Island, Nunavut, NE Canada
Brodnica 73 E2 N Poland
Broek-in-Waterland 60 D3 C Netherlands
Broken Hill 117 F5 NSW, SE Australia
Bromberg see Bydgoszcz
Brooks Range 35 D3 ▲▲ Alaska, USA
Brookton 117 B5 Western Australia
Broome 117 C2 Western Australia
Brownsville 39 G6 Texas, USA
Bruges 60 B6 NW Belgium
Brugge see Bruges
Brummen 60 E4 E Netherlands
Brunei 101 D5 ◆ *Monarchy,* SE Asia
Brunner, Lake 119 C6 ◎ South Island, NZ
Brus Laguna 43 E2 E Honduras
Brussel/Bruxelles see Brussels
Brussels 60 C6 ● C Belgium
Bryan 39 G5 Texas, USA
Bryansk 79 A6 W Russ. Fed.
Brzeg 73 D4 SW Poland
Buala 121 E2 E Solomon Islands
Bucaramanga 51 C2 N Colombia
Buchanan 108 B5 SW Liberia
Bucharest 77 C7 ● S Romania
Bucureşti see Bucharest
Budapest 73 E7 ● N Hungary
Budaun 99 E3 N India
Buenaventura 51 B3 W Colombia
Buena Vista 53 B2 C Bolivia
Buenos Aires 43 F6 SE Costa Rica
Buenos Aires 53 C5 ● E Argentina
Buenos Aires, Lago 53 A8 ◎ Argentina/Chile
Buffalo 37 F3 New York, USA
Buffalo Narrows 35 G6 Saskatchewan, C Canada
Bug 77 B3 ≈ E Europe
Buguruslan 79 D6 W Russ. Fed.
Bujalance 67 D5 S Spain
Bujanovac 75 D3 SE Serbia and Montenegro (Yugoslavia)
Bujumbura 111 B6 ● W Burundi
Buka Island 121 D2 *Island,* NE PNG
Bukavu 112 D2 E Dem. Rep. Congo
Bukoba 111 C5 NW Tanzania
Bülach 69 B7 NW Switzerland
Bulawayo 112 D5 SW Zimbabwe
Bulgaria 75 E3 ◆ *Republic,* SE Europe
Bulukumba 101 E7 Celebes, C Indonesia
Bumba 112 C1 N Dem. Rep. Congo
Bunbury 117 B6 Western Australia
Bundaberg 117 H4 Queensland, E Australia
Bungo-suido 95 D7 *Strait,* SW Japan
Bünyan 89 D3 C Turkey
Buon Ma Thuot 101 C4 S Vietnam
Buraydah 91 C4 N Saudi Arabia
Burco 111 F3 NW Somalia
Burdur 89 B4 SW Turkey
Burdur Gölü 89 B4 *Salt lake,* SW Turkey
Bure 111 D3 NW Ethiopia
Burgas 75 G3 E Bulgaria
Burgaski Zaliv 89 A1 *Gulf,* E Bulgaria
Burgos 67 D2 N Spain
Burgundy see Bourgogne
Burhan Budai Shan 97 D4 ▲▲ C China
Burjassot 67 F4 E Spain
Burketown 117 F2 Queensland, NE Australia
Burkina 108 C4 ◆ *Republic,* W Africa
Burkina Faso see Burkina
Burma 101 A2 ◆ *military dictatorship,* SE Asia
Burnie 117 F7 Tasmania, SE Australia
Burnside 35 G4 ≈ Nunavut, NW Canada
Burriana 67 F3 E Spain
Bursa 89 B3 NW Turkey
Burundi 111 B6 ◆ *Republic,* C Africa
Buru, Pulau 101 F7 *Island,* E Indonesia
Bushire 91 D3 S Iran
Busselton 117 B6 Western Australia
Buta 112 D1 N Dem. Rep. Congo
Buton, Pulau 101 F7 *Island,* C Indonesia
Button Islands 33 E1 *Island group,* Québec, NE Canada
Butuan 101 F5 S Philippines
Buulobarde 111 F4 C Somalia
Buur Gaabo 111 E5 S Somalia
Buxoro 93 E3 C Uzbekistan
Buynaksk 79 B9 SW Russ. Fed.
Büyükmenderes Nehri 89 A4 ≈ SW Turkey
Buzău 77 C7 SE Romania
Büzmeýin 93 C3 C Turkmenistan
Buzuluk 79 C6 W Russ. Fed.
Bydgoszcz 73 D3 W Poland
Byelaruskaya Hrada 77 C3 *Ridge,* N Belarus
Byerezino 77 D2 ≈ C Belarus
Bytâa 73 D6 NW Slovakia
Bytów 73 D2 N Poland
Byzantium see Istanbul

C

Caazapá 53 C4 S Paraguay
Cabañaquinta 67 C1 N Spain
Cabanatuan 101 F3 N Philippines
Cabinda 112 B3 *Province,* NW Angola
Cabinda 112 B2 NW Angola
Cabora Bassa, Lake 112 E4 ▣ NW Mozambique
Caborca 41 B2 NW Mexico
Cabot Strait 33 G4 *Strait,* E Canada
Cabrera 67 G4 *Island,* Balearic Islands, Spain
Cáceres 67 C4 W Spain
Cachimbo, Serra do 51 E4 ▲▲ C Brazil
Caconda 112 B4 C Angola
Čadca 73 D6 N Slovakia
Cadiz 101 F4 C Philippines
Cádiz 67 C6 SW Spain
Cádiz 67 C6 *Province,* SW Spain
Cádiz, Golfo de see Cadiz, Gulf of
Cadiz, Gulf of 67 B6 *Gulf,* Portugal/Spain
Caen 65 C2 N France
Cafayate 53 B4 N Argentina
Cagayan de Oro 101 F5 S Philippines
Cagliari 71 A6 Sardinia, Italy
Caguas 45 I4 E Puerto Rico
Cahors 65 C6 S France
Cahul 77 D6 S Moldova
Caicos Passage 45 F3 *Strait,* Bahamas/Turks and Caicos Islands
Cairns 117 G2 Queensland, NE Australia
Cairo 106 I2 ● N Egypt
Cajamarca 51 B5 NW Peru
Calabar 108 F5 S Nigeria
Calahorra 67 E2 N Spain
Calais 65 D1 N France
Calama 53 A3 N Chile
Călăraşi 77 C7 SE Romania
Calatayud 67 E3 NE Spain
Calbayog 101 F4 Samar, C Philippines
Calcutta see Kolkata
Caldas da Rainha 67 A4 W Portugal
Caldera 53 A4 N Chile
Caledonia 43 C1 N Belize
Caleta Olivia 53 B8 SE Argentina
Calgary 35 G7 Alberta, SW Canada
Cali 51 B3 W Colombia
Calicut 99 D7 SW India
California 39 B3 *State,* W USA
California, Gulf of 41 B2 *Gulf,* NE Mexico
Callabonna, Lake 117 F5 ◎ South Australia
Callao 51 B5 W Peru
Callosa de Segura 67 F5 E Spain
Caloundra 117 H4 Queensland, E Australia
Caltanissetta 71 D8 Sicily, Italy
Caluula 111 G3 NE Somalia
Camabatela 112 B3 NW Angola
Camacupa 112 B4 C Angola
Camagüey 45 D3 C Cuba
Camagüey, Archipiélago de 45 D3 *Island group,* C Cuba
Camargue 65 E6 *Physical region,* SE France
Ca Mau 101 C5 S Vietnam
Cambodia 101 C4 ◆ *Republic,* SE Asia
Cambrai 65 D1 N France
Cambridge 63 F7 E England, UK
Cambridge 119 D3 North Island, NZ
Cambridge Bay 35 G4 Victoria Island, Nunavut, NW Canada
Cameroon 108 F5 ◆ *Republic,* W Africa
Cameroon Mountain 108 E5 ▲ SW Cameroon
Camocim 51 H4 E Brazil
Camorta 99 H6 *Island,* Nicobar Islands, India
Campamento 43 D3 C Honduras
Campbell, Cape 119 D5 *Headland,* South Island, NZ
Campbell Plateau 15 *Undersea feature,* SW Pacific Ocean
Campbell River 35 E7 Vancouver Island, British Columbia, SW Canada
Campeche 41 H4 SE Mexico
Campeche, Bay of 41 G4 *Bay,* E Mexico
Câm Pha 101 C2 N Vietnam
Campina Grande 51 I5 E Brazil
Campinas 51 G7 S Brazil
Campobasso 71 D5 C Italy
Campo de Criptana 67 D4 C Spain
Campo Grande 51 F7 SW Brazil
Campos 51 H7 SE Brazil
Cam Ranh 101 D4 S Vietnam
Canada 29 ◆ *Commonwealth Republic,* N North America
Canada Basin 123 B3 *Undersea feature,* Arctic Ocean
Canadian River 39 F4 ≈ SW USA
Canadian Shield 33 B3 *Physical region,* Canada
Çanakkale 89 A2 W Turkey
Cananea 41 B2 NW Mexico
Canarreos, Archipiélago de los 45 B3 *Island group,* W Cuba
Canary Islands 106 A2 *Island group,* Spain, NE Atlantic Ocean

CAR Central African Republic FYR Former Yugoslavian Rebublic NSW New South Wales NZ New Zealand PNG Papua New Guinea Russ. Fed. Russian Federation UAE United Arab Emirates UK United Kingdom USA United States of America 127

128

Corinth, Isthmus of 75 D5 *Isthmus,* S Greece
Corinto 43 C4 NW Nicaragua
Cork 63 B7 S Ireland
Çorlu 89 A2 NW Turkey
Corner Brook 33 G4 Newfoundland, E Canada
Corn Islands 43 F4 *Island group,* SE Nicaragua
Cornwallis Island 35 G2 *Island,* Parry Islands, Nunavut, N Canada
Coro 51 C1 NW Venezuela
Corocoro 53 A2 W Bolivia
Coromandel 119 D2 North Island, NZ
Coronado, Bahía de 43 E6 *Bay,* S Costa Rica
Coronel Dorrego 53 B6 E Argentina
Corozal 43 C1 N Belize
Corpus Christi 39 G5 Texas, USA
Corrib, Lough 63 A6 ◎ W Ireland
Corrientes 53 C4 NE Argentina
Corsica 65 F7 *Island* France, C Mediterranean Sea
Cortegana 67 B5 S Spain
Cortés 43 F6 SE Costa Rica
Cortina d'Ampezzo 71 D2 NE Italy
Coruche 67 B4 C Portugal
Çoruh Nehri 89 F2 ≈ Georgia/Turkey
Çorum 89 D2 N Turkey
Cosenza 71 E7 SW Italy
Cosne-Cours-sur-Loire 65 D3 C France
Costa Rica 43 E5 ◆ *Republic,* Central America
Cotagaita 53 B3 S Bolivia
Côte d'Azur 65 F7 ✕ SE France
Côte d'Or 65 E3 *Cultural region,* C France
Cotonou 108 E5 S Benin
Cotswold Hills 63 E7 *Hill range,* S England, UK
Cottbus 69 E4 E Germany
Council Bluffs 39 G2 Iowa, USA
Courland Lagoon 59 D7 *Lagoon,* Lithuania/Russ. Fed.
Coutances 65 B2 N France
Couvin 60 C8 S Belgium
Coventry 63 E7 C England, UK
Covilhã 67 B3 E Portugal
Cowan, Lake 117 C5 ◎ Western Australia
Cozumel, Isla 41 I4 *Island,* SE Mexico
Cracow *see* Kraków
Cradock 112 D7 S South Africa
Craiova 77 B7 SW Romania
Cranbrook 35 F7 British Columbia, SW Canada
Crawley 63 E8 SE England, UK
Cremona 71 B2 N Italy
Cres 75 B2 *Island,* W Croatia
Crescent City 39 B2 California, USA
Crete 75 F7 *Island,* Greece
Créteil 65 D2 N France
Crete, Sea of 75 F6 *Sea,* Greece, Aegean Sea
Creuse 65 C4 ≈ C France
Crewe 63 D6 C England, UK
Crimea 77 F6 *Peninsula,* SE Ukraine
Cristóbal 43 H6 C Panama
Crna Reka 75 D4 ≈ S FYR Macedonia
Croatia 75 B1 ◆ *Republic,* SE Europe
Croker Island 117 D1 *Island,* Northern Territory, N Australia
Cromwell 119 B7 South Island, NZ
Crooked Island 45 E2 *Island,* SE Bahamas
Crooked Island Passage 45 E2 *Channel,* SE Bahamas
Crookston 39 F1 Minnesota, USA
Crotone 71 E7 SW Italy
Croydon 63 E7 SE England, UK
Crozet Islands 15 *Island group,* French Southern and Antarctic Territories
Csorna 73 D7 NW Hungary
Csurgó 73 D8 SW Hungary
Cuando 112 C4 ≈ S Africa
Cuango 112 B3 ≈ Angola/Dem. Rep. Congo
Cuanza 112 B3 ≈ C Angola
Cuauhtémoc 41 C2 N Mexico
Cuautla 41 F5 S Mexico
Cuba 45 D3 ◆ *Republic,* W West Indies
Cubal 112 B4 W Angola
Cubango 112 B4 ≈ S Africa
Cubango 112 B4 SW Angola
Cúcuta 51 C2 N Colombia
Cuddapah 99 E6 S India
Cuenca 67 E3 C Spain
Cuenca 51 B4 S Ecuador
Cuernavaca 41 F5 S Mexico
Cuiabá 51 E6 SW Brazil
Cuijck 60 E5 SE Netherlands
Cuito 112 C4 ≈ SE Angola
Culiacán 41 C3 C Mexico
Cullera 67 F4 E Spain
Cumberland, Lake 37 E4 ▣ Kentucky, USA
Cumberland Sound 35 J3 *Inlet,* Baffin Island, Nunavut, NE Canada
Cumpas 41 C2 NW Mexico
Cunene 112 B4 ≈ Angola/Namibia
Cuneo 71 A3 NW Italy
Cunnamulla 117 G4 Queensland, E Australia
Curaçao 45 H7 *Island,* Netherlands Antilles
Curicó 53 A6 C Chile
Curitiba 51 F8 S Brazil
Curtis Island 117 H4 *Island,* Queensland, SE Australia
Cusco 51 C6 C Peru
Cusset 65 D4 C France
Cuttack 99 F4 E India
Cuxhaven 69 B2 NW Germany
Cyclades 75 F6 *Island group,* SE Greece
Cymru *see* Wales
Cyprus 80 C5 ◆ *Republic,* E Mediterranean Sea
Czechoslovakia *see* Czech Republic/Slovakia
Czech Republic 73 B6 ◆ *Republic,* C Europe
Częstochowa 73 E5 S Poland
Człuchów 73 D2 NW Poland

D

Dąbrowa Tarnowska 73 F5 SE Poland
Dacca *see* Dhaka
Dagana 108 A3 N Senegal
Dagda 59 F6 SE Latvia
Dagupan 101 F3 N Philippines
Dahm, Ramlat 91 C6 *Desert,* NW Yemen
Daimiel 67 D4 C Spain
Dakar 108 A3 ● W Senegal
Dakoro 108 E3 S Niger
Dalaman 89 A5 SW Turkey
Dalandzadgad 97 E2 S Mongolia
Da Lat 101 C4 S Vietnam
Dalby 117 H4 Queensland, E Australia
Dali 97 D5 SW China
Dalian 97 G3 NE China
Dallas 39 G4 Texas, USA
Dalmatia 75 B2 *Cultural region,* S Croatia
Daly Waters 117 E2 Northern Territory, N Australia
Daman 99 C4 W India
Damara 108 H5 S CAR
Damascus 91 A2 ● SW Syria
Damavand, Qolleh-ye 91 D2 ▲ N Iran
Dampier 117 B3 Western Australia
Dampier, Selat 101 G6 *Strait,* E Indonesia
Damqawt 91 E6 E Yemen
Damxung 97 C4 W China
Danakil Desert 111 E3 *Desert,* E Africa
Danané 108 C5 W Ivory Coast
Da Nang 101 C3 C Vietnam
Dandong 97 G3 NE China
Daneborg 123 B6 N Greenland
Danghara 93 F4 SW Tajikistan
Dangriga 43 C2 E Belize
Danlí 43 D3 S Honduras
Danmark *see* Denmark
Dannenberg 69 C3 N Germany
Dannevirke 119 D4 North Island, NZ
Danube 54 ≈ C Europe
Danubian Plain 75 E2 *Plain,* N Bulgaria
Danzhou 97 F6 S China
Danzig, Gulf of 73 D1 *Gulf,* N Poland
Dardanelles 89 A3 *Strait,* Marmara Denizi/Mediterranean Sea
Dar es Salaam 111 D6 E Tanzania
Darfield 119 C6 South Island, NZ
Darfur 111 B3 *Cultural region,* W Sudan
Darhan 97 E2 N Mongolia
Darien, Gulf of 51 B2 *Gulf,* S Caribbean Sea
Darién, Serranía del 43 I6 ▲ Colombia/Panama
Darjiling 99 G3 NE India
Darling River 117 F5 ≈ NSW, SE Australia
Darlington 63 E5 N England, UK
Darmstadt 69 B5 SW Germany
Darnah 106 H2 NE Libya
Darnley, Cape 122 E4 *Headland,* Antarctica
Daroca 67 E3 NE Spain
Daroot-Korgon 93 G3 SW Kyrgyzstan
Dartmouth 33 G5 Nova Scotia, SE Canada
Daru 121 A3 SW PNG
Darvishan 93 E6 S Afghanistan
Darwaza 93 C3 C Turkmenistan
Darwin 117 D1 *Territory capital,* Northern Territory, N Australia
Darwin, Isla 51 A6 *Island,* Galapagos Islands, Ecuador
Daşogz 93 D2 N Turkmenistan
Datong 97 F3 C China
Daugava *see* Western Dvina
Daugavpils 59 F7 SE Latvia
Dauphiné 65 E6 *Cultural region,* E France
Davangere 99 D6 W India
Davao 101 F5 S Philippines
Davao Gulf 101 G5 *Gulf,* S Philippines
Davenport 39 H2 Iowa, USA
David 43 F7 W Panama
Davis 122 E4 *Australian research station,* Antarctica
Davis Sea 122 E4 *Sea,* Antarctica
Davis Strait 35 J2 *Strait,* Baffin Bay/Labrador Sea
Dax 65 B6 SW France
Dayton 37 E3 Ohio, USA
Daytona Beach 37 E6 Florida, USA
De Aar 112 C7 C South Africa
Dead Sea 91 H6 *Salt lake,* Israel/Jordan
Deán Funes 53 B5 C Argentina
Death Valley 39 C4 *Valley,* California, USA
De Bilt 60 D4 C Netherlands
Debrecen 73 F7 E Hungary
Decatur 37 D3 Illinois, USA
Deccan 99 D5 *Plateau,* C India
Děčín 73 B5 NW Czech Republic
Dedemsvaart 60 E3 E Netherlands
Dee 63 D3 ≈ NE Scotland, UK
Deering 35 D3 Alaska, USA
Deggendorf 69 D6 SE Germany
Deh Shu 93 D6 S Afghanistan
Deinze 60 B6 NW Belgium
Dékoa 108 H5 C CAR
Delaram 93 E5 SW Afghanistan
Delaware 37 G4 *State,* NE USA
Delft 60 C4 W Netherlands
Delfzijl 60 F2 NE Netherlands
Delgo 111 C1 N Sudan
Delhi 99 D3 N India
Delicias 41 D2 N Mexico
Delmenhorst 69 B3 NW Germany
Del Norte 41 C2 California, USA
Demba 112 C2 C Dem. Rep. Congo
Dembia 108 I5 SE CAR
Demchok 99 E2 *Disputed region,* China/India
Demmin 69 D2 NE Germany
Dêmqog 97 A4 *Disputed region,* China/India
Denali *see* McKinley, Mount
Dender 60 B7 ≈ W Belgium
Denekamp 60 F3 E Netherlands
Den Ham 60 F3 E Netherlands
Denham 117 A4 Western Australia
Den Helder 60 C2 NW Netherlands
Dénia 67 F4 E Spain
Deniliquin 117 F6 NSW, SE Australia
Denizli 89 B4 SW Turkey
Denmark 59 B7 ◆ *Monarchy,* N Europe
Denov 93 F3 S Uzbekistan
Denpasar 101 E8 Bali, C Indonesia
Denton 39 G4 Texas, USA
D'Entrecasteaux Islands 121 C3 *Island group,* SE PNG
Denver 39 E3 Colorado, USA
Dera Ghazi Khan 99 C2 C Pakistan
Đeravica 75 D3 ▲ S Serbia and Montenegro (Yugoslavia)
Derbent 79 B9 SW Russ. Fed.
Derby 63 E6 C England, UK
Derby 117 C2 Western Australia
Derg, Lough 63 A6 ◎ W Ireland
Dese 111 E3 N Ethiopia
Deseado, Río 53 B8 ≈ S Argentina
Des Moines 39 G2 Iowa, USA
Desna 79 A6 ≈ Russian Federation/Ukraine
Dessau 69 D4 E Germany
Detroit 37 E3 Michigan, USA
Deurne 60 E5 SE Netherlands
Deva 77 B6 W Romania
Deventer 60 E4 E Netherlands
Devon Island 35 H2 *Island,* Parry Islands, Nunavut, NE Canada
Devonport 117 F7 Tasmania, SE Australia
Devrek 89 C2 N Turkey
Dezful 91 D2 SW Iran
Dezhou 97 G3 E China
Değirmenlik *see* Kythrea
Dhaka 99 G4 ● C Bangladesh
Dhanbad 99 F4 NE India
Dhekelia Soverign Base Area 80 D6 *Air base,* SE Cyprus
Dhuusa Marreeb 111 F4 C Somalia
Diamantina, Chapada 51 H5 ▲ E Brazil
Dibrugarh 99 H3 NE India
Dickinson 39 E1 North Dakota, USA
Didymóteicho 75 F3 NE Greece
Diekirch 60 E8 C Luxembourg
Diepenbeek 60 D6 NE Belgium
Diepholz 69 B3 NW Germany
Dieppe 65 C1 N France
Dieren 60 E4 E Netherlands
Differdange 60 E9 SW Luxembourg
Digne 65 E6 SE France
Digoin 65 E4 C France
Digul, Sungai 101 I7 ≈ E Indonesia
Dijon 65 E4 C France
Dikhil 111 E3 SW Djibouti
Dikson 86 E2 N Russ. Fed.
Díkti 75 F7 ▲ Crete, Greece
Dili 101 F8 ● N East Timor
Dilia 108 G3 ≈ SE Niger
Dilling 111 C3 C Sudan
Dilolo 112 C3 S Dem. Rep. Congo
Dimashq *see* Damascus
Dimitrovgrad 75 F3 S Bulgaria
Dimitrovgrad 79 C6 W Russ. Fed.
Dimovo 75 E2 NW Bulgaria
Dinajpur 99 G3 NW Bangladesh
Dinan 65 B2 NW France
Dinant 60 D8 S Belgium
Dinar 89 B4 SW Turkey
Dinaric Alps 75 C2 ▲ Bosnia and Herzegovina/Croatia
Dindigul 99 D7 SE India
Dingle Bay 63 A7 *Bay,* SW Ireland
Dinguiraye 108 B4 N Guinea
Diourbel 108 A3 W Senegal
Dire Dawa 111 E3 E Ethiopia
Dirk Hartog Island 117 A4 *Island,* Western Australia
Disappointment, Lake 117 B3 *Salt lake,* Western Australia
Divinópolis 51 G7 SE Brazil
Divo 108 C5 S Ivory Coast
Diyarbakır 89 F4 SE Turkey
Djambala 112 B2 C Congo
Djanet 106 E4 SE Algeria
Djelfa 106 E1 N Algeria
Djéma 108 I5 E CAR
Djerba 106 F2 *Island,* E Tunisia
Djérem 108 G5 ≈ C Cameroon
Djibouti 111 E3 ● E Djibouti
Djibouti 111 E3 ◆ *Republic,* E Africa
Djourab, Erg du 108 H3 *Dunes,* N Chad
Djúpivogur 59 B1 SE Iceland
Dnieper 54 ≈ E Europe
Dnieper Lowland 77 E4 *Lowlands,* Belarus/Ukraine
Dniester 77 D5 ≈ Moldova/Ukraine
Dniprodzerzhyns'k 77 F5 E Ukraine
Dniprodzerzhyns'ke Vodoskhovyshche 77 F5 ▣ C Ukraine
Dnipropetrovs'k 77 F5 E Ukraine
Dniprorudne 77 F5 SE Ukraine
Doba 108 G4 S Chad
Döbeln 69 D4 E Germany
Doberai Peninsula 101 G7 *Peninsula,* E Indonesia
Dobre Miasto 73 E2 N Poland
Dobrich 75 G2 NE Bulgaria
Dodecanese 75 F6 *Island group,* SE Greece
Dodekánisa *see* Dodecanese
Dodge City 39 F3 Kansas, USA
Dodoma 111 D6 ● C Tanzania
Dogai Coring 97 C4 ◎ W China
Dogo 95 D6 *Island,* Oki-shotō, SW Japan
Dogondoutchi 108 E3 SW Niger
Doğubayazıt 89 H3 E Turkey
Doğu Karadeniz Dağları 89 F2 ▲ NE Turkey
Doha 91 D4 ● C Qatar
Dokkum 60 E2 N Netherlands
Dôle 65 E4 E France
Dolisie 112 B2 S Congo
Dolomites 71 C2 ▲ Italy
Dolomiti *see* Dolomites
Dolores 43 B2 N Guatemala
Dolores 53 C5 SW Uruguay
Dolores 53 C6 E Argentina
Dolores Hidalgo 41 E4 C Mexico
Dombås 59 B4 S Norway
Domeyko 53 A4 N Chile
Dominica 45 K5 ◆ *Republic,* E West Indies
Dominican Republic 45 F5 ◆ *Republic,* C West Indies
Don 79 B7 ≈ SW Russ. Fed.
Donau *see* Danube
Donauwörth 69 C6 S Germany
Donawitz 69 E7 SE Austria
Donbass 77 G5 *Industrial region,* Russ. Fed./Ukraine
Don Benito 67 C4 W Spain
Doncaster 63 E6 N England, UK
Dondo 112 B3 NW Angola
Donegal 63 B5 NW Ireland
Donegal Bay 63 B5 *Bay,* NW Ireland
Donets 79 A7 ≈ Russ. Fed./Ukraine
Donets'k 77 G5 E Ukraine
Dongfang 97 F6 S China
Dongola 111 C1 N Sudan
Dongou 112 B1 NE Congo
Dongting Hu 97 F5 ◎ S China
Donostia *see* Donostia-San Sebastián
Donostia-San Sebastián 67 E1 N Spain
Doolow 111 E4 SE Ethiopia
Dordogne 65 C5 *Cultural region,* SW France
Dordogne 65 C5 ≈ W France
Dordrecht 60 C5 SW Netherlands
Dorotea 59 C3 N Sweden
Dorre Island 117 A4 *Island,* Western Australia
Dortmund 69 B4 W Germany
Dos Hermanas 67 C5 S Spain
Dotnuva 59 E7 C Lithuania
Douai 65 D1 N France
Douala 108 F5 W Cameroon
Douglas 63 C6 ○ E Isle of Man
Douro 67 B3 ≈ Portugal/Spain
Dover 37 G4 Delaware, USA
Dover 63 F8 SE England, UK
Dover, Strait of 65 D1 *Strait,* England, UK/France
Dovrefjell 59 B4 *Plateau,* S Norway
Downpatrick 63 C5 SE Northern Ireland, UK
Dozen 95 D6 *Island,* Oki-shotō, SW Japan
Drachten 60 E2 N Netherlands
Dra, Hamada du 106 C2 *Plateau,* W Algeria
Drahichyn 77 C3 SW Belarus
Drakensberg 112 D7 ▲ Lesotho/South Africa
Drake Passage 53 B9 *Passage,* Atlantic Ocean/Pacific Ocean
Dráma 75 E4 NE Greece
Drammen 59 B5 S Norway
Drau *see* Drava
Drava 73 C9 ≈ C Europe
Drave *see* Drava
Drawsko Pomorskie 73 C2 NW Poland
Dresden 69 D5 E Germany
Drina 75 D2 ≈ Bosnia and Herzegovina/Serbia and Montenegro (Yugoslavia)
Drinit, Lumi i 75 D3 ≈ NW Albania
Drobeta-Turnu Severin 77 B7 SW Romania
Drogheda 63 C6 NE Ireland
Drôme 65 E6 *Cultural region,* SE France
Dronning Maud Land 122 C3 *Physical region,* Antarctica
Drummondville 33 E5 Québec, SE Canada
Dryden 33 A4 Ontario, C Canada
Drysa 77 D1 ≈ N Belarus
Duarte, Pico 45 G4 ▲ C Dominican Republic
Dubai 91 E4 *Emirate capital,* NE UAE
Dubawnt 35 G5 ≈ NW Terr., NW Canada
Dubbo 117 G5 NSW, SE Australia
Dublin 63 C6 ● E Ireland
Dubno 77 C4 NW Ukraine
Dubrovnik 75 C3 SE Croatia
Dubuque 39 G2 Iowa, USA
Dudelange 60 E9 S Luxembourg
Duero 67 D2 ≈ Portugal/Spain
Duffel 60 C6 C Belgium
Duff Islands 121 G3 *Island group,* E Solomon Islands
Dugi Otok 75 B2 *Island,* W Croatia
Duisburg 69 A4 W Germany
Duiven 60 E4 E Netherlands
Duk Faiwil 111 C4 SE Sudan
Dulan 97 D4 C China
Dulce, Golfo 43 F7 *Gulf,* S Costa Rica
Dülmen 69 B4 W Germany
Dulovo 75 F2 NE Bulgaria
Duluth 39 G1 Minnesota, USA
Duma 91 A2 SW Syria
Dumfries 63 D5 S Scotland, UK
Dumont d'Urville 122 E6 *French research station,* Antarctica
Dumyât 106 I2 N Egypt
Duna *see* Danube
Düna *see* Western Dvina
Dunaj *see* Danube
Dunaújváros 73 E8 C Hungary
Dunav *see* Danube
Dundalk 63 C6 NE Ireland
Dundee 63 D4 E Scotland, UK
Dundee 112 D6 E South Africa
Dunedin 119 B7 South Island, NZ
Dunfermline 63 D4 C Scotland, UK
Dungu 112 D1 NE Dem. Rep. Congo
Dunkerque 65 D1 N France
Dunkirk *see* Dunkerque
Dún Laoghaire 63 C6 E Ireland
Dunărea *see* Danube
Duqm 91 F5 E Oman
Durance 65 E6 ≈ SE France
Durango 41 D4 W Mexico
Durban 112 D7 E South Africa
Durg 99 E4 C India
Durham 37 F4 North Carolina, USA
Durham 63 E5 N England, UK
Durrës 75 C4 W Albania
D'Urville Island 119 C4 *Island,* C NZ
Dushanbe 93 F3 ✕ W Tajikistan
Dushanbe 93 F3 ● W Tajikistan
Düsseldorf 69 A4 W Germany
Dusti 93 F4 SW Tajikistan
Dutch Guiana *see* Surinam
Dutch Harbor 35 B4 Unalaska Island, Alaska, USA
Dutch West Indies *see* Netherlands Antilles
Dzerzhinsk 79 B5 W Russ. Fed.
Dzhalal-Abad 93 G3 W Kyrgyzstan
Dzhankoy 77 F6 S Ukraine
Dzhelandy 93 G4 SE Tajikistan
Dzhergalan 93 I2 NE Kyrgyzstan
Dzhugdzhur, Khrebet 86 H4 ▲ E Russ. Fed.
Dzhusaly 86 B5 SW Kazakhstan
Działdowo 73 E3 C Poland

E

East Anglia 63 F7 *Physical region,* E England, UK
Eastbourne 63 F8 SE England, UK
East Cape 119 E3 *Headland,* North Island, NZ
East China Sea 82 *Sea,* W Pacific Ocean
Easter Island 121 D5 *Island,* E Pacific Ocean
Eastern Ghats 99 E5 ▲ SE India
Eastern Sayans 86 E5 ▲ Mongolia/Russ. Fed.
East Falkland 53 C9 *Island,* E Falkland Islands
East Frisian Islands 69 A2 *Island group,* NW Germany
East Kilbride 63 D4 S Scotland, UK
East Korea Bay 95 B5 *Bay,* E North Korea
Eastleigh 63 E8 S England, UK
East London 112 D7 S South Africa
Eastmain 33 D4 ≈ Québec, C Canada
East Novaya Zemlya Trough 123 E5 *Undersea feature,* W Kara Sea
East Pacific Rise 14 *Undersea rise,* E Pacific Ocean
East Pakistan *see* Bangladesh
East Saint Louis 37 C4 Illinois, USA
East Siberian Sea 123 C2 *Sea,* Arctic Ocean
East Timor 101 G8 ◆ *Country,* SE Asia
Eau Claire 37 C2 Wisconsin, USA
Ebensee 69 E7 N Austria
Eberswalde-Finow 69 D3 E Germany
Ebetsu 95 F2 NE Japan
Eblana *see* Dublin
Ebolowa 108 F6 S Cameroon
Ebro 67 E2 ≈ NE Spain
Echo Bay 35 G4 NW Terr., NW Canada
Echt 60 E6 SE Netherlands
Ecija 67 C5 SW Spain
Ecuador 51 B3 ◆ *Republic,* NW South America
Ed Da'ein 111 B3 W Sudan
Ed Damazin 111 C3 E Sudan
Ed Damer 111 C2 NE Sudan
Ed Debba 111 C2 N Sudan
Ede 60 E4 C Netherlands
Ede 108 E5 SW Nigeria
Edinburgh 63 D4 *National region capital,* S Scotland, UK
Edirne 89 A2 NW Turkey
Edmonton 35 G6 Alberta, SW Canada
Edmundston 33 F5 New Brunswick, SE Canada
Edolo 71 C2 N Italy
Edremit 89 A3 NW Turkey
Edward, Lake 112 D2 ◎ Dem. Rep. Congo/Uganda
Edwards Plateau 39 F5 *Plain,* Texas, USA
Eeklo 60 B6 NW Belgium
Eemshaven 60 F1 NE Netherlands
Eersel 60 D5 S Netherlands
Efate 121 H5 *Island,* C Vanuatu
Efstratios, Agios 75 F5 *Island,* Vóreion Aigaíon, E Greece
Egadi Island 71 B8 *Island group,* S Italy
Ege Denizi *see* Aegean Sea
Eger 73 E7 NE Hungary
Éghezèe 60 D7 C Belgium
Egmont, Cape 119 C4 *Headland,* North Island, NZ
Egmount, Mount *see* Taranaki, Mount
Egypt 106 I4 ◆ *Republic,* NE Africa
Eibar 67 E1 N Spain
Eibergen 60 F4 E Netherlands
Eidfjord 59 A5 S Norway
Eifel 69 A5 *Plateau,* W Germany
Eiger 69 B8 ▲ C Switzerland
Eigg 63 C4 *Island,* W Scotland, UK

CAR Central African Republic **FYR** Former Yugoslavian Rebublic **NSW** New South Wales **NZ** New Zealand **PNG** Papua New Guinea **Russ. Fed.** Russian Federation **UAE** United Arab Emirates **UK** United Kingdom **USA** United States of America 129

EIGHT DEGREE CHANNEL

Eight Degree Channel 99 C8 *Channel*, India/Maldives
Eighty Mile Beach 117 B3 *Beach*, Western Australia
Eijsden 60 E7 SE Netherlands
Edzo 33 F5 NW Terr., NW Canada
Eindhoven 60 D5 S Netherlands
Eire *see* Ireland, Republic of
Eisenhüttenstadt 69 E4 E Germany
Eisenstadt 69 F7 E Austria
Eisleben 69 C4 C Germany
Eivissa *see* Ibiza
Ejea de los Caballeros 67 E2 NE Spain
Ejin Qi 97 E3 N China
El 'Alamein 106 I2 N Egypt
Elat 91 G7 S Israel
El'Atrun 111 B2 NW Sudan
Elâzığ 89 F3 E Turkey
Elba 71 B4 *Island*, Archipelago Toscano, C Italy
Elbe 69 C3 ≈ Czech Republic/Germany
Elbert, Mount 39 D3 ▲ Colorado, USA
Elbląg 73 E2 N Poland
El'brus 79 A8 ▲ SW Russ. Fed.
El Burgo de Osma 67 E2 C Spain
Elburz Mountains 91 D2 ⛰ N Iran
El Calafate 53 A8 S Argentina
Elche 67 F5 E Spain
El Chichónal, Volcán 41 G5 ✷ SE Mexico
Elda 67 F4 E Spain
El Dorado 41 C4 C Mexico
Eldorado 53 D4 NE Argentina
Eldoret 111 D5 W Kenya
Elektrostal' 79 B5 W Russ. Fed.
Elemi Triangle 111 C4 *Disputed region*, Kenya/Sudan
Eleuthera Island 45 D1 *Island*, N Bahamas
El Fasher 111 B3 W Sudan
El Geneina 111 A3 W Sudan
Elgin 37 D3 Illinois, USA
Elgin 63 D3 NE Scotland, UK
El Giza 106 I2 N Egypt
El Goléa 106 D2 C Algeria
El Hank 108 C1 *Cliff*, N Mauritania
Elista 79 B8 SW Russ. Fed.
Elizabeth 117 E6 South Australia
Ełk 73 F2 NE Poland
El Khârga 106 I3 C Egypt
Ellef Ringnes Island 35 G2 *Island*, NW Terr., N Canada
Ellen, Mount 39 D3 ▲ Utah, USA
Ellesmere Island 35 H1 *Island*, Queen Elizabeth Islands, Nunavut, N Canada
Ellesmere, Lake 119 C6 ◎ South Island, NZ
Elliston 117 E5 South Australia
Ellsworth Land 122 A5 *Physical region*, Antarctica
El Mahbas 106 B3 SW Western Sahara
El Minya 106 I3 C Egypt
El Mreyyé 108 C2 *Desert*, E Mauritania
Elmshorn 69 C2 N Germany
El Muglad 111 B3 C Sudan
El Obeid 111 C3 C Sudan
El Oued 106 E2 NE Algeria
El Paso 39 E5 Texas, USA
El Porvenir 43 H6 *Special territory capital*, N Panama
El Progreso 43 C3 NW Honduras
El Puerto de Santa María 67 C6 S Spain
El Rama 43 E4 SE Nicaragua
El Real 43 I6 SE Panama
El Salvador 43 B4 ◆ *Republic*, Central America
El Sáuz 41 C2 N Mexico
Elst 60 E4 E Netherlands
El Sueco 41 C2 N Mexico
El Suweis *see* Suez
El Tigre 51 D2 W Colombia
Elvas 67 B4 C Portugal
El Vendrell 67 G3 NE Spain
Elx *see* Elche
Emba 86 B5 W Kazakhstan
Emden 69 B3 NW Germany
Emerald 117 G4 Queensland, E Australia
Emeti 121 A2 SW PNG
Emi Koussi 108 H2 ▲ N Chad
Emmeloord 60 E3 N Netherlands
Emmen 60 F3 NE Netherlands
Emmendingen 69 B7 SW Germany
Emory Peak 39 E5 ▲ Texas, USA
Empalme 41 B3 NW Mexico
Emperor Seamounts 15 *Undersea feature*, NW Pacific Ocean
Ems 69 B3 ≈ NW Germany
Encarnación 53 C4 S Paraguay
Encs 73 F6 NE Hungary
Endeavour Strait 117 F1 *Strait*, Queensland, NE Australia
Enderby Land 122 D3 *Physical region*, Antarctica
Enghien 60 C7 SW Belgium
England 63 D6 *National region*, United Kingdom
English Channel 63 E8 *Channel*, NW Europe
Enguri 89 G1 ≈ NW Georgia
Enid 39 F4 Oklahoma, USA
Ennedi 108 H2 *Plateau*, E Chad
Ennis 63 A6 W Ireland
Enniskillen 63 B5 SW Northern Ireland, UK
Enns 69 E7 ≈ C Austria
Enschede 60 F4 E Netherlands
Ensenada 41 A1 NW Mexico
Entebbe 111 C5 S Uganda
Entroncamento 67 B4 C Portugal
Enugu 108 F5 S Nigeria
Eolie, Isole *see* Aeolian Islands
Epéna 112 B1 NE Congo
Epi 121 H5 *Island*, C Vanuatu
Épinal 65 F3 NE France
Equatorial Guinea 108 F6 ◆ *Republic*, C Africa
Erciş 89 G3 E Turkey
Erdenet 97 E2 N Mongolia
Erdi 108 H2 *Plateau*, NE Chad
Erebus, Mount 122 C6 ✷ Ross Island, Antarctica
Ereğli 89 D4 S Turkey
Erenhot 97 F2 NE China
Erfurt 69 C5 C Germany
Ergene Nehri 89 A2 ≈ NW Turkey
Ergun He *see* Argun
Erie 37 F3 Pennsylvania, USA
Erie, Lake 37 E3 ◎ Canada/USA
Eritrea 111 D2 ◆ *Transitional government*, E Africa
Erlangen 69 C6 S Germany
Ermelo 60 E3 C Netherlands
Ermióni 75 E6 S Greece
Ernakulam 99 D7 SW India
Erode 99 D7 SE India
Erquelinnes 60 C7 S Belgium
Er-Rachidia 106 C2 E Morocco
Er Rahad 111 C3 C Sudan
Erromango 121 G5 *Island*, S Vanuatu
Erzgebirge *see* Ore Mountains
Erzincan 89 F3 E Turkey
Erzurum 89 G3 NE Turkey
Esbjerg 59 A7 W Denmark
Esch-sur-Alzette 60 E9 S Luxembourg
Escuinapa 41 D4 C Mexico
Escuintla 43 A3 S Guatemala
Escuintla 41 H6 SE Mexico
Eshkamesh 93 F4 NE Afghanistan
Esh Sham *see* Damascus
Eskişehir 89 B3 W Turkey
Esmeraldas 51 B3 N Ecuador
Esperance 117 C5 Western Australia
Esperanza 41 C3 NW Mexico
Esperanza 122 A3 *Argentinian research station*, Antarctica
Espírito Santo 51 G7 *State*, E Brazil
Espiritu Santo 121 G4 *Island*, W Vanuatu
Espoo 59 E5 S Finland
Esquel 53 A7 SW Argentina
Essaouira 106 B2 W Morocco
Essen 60 C5 N Belgium
Essen 69 A4 W Germany
Estacado, Llano 39 E4 *Plain*, SW USA
Estados, Isla de los 53 B9 *Island*, S Argentina
Estância 51 I5 E Brazil
Estelí 43 D4 NW Nicaragua
Estella-Lizarra 67 E2 N Spain
Estepona 67 C6 S Spain
Estevan 35 H7 Saskatchewan, S Canada
Estonia 59 F6 ◆ *Republic*, NE Europe
Estrela, Serra da 67 B3 ⛰ C Portugal
Estremoz 67 B4 S Portugal
Esztergom 73 D7 N Hungary
Étalle 60 D9 SE Belgium
Etawah 99 E3 N India
Ethiopia 111 D4 ◆ *Republic*, E Africa
Ethiopian Highlands 111 D4 *Plateau*, N Ethiopia
Etna, Monte 71 D8 ✷ Sicily, Italy
Etna, Mount *see* Etna, Monte
Etosha Pan 112 B5 *Salt lake*, N Namibia
Etrek 93 B3 ≈ Iran/Turkmenistan
Ettelbrück 60 E8 C Luxembourg
Euboea 75 E5 *Island*, C Greece
Eucla 117 D5 Western Australia
Euclid 37 E3 Ohio, USA
Eugene 39 B2 Oregon, USA
Eupen 60 E7 E Belgium
Euphrates 91 C3 ≈ SW Asia
Europe 54 *Continent*,
Eutin 69 C2 N Germany
Evansville 37 D4 Indiana, USA
Everard, Lake 117 D5 *Salt lake*, South Australia
Everest, Mount 97 B5 ▲ China/Nepal
Everett 39 B1 Washington, USA
Everglades, The 37 E7 *Wetland*, SE USA
Evje 59 B6 S Norway
Évora 67 B4 C Portugal
Évreux 65 D2 N France
Évros 75 F4 ≈ SE Europe
Evvoia *see* Euboea
Exe 63 D8 ≈ SW England, UK
Exeter 63 D8 SW England, UK
Exmouth 63 D8 SW England, UK
Exmouth 117 A3 Western Australia
Exmouth Gulf 117 A3 *Gulf*, Western Australia
Extremadura 67 C4 *Autonomous community*, W Spain
Exuma Cays 45 D2 *Islets*, C Bahamas
Exuma Sound 45 D2 *Sound*, C Bahamas
Eyre Basin, Lake 117 E4 *Salt lake*, South Australia
Eyre Mountains 119 B7 ⛰ South Island, NZ
Eyre North, Lake 117 E4 *Salt lake*, South Australia
Eyre Peninsula 117 E5 *Peninsula*, South Australia
Eyre South, Lake 117 E5 *Salt lake*, South Australia

F

Faaa 121 A6 W French Polynesia
Faadhippolhu Atoll 99 C8 Atoll, N Maldives
Fada 108 H2 E Chad
Fada-Ngourma 108 D4 E Burkina
Faenza 71 C3 N Italy
Fagamalo 121 A4 N Samoa
Fagne 60 C8 *Hill range*, S Belgium
Faguibine, Lac 108 C3 ◎ NW Mali
Fairbanks 35 D4 Alaska, USA
Fair Isle 63 E2 *Island*, NE Scotland, UK
Fairlie 119 B6 South Island, NZ
Faisalabad 99 D2 NE Pakistan
Faizabad 99 E3 N India
Fakfak 101 H7 E Indonesia
Falam 101 A2 W Burma
Falconara Marittima 71 D4 C Italy
Falealupo 121 A4 NW Samoa
Falkland Islands 53 C8 *UK* ◇, SW Atlantic Ocean
Falmouth 63 C8 SW England, UK
Falster 59 B7 *Island*, SE Denmark
Falun 59 C5 C Sweden
Famagusta 80 D6 E Cyprus
Famagusta Bay 80 D6 *Bay*, E Cyprus
Famenne 60 D8 *Physical region*, SE Belgium
Fano 71 D3 C Italy
Farafangana 112 G6 SE Madagascar
Farah 93 D5 W Afghanistan
Farah Rud 93 D5 ≈ W Afghanistan
Faranah 108 B4 S Guinea
Farasan, Jaza'ir 91 B6 *Island group*, SW Saudi Arabia
Farewell, Cape 119 C4 *Headland*, South Island, NZ
Fargo 39 F1 North Dakota, USA
Farg'ona 93 G3 E Uzbekistan
Faridabad 99 D3 N India Asia
Farkhor 93 F4 SW Tajikistan
Farmington 39 D4 New Mexico, USA
Faro 67 B5 S Portugal
Farquhar Group 112 H3 *Island group*, S Seychelles
Fastiv 77 D4 NW Ukraine
Fauske 59 C2 C Norway
Faxaflói 59 A1 *Bay*, W Iceland
Faya 108 H2 N Chad
Fayaoué 121 G6 C New Caledonia
Fayetteville 37 F5 North Carolina, USA
Fdérik 108 B1 NW Mauritania
Fear, Cape 37 F5 *Headland*, Bald Head Island, North Carolina, USA
Fécamp 65 C1 N France
Fehérgyarmat 73 G7 E Hungary
Fehmarn 69 C2 *Island*, N Germany
Fehmarn Belt 69 C2 *Strait*, Denmark/Germany
Feijó 51 C5 W Brazil
Feilding 119 D4 North Island, NZ
Feira de Santana 51 H5 E Brazil
Felanitx 67 H4 Majorca, Spain
Felipe Carrillo Puerto 41 I4 SE Mexico
Felixstowe 63 F7 E England, UK
Femunden 59 B4 ◎ S Norway
Fenoarivo 112 G5 E Madagascar
Feodosiya 77 F6 S Ukraine
Fergana Valley 93 G3 *Basin*, Tajikistan/Uzbekistan
Ferkessédougou 108 C4 N Ivory Coast
Fermo 71 D4 C Italy
Ferrara 71 C3 N Italy
Ferrol 67 B1 NW Spain
Ferwerd 60 E2 N Netherlands
Fethiye 89 B5 SW Turkey
Fetlar 63 E1 *Island*, NE Scotland, UK
Feyzabad 93 G4 NE Afghanistan
Fez 106 C1 N Morocco
Fianarantsoa 112 G5 C Madagascar
Fianga 108 G4 SW Chad
Fier 75 D4 SW Albania
Figeac 65 D5 S France
Figueira da Foz 67 A3 W Portugal
Figueres 67 H2 E Spain
Figuig 106 D2 E Morocco
Fiji 121 I5 ◆ *Republic*, SW Pacific Ocean
Filadelfia 43 D6 W Costa Rica
Filipstad 59 C5 C Sweden
Finale Ligure 71 B3 NW Italy
Finike 89 B5 SW Turkey
Finland 59 E4 ◆ *Republic*, N Europe
Finland, Gulf of 59 E5 *Gulf*, E Baltic Sea
Finnmarksvidda 59 D1 *Physical region*, N Norway
Finschhafen 121 C2 C PNG
Finsterwalde 69 D4 E Germany
Fiordland 119 A7 *Physical region*, South Island, NZ
Firenze *see* Florence
Fischbacher Alpen 69 F7 ⛰ E Austria
Fish 112 C6 ≈ S Namibia
Fishguard 63 C7 SW Wales, UK
Fisterra, Cabo 67 A1 *Headland*, NW Spain
Fito 121 B5 ▲ C Samoa
Fitzroy Crossing 117 C2 Western Australia
Fitzroy River 117 C2 ≈ Western Australia
Fläming 73 A3 *Hill range*, NE Germany
Flanders 60 A6 *Cultural region*, Belgium/France
Flathead Lake 39 D1 ◎ Montana, USA
Flattery, Cape 39 B1 *Headland*, Washington, USA
Flensburg 69 C2 N Germany
Flinders Island 117 G7 *Island*, Tasmania, SE Australia
Flinders Ranges 117 F5 ⛰ South Australia
Flinders River 117 F3 ≈ Queensland, N Australia
Flin Flon 35 H6 Manitoba, C Canada
Flint 37 E3 Michigan, USA
Flint Island 115 *Island*, Line Islands, E Kiribati
Florence 71 D3 C Italy
Florencia 51 B3 S Colombia
Flores 43 B2 N Guatemala
Flores 101 F8 *Island*, Nusa Tenggara, C Indonesia
Flores Sea 101 E8 *Sea*, C Indonesia
Floriano 51 H4 E Brazil
Florianópolis 51 G8 S Brazil
Florida 37 E6 *State*, SE USA
Florida 53 C5 S Uruguay
Florida Keys 37 E7 *Island group*, SE USA
Florida, Straits of 37 F7 *Strait*, Atlantic Ocean/Gulf of Mexico
Florissant 39 H3 Missouri, USA
Fly 121 A2 ≈ Indonesia/PNG
Foča 75 C2 SE Bosnia and Herzegovina
Focşani 77 C6 E Romania
Foggia 71 E5 SE Italy
Foix 65 C7 S France
Foleyet 33 C5 Ontario, S Canada
Foligno 71 D4 C Italy
Folkestone 63 F7 SE England, UK
Fongafale 121 J3 ● Funafuti Atoll, SE Tuvalu
Fonseca, Gulf of 43 C4 *Gulf*, C Central America
Fontainebleau 65 D3 N France
Fontenay-le-Comte 65 C4 NW France
Fonyód 73 D8 W Hungary
Forchheim 69 C6 SE Germany
Forfar 63 D4 E Scotland, UK
Forlì 71 C3 N Italy
Formentera 67 G4 *Island*, Balearic Islands, Spain
Formosa 53 C4 NE Argentina
Formosa *see* Taiwan
Formosa, Serra 51 F5 ⛰ C Brazil
Fort Albany 33 C4 Ontario, C Canada
Fortaleza 51 H4 NE Brazil
Fortaleza 53 B1 N Bolivia
Fort Collins 39 E3 Colorado, USA
Fort-de-France 45 K5 ○ W Martinique
Fortescue River 117 B3 ≈ Western Australia
Fort Frances 33 A4 Ontario, S Canada
Fort Good Hope 35 F4 NW Terr., NW Canada
Forth 63 C4 ≈ C Scotland, UK
Forth, Firth of 63 D4 *Estuary*, E Scotland, UK
Fort Lauderdale 37 F7 Florida, USA
Fort Liard 35 F5 NW Terr., W Canada
Fort McMurray 35 G6 Alberta, C Canada
Fort McPherson 35 E4 NW Terr., NW Canada
Fort Nelson 35 F5 British Columbia, W Canada
Fort Peck Lake 39 E1 ⊠ Montana, USA
Fort Providence 35 F5 NW Terr., W Canada
Fort St.John 35 F6 British Columbia, W Canada
Fort Severn 33 B2 Ontario, C Canada
Fort-Shevchenko 86 A5 W Kazakhstan
Fort Simpson 35 F5 NW Terr., W Canada
Fort Smith 35 G5 NW Terr., W Canada
Fort Smith 39 G4 Arkansas, USA
Fort Vermilion 35 F6 Alberta, W Canada
Fort Wayne 37 E3 Indiana, USA
Fort William 63 C4 N Scotland, UK
Fort Worth 39 G4 Texas, USA
Fort Yukon 35 E3 Alaska, USA
Fougères 65 C2 NW France
Foulwind, Cape 119 B5 *Headland*, South Island, NZ
Foumban 108 F5 NW Cameroon
Foveaux Strait 119 A8 *Strait*, S NZ
Foxe Basin 35 I3 *Sea*, Nunavut, N Canada
Fox Glacier 119 B6 South Island, NZ
Fox Mine 35 H6 Manitoba, C Canada
Fraga 67 F2 NE Spain
Fram Basin 123 C4 *Undersea feature*, Arctic Ocean
France 65 C4 ◆ *Republic*, W Europe
Franceville 112 B2 E Gabon
Franche-Comté 65 E4 *Region*, E France
Francis Case, Lake 39 F2 ⊠ South Dakota, USA
Francisco Escárcega 41 H5 SE Mexico
Francistown 112 D5 North East, NE Botswana
Frankfort 37 E4 Kentucky, USA
Frankfurt am Main 69 B5 SW Germany
Frankfurt an der Oder 69 E4 E Germany
Fränkische Alb 69 C6 ⛰ S Germany
Franz Josef Land 86 D1 *Island group*, N Russ. Fed.
Fraserburgh 63 D3 NE Scotland, UK
Fraser Island 117 H4 *Island*, Queensland, E Australia
Fray Bentos 53 C5 W Uruguay
Fredericton 33 F5 New Brunswick, SE Canada
Fredrikstad 59 B5 S Norway
Freeport 45 D1 N Bahamas
Freetown 108 B4 ● W Sierra Leone
Freiburg im Breisgau 69 B7 SW Germany
Fremantle 117 B5 Western Australia
French Guiana 51 F2 *French* ◇, N South America
French Polynesia 115 *French* ◇, S Pacific Ocean
French Sudan *see* Mali
Fresnillo 41 E4 C Mexico
Fresno 39 B3 California, USA
Frías 53 B4 N Argentina
Friedrichshafen 69 B7 S Germany
Frohavet 59 B4 *Sound*, C Norway
Frome, Lake 117 F5 *Salt lake*, South Australia
Frontera 41 H5 SE Mexico
Frontignan 65 D6 S France
Frøya 59 B4 *Island*, W Norway
Frýdek-Místek 73 D6 SE Czech Republic
Fuengirola 67 D6 S Spain
Fuerte Olimpo 53 C3 NE Paraguay
Fuji, Mount 95 F6 ▲ Honshū, SE Japan
Fukui 95 F6 SW Japan
Fukuoka 95 D7 SW Japan
Fukushima 95 G4 C Japan
Fulda 69 C5 C Germany
Funafuti Atoll 121 J3 *Atoll*, C Tuvalu
Fundy, Bay of 33 F5 *Bay*, Canada/USA
Fünen *see* Fyn
Fürth 69 C6 S Germany
Furukawa 95 G4 C Japan
Fushun 97 G2 NE China
Füssen 69 C7 S Germany
Futuna 121 H5 *Island*, S Vanuatu
Futuna, Île 121 J4 *Island*, S Wallis and Futuna
Fuxin 97 G2 NE China
Fuzhou 97 G5 SE China
Fyn 59 B7 *Island*, C Denmark

G

Gaalkacyo 111 F4 C Somalia
Gabela 112 B3 W Angola
Gabès 106 F2 E Tunisia
Gabès, Golfe de 106 F2 *Gulf*, E Tunisia
Gabon 112 A1 ◆ *Republic*, C Africa
Gaborone 112 D6 ● SE Botswana
Gabrovo 75 F3 C Bulgaria
Gadag 99 D6 W India
Gaeta 71 D5 C Italy
Gaeta, Gulf of 71 C5 *Gulf*, C Italy
Gafsa 106 E2 W Tunisia
Gagnoa 108 C5 C Ivory Coast
Gagra 89 F1 NW Georgia
Gaillac 65 C6 S France
Gairdner, Lake 117 E5 *Salt lake*, South Australia
Galán, Cerro 53 A4 ▲ NW Argentina
Galanta 73 D7 SW Slovakia
Galapagos Islands 51 A7 *Island group*, Ecuador
Galashiels 63 D5 SE Scotland, UK
Galaţi 77 D7 E Romania
Galicia 67 B1 *Autonomous community*, NW Spain
Galilee, Sea of *see* Tiberias, Lake
Galkynyş 93 E3 NE Turkmenistan
Galle 99 E8 SW Sri Lanka
Gallipoli 71 F6 SE Italy
Gällivare 59 D2 N Sweden
Gallup 39 D4 New Mexico, USA
Galtat-Zemmour 106 B3 C Western Sahara
Galveston 39 G5 Texas, USA
Galway 63 A6 W Ireland
Galway Bay 63 A6 *Bay*, W Ireland
Gambell 35 C2 Saint Lawrence Island, Alaska, USA
Gambia 108 A3 ◆ *Republic*, W Africa
Gambia 108 B3 ≈ W Africa
Gambier, Îles 115 *Island group*, E French Polynesia
Gamboma 112 B2 E Congo
Gäncä 89 H2 W Azerbaijan
Gandajika 112 C3 S Dem. Rep. Congo
Gander 33 H4 Newfoundland, SE Canada
Gandhidham 99 C4 W India
Gandía 67 F4 E Spain
Ganges 99 G3 ≈ Bangladesh/India
Ganges, Mouths of the 99 G4 *Delta*, Bangladesh/India
Gangtok 99 G3 N India
Ganzhou 97 G5 S China
Gao 108 D3 E Mali
Gaoual 108 B4 N Guinea
Gap 65 E6 SE France
Gar 97 A4 W China
Garabil Belentligi 93 D4 ⛰ S Turkmenistan
Garachiné 43 I7 SE Panama
Garagum 93 D3 *Desert*, C Turkmenistan
Garagum Canal 93 E4 *Canal*, C Turkmenistan
Garda, Lake 71 C2 ◎ Italy
Gardez 93 F5 E Afghanistan
Garissa 111 E5 E Kenya
Garonne 65 C5 ≈ S France
Garoowe 111 F3 N Somalia
Garoua 108 G4 N Cameroon
Garry Lake 35 H4 ◎ Nunavut, N Canada
Garsen 111 E6 S Kenya
Garrygala 93 C3 W Turkmenistan
Garwolin 73 F4 E Poland
Gary 37 D3 Indiana, USA
Gascogne *see* Gascony
Gascony 65 C6 *Cultural region*, France
Gascoyne River 117 B4 ≈ Western Australia
Gasmata 121 C2 E PNG
Gaspé 33 F4 Québec, SE Canada
Gaspé, Péninsule de 33 F4 *Peninsula*, Québec, SE Canada
Gatchina 79 A4 NW Russ. Fed.
Gatineau 33 D5 Québec, SE Canada
Gatún, Lago 43 G6 ⊠ C Panama
Gavbandi 91 E4 S Iran
Gavere 60 B6 NW Belgium
Gävle 59 D5 C Sweden
Gawler 117 E6 South Australia
Gaya 99 F3 N India
Gayndah 117 H4 Queensland, E Australia
Gaza 91 G6 NE Gaza Strip
Gaza Strip 91 G6 *Disputed region*, SW Asia
Gaziantep 89 E4 S Turkey
Gazimağusa *see* Famagusta
Gazli 93 E3 C Uzbekistan
Gazojak 93 D2 NE Turkmenistan
Gbanga 108 B5 N Liberia
Gdańsk 73 D2 N Poland
Gdynia 73 D1 N Poland
Gedaref 111 D2 E Sudan
Gediz 89 B3 W Turkey
Gediz Nehri 89 A3 ≈ W Turkey
Geel 60 D6 N Belgium
Geelong 117 F6 Victoria, SE Australia

◆ Country ● Country capital ◇ Dependent territory ○ Dependent territory capital ⛰ Mountain range ▲ Mountain ✷ Volcano ≈ River ◎ Lake ⊠ Reservoir

HERMANSVERK

Geilo 59 B5 S Norway
Gejiu 97 E6 S China
Gela 71 D8 Sicily, Italy
Geldermalsen 60 A4 C Netherlands
Geleen 60 E6 SE Netherlands
Gellinsoor 111 F4 NE Somalia
Gembloux 60 C7 SE Belgium
Gemena 112 C1 NW Dem. Rep. Congo
Gemona del Friuli 71 D2 NE Italy
General Alvear 53 B5 W Argentina
General Eugenio A.Garay 53 B3 S Paraguay
General Santos 101 F5 S Philippines
Geneva 69 A8 SW Switzerland
Geneva, Lake 69 A8 ⊗ France/Switzerland
Genève *see* Geneva
Genk 60 D6 NE Belgium
Gennep 60 E5 SE Netherlands
Genoa 71 B3 NW Italy
Genoa, Gulf of 71 B3 *Gulf,* NW Italy
Genova *see* Genoa
Gent *see* Ghent
Gökdepe 93 C3 C Turkmenistan
George Town 45 B4 ○ SW Cayman Islands
George Town 45 D2 C Bahamas
George Town 101 B5 Peninsular Malaysia
Georgetown 51 E2 ● N Guyana
George V Land 122 C6 *Physical region,* Antarctica
Georgia 37 E5 *State,* SE USA
Georgia 89 G1 ◆ *Republic,* SW Asia
Georgian Bay 33 C5 *Lake bay,* Ontario, S Canada
Georg von Neumayer 122 B3 *German research station,* Antarctica
Gera 69 D5 E Germany
Geraldine 119 C6 South Island, NZ
Geraldton 117 B5 Western Australia
Gerede 89 C2 N Turkey
Gereshk 93 E6 SW Afghanistan
Gerlachovský štít 73 E6 ▲ N Slovakia
Germany 69 B5 ◆ *Federal Republic,* N Europe
Gerona *see* Girona
Gerpinnes 60 C7 S Belgium
Gerze 89 D2 N Turkey
Getafe 67 D3 C Spain
Gevaş 89 G4 SE Turkey
Ghana 108 D5 ◆ *Republic,* W Africa
Ghanzi 112 C5 W Botswana
Ghardaïa 106 E2 N Algeria
Gharyan 106 F2 NW Libya
Ghazni 93 F5 E Afghanistan
Ghent 60 B6 NW Belgium
Ghudara 93 G3 SE Tajikistan
Ghurian 93 D5 W Afghanistan
Giannitsá 75 E4 N Greece
Gibraltar 67 C6 *UK* ◇, SW Europe
Gibraltar, Strait of 67 *Strait,* Atlantic Ocean/Mediterranean Sea
Gibson Desert 117 C4 *Desert,* Western Australia
Giedraičiai 59 F7 E Lithuania
Giessen 69 B5 W Germany
Gifu 95 F6 SW Japan
Giganta, Sierra de la 41 B3 ⛰ W Mexico
G'ijduvon 93 E3 C Uzbekistan
Gijón 67 C1 NW Spain
Gilf Kebir Plateau 106 H4 *Plateau,* SW Egypt
Gillette 39 E2 Wyoming, USA
Giluwe, Mount 121 B2 ▲ W PNG
Gingin 117 B5 Western Australia
Giresun 89 E2 NE Turkey
Girne *see* Kyrenia
Girona 67 H2 NE Spain
Gisborne 119 E3 North Island, NZ
Gissar Range 93 F3 ⛰ Tajikistan/Uzbekistan
Giulianova 71 D4 C Italy
Giurgiu 77 C7 S Romania
Gizo 121 E2 NW Solomon Islands
Gjirokastër 75 D4 S Albania
Gjoa Haven 35 H3 King William Island, Nunavut, NW Canada
Gjøvik 59 B5 S Norway
Glace Bay 33 G5 Cape Breton Island, Nova Scotia, SE Canada
Gladstone 117 H4 Queensland, E Australia
Glåma 59 B5 ≈ SE Norway
Glasgow 63 D4 S Scotland, UK
Glazov 79 D5 NW Russ. Fed.
Glittertind 59 B4 ▲ S Norway
Gliwice 73 D5 S Poland
Głogów 73 C4 W Poland
Gloucester 63 D7 C England, UK
Gloucester 121 C2 E PNG
Glovers Reef 43 C2 *Reef,* E Belize
Głowno 73 E3 C Poland
Gniezno 73 D3 C Poland
Gobabis 112 C5 E Namibia
Gobi 97 E3 *Desert,* China/Mongolia
Gobo 95 E7 SW Japan
Godavari 99 E5 ≈ C India
Godhra 99 D4 W India
Godoy Cruz 53 A5 W Argentina
Goeree 60 B5 *Island,* SW Netherlands
Goes 60 B5 SW Netherlands
Goiânia 51 G6 C Brazil
Goiás 51 F6 *State,* C Brazil
Gojome 95 F3 NW Japan
Göksun 89 E4 C Turkey
Gol 59 B5 S Norway
Golan Heights 91 H5 ⛰ SW Syria
Gołdap 73 F2 NE Poland
Gold Coast 117 H5 *Cultural region,* Queensland, E Australia
Gold Coast *see* Ghana
Golden Bay 119 C4 *Bay,* South Island, NZ
Goleniów 73 B2 NW Poland
Golmud 97 D3 C China
Goma 112 D2 NE Dem. Rep. Congo
Gombi 108 G4 E Nigeria
Gómez Palacio 41 D3 C Mexico
Gonaïves 45 F4 N Haiti
Gonâve, Île de la 45 E4 *Island,* C Haiti
Gonder 111 D3 NW Ethiopia
Gondia 99 E4 C India
Gongola 108 F4 ≈ E Nigeria
Good Hope, Cape of 112 B7 *Headland,* SW South Africa
Goondiwindi 117 G5 Queensland, E Australia
Goor 60 F4 E Netherlands
Goose Green 53 C9 East Falkland, Falkland Islands
Göppingen 69 C6 SW Germany
Gorakhpur 99 F3 N India
Gore 111 D4 W Ethiopia
Gore 119 B8 South Island, NZ
Goré 108 G5 S Chad
Gorgan 91 E1 N Iran
Gori 89 H1 C Georgia
Gorinchem 60 D5 C Netherlands
Goris 89 I3 SE Armenia
Görlitz 69 E4 E Germany
Goroka 121 B2 C PNG
Gorontalo 101 F6 Celebes, C Indonesia
Gorssel 60 E4 E Netherlands
Gorzów Wielkopolski 73 C3 W Poland
Goshogawara 95 F3 C Japan
Göteborg *see* Gothenburg
Gotha 69 C5 C Germany
Gothenburg 59 B6 S Sweden
Gotland 59 D6 *Island,* SE Sweden
Goto-retto 95 C8 *Island group,* SW Japan
Gotsu 95 D6 SW Japan
Göttingen 69 C4 C Germany
Gouda 60 C4 C Netherlands
Gouin, Réservoir 33 D4 ⊠ Québec, SE Canada
Goulburn 117 G6 NSW, SE Australia
Goundam 108 D3 NW Mali
Gouré 108 F3 SE Niger
Governador Valadares 51 H7 SE Brazil
Govi Altayn Nuruu 97 E2 ⛰ S Mongolia
Goya 53 C4 NE Argentina
Goz Beïda 108 H4 SE Chad
Gozo 80 A6 *Island,* N Malta
Gradačac 75 C2 N Bosnia and Herzegovina
Gradas, Serra dos 51 F5 ⛰ C Brazil
Grafton 117 H5 NSW, SE Australia
Graham Land 122 A4 *Physical region,* Antarctica
Grajewo 73 F2 NE Poland
Granada 67 D5 S Spain
Granada 43 D5 SW Nicaragua
Gran Chaco 53 B3 *Lowland plain,* South America
Grand Bahama Island 45 C1 *Island,* N Bahamas
Grand Canyon 39 C4 *Canyon,* Arizona, USA
Grand Cayman 45 C4 *Island,* SW Cayman Islands
Grande, Bahía 53 B8 *Bay,* S Argentina
Grande Comore 112 G4 *Island,* NW Comoros
Grande de Matagalpa, Río 43 E4 ≈ C Nicaragua
Grande Prairie 35 F6 Alberta, W Canada
Grand Erg Occidental 106 D2 *Desert,* W Algeria
Grand Erg Oriental 106 E3 *Desert,* Algeria/Tunisia
Grande, Rio 37 A7 ≈ Mexico/USA
Grande, Río 41 E2 ≈ S Mexico
Grande Terre 45 K5 *Island,* E West Indies
Grand Falls 33 H4 Newfoundland, SE Canada
Grand Forks 39 F1 North Dakota, USA
Grand Rapids 37 D3 Michigan, USA
Gran Paradiso 71 A2 ▲ NW Italy
Granville 65 B2 N France
Graulhet 65 C7 S France
Grave 60 E5 SE Netherlands
Grayling 35 C3 Alaska, USA
Graz 69 E8 SE Austria
Great Abaco 45 D1 *Island,* N Bahamas
Great Ararat *see* Ararat, Mount
Great Artesian Basin 117 F4 *Lowlands,* Queensland, C Australia
Great Australian Bight 117 D5 *Bight,* S Australia
Great Barrier Island 119 D2 *Island,* N NZ
Great Barrier Reef 117 G2 *Reef,* Queensland, NE Australia
Great Basin 39 C3 *Basin,* W USA
Great Bear Lake 35 F4 ⊗ NW Terr., NW Canada
Great Belt 59 B7 *Sea waterway,* Denmark
Great Dividing Range 114 ⛰ NE Australia
Greater Antarctica 122 D4 *Physical region,* Antarctica
Greater Antilles 45 E5 *Island group,* West Indies
Great Exhibition Bay 119 C1 *Inlet,* North Island, NZ
Great Exuma Island 45 D2 *Island,* C Bahamas
Great Falls 39 D1 Montana, USA
Great Hungarian Plain 73 D8 *Plain,* SE Europe
Great Inagua 45 F3 *Island,* S Bahamas
Great Karoo 112 C7 *Plateau region,* S South Africa
Great Khingan Range 97 G1 ⛰ NE China
Great Lakes 37 E2 *Lakes,* Canada/USA
Great Nicobar 99 H6 *Island,* Nicobar Islands, India
Great Rift Valley 53 *Depression,* Asia/Africa
Great Ruaha 111 D7 ≈ S Tanzania
Great Saint Bernard Pass 71 A1 *Pass,* Italy/Switzerland
Great Salt Lake 39 C3 *Salt lake,* Utah, USA
Great Salt Lake Desert 39 C3 *Plain,* Utah, USA
Great Sand Sea 106 H3 *Desert,* Egypt/Libya
Great Sandy Desert 117 C3 *Desert,* Western Australia
Great Slave Lake 35 G5 ⊗ NW Terr., NW Canada
Great Victoria Desert 117 C4 *Desert,* South Australia/Western Australia
Great Wall of China 97 E3 *Ancient monument,* N China
Great Yarmouth 63 F7 E England, UK
Gredos, Sierra de 67 C3 ⛰ W Spain
Greece 75 D5 ◆ *Republic,* SE Europe
Greeley 39 E3 Colorado, USA
Green Bay 37 D2 *Lake bay,* N USA
Green Bay 37 D2 Wisconsin, USA
Green Islands 121 D2 *Island group,* NE PNG
Greenland 28 *Danish* ◇, NE North America
Greenland Sea 123 C5 *Sea,* Arctic Ocean
Green Mountains 37 G2 ⛰ Vermont, USA
Greenock 63 C4 W Scotland, UK
Green River 39 D3 ≈ W USA
Green River 39 D2 Wyoming, USA
Green River 121 A1 NW PNG
Greensboro 37 F4 North Carolina, USA
Greenville 37 E5 South Carolina, USA
Gregory Range 117 G3 ⛰ Queensland, E Australia
Greifswald 69 D2 NE Germany
Grenada 45 K7 *Island,* Grenada
Grenada 45 J6 ● SE West Indies
Grenadines, The 45 K6 *Island group,* Grenada/St Vincent and the Grenadines
Grenoble 65 E5 E France
Grevenmacher 60 E9 E Luxembourg
Greymouth 119 B6 South Island, NZ
Grey Range 117 F4 ⛰ NSW/Queensland, E Australia
Grimari 108 H5 C CAR
Grimsby 63 E6 E England, UK
Groesbeek 60 E5 SE Netherlands
Grójec 73 F4 C Poland
Groningen 60 F2 NE Netherlands
Groote Eylandt 117 E2 *Island,* Northern Territory, N Australia
Grootfontein 112 C5 N Namibia
Groot Karasberge 112 C6 ⛰ S Namibia
Grosseto 71 C4 C Italy
Grossglockner 69 D8 ▲ W Austria
Groznyy 79 B9 SW Russ. Fed.
Grudziądz 73 D2 N Poland
Grums 59 C5 C Sweden
Gryazi 79 B6 W Russ. Fed.
Gryfice 73 C2 NW Poland
Guabito 43 F6 NW Panama
Guadalajara 67 D3 C Spain
Guadalajara 41 D5 C Mexico
Guadalcanal 121 E3 *Island,* C Solomon Islands
Guadalquivir 67 C5 ≈ W Spain
Guadalupe 41 D4 C Mexico
Guadalupe Peak 39 E5 ▲ Texas, USA
Guadarrama, Sierra de 67 E3 ⛰ C Spain
Guadeloupe 45 K5 *French* ◇, E West Indies
Guadiana 67 B4 *River,* Portugal/Spain
Guadix 67 D5 S Spain
Guaimaca 43 D3 C Honduras
Gualaco 43 D3 C Honduras
Gualán 43 B3 C Guatemala
Gualeguaychú 53 C5 E Argentina
Guamúchil 41 C3 C Mexico
Guanabacoa 45 B2 W Cuba
Guanajuato 41 E4 C Mexico
Guanare 51 C2 N Venezuela
Guangyuan 97 E4 C China
Guangzhou 97 F6 S China
Guantánamo 45 E4 SE Cuba
Guaporé, Rio 51 D5 ≈ Bolivia/Brazil
Guarda 67 B3 N Portugal
Guarumal 43 G7 S Panama
Guasave 41 C3 C Mexico
Guasopa 121 D3 SE PNG
Guatemala 43 A3 ◆ *Republic,* Central America
Guatemala Basin 14 *Undersea feature,* E Pacific Ocean
Guatemala City 43 B3 ● C Guatemala
Guaviare, Río 51 C2 ≈ E Colombia
Guayaquil 51 A4 SW Ecuador
Guayaquil, Golfo de 51 A4 *Gulf,* SW Ecuador
Guaymas 41 B3 NW Mexico
Gubadag 93 D2 N Turkmenistan
Guben 69 E4 E Germany
Gubkin 79 A6 W Russ. Fed.
Gudaut'a 89 F1 NW Georgia
Guéret 65 D4 C France
Guernsey 63 D9 *UK* ◇, NW Europe
Guerrero Negro 41 A3 NW Mexico
Guiana Basin 14 *Undersea feature,* W Atlantic Ocean
Guiana Highlands 51 E3 ⛰ N South America
Guider 108 G4 N Cameroon
Guidimouni 108 F3 S Niger
Guildford 63 E8 SE England, UK
Guilin 97 F5 S China
Guimarães 67 B2 N Portugal
Guinea 108 B4 ◆ *Republic,* W Africa
Guinea-Bissau 108 A4 ◆ *Republic,* W Africa
Guinea, Gulf of 108 E6 *Gulf,* E Atlantic Ocean
Guiyang 97 E5 S China
Gujarat 99 C4 *State,* W India
Gujranwala 99 D2 NE Pakistan
Gujrat 99 D2 E Pakistan
Gulbarga 99 D5 C India
Gulfport 37 C6 Mississippi, USA
Gulf, The 91 D3 *Gulf,* SW Asia
Guliston 93 F3 E Uzbekistan
Gulkana 35 D4 Alaska, USA
Gulu 111 C5 N Uganda
Gümüşhane 89 F2 NE Turkey
Güney Doğu Toroslar 89 F4 ⛰ SE Turkey
Gunnbjørn Fjeld 123 A6 ▲ C Greenland
Gunnedah 117 G5 NSW, SE Australia
Gurbantünggüt Shamo 97 C2 *Desert,* NW China
Gurktaler Alpen 69 E8 ⛰ S Austria
Gürün 89 E3 C Turkey
Gusau 108 E4 N Nigeria
Gusev 59 E7 W Russ. Fed.
Gustavus 35 E5 Alaska, USA
Güstrow 69 D2 NE Germany
Gütersloh 69 B4 W Germany
Guwahati 99 G3 NE India
Guyana 51 E2 ◆ *Republic,* N South America
Güzelyurt *see* Morfou
Gwadar 99 A3 SW Pakistan
Gwalior 99 E3 C India
Gwanda 112 D5 SW Zimbabwe
Gyangzê 97 C5 W China
Gyaring Co 97 C4 ⊗ W China
Gympie 117 H4 Queensland, E Australia
Gyomaendrőd 73 F8 SE Hungary
Gyöngyös 73 E7 NE Hungary
Győr 73 D7 NW Hungary
Gyumri 89 G2 W Armenia

H

Haacht 60 C6 C Belgium
Haaksbergen 60 F4 E Netherlands
Haarlem 60 C3 W Netherlands
Haast 119 B6 South Island, NZ
Hachijo-jima 95 G7 *Island,* Izu-shotō, SE Japan
Hachinohe 95 G3 C Japan
Hadejia 108 F4 ≈ N Nigeria
Hadejia 108 F4 N Nigeria
Hadhdhunmathi Atoll 99 C9 Atoll, S Maldives
Ha Dong 101 C2 N Vietnam
Hadramaut 91 D7 ⛰ S Yemen
Haeju 95 A5 S North Korea
Hagåtña 114 ○ NW Guam
Hagondange 65 F2 NE France
Haguenau 65 F2 NE France
Haicheng 97 G3 NE China
Haifa 91 G5 N Israel
Haikou 97 F6 S China
Ha'il 91 B3 NW Saudi Arabia
Hailar 97 G1 N China
Hailuoto 59 E3 *Island,* W Finland
Hainan Dao 97 F6 *Island,* S China
Haines 35 E5 Alaska, USA
Hainichen 69 D5 E Germany
Hai Phong 101 C2 N Vietnam
Haiti 45 F4 ◆ *Republic,* C West Indies
Haiya 111 D2 NE Sudan
Hajdarken *see* Khaydarkan
Hajdúhadház 73 F7 E Hungary
Hakodate 95 F2 NE Japan
Halab *see* Aleppo
Halberstadt 69 C4 C Germany
Halden 59 B5 S Norway
Halfmoon Bay 119 B8 Stewart Island, Southland, NZ
Halifax 33 G5 Nova Scotia, SE Canada
Halle 60 C7 C Belgium
Halle 69 D4 C Germany
Halle-Neustadt 69 D4 C Germany
Halley 122 B3 *UK research station,* Antarctica
Halls Creek 117 D2 Western Australia
Halmahera, Pulau 101 G6 *Island,* E Indonesia
Halmahera Sea 101 G6 *Sea,* E Indonesia
Halmstad 59 C6 S Sweden
Hamada 95 D6 SW Japan
Hamadan 91 D2 W Iran
Hamah 91 B2 W Syria
Hamamatsu 95 F6 S Japan
Hamar 59 B5 S Norway
Hamburg 69 C3 N Germany
Hamd, Wadi al 91 A4 *Dry watercourse,* W Saudi Arabia
Hämeenlinna 59 E5 SW Finland
Hamersley Range 117 B3 ⛰ Western Australia
Hamgyong-sanmaek 95 B4 ⛰ N North Korea
Hamhung 95 B4 C North Korea
Hami 97 D2 NW China
Hamilton 63 D4 S Scotland, UK
Hamilton 33 D6 Ontario, S Canada
Hamilton 119 D3 North Island, NZ
Hamim, Wadi al 106 G3 ≈ NE Libya
Hamm 69 B4 W Germany
Hammamet, Golfe de 80 E4 *Gulf,* NE Tunisia
Hammar, Hawr al 91 C3 ⊗ SE Iraq
Hampden 119 B7 South Island, NZ
Hamrun 80 B6 C Malta
Handan 97 E4 E China
Hangayn Nuruu 97 D2 ⛰ C Mongolia
Hangö *see* Hanko
Hangzhou 97 G4 SE China
Hanko 59 E5 SW Finland
Hanmer Springs 119 C6 South Island, NZ
Hannover *see* Hanover
Hanöbukten 59 C7 *Bay,* S Sweden
Hanoi 101 C2 ● N Vietnam
Hanover 69 C4 NW Germany
Han Shui 97 F4 ≈ C China
Hanzhong 97 E4 C China
Haora 99 G4 NE India
Haparanda 59 E3 N Sweden
Haradok 77 D1 N Belarus
Haramachi 95 G4 E Japan
Harare 112 E4 ● NE Zimbabwe
Harbel 108 B5 W Liberia
Harbin 97 H2 NE China
Hardangerfjorden 59 A5 *Fjord,* S Norway
Hardangervidda 59 B5 *Plateau,* S Norway
Hardenberg 60 F3 E Netherlands
Harelbeke 60 B6 W Belgium
Haren 60 F2 NE Netherlands
Harer 111 E3 E Ethiopia
Hargeysa 111 E3 NW Somalia
Harima-nada 95 E6 *Sea,* S Japan
Harirud 93 E5 ≈ Afghanistan/Iran
Harlingen 60 D2 N Netherlands
Harlow 63 F7 E England, UK
Harney Basin 39 B2 *Basin,* Oregon, USA
Härnösand 59 D4 C Sweden
Har Nuur 97 D2 ⊗ NW Mongolia
Harper 108 C5 NE Liberia
Harricana 33 D4 ≈ Québec, SE Canada
Harrisburg 37 F3 Pennsylvania, USA
Harrison, Cape 33 G2 *Headland,* Newfoundland and Labrador, E Canada
Harrogate 63 E6 N England, UK
Harstad 59 C2 N Norway
Hartford 37 G3 Connecticut, USA
Hartlepool 63 E5 N England, UK
Harwich 63 F7 E England, UK
Haryana 99 D2 *State,* N India
Harz 69 C4 ⛰ C Germany
Hasselt 60 D6 NE Belgium
Hastings 63 F8 SE England, UK
Hastings 119 E4 North Island, NZ
Hatay *see* Antakya
Hattem 60 E3 E Netherlands
Hatteras, Cape 37 G5 *Headland,* North Carolina, USA
Hattiesburg 37 C6 Mississippi, USA
Hat Yai 101 B5 SW Thailand
Haugesund 59 A5 S Norway
Haukeligrend 59 B5 S Norway
Haukivesi 59 F4 ⊗ SE Finland
Hauraki Gulf 119 D2 *Gulf,* North Island, N NZ
Hauroko, Lake 119 A8 ⊗ South Island, NZ
Hautes Fagnes 60 E7 ⛰ E Belgium
Hauts Plateaux 106 D2 *Plateau,* Algeria/Morocco
Hauzenberg 69 E6 SE Germany
Havana 45 B2 ● W Cuba
Havant 63 E8 S England, UK
Havelock North 119 E4 North Island, NZ
Haverfordwest 63 C7 SW Wales, UK
Havířov 73 D5 E Czech Republic
Havre 39 D1 Montana, USA
Havre-St-Pierre 33 F4 Québec, E Canada
Hawaii 39 B6 *State,* USA, C Pacific Ocean
Hawea, Lake 119 B7 ⊗ South Island, NZ
Hawera 119 D4 North Island, NZ
Hawick 63 D5 SE Scotland, UK
Hawke Bay 119 E4 *Bay,* North Island, NZ
Hawthorne 39 B3 Nevada, USA
Hay 117 F6 NSW, SE Australia
Hayes 33 A2 ≈ Manitoba, C Canada
Hay River 35 G5 NW Terr., W Canada
Hays 39 F3 Kansas, USA
Haysyn 77 D5 C Ukraine
Hazar 93 B3 W Turkmenistan
Hearst 33 C4 Ontario, S Canada
Hebron 91 H6 S West Bank
Heemskerk 60 C3 W Netherlands
Heerde 60 E3 E Netherlands
Heerenveen 60 E2 N Netherlands
Heerhugowaard 60 D3 NW Netherlands
Heerlen 60 E6 SE Netherlands
Hefa *see* Haifa
Hefei 97 G4 E China
Hegang 97 H1 NE China
Heide 69 B2 N Germany
Heidelberg 69 B6 SW Germany
Heidenheim an der Brenz 69 C6 S Germany
Heilbronn 69 B6 SW Germany
Heilong Jiang *see* Amur
Heiloo 60 C3 NW Netherlands
Heimdal 59 B4 S Norway
Hekimhan 89 E3 C Turkey
Helena 39 D1 Montana, USA
Helensville 119 D2 North Island, NZ
Helgoländer Bucht 69 B2 *Bay,* NW Germany
Hellevoetsluis 60 C5 SW Netherlands
Hellín 67 E4 C Spain
Helmand, Darya-ye 93 D6 ≈ Afghanistan/Iran
Helmond 60 E5 S Netherlands
Helsingborg 59 C7 S Sweden
Helsinki 59 E5 ● S Finland
Hengduan Shan 97 D5 ⛰ SW China
Hengelo 60 F4 E Netherlands
Hengyang 97 F5 S China
Heniches'k 77 F6 S Ukraine
Hennebont 65 B3 NW France
Henzada 101 A3 SW Burma
Herat 93 D5 W Afghanistan
Heredia 43 E6 C Costa Rica
Herford 69 B4 NW Germany
Herk-de-Stad 60 D6 NE Belgium
Hermansverk 59 B5 S Norway

CAR Central African Republic **FYR** Former Yugoslavian Rebublic **NSW** New South Wales **NZ** New Zealand **PNG** Papua New Guinea **Russ. Fed.** Russian Federation **UAE** United Arab Emirates **UK** United Kingdom **USA** United States of America 131

HERMIT ISLANDS

Hermit Islands 121 B1 *Island group,* N PNG
Hermon, Mount 91 H5 ▲ S Syria
Hermosillo 41 B2 NW Mexico
Herrera del Duque 67 C4 W Spain
Herselt 60 D6 C Belgium
Herstal 60 E7 E Belgium
Hessen 69 C5 *State,* C Germany
Hidalgo del Parral 41 D3 N Mexico
Hida-sanmyaku 95 E5 ⛰ Honshū, S Japan
Hienghène 121 G6 C New Caledonia
Hierosolyma *see* Jerusalem
High Atlas 106 C2 ⛰ C Morocco
High Point 37 F4 North Carolina, USA
Hiiumaa 59 D6 *Island,* W Estonia
Hikurangi 119 D2 North Island, NZ
Hildesheim 69 C4 N Germany
Hill Bank 43 B1 N Belize
Hillegom 60 C4 W Netherlands
Hilo 39 B6 Hawaii, USA
Hilversum 60 D4 C Netherlands
Himalayas 99 E2 ⛰ S Asia
Himeji 95 E6 SW Japan
Hims 91 B2 C Syria
Hinchinbrook Island 117 G2 *Island,* Queensland, NE Australia
Hinds 119 C6 South Island, NZ
Hindu Kush 93 F4 ⛰ Afghanistan/Pakistan
Hinnøya 59 C2 *Island,* C Norway
Hirfanli Baraji 89 C3 ⊠ C Turkey
Hirosaki 95 F3 C Japan
Hiroshima 95 D7 SW Japan
Hirson 65 E2 N France
Hisiu 121 B3 SW PNG
Hispania *see* Spain
Hispaniola 45 F4 *Island,* Dominion Republic/Haiti
Hitachi 95 G5 S Japan
Hitra 59 B4 *Island,* S Norway
Hjälmaren 59 C6 ◎ C Sweden
Hjørring 59 B6 N Denmark
Hkakabo Razi 101 A1 ▲ Burma/China
Hlukhiv 77 E3 NE Ukraine
Hlybokaye 77 C2 N Belarus
Hoang Liên Son 101 C2 ⛰ N Vietnam
Hobart 117 G7 Tasmania, SE Australia
Hobro 59 B6 N Denmark
Hô Chi Minh 101 C4 S Vietnam
Hodeida 91 B6 W Yemen
Hódmezővásárhely 73 E8 SE Hungary
Hodna, Chott El 80 D4 *Salt lake,* N Algeria
Hodonín 73 D6 SE Czech Republic
Hoeryong 95 C3 NE North Korea
Hof 69 D5 SE Germany
Hofu 95 D7 SW Japan
Hohenems 69 C7 W Austria
Hohe Tauern 69 D8 ⛰ W Austria
Hohhot 97 F3 N China
Hokianga Harbour 119 C2 *Inlet,* SE Tasman Sea
Hokitika 119 B6 South Island, NZ
Hokkaido 95 F1 *Island,* NE Japan
Holguín 45 D3 SE Cuba
Hollabrunn 69 F6 NE Austria
Holland *see* Netherlands
Holman 35 G3 Victoria Island, NW Terr., N Canada
Holmsund 59 D4 N Sweden
Holon 91 G6 C Israel
Holstebro 59 B6 W Denmark
Holyhead 63 C5 N Wales, UK
Hombori 108 D3 S Mali
Homyel' 77 D3 SE Belarus
Hondo 43 B1 ∽ Central America
Honduras 43 C3 ◆ *Republic,* Central America
Honduras, Gulf of 43 C2 *Gulf,* W Caribbean Sea
Hønefoss 59 B5 S Norway
Hông Gai 101 C2 N Vietnam
Hong Kong (Xianggang) 97 H6 *Special Administrative Region of China, Former UK dependency,* S China
Honiara 121 E3 ● C Solomon Islands
Honjo 95 F4 C Japan
Honolulu 39 B6 Oahu, Hawaii, USA
Honshu 95 G5 *Island,* SW Japan
Hoogeveen 60 E3 NE Netherlands
Hoogezand-Sappemeer 60 F2 NE Netherlands
Hoorn 60 D3 NW Netherlands
Hopa 89 G2 NE Turkey
Hope 35 D4 British Columbia, SW Canada
Hopedale 33 F2 Newfoundland and Labrador, NE Canada
Horasan 89 G3 NE Turkey
Horki 77 D2 E Belarus
Horlivka 77 G5 E Ukraine
Hormuz, Strait of 91 E4 *Strait,* Iran/Oman
Horn, Cape 53 B9 *Headland,* S Chile
Horoshiri-dake 95 G2 ▲ N Japan
Horsham 117 F6 Victoria, SE Australia
Horst 60 E5 SE Netherlands
Horten 59 B5 S Norway
Horyn' 77 C4 ∽ NW Ukraine
Hosingen 60 E8 NE Luxembourg
Hotan 97 B3 NW China
Hotazel 112 C6 N South Africa
Hoting 59 C4 C Sweden
Houayxay 101 B2 N Laos
Houghton 37 D1 Michigan, USA
Houilles 65 C6 N France
Houlton 37 H2 Maine, USA
Houston 39 G5 Texas, USA
Hovd 97 C2 W Mongolia
Hove 63 E8 SE England, UK
Hoverla, Hora 77 B5 ▲ W Ukraine
Hövsgöl Nuur 97 D1 ◎ N Mongolia
Howar, Wadi 111 B2 ∽ Chad/Sudan
Hoy 63 D2 *Island,* N Scotland, UK
Hoyerswerda 69 E4 E Germany
Hradec Králové 73 C5 NE Czech Republic
Hranice 73 D6 E Czech Republic
Hrodna 77 B2 W Belarus
Hrvatska *see* Croatia
Huaihua 97 F5 S China
Huajuapan 41 F5 SE Mexico
Huambo 112 B4 C Angola
Huancayo 51 B5 C Peru
Huangshi 97 G4 C China
Huánuco 51 B5 C Peru
Huanuni 53 A2 W Bolivia
Huaraz 51 B5 W Peru
Huatabampo 41 C3 NW Mexico
Hubli 99 D6 SW India
Huch'ang 95 B4 N North Korea
Huddersfield 63 E6 N England, UK
Hudiksvall 59 D4 C Sweden
Hudson Bay 33 B2 *Bay,* NE Canada
Hudson River 37 G2 ∽ NE USA
Hudson Strait 35 J4 *Strait,* NW Terr./Québec, NE Canada
Huê 101 C3 C Vietnam
Huehuetenango 43 A3 W Guatemala
Huelva 67 B5 SW Spain
Huesca 67 F2 NE Spain
Huéscar 67 E5 S Spain
Hughenden 117 G3 Queensland, NE Australia
Huich'on 95 B4 C North Korea
Huíla Plateau 112 B4 *Plateau,* S Angola
Huixtla 41 H6 SE Mexico
Hulingol 97 G2 N China
Hull 33 D5 Québec, SE Canada
Hulst 60 C6 SW Netherlands
Hulun Nur 97 F2 ◎ NE China
Humaitá 51 D4 N Brazil
Humboldt River 39 B3 ∽ Nevada, USA
Humphreys Peak 39 D4 ▲ Arizona, USA
Humpolec 73 C6 C Czech Republic
Hunedoara 77 B6 SW Romania
Hünfeld 69 C5 C Germany
Hungary 73 D8 ◆ *Republic,* C Europe
Hunter Island 117 F7 *Island,* Tasmania, SE Australia
Huntington 37 E4 West Virginia, USA
Huntly 119 D3 North Island, NZ
Huntsville 37 D5 Alabama, USA
Huon Gulf 121 B2 *Gulf,* E PNG
Hurghada 106 J3 E Egypt
Huron, Lake 37 E2 ◎ Canada/USA
Hurunui 119 C6 ∽ South Island, NZ
Húsavík 59 A1 NE Iceland
Husum 69 B2 N Germany
Huy 60 D7 E Belgium
Hvannadalshnúkur 59 B1 🌋 S Iceland
Hvar 75 B3 *Island,* S Croatia
Hwange 112 D5 W Zimbabwe
Hyargas Nuur 97 D2 ◎ NW Mongolia
Hyderabad 99 E5 C India
Hyderabad 99 B3 SE Pakistan
Hyères 65 E7 SE France
Hyères, Îles d' 65 E7 *Island group,* S France
Hyesan 95 B4 NE North Korea
Hyvinkää 59 E5 S Finland

I

Ialomiţa 77 C7 ∽ SE Romania
Iaşi 77 C6 NE Romania
Ibadan 108 E5 SW Nigeria
Ibar 75 D2 ∽ C Serbia and Montenegro (Yugoslavia)
Ibarra 51 B3 N Ecuador
Iberian Peninsula 54 *Physical region,* Portugal/Spain
Ibérico, Sistema 67 E2 ⛰ NE Spain
Ibiza 67 G4 *Island,* Balearic Islands, Spain
Ica 51 B6 SW Peru
Iceland 59 A1 ◆ *Republic,* N Atlantic Ocean
Iceland Plateau 123 B6 *Undersea feature,* S Greenland Sea
Idaho 39 C2 *State,* NW USA
Idfu 106 J3 SE Egypt
Idîni 108 A2 W Mauritania
Idlib 91 B2 NW Syria
Idre 59 C4 C Sweden
Ieper 60 A6 W Belgium
Iferouâne 108 F2 N Niger
Ifôghas, Adrar des 108 E2 ⛰ NE Mali
Igarka 86 E3 N Russ. Fed.
Iglesias 71 A6 Sardinia, Italy
Igloolik 35 I3 Nunavut, N Canada
Igoumenitsa 75 D5 W Greece
Iguaçu, Rio 51 F8 ∽ Argentina/Brazil
Iguala 41 F5 S Mexico
Iguazu Falls 53 D4 *Waterfall,* Argentina/Brazil
Iguidi, 'Erg 106 C3 *Desert,* Algeria/Mauritania
Ihosy 112 G5 S Madagascar
Iisalmi 59 E4 C Finland
IJssel 60 E4 ∽ Netherlands
IJsselmeer 60 D3 ◎ N Netherlands
IJsselmuiden 60 E3 E Netherlands
Ijzer 60 A6 ∽ W Belgium
Ikaría 75 F6 *Island,* Dodecanese, Greece
Ikela 112 C2 C Congo
Iki 95 C7 *Island,* SW Japan
Ilagan 101 F3 N Philippines
Iława 73 E2 N Poland
Ilebo 112 C2 W Congo
Île-de-France 65 D3 *Region,* N France
Ilfracombe 63 D8 SW England, UK
Ílhavo 67 B3 N Portugal
Ili 93 H1 ∽ China/Kazakhstan
Iliamna Lake 35 D2 *Lake,* Alaska, USA
Iligan 101 F5 S Philippines
Illapel 53 A5 C Chile
Illichivs'k 77 E6 SW Ukraine
Illinois 37 C3 *State,* C USA
Iloilo 101 F4 C Philippines
Ilorin 108 E4 W Nigeria
Ilovlya 79 B7 SW Russ. Fed.
Imatra 59 F4 SE Finland
Imisli 89 I2 C Azerbaijan
Imola 71 C3 N Italy
Imperatriz 51 G4 NE Brazil
Imperia 71 A3 NW Italy
Imphal 99 H3 NE India
Inarijärvi 59 E1 ◎ N Finland
Inawashiro-ko 95 F5 ◎ Honshū, C Japan
İncesu 89 D4 C Turkey
Inch'on 95 B5 NW South Korea
India 99 D4 ◆ *Republic,* S Asia
Indiana 37 D3 *State,* N USA
Indianapolis 37 D3 Indiana, USA
Indian Church 43 B1 N Belize
Indian Desert *see* Thar Desert
Indian Ocean 15 *Ocean*
Indigirka 86 G2 ∽ NE Russ. Fed.
Indira Point 99 H6 *Headland,* Andaman and Nicobar Islands, India
Indonesia 101 C7 ◆ *Republic,* SE Asia
Indore 99 D4 C India
Indus 99 B3 ∽ S Asia
Indus, Mouths of the 99 B3 *Delta,* S Pakistan
İnebolu 89 D2 N Turkey
Infiernillo, Presa del 41 E5 ⊠ S Mexico
Ingolstadt 69 C6 S Germany
Inhambane 112 E6 SE Mozambique
Inn 69 D7 ∽ C Europe
Inner Hebrides 63 B4 *Island group,* W Scotland, UK
Innisfail 117 G2 Queensland, NE Australia
Innsbruck 69 C7 W Austria
Inowrocław 73 D3 C Poland
I-n-Salah 106 D3 C Algeria
Inta 79 E3 NW Russ. Fed.
Interlaken 69 B8 SW Switzerland
Inukjuak 33 D2 Québec, NE Canada
Inuvik 35 F4 NW Terr., NW Canada
Invercargill 119 B8 South Island, NZ
Inverness 63 D3 N Scotland, UK
Investigator Strait 117 E6 *Strait,* South Australia
Inyangani 112 E5 ▲ NE Zimbabwe
Ioánnina 75 D5 W Greece
Ionian Islands 75 D5 *Island group,* W Greece
Ionian Sea 80 G3 *Sea,* C Mediterranean Sea
Iónia Nisiá *see* Ionian Islands
Íos 75 F6 *Island,* Cyclades, Greece
Iowa 39 G2 *State,* C USA
Iowa City 39 G2 Iowa, USA
Ipel' 73 E7 ∽ Hungary/Slovakia
Ipoh 101 B5 Peninsular Malaysia
Ippy 108 H5 C CAR
Ipswich 63 F7 E England, UK
Ipswich 117 H5 Queensland, E Australia
Iqaluit 35 J3 Baffin Island, Nunavut, NE Canada
Iquique 53 A3 N Chile
Iquitos 51 C4 N Peru
Irákleio 75 F7 Crete, Greece
Iran 91 E2 ◆ *Republic,* SW Asia
Iranian Plateau 91 E3 *Plateau,* N Iran
Irapuato 41 E4 C Mexico
Iraq 91 B2 ◆ *Republic,* SW Asia
Irbid 91 A2 N Jordan
Ireland, Republic of 63 A6 ◆ *Republic,* NW Europe
Irian Jaya *see* Papua
Iringa 111 D7 C Tanzania
Iriomote-jima 95 A8 *Island,* Sakishima-shotō, SW Japan
Iriona 43 D2 NE Honduras
Irish Sea 63 C6 *Sea,* C British Isles
Irkutsk 86 F5 S Russ. Fed.
Iroise 65 A2 *Sea,* NW France
Irrawaddy 101 A2 ∽ W Burma
Irrawaddy, Mouths of the 101 A3 *Delta,* SW Burma
Irtysh 86 D4 ∽ C Asia
Irún 67 E1 N Spain
Iruña *see* Pamplona
Isabela, Isla 51 A7 *Island,* Galapagos Islands, Ecuador
Isabella, Cordillera 43 D4 ⛰ NW Nicaragua
Isachsen 35 G2 Ellef Ringnes Island, Nunavut, N Canada
Ísafjördhur 59 A1 NW Iceland
Ise 95 F6 SW Japan
Isère 65 E5 ∽ E France
Isernia 71 D5 C Italy
Ise-wan 95 F6 *Bay,* S Japan
Isfahan 91 D2 C Iran
Ishigaki-jima 95 A8 *Island,* Sakishima-shotō, SW Japan
Ishikari-wan 95 F2 *Bay,* NE Japan
Ishim 86 D4 ∽ Kazakhstan/Russ. Fed.
Ishim 86 C4 C Russ. Fed.
Ishinomaki 95 G4 C Japan
Ishkoshim 93 G4 S Tajikistan
Isiro 112 D1 NE Congo
İskenderun 89 E5 S Turkey
Iskur 75 E3 ∽ NW Bulgaria
Iskur, Yazovir 75 E3 ⊠ W Bulgaria
Isla Cristina 67 B5 S Spain
Islamabad 99 D1 ● NE Pakistan
I-n-Sakane, 'Erg 108 D2 *Desert,* N Mali
Islay 63 B4 *Island,* SW Scotland, UK
Isle 65 C5 ∽ W France
Isle of Man 63 C6 *UK* ◇, NW Europe
Isle of Wight 63 E8 *Unitary auth.,* S England, UK
Ismâ'ilîya 106 I2 N Egypt
Isna 106 J3 SE Egypt
Isoka 112 D3 NE Zambia
İsparta 89 B4 Isparta, SW Turkey
İspir 89 F2 NE Turkey
Israel 91 G6 ◆ *Republic,* SW Asia
Issoire 65 D5 C France
Issyk-Kul', Ozero 93 H2 ◎ E Kyrgyzstan
İstanbul 89 B2 NW Turkey
İstanbul Boğazı *see* Bosporus
Istra 71 D3 *Peninsula,* Slovenia/Serbia and Montenegro (Yugoslavia)
Istra 75 A1 *Cultural region,* NW Croatia
Itabuna 51 H6 E Brazil
Itagüí 51 B2 W Colombia
Itaipú Dam 53 C4 *Dam,* Brazil/Paraguay
Itaipú, Represa de 51 F7 ⊠ Brazil/Paraguay
Itaituba 51 F4 NE Brazil
Italy 71 C4 ◆ *Republic,* S Europe
Itoigawa 95 F5 C Japan
Iturup, Ostrov 86 I5 *Island,* Kurile Islands, SE Russ. Fed.
Itzehoe 69 C2 N Germany
Ivalo 59 E2 N Finland
Ivanhoe 117 F5 NSW, SE Australia
Ivano-Frankivs'k 77 B5 W Ukraine
Ivanovo 79 B5 W Russ. Fed.
Ivoire, Côte d' *see* Ivory Coast
Ivory Coast 108 C5 ◆ *Republic,* W Africa
Ivujivik 33 D1 Québec, NE Canada
Iwaki 95 G5 N Japan
Iwakuni 95 D7 SW Japan
Iwanai 95 F2 NE Japan
Iwate 95 G3 N Japan
Ixtapa 41 E5 S Mexico
Ixtepec 41 G5 SE Mexico
Iyo-nada 95 D7 *Sea,* S Japan
Izabal, Lago de 43 B3 ◎ E Guatemala
Izad Khvast 91 D3 C Iran
Izegem 60 B6 W Belgium
Izhevsk 79 D6 NW Russ. Fed.
Izmayil 77 D7 SW Ukraine
İzmir 89 A4 W Turkey
İzmit 89 B2 NW Turkey
İznik Gölü 89 B2 ◎ NW Turkey
Izu-hanto 95 G6 *Peninsula,* Honshū, S Japan
Izu-shoto 95 G6 *Island group,* S Japan

J

Jabal ash Shifa 91 A3 *Desert,* NW Saudi Arabia
Jabalpur 99 E4 C India
Jaca 67 F2 NE Spain
Jacaltenango 43 A3 W Guatemala
Jackson 37 C5 Mississippi, USA
Jacksonville 37 E6 Florida, USA
Jacmel 45 F4 S Haiti
Jacobabad 99 C3 SE Pakistan
Jaén 67 D5 SW Spain
Jaffna 99 E7 N Sri Lanka
Jagdalpur 99 E5 C India
Jagdaqi 97 G1 N China
Jaipur 99 D3 N India
Jaisalmer 99 C3 NW India
Jakarta 101 C7 ● Java, C Indonesia
Jakobstad 59 E4 W Finland
Jalalabad 93 G5 E Afghanistan
Jalandhar 99 D2 N India
Jalapa 43 D3 NW Nicaragua
Jalpa 41 E4 C Mexico
Jalu 106 H3 NE Libya
Jamaame 111 E5 S Somalia
Jamaica 45 C5 ◆ *Commonwealth Republic,* W West Indies
Jamaica Channel 45 E4 *Channel,* Haiti/Jamaica
Jambi 101 C7 Sumatra, W Indonesia
James Bay 33 C3 *Bay,* Ontario/Québec, E Canada
James River 39 F2 ∽ N USA
Jammu 99 D2 NW India
Jammu and Kashmir 99 D2 *disputed region,* India/Pakistan
Jamnagar 99 C4 W India
Jamshedpur 99 F4 NE India
Jamuna 41 G4 ∽ Bangladesh
Janesville 37 D3 Wisconsin, USA
Jan Mayen 123 C6 *Norwegian* ◇, N Atlantic Ocean
Jánoshalma 73 E8 S Hungary
Japan 95 G4 ◆ *Monarchy,* E Asia
Japan, Sea of 95 D5 *Sea,* NW Pacific Ocean
Japiim 51 C5 W Brazil
Japurá, Rio 51 C3 ∽ Brazil/Colombia
Jaqué 43 I7 SE Panama
Jardines de la Reina, Archipiélago de los 45 C3 *Island group,* C Cuba
Jarocin 73 D4 C Poland
Jarosław 73 G5 SE Poland
Jarqo'rg'on 93 F4 S Uzbekistan
Jarvis Island 115 *US* ◇, C Pacific Ocean
Jasło 73 F5 SE Poland
Jastrzębie-Zdrój 73 D5 S Poland
Jataí 51 F6 C Brazil
Jaunpur 99 F3 N India
Java 101 C8 *Island,* C Indonesia
Javalambre 67 E3 ▲ E Spain
Javari, Rio 51 C4 ∽ Brazil/Peru
Java Sea 101 D7 *Sea,* W Indonesia
Jawhar 111 F5 S Somalia
Jaya, Puncak 101 H7 ▲ E Indonesia
Jayapura 101 I7 E Indonesia
Jaz Murian, Hamun-e 91 F3 ◎ SE Iran
Jebba 108 E4 W Nigeria
Jedda 91 B5 ● W Saudi Arabia
Jędrzejów 73 E5 S Poland
Jefferson City 39 G3 Missouri, USA
Jelenia Góra 73 C4 SW Poland
Jelgava 59 E6 C Latvia
Jemappes 60 B7 S Belgium
Jember 101 D8 Java, C Indonesia
Jena 69 C5 C Germany
Jenin 91 H6 N West Bank
Jérémie 45 E4 SW Haiti
Jeréz de la Frontera 67 C6 SW Spain
Jeréz de los Caballeros 67 C5 W Spain
Jericho 91 H6 E West Bank
Jerid, Chott el 106 E2 *Salt lake,* SW Tunisia
Jersey 63 E9 *UK* ◇, NW Europe
Jerusalem 91 H6 ● NE Israel
Jesenice 69 E8 NW Slovenia
Jessore 99 G4 W Bangladesh
Jesús María 53 B5 C Argentina
Jhansi 99 E3 N India
Jhelum 99 D2 NE Pakistan
Jiamusi 97 H2 NE China
Jiangmen 97 F6 S China
Jiaxing 97 G4 SE China
Jiddah *see* Jedda
Jihlava 73 C6 S Czech Republic
Jilib 111 E5 S Somalia
Jilin 97 H2 NE China
Jima 111 D4 SW Ethiopia
Jiménez 41 D3 N Mexico
Jinan 97 G3 E China
Jingdezhen 97 G5 S China
Jinghong 97 D6 SW China
Jinhua 97 G4 SE China
Jining 97 G4 E China
Jinja 111 C5 S Uganda
Jinotega 43 D4 NW Nicaragua
Jinotepe 43 D5 SW Nicaragua
Jinsha Jiang 97 D4 ∽ SW China
Jinzhou 97 G3 NE China
Jiu 77 B7 ∽ S Romania
Jiujiang 97 G4 S China
Jixi 97 H2 NE China
Jizan 91 B6 SW Saudi Arabia
Jizzax 93 F3 C Uzbekistan
João Pessoa 51 I5 E Brazil
Jodhpur 99 C3 NW India
Joensuu 59 F4 SE Finland
Joetsu 95 F5 C Japan
Johannesburg 112 C6 NE South Africa
John o'Groats 63 D2 N Scotland, UK
Johnston Atoll 26 *US* ◇, C Pacific Ocean
Johor Bahru 101 C6 Peninsular Malaysia
Joinville 51 G8 S Brazil
Jokkmokk 59 D3 N Sweden
Joliet 37 D3 Illinois, USA
Jonava 59 E7 C Lithuania
Jönköping 59 C6 S Sweden
Jonquière 33 E4 Québec, SE Canada
Jordan 91 A3 ◆ *Monarchy,* SW Asia
Jordan 93 G3 E Uzbekistan
Jorhat 99 H3 NE India
Jos 108 F4 C Nigeria
Jos Plateau 108 F4 *Plateau,* C Nigeria
Jotunheimen 59 B5 ⛰ S Norway
Joure 60 E2 N Netherlands
Joutseno 59 F5 SE Finland
Juan Aldama 41 D3 C Mexico
Juazeiro 51 H5 E Brazil
Juazeiro do Norte 51 H5 E Brazil
Juba 111 E5 ∽ Ethiopia/Somalia
Juba 111 C4 S Sudan
Júcar 67 E4 ∽ C Spain
Juchitán 41 G5 SE Mexico
Judenburg 69 E8 C Austria
Juigalpa 43 D5 S Nicaragua
Juiz de Fora 51 G7 SE Brazil
Juliaca 51 C6 SE Peru
Jumilla 67 E4 SE Spain
Juneau 35 E5 Alaska, USA
Junín 53 B5 E Argentina
Jur 111 B3 ∽ C Sudan
Jura 63 C4 *Island,* SW Scotland, UK
Jura 69 A8 NW Switzerland
Jura 65 F4 E France
Jūrmala 59 E6 C Latvia
Juruá, Rio 51 C4 ∽ Brazil/Peru
Juruena, Rio 51 E5 ∽ W Brazil
Jutiapa 43 B3 S Guatemala
Juticalpa 43 D3 C Honduras
Jutland 59 B7 *Island,* W Denmark
Jylland *see* Jutland
Jyväskylä 59 E4 C Finland

K

K2 99 D1 ▲ China/Pakistan
Kaamanen 59 E1 N Finland
Kaaresuvanto 59 D2 N Finland
Kabale 111 C5 SW Uganda
Kabinda 112 D3 SE Congo
Kabompo 112 D4 ∽ W Zambia
Kabul 93 F5 ● E Afghanistan
Kabwe 112 D4 C Zambia
Kachchh, Gulf of 99 B4 *Gulf,* W India
Kachchh, Rann of 99 C4 *Salt marsh,* India/Pakistan
Kadavu 121 J5 *Island,* S Fiji
Kadavu Passage 121 J5 *Channel,* S Fiji
Kadugli 111 C3 S Sudan
Kaduna 108 F4 C Nigeria
Kadzhi-Say 93 H2 NE Kyrgyzstan
Kaédi 108 B3 S Mauritania
Kaesong 95 B5 S North Korea
Kafue 112 D4 ∽ C Zambia
Kafue 112 D4 SE Zambia
Kaga Bandoro 108 G5 C CAR
Kâghet 108 C1 *Physical region,* N Mauritania
Kagoshima 95 D8 SW Japan
Kahmard, Darya-ye 93 F4 ∽ NE Afghanistan
Kahramanmaraş 89 E4 S Turkey
Kaiapoi 119 C6 South Island, NZ
Kaifeng 97 F4 C China
Kai, Kepulauan 101 G7 *Island group,* Maluku, SE Indonesia
Kaikohe 119 C1 North Island, NZ
Kaikoura 119 C5 South Island, NZ
Kainji Reservoir 108 E4 ⊠ W Nigeria
Kaipara Harbour 119 C2 *Harbour,* North Island, NZ
Kairouan 106 F1 E Tunisia

◆ Country ● Country capital ◇ Dependent territory ○ Dependent territory capital ⛰ Mountain range ▲ Mountain 🌋 Volcano ∽ River ◎ Lake ⊠ Reservoir

KRONACH

Kaiserslautern 69 B6 SW Germany
Kaitaia 119 C1 North Island, NZ
Kajaani 59 F3 C Finland
Kaka 93 D4 S Turkmenistan
Kake 35 E5 Kupreanof Island, Alaska, USA
Kakhovs'ke Vodoskhovyshche 77 E5 ⊠ SE Ukraine
Kakinada 99 E5 E India
Kaktovik 35 E3 Alaska, USA
Kalahari Desert 112 C6 *Desert,* Southern Africa
Kalamariá 75 E4 N Greece
Kalamáta 75 E6 S Greece
Kalamazoo 37 D3 Michigan, USA
Kalat 93 F6 S Afghanistan
Kālat 99 B2 SW Pakistan
Kalbarri 117 A5 Western Australia
Kalecik 89 C3 N Turkey
Kalemie 112 D2 SE Congo
Kalgoorlie 117 C5 Western Australia
Kalima 112 D2 E Congo
Kalimantan 101 D6 *Geopolitical region,* C Indonesia
Kaliningrad 59 E7 W Russ. Fed.
Kaliningrad 59 F7 *Province,* W Russ. Fed.
Kalisz 73 D4 C Poland
Kalix 59 E3 N Sweden
Kalixälven 59 E3 ≈ N Sweden
Kalkarindji 117 D2 Northern Territory, N Australia
Kallavesi 59 F4 ◎ SE Finland
Kalloní 75 F5 Lesbos, E Greece
Kalmar 59 C6 S Sweden
Kalmthout 60 C5 N Belgium
Kaluga 79 A5 W Russ. Fed.
Kalyan 99 C5 W India
Kálymnos 75 F6 *Island,* Dodecanese, Greece
Kama 79 D5 ≈ NW Russ. Fed.
Kamchatka 86 I3 *Peninsula,* E Russ. Fed.
Kamensk-Shakhtinskiy 79 A7 SW Russ. Fed.
Kamina 112 D3 S Congo
Kamloops 35 F7 British Columbia, SW Canada
Kampala 111 C5 ● S Uganda
Kâmpóng Cham 101 C4 C Cambodia
Kâmpóng Saôm 101 C4 SW Cambodia
Kampuchea *see* Cambodia
Kam"yanets'-Podil's'kyy 77 C5 W Ukraine
Kamyshin 79 B7 SW Russ. Fed.
Kananga 112 C2 S Congo
Kanash 79 C6 W Russ. Fed.
Kanazawa 95 F5 SW Japan
Kanchipuram 99 E6 SE India
Kandahar 93 E6 S Afghanistan
Kandalaksha 79 B2 NW Russ. Fed.
Kandangan 101 E7 C Indonesia
Kandi 108 E4 N Benin
Kandy 99 E8 C Sri Lanka
Kaneohe 39 B6 Oahu, Hawaii, USA
Kangan 91 D3 S Iran
Kangaroo Island 117 E6 *Island,* South Australia
Kanggye 95 B4 N North Korea
Kangnung 95 C5 NE South Korea
Kanivs'ke Vodoskhovyshche 77 D4 ⊠ C Ukraine
Kankaanpää 59 E4 SW Finland
Kankan 108 B4 E Guinea
Kano 108 F4 N Nigeria
Kanpur 99 E3 N India
Kansas 39 F3 *State,* C USA
Kansas City 39 G3 Kansas, USA
Kansas City 39 G3 Missouri, USA
Kansk 86 E5 S Russ. Fed.
Kantemirovka 79 A7 W Russ. Fed.
Kanto Plain 95 G5 *Plain,* Honshū, C Japan
Kanye 112 D6 SE Botswana
Kaohsiung 97 H6 S Taiwan
Kaolack 108 A3 W Senegal
Kapelle 60 C5 SW Netherlands
Kapellen 60 C6 N Belgium
Kaplangky, Plato 93 C2 *Ridge,* Turkmenistan/Uzbekistan
Kapoeta 111 C4 SE Sudan
Kaposvár 73 D8 SW Hungary
Kappeln 69 C2 N Germany
Kapuas, Sungai 101 D6 ≈ C Indonesia
Kapuskasing 33 C4 Ontario, S Canada
Kara-Balta 93 H2 N Kyrgyzstan
Karabük 89 C2 N Turkey
Karachi 99 B3 SE Pakistan
Karaganda 86 C5 C Kazakhstan
Karaginskiy, Ostrov 86 I3 *Island,* E Russ. Fed.
Karakol 93 H2 NE Kyrgyzstan
Karakol 93 I2 NE Kyrgyzstan
Karakoram Range 99 D1 ▲▲ C Asia
Karaman 89 C4 S Turkey
Karamay 97 C2 NW China
Karamea Bight 119 C5 *Gulf,* South Island, NZ
Kara-Say 93 I2 NE Kyrgyzstan
Karasburg 112 C6 S Namibia
Kara Sea 86 D2 *Sea,* Arctic Ocean
Kara Strait 79 E2 *Strait,* N Russ. Fed.
Karatau 86 C6 S Kazakhstan
Karatau, Khrebet 93 F2 ▲▲ S Kazakhstan
Karbala' 91 C2 S Iraq
Kardítsa 75 D5 C Greece
Kargı 89 D2 N Turkey
Kariba 112 D4 N Zimbabwe
Kariba, Lake 112 D4 ⊠ Zambia/Zimbabwe
Karibib 112 B5 C Namibia
Karigasniemi 59 E1 N Finland
Karimata, Selat 101 C6 *Strait,* W Indonesia
Karimnagar 99 E5 C India
Karin 111 F3 N Somalia
Karkar Island 121 B2 *Island,* N PNG
Karkinits'ka Zatoka 77 E6 *Gulf,* S Ukraine
Karleby *see* Kokkola
Karlovac 75 B1 C Croatia
Karlovy Vary 73 A5 W Czech Republic
Karlskrona 59 C7 S Sweden
Karlsruhe 69 B6 SW Germany
Karlstad 59 C5 C Sweden
Karnal 99 D2 N India
Karnataka 99 D6 *State,* W India
Kárpathos 75 G7 *Island,* SE Greece
Kárpathos 75 G7 Kárpathos, SE Greece
Karpenísi 75 D5 C Greece
Kars 89 G2 NE Turkey
Karskoye More *see* Kara Sea
Karst 69 E8 *Physical region,* Croatia/Slovenia
Karyés 75 E4 N Greece
Kaş 89 B5 SW Turkey
Kasai 112 C3 ≈ Angola/Congo
Kasaji 112 C3 S Congo
Kasama 112 E3 N Zambia
Kasese 111 C5 SW Uganda
Kashan 91 D2 C Iran
Kashi 97 A3 NW China
Kasongo 112 D2 E Congo
Kasongo-Lunda 112 B3 SW Congo
Kásos 75 F7 *Island,* S Greece
Kaspiysk 79 B9 SW Russ. Fed.
Kassala 111 D2 E Sudan
Kassel 69 C4 C Germany
Kastamonu 89 D2 N Turkey
Kastsyukovichy 77 E2 E Belarus
Kasulu 111 C6 W Tanzania
Kasumiga-ura 95 G5 ◎ Honshū, S Japan
Katahdin, Mount 37 H1 ▲ Maine, USA
Katalla 35 D4 Alaska, USA
Katanning 117 B6 Western Australia
Katchall Island 99 H6 *Island,* Nicobar Islands, India
Kateríni 75 E4 N Greece
Katherine 117 D1 Northern Territory, N Australia
Kathmandu 99 F3 ● C Nepal
Katikati 119 D3 North Island, NZ
Katima Mulilo 112 D4 NE Namibia
Katiola 108 C5 C Ivory Coast
Katowice 73 E5 S Poland
Katsina 108 F4 N Nigeria
Kattaqo'rg'on 93 E3 C Uzbekistan
Kattegat 59 B7 *Strait,* N Europe
Kauai 39 A5 *Island,* Hawaii, USA
Kaufbeuren 69 C7 S Germany
Kaunas 59 E7 C Lithuania
Kauno Marios 73 G1 ⊠ S Lithuania
Kavála 75 E4 NE Greece
Kavali 99 E6 E India
Kavaratti 99 C7 Laccadive Islands, SW India
Kavarna 75 G2 NE Bulgaria
Kavieng 121 C1 NE PNG
Kavir, Dasht-e 91 E2 *Salt pan,* N Iran
Kawagoe 95 G5 S Japan
Kawasaki 95 G5 S Japan
Kawerau 119 E3 North Island, NZ
Kaya 108 D4 C Burkina
Kayan, Sungai 101 E6 ≈ C Indonesia
Kayes 108 B3 W Mali
Kayseri 89 D4 C Turkey
Kazach'ye 86 G3 NE Russ. Fed.
Kazakhstan 86 B5 ◆ *Republic,* C Asia
Kazakh Uplands 86 C5 *Plateau,* Kazakhstan
Kazan' 79 C6 W Russ. Fed.
Kazanlŭk 75 F3 C Bulgaria
Kazbek 89 G1 ▲ N Georgia
Kazerun 91 D3 S Iran
Kéa 75 F6 *Island,* Cyclades, Greece
Kea, Mauna 39 B6 ▲ Hawaii, USA
Keban Baraji 89 F3 ◎ Turkey Asia
Kebkabiya 111 A2 W Sudan
Kebnekaise 59 C2 ▲ N Sweden
Kecskemét 73 E8 C Hungary
Kediri 101 D8 Java, C Indonesia
Keetmanshoop 112 C6 S Namibia
Kefalonía 75 D5 *Island,* Ionian Islands, Greece
Kehl 69 B6 SW Germany
Keïta 108 E3 C Niger
Keitele 59 E4 ◎ C Finland
Keith 117 F6 South Australia
Këk-Art 93 H3 SW Kyrgyzstan
Kékes 73 E7 ▲ N Hungary
Kélo 108 G4 SW Chad
Kelowna 35 F7 British Columbia, SW Canada
Keluang 101 C6 Peninsular Malaysia
Kem' 79 B3 NW Russ. Fed.
Kemah 89 F3 E Turkey
Kemerovo 86 E5 C Russ. Fed.
Kemi 59 E3 NW Finland
Kemijärvi 59 E2 N Finland
Kemijoki 59 E3 ≈ NW Finland
Kemin 93 H2 N Kyrgyzstan
Kempele 59 E3 C Finland
Kemp Land 122 D4 *Physical region,* Antarctica
Kempten 69 C7 S Germany
Kendal 63 D5 NW England, UK
Kendari 101 F7 Celebes, C Indonesia
Kenema 108 B5 SE Sierra Leone
Keng Tung 101 B2 E Burma
Kénitra 106 C1 NW Morocco
Kenora 33 A4 Ontario, S Canada
Kentau 86 C6 S Kazakhstan
Kentucky 37 D4 *State,* C USA
Kentucky Lake 37 C4 ⊠ S USA
Kenya 111 D5 ◆ *Republic,* E Africa
Kępno 73 D4 C Poland
Kerala 99 D7 *State,* S India
Kerch 77 G6 SE Ukraine
Kerch Strait 77 G7 *Strait,* Black Sea/Sea of Azov
Kerema 121 B2 S PNG
Kerguelen 15 *Island,* C French Southern and Antarctic Territories
Kerí 75 D6 Zákynthos, Greece
Kerikeri 119 D1 North Island, NZ
Kerkenah, Îles de 80 E4 *Island group,* E Tunisia
Kerkrade 60 E6 SE Netherlands
Kerkyra *see* Corfu
Kermadec Islands 115 *Island group,* NE New Zealand
Kerman 91 E3 C Iran
Kerulen 97 F2 ≈ China/Mongolia
Kesennuma 95 G4 C Japan
Keszthely 73 D8 SW Hungary
Ketchikan 35 E6 Revillagigedo Island, Alaska, USA
Kettering 63 E7 C England, UK
Keuruu 59 E4 C Finland
Key Largo 37 F7 Key Largo, Florida, USA
Key West 37 E7 Florida Keys, Florida, USA
Khabarovsk 86 H5 SE Russ. Fed.
Khairpur 99 C3 SE Pakistan
Khambhat, Gulf of 99 C4 *Gulf,* W India
Khandwa 99 D4 C India
Khanka, Lake 86 H5 ◎ China/Russ. Fed.
Khanthabouli 101 C3 S Laos
Khanty-Mansiysk 86 D4 C Russ. Fed.
Khao Laem Reservoir 101 A3 ⊠ W Thailand
Kharagpur 99 G4 NE India
Kharkiv 77 F4 NE Ukraine
Khartoum 111 C2 ● C Sudan
Khartoum North 111 C2 C Sudan
Khasavyurt 79 B9 SW Russ. Fed.
Khash, Dasht-e 93 D6 *Desert,* SW Afghanistan
Khashm el Girba 111 D2 E Sudan
Khaskovo 75 F3 S Bulgaria
Khatanga 123 E3 N Russ. Fed.
Khaydarkan 93 G3 SW Kyrgyzstan
Kherson 77 E6 S Ukraine
Kheta 86 E3 ≈ N Russ. Fed.
Khiwa 93 D2 W Uzbekistan
Khmel'nyts'kyy 77 C5 W Ukraine
Kholm 93 F4 N Afghanistan
Khon Kaen 101 B3 E Thailand
Khor 86 H5 SE Russ. Fed.
Khorugh 93 G4 S Tajikistan
Khouribga 106 C2 C Morocco
Khowst 93 F5 E Afghanistan
Khujand 93 F3 N Tajikistan
Khulna 99 G4 SW Bangladesh
Khust 77 B5 W Ukraine
Khvoy 91 C1 NW Iran
Khyber Pass 99 C1 *Pass,* Afghanistan/Pakistan
Kia 121 E2 N Solomon Islands
Kibangou 112 B2 SW Congo
Kibombo 112 D2 E Congo
Kidderminster 63 D7 C England, UK
Kiel 69 C2 N Germany
Kielce 73 E4 SE Poland
Kieler Bucht 69 C2 *Bay,* N Germany
Kiev 77 D4 ● N Ukraine
Kiev Reservoir 77 D4 ⊠ N Ukraine
Kiffa 108 B3 S Mauritania
Kigali 111 C6 ● C Rwanda
Kigoma 111 B6 W Tanzania
Kii-suido 95 E7 *Strait,* S Japan
Kikinda 75 D1 N Serbia and Montenegro (Yugoslavia)
Kikwit 112 C2 W Congo
Kilchu 95 C4 NE North Korea
Kilimanjaro 111 D6 ⛰ NE Tanzania
Kilis 89 E5 S Turkey
Kilkenny 63 B7 S Ireland
Kilkís 75 E4 N Greece
Killarney 63 A7 SW Ireland
Killeen 39 F5 Texas, USA
Kilmarnock 63 C5 W Scotland, UK
Kilwa Kivinje 111 D7 SE Tanzania
Kimbe 121 C2 E PNG
Kimberley 112 D6 C South Africa
Kimberley Plateau 117 C2 *Plateau,* Western Australia
Kimch'aek 95 C4 E North Korea
Kinabalu, Gunung 101 E5 ▲ East Malaysia
Kindersley 35 G7 Saskatchewan, S Canada
Kindia 108 B4 SW Guinea
Kindu 112 D2 C Congo
Kineshma 79 B5 W Russ. Fed.
King Island 117 F7 *Island,* Tasmania, SE Australia
Kingman Reef 115 US ◇, C Pacific Ocean
King's Lynn 63 F6 E England, UK
King Sound 117 C2 *Sound,* Western Australia
Kingston 33 D6 Ontario, SE Canada
Kingston 45 D5 ● E Jamaica
Kingston upon Hull 63 E6 E England, UK
Kingstown 45 K6 ● Saint Vincent, Saint Vincent and the Grenadines
King William Island 35 H3 *Island,* Nunavut, N Canada
Kinrooi 60 E6 NE Belgium
Kinshasa 112 B2 ● W Congo
Kintyre 63 C5 *Peninsula,* W Scotland, UK
Kinyeti 111 C4 ▲ S Sudan
Kipili 111 C7 W Tanzania
Kipushi 112 D3 SE Congo
Kirakira 121 F3 SE Solomon Islands
Kirghiz Range 93 G2 ▲▲ Kazakhstan/Kyrgyzstan
Kirghiz Steppe 86 C5 *Uplands,* C Kazakhstan
Kiribati 121 J1 ◆ *Republic,* C Pacific Ocean
Kırıkhan 89 E5 S Turkey
Kırıkkale 89 D3 C Turkey
Kirinyaga 111 D5 ⛰ C Kenya
Kirishi 79 A4 NW Russ. Fed.
Kiritimati 115 *Island,* E Kiribati
Kiriwina Islands 121 C2 *Island group,* S PNG
Kirkenes 59 E1 N Norway
Kirkland Lake 33 C5 Ontario, S Canada
Kırklareli 89 A2 NW Turkey
Kirkpatrick, Mount 122 C5 ▲ Antarctica
Kirksville 39 G3 Missouri, USA
Kirkuk 91 C2 N Iraq
Kirkwall 63 D2 NE Scotland, UK
Kirov 79 C5 W Russ. Fed.
Kirovo-Chepetsk 79 C5 NW Russ. Fed.
Kirovohrad 77 E5 C Ukraine
Kiruna 59 D2 N Sweden
Kisangani 112 D1 NE Congo
Kiskörei-víztároló 73 E7 ⊠ E Hungary
Kiskunfélegyháza 73 E8 C Hungary
Kislovodsk 79 A8 SW Russ. Fed.
Kismayo 111 E5 S Somalia
Kissidougou 108 B4 S Guinea
Kissimmee, Lake 37 E7 ◎ SE USA
Kisumu 111 D5 W Kenya
Kisvárda 73 F7 E Hungary
Kita 108 B4 W Mali
Kitakyushu 95 C7 SW Japan
Kitami 95 G1 NE Japan
Kitchener 33 C6 Ontario, S Canada
Kitimat 35 E6 British Columbia, SW Canada
Kitinen 59 E2 ≈ N Finland
Kitob 93 F3 S Uzbekistan
Kitwe 112 D4 C Zambia
Kitzbühler Alpen 69 D7 ▲▲ W Austria
Kiunga 121 A2 SW PNG
Kivalina 35 D3 Alaska, USA
Kivalo 59 E3 *Ridge,* C Finland
Kivu, Lake 112 D2 ◎ Congo/Rwanda
Kiwai Island 121 A3 *Island,* SW PNG
Kızıl Irmak 89 D2 ≈ C Turkey
Kladno 73 B5 NW Czech Republic
Klagenfurt 69 E8 S Austria
Klaipėda 59 E7 NW Lithuania
Klang 101 B6 Selangor, Peninsular Malaysia
Klarälven 59 C5 ≈ Norway/Sweden
Klatovy 73 A6 SW Czech Republic
Klazienaveen 60 F3 NE Netherlands
Klintsy 79 A5 W Russ. Fed.
Kłobuck 73 E4 S Poland
Klosters 69 C8 SE Switzerland
Kluczbork 73 D4 SW Poland
Klyuchevka 93 G2 NW Kyrgyzstan
Klyuchevskaya Sopka, Vulkan 86 H3 ⛰ E Russ. Fed.
Knokke-Heist 60 B5 NW Belgium
Knoxville 37 E4 Tennessee, USA
Knud Rasmussen Land 35 I1 *Physical region,* N Greenland
Kobe 95 F6 SW Japan
København *see* Copenhagen
Kobenni 108 B3 S Mauritania
Koblenz 69 B5 W Germany
Kobryn 77 B3 SW Belarus
K'obulet'i 89 G2 W Georgia
Kočevje 69 E9 S Slovenia
Koch Bihar 99 G3 NE India
Kochi 95 E7 Shikoku, SW Japan
Kodiak 35 D4 Kodiak Island, Alaska, USA
Kodiak Island 35 D5 *Island,* Alaska, USA
Kofu 95 F5 S Japan
Kogon 93 E3 C Uzbekistan
Kogum-do 95 B7 *Island,* S South Korea
Kohima 99 H3 E India
Kohtla-Järve 59 F5 NE Estonia
Koician 73 C3 W Poland
Koidu 108 B4 E Sierra Leone
Koje-do 95 C7 *Island,* S South Korea
Kokkola 59 E4 W Finland
Koko 108 E4 W Nigeria
Kokrines 35 D3 Alaska, USA
Kokshaal-Tau 93 H3 ▲▲ China/Kyrgyzstan
Kokshetau 86 C5 N Kazakhstan
Koksijde 60 A6 W Belgium
Koksoak 33 D2 ≈ Québec, E Canada
Kokstad 112 D7 E South Africa
Kola Peninsula 79 C3 *Peninsula,* NW Russ. Fed.
Kolari 59 E2 NW Finland
Kolárovo 73 D7 SW Slovakia
Kolda 108 A3 S Senegal
Kolding 59 B7 C Denmark
Kolguyev, Ostrov 79 C2 *Island,* NW Russ. Fed.
Kolhapur 99 D5 SW India
Kolín 73 B5 C Czech Republic
Kolka 59 E6 NW Latvia
Kolkata 99 G4 NE India
Köln *see* Cologne
Koło 73 D3 C Poland
Kołobrzeg 73 C2 NW Poland
Kolokani 108 C3 W Mali
Kolomna 79 B5 W Russ. Fed.
Kolpa 75 B1 ≈ Croatia/Slovenia
Kolpino 79 A4 NW Russ. Fed.
Kol'skiy Poluostrov *see* Kola Peninsula
Kolwezi 112 D3 S Congo
Kolyma 86 H2 ≈ NE Russ. Fed.
Kolyma Range 86 H3 ▲▲ E Russ. Fed.
Komatsu 95 F5 SW Japan
Komoé 108 C4 ≈ E Ivory Coast
Komotiní 75 F4 NE Greece
Komsomolets, Ostrov 86 E1 *Island,* N Russ. Fed.
Komsomol'sk-na-Amure 86 H5 SE Russ. Fed.
Kondopoga 79 B4 NW Russ. Fed.
Koné 121 G6 W New Caledonia
Köneürgenç 93 D2 N Turkmenistan
Kong Frederik VIII Land 123 B5 *Physical region,* NE Greenland
Kongolo 112 D2 E Congo
Kongor 111 C4 SE Sudan
Kongsberg 59 B5 S Norway
Konin 73 D3 C Poland
Kónitsa 75 D4 W Greece
Konosha 79 B4 NW Russ. Fed.
Konotop 77 E3 NE Ukraine
Konstanz 69 B7 S Germany
Konya 89 C4 C Turkey
Kopaonik 75 D3 ▲▲ S Serbia and Montenegro (Yugoslavia)
Koper 69 E9 SW Slovenia
Köpetdag Gershi 93 C3 ▲▲ Iran/Turkmenistan
Koppeh Dagh 91 E1 ▲▲ Iran/Turkmenistan
Korat Plateau 101 B3 *Plateau,* E Thailand
Korçë 75 D4 SE Albania
Korčula 75 B3 *Island,* S Croatia
Korea Bay 97 G3 *Bay,* China/North Korea
Korea Strait 95 C7 *Channel,* Japan/South Korea
Korhogo 108 C4 N Ivory Coast
Korinthos *see* Corinth
Koriyama 95 G4 C Japan
Korla 97 C2 NW China
Körmend 73 C8 W Hungary
Koro 121 J5 *Island,* C Fiji
Koróni 75 E6 S Greece
Koror 114 ● N Palau
Koro Sea 121 J5 *Sea,* C Fiji
Korosten' 77 D4 NW Ukraine
Koro Toro 108 H3 N Chad
Kortrijk 60 B6 W Belgium
Koryak Range 86 I2 ▲▲ NE Russ. Fed.
Koryazhma 79 C4 NW Russ. Fed.
Kos 75 G6 *Island,* Dodecanese, Greece
Ko-saki 95 C7 *Headland,* Tsushima, SW Japan
Kościerzyna 73 D2 NW Poland
Kosciuszko, Mount 117 G6 ▲ NSW, SE Australia
Koshikijima-retto 95 C8 *Island group,* SW Japan
Košice 73 F6 E Slovakia
Koson 93 E3 S Uzbekistan
Kosong 95 B5 SE North Korea
Kosovo 75 D3 *Cultural region,* S Serbia and Montenegro (Yugoslavia)
Kosovska Mitrovica 75 D3 S Serbia and Montenegro (Yugoslavia)
Kossou, Lac de 108 C5 ⊠ C Ivory Coast
Kostanay 86 C4 N Kazakhstan
Kostroma 79 B5 NW Russ. Fed.
Kostyantynivka 77 G5 SE Ukraine
Koszalin 73 C2 NW Poland
Kota 99 D3 N India
Kota Bharu 101 B5 Peninsular Malaysia
Kota Kinabalu 101 D5 East Malaysia
Kotel'nyy, Ostrov 86 F2 *Island,* N Russ. Fed.
Kotka 59 F5 S Finland
Kotlas 79 C4 NW Russ. Fed.
Kotovs'k 77 D5 SW Ukraine
Kotto 108 I5 ≈ CAR/Congo
Kotuy 86 F3 ≈ N Russ. Fed.
Koudougou 108 D4 C Burkina
Koulamoutou 112 B2 C Gabon
Koulikoro 108 C4 SW Mali
Koumac 121 G6 W New Caledonia
Koumra 108 H4 S Chad
Kourou 51 F2 N French Guiana
Kousséri 108 G4 NE Cameroon
Koutiala 108 C4 S Mali
Kouvola 59 F5 S Finland
Kovel' 77 B4 NW Ukraine
Kozáni 75 D4 N Greece
Kozara 75 B2 ▲▲ NW Bosnia and Herzegovina
Kozloduy 75 E2 NW Bulgaria
Kozu-shima 95 F6 *Island,* E Japan
Kpalimé 108 D5 SW Togo
Kragujevac 75 D2 C Serbia and Montenegro (Yugoslavia)
Kra, Isthmus of 101 B5 *Isthmus,* Malaysia/Thailand
Kraków 73 E5 S Poland
Kraljevo 75 D2 C Serbia and Montenegro (Yugoslavia)
Kramators'k 77 G5 SE Ukraine
Kramfors 59 D4 C Sweden
Kranj 69 E8 NW Slovenia
Krasnoarmeysk 79 B7 W Russ. Fed.
Krasnodar 79 A8 SW Russ. Fed.
Krasnokamensk 86 G5 S Russ. Fed.
Krasnokamsk 79 D5 W Russ. Fed.
Krasnoyarsk 86 E5 S Russ. Fed.
Krasnystaw 73 G4 SE Poland
Krasnyy Kut 79 C7 W Russ. Fed.
Krasnyy Luch 77 G5 E Ukraine
Krefeld 69 A4 W Germany
Kremenchuk 77 E5 NE Ukraine
Kremenchuk Reservoir 77 D5 ⊠ C Ukraine
Kreminna 77 G4 E Ukraine
Krishna 99 E5 ≈ C India
Krishnagiri 99 D6 SE India
Kristiansand 59 B6 S Norway
Kristianstad 59 C7 S Sweden
Kristiansund 59 B4 S Norway
Kriti *see* Crete
Kritikó Pélagos *see* Crete, Sea of
Krk 75 B1 *Island,* NW Croatia
Kronach 69 C5 E Germany

◆ Country   ● Country capital   ◇ Dependent territory   ○ Dependent territory capital   ▲ Mountain range   ▲ Mountain   ☒ Volcano   ✍ River   ◎ Lake   ▤ Reservoir

Column 1

Lower Tunguska 86 E4 ↔ N Russ. Fed.
Lowestoft 63 F7 E England, UK
Loyauté, Îles 121 G6 *Island group,* S New Caledonia
Lualaba 112 D2 ↔ SE Congo
Luanda 112 B3 ● NW Angola
Luangwa 112 E4 ↔ Mozambique/Zambia
Luanshya 112 D4 C Zambia
Luarca 67 C1 N Spain
Lubaczów 73 G5 E Poland, UK
Lubań 73 B4 SW Poland
Lubango 112 B4 SW Angola
Lubao 112 D2 C Congo
Lübben 69 E4 E Germany
Lübbenau 69 E4 E Germany
Lubbock 39 F4 Texas, USA
Lübeck 69 C2 N Germany
Lubelska, Wyżyna 73 F4 *Plateau,* SE Poland
Lubin 73 C4 W Poland
Lublin 73 F4 E Poland
Lubliniec 73 D5 S Poland
Lubny 77 E4 NE Ukraine
Lubsko 73 B4 W Poland
Lubumbashi 112 D3 SE Congo
Lucan 63 C6 E Ireland
Lucano, Appennino 71 E6 ▲ S Italy
Lucapa 112 C3 NE Angola
Lucca 71 C3 C Italy
Lucena 67 D5 S Spain
Lucena 101 F4 N Philippines
Lučenec 73 E7 S Slovakia
Lucerne *see* Luzern
Lucknow 99 E3 N India
Luda Kamchiya 75 F3 ↔ E Bulgaria
Lüderitz 112 B6 SW Namibia
Ludhiana 99 D2 N India
Ludvika 59 C5 C Sweden
Ludwigsburg 69 B6 SW Germany
Lüdwigsfelde 69 D4 NE Germany
Ludwigshafen 69 B6 W Germany
Ludwigslust 69 C3 N Germany
Ludza 59 F6 E Latvia
Luena 112 C3 E Angola
Lufira 112 D3 ↔ SE Congo
Luga 79 A4 NW Russ. Fed.
Lugano 69 B8 S Switzerland
Luganville 121 G4 C Vanuatu
Lugenda, Rio 112 F4 ↔ N Mozambique
Lugo 67 B1 NW Spain
Lugoj 77 A6 W Romania
Luhans'k 77 G5 E Ukraine
Luik *see* Liège
Lukenie 112 C2 ↔ C Congo
Łuków 73 F4 E Poland
Lukuga 112 D3 ↔ SE Congo
Luleå 59 D3 N Sweden
Luleälven 59 D3 ↔ N Sweden
Lulimba 112 D2 E Congo
Lulonga 112 C1 ↔ NW Congo
Lumbo 112 F4 NE Mozambique
Lumi 121 A1 NW PNG
Lumsden 119 B7 South Island, NZ
Lund 59 C7 S Sweden
Lüneburg 69 C3 N Germany
Lungué-Bungo 112 C4 ↔ Angola/Zambia
Luninyets 77 C3 SW Belarus
Lunteren 60 D4 C Netherlands
Luoyang 97 F4 C China
Lúrio 112 F4 NE Mozambique
Lúrio, Rio 112 F4 ↔ NE Mozambique
Lusaka 112 D4 ● SE Zambia
Lut, Dasht-e 91 F3 *Desert,* E Iran
Luti 121 E2 NW Solomon Islands
Luton 63 E7 E England, UK
Łutselk'e 35 G5 NW Terr., W Canada
Luts'k 77 C4 NW Ukraine
Lützow-Holm Bay 122 D3 *Bay,* Antarctica
Luuq 111 E4 SW Somalia
Luwego 111 D7 ↔ S Tanzania
Luxembourg 60 E8 ◆ *Monarchy,* NW Europe
Luxembourg 60 E9 *District,* S Luxembourg
Luxembourg 60 E9 ● S Luxembourg
Luxor 106 J3 E Egypt
Luza 79 C4 NW Russ. Fed.
Luzern 69 B8 C Switzerland
Luzon 101 F3 *Island,* N Philippines
Luzon Strait 101 F1 *Strait,* Philippines/Taiwan
L'viv 77 B4 W Ukraine
Lyckseله 59 D3 N Sweden
Lyepyel' 77 D2 N Belarus
Lyme Bay 63 D8 *Bay,* S England, UK
Lyon 65 E5 E France
Lysychans'k 77 G4 E Ukraine
Lyttelton 119 C6 South Island, NZ

M

Column 2

Maaseik 60 E6 NE Belgium
Maastricht 60 E6 SE Netherlands
Macao 97 E6 S China
Macapá 51 F3 N Brazil
Macdonnell Ranges 117 D3 ▲ Northern Territory, C Australia
Maceió 51 I5 E Brazil
Machala 51 A4 SW Ecuador
Machanga 112 E5 E Mozambique
Machilipatnam 99 E5 E India
Mackay 117 G3 Queensland, NE Australia
Mackay, Lake 117 D3 *Salt lake,* Northern Territory/ Western Australia
Mackenzie 35 F4 ↔ NW Terr., NW Canada
Mackenzie Bay 122 E4 *Bay,* Antarctica
Mackenzie Mountains 35 E4 ▲ NW Terr., NW Canada
Macleod, Lake 117 A4 Western Australia
Macomer 71 A6 Sardinia, Italy
Mâcon 65 E4 C France
Macuspana 41 H5 SE Mexico
Ma'daba 91 A2 NW Jordan
Madagascar 112 G5 ◆ *Republic,* W Indian Ocean
Madang 121 B2 N PNG
Made 60 C5 S Netherlands
Madeira, Rio 51 E4 ↔ Bolivia/Brazil
Madeleine, Îles de la 33 F4 *Island group,* Québec, E Canada
Madhya Pradesh 99 E4 *State,* C India
Madison 37 D2 Wisconsin, USA
Madiun 101 D8 Java, C Indonesia
Madras 99 E6 S India
Madras *see* Chennai
Madre de Dios, Río 53 A1 ↔ Bolivia/Peru
Madre del Sur, Sierra 41 F5 ▲ S Mexico
Madre, Laguna 41 F3 *Lagoon,* NE Mexico
Madre Occidental, Sierra *see* Western Sierra Madre
Madre Oriental, Sierra *see* Eastern Sierra Madre
Madrid 67 D3 *Autonomous community,* C Spain
Madrid 67 D3 ● C Spain
Madurai 99 D7 S India
Madura, Pulau 101 E8 *Island,* C Indonesia
Maebashi 95 G5 S Japan
Mae Nam Nan 101 B3 ↔ NW Thailand
Maéwo 121 G4 *Island,* C Vanuatu
Mafia 111 E7 *Island,* E Tanzania
Magadan 86 H3 E Russ. Fed.
Magarida 121 C3 SW PNG
Magdalena 41 B2 NW Mexico
Magdalena 53 B1 N Bolivia
Magdalena, Isla 41 B4 *Island,* W Mexico
Magdalena, Río 51 B3 ↔ C Colombia
Magdeburg 69 D4 C Germany
Magelang 101 C8 Java, C Indonesia
Magellan, Strait of 53 B9 *Strait,* Argentina/Chile
Magerøya 59 D1 *Island,* N Norway
Maggiore, Lake 71 B1 ◎ Italy/Switzerland
Maglie 71 F6 SE Italy
Magnitogorsk 86 C4 C Russ. Fed.
Magta' Lahjar 108 B3 SW Mauritania
Mahajanga 112 G4 NW Madagascar
Mahakam, Sungai 101 E6 ↔ C Indonesia
Mahalapye 112 D5 SE Botswana
Mahānadi 99 F4 ↔ E India
Maharashtra 99 D5 *State,* W India
Mahbubnagar 99 D5 C India
Mahia Peninsula 119 E4 *Peninsula,* North Island, NZ
Mahilyow 77 D2 E Belarus
Mahmud-e Raqi 93 F5 NE Afghanistan
Mahón 67 H3 Minorca, Spain
Maidenhead 63 E7 E England, UK
Maiduguri 108 G4 NE Nigeria
Main 69 C5 ↔ C Germany
Mai-Ndombe, Lac 112 C2 ◎ W Congo
Maine 37 H2 *State,* NE USA
Maine 65 C2 *Cultural region,* NW France
Maine, Gulf of 37 H2 *Gulf,* NE USA
Mainland 63 D2 *Island,* N Scotland, UK

Column 3

Mainland 63 E1 *Island,* NE Scotland, UK
Mainz 69 B5 SW Germany
Maitri 122 C3 *Indian research station,* Antarctica
Maizhokunggar 97 C4 W China
Majorca 67 H4 *Island,* Balearic Islands, Spain
Makarov Basin 123 C4 *Undersea feature,* Arctic Ocean
Makassar Strait 101 E7 *Strait,* C Indonesia
Makay 112 G5 ▲ SW Madagascar
Makedonija *see* Macedonia
Makeni 108 B4 C Sierra Leone
Makhachkala 79 B9 SW Russ. Fed.
Makiyivka 77 G5 E Ukraine
Makkovik 33 G2 Newfoundland and Labrador, NE Canada
Makó 73 F8 SE Hungary
Makoua 112 B2 C Congo
Makran Coast 91 F4 *Coastal region,* SE Iran
Makrany 77 B3 SW Belarus
Makurdi 108 F5 C Nigeria
Malabo 112 B1 ● Isla de Bioco, NW Equatorial Guinea
Malacca *see* Melaka
Malacca, Strait of 101 B6 *Strait,* Indonesia/Malaysia
Malacky 73 C7 W Slovakia
Maladzyechna 77 C2 C Belarus
Málaga 67 D6 S Spain
Malaita 121 F4 *Island,* N Solomon Islands
Malakal 111 C3 S Sudan
Malang 101 D8 Java, C Indonesia
Malanje 112 B3 NW Angola
Mälaren 59 D5 ◎ C Sweden
Malatya 89 E4 SE Turkey
Malawi 112 E4 ◆ *Republic,* S Africa
Malaya *see* Malaysia
Malay Peninsula 101 B5 *Peninsula,* Malaysia/Thailand
Malaysia 101 C5 ◆ *Monarchy,* SE Asia
Malbork 73 E2 N Poland
Malchin 69 D2 N Germany
Malden Island 115 *Atoll,* E Kiribati
Maldives 99 C9 ◆ *Republic,* N Indian Ocean
Male' 99 C8 ● N India
Malekula 121 G5 *Island,* W Vanuatu
Malheur Lake 39 C2 ◎ Oregon, USA
Mali 108 D3 ◆ *Republic,* W Africa
Mali Kyun 101 A4 *Island,* Mergui Archipelago, S Burma
Malindi 111 E6 SE Kenya
Mallaig 63 C4 N Scotland, UK
Mallawi 106 I3 C Egypt
Mallorca *see* Majorca
Malmberget 59 D2 N Sweden
Malmédy 60 E7 E Belgium
Malmö 59 C7 S Sweden
Małopolska 73 F5 *Plateau,* S Poland
Malozemel'skaya Tundra 79 D3 *Physical region,* NW Russ. Fed.
Malta 80 A6 ◆ *Republic,* C Mediterranean Sea
Malta Channel 71 D9 *Strait,* Italy/Malta
Maluku *see* Moluccas
Malung 59 C5 C Sweden
Mamberamo, Sungai 101 I7 ↔ E Indonesia
Mamonovo 59 D7 W Russ. Fed.
Mamoré, Rio 53 D1 ↔ Bolivia/Brazil
Mamou 108 B4 W Guinea
Mamoudzou 112 G4 ○ C Mayotte
Mamuno 112 C5 W Botswana
Manacor 67 H4 Majorca, Spain
Manado 101 F6 Celebes, C Indonesia
Managua 43 D5 ● W Nicaragua
Managua, Lake 43 D4 ◎ W Nicaragua
Manakara 112 G5 SE Madagascar
Manama 91 D4 ● N Bahrain
Mananjary 112 G5 SE Madagascar
Manapouri, Lake 119 A7 ◎ South Island, NZ
Manas, Gora 93 F2 ▲ Kyrgyzstan/Uzbekistan
Manau 121 C2 S PNG
Manaus 51 E4 NW Brazil
Manavgat 89 C5 SW Turkey
Manbij 91 B1 N Syria
Manchester 37 G2 New Hampshire, USA
Manchester 63 D6 NW England, UK
Mandalay 101 A2 C Burma
Mand, Rud-e 91 D3 ↔ S Iran
Mandurah 117 B5 Western Australia
Manduria 71 F6 SE Italy
Mandya 99 D6 C India

Column 4

Manfredonia 71 E5 SE Italy
Mangai 112 C2 W Congo
Mangalmé 108 H4 SE Chad
Mangalore 99 D6 W India
Mangoky 112 F5 ↔ W Madagascar
Manicouagan, Réservoir 33 E4 ◎ Québec, E Canada
Manihiki 115 *Atoll,* N Cook Islands
Manila 111 ● N Philippines
Manisa 89 A3 W Turkey
Manitoba 35 H6 *Province,* S Canada
Manitoba, Lake 35 H6 ◎ Manitoba, S Canada
Manitoulin Island 33 C5 *Island,* Ontario, S Canada
Manizales 51 B2 W Colombia
Manjimup 117 B6 Western Australia
Manlleu 67 G2 NE Spain
Manmad 99 D4 W India
Mannar 99 E7 NW Sri Lanka
Mannar, Gulf of 99 D8 *Gulf,* India/Sri Lanka
Mannheim 69 B6 SW Germany
Manono 112 D3 SE Congo
Manosque 65 E6 SE France
Mansa 112 D3 N Zambia
Mansel Island 35 I4 *Island,* Nunavut, NE Canada
Mansfield 37 E3 Ohio, USA
Mantova 71 C2 NW Italy
Mantua *see* Mantova
Manurewa 119 D2 North Island, NZ
Manus Island 121 B1 *Island,* N PNG
Manzanares 67 D4 C Spain
Manzanillo 45 D3 E Cuba
Manzanillo 45 D3 SW Mexico
Manzhouli 97 F1 N China
Mao 108 G3 W Chad
Maoke, Pegunungan 101 I7 ▲ E Indonesia
Maoming 97 F6 S China
Maputo 112 E6 ● S Mozambique
Maraa 121 A6 W French Polynesia
Marabá 51 G4 NE Brazil
Maracaibo 51 C1 NW Venezuela
Maracaibo, Lake 51 B2 *Inlet,* NW Venezuela
Maradah 106 G3 N Libya
Maradi 108 F3 S Niger
Maragheh 91 C1 NW Iran
Marajó, Baía de 51 G3 *Bay,* N Brazil
Marajó, Ilha de 51 F3 *Island,* N Brazil
Maramba *see* Livingstone
Maranhão 51 G4 *State,* E Brazil
Marañón, Río 51 B4 ↔ N Peru
Marathon 33 B4 Ontario, S Canada
Marbella 67 D6 S Spain
Marble Bar 117 B4 Western Australia
Marburg an der Lahn 69 B5 W Germany
Marche 65 D4 *Cultural region,* C France
Marche-en-Famenne 60 D8 SE Belgium
Mar Chiquita, Laguna 53 B5 ◎ C Argentina
Mardan 99 C1 N Pakistan
Mar del Plata 53 C6 E Argentina
Mardin 89 F4 SE Turkey
Maré 121 G6 *Island,* Îles Loyauté, E New Caledonia
Mareeba 117 G2 Queensland, NE Australia
Margarita, Isla de 51 D1 *Island,* N Venezuela
Margate 63 F7 SE England, UK
Margherita, Lake 111 D4 ◎ SW Ethiopia
Margow, Dasht-e 93 D6 *Desert,* SW Afghanistan
Mari 121 A3 SW PNG
María Cleofas, Isla 41 C5 *Island,* C Mexico
Maria Island 117 G7 *Island,* Tasmania, SE Australia
María Madre, Isla 41 C4 *Island,* C Mexico
María Magdalena, Isla 41 C4 *Island,* C Mexico
Mariana Islands 15 *Island group,* Guam/Northern Mariana Islands
Mariana Trench 15 *Trench,* W Pacific Ocean
Mariánské Lázně 73 A5 W Czech Republic
Maribor 69 F8 NE Slovenia
Maridi 111 B5 S Sudan
Marie Byrd Land 122 B5 *Physical region,* Antarctica
Marie-Galante 45 K5 *Island,* SE Guadeloupe
Mariental 112 C6 SW Namibia
Marietta 37 E4 NE Venezuela
Maturín 51 D1 NE Venezuela
Maui 39 B6 *Island,* Hawaii, USA
Maun 112 C5 C Botswana

Column 5

Marília 51 F7 S Brazil
Marín 67 B2 NW Spain
Maringá 51 F7 S Brazil
Maritsa 75 F3 ↔ SW Europe
Mariupol' 77 G5 SE Ukraine
Marka 111 D5 S Somalia
Markham, Mount 122 C5 ▲ Antarctica
Markounda 108 H5 NW CAR
Marktredwitz 69 D5 E Germany
Marmande 65 C5 SW France
Marmara, Sea of 89 A2 *Sea,* NW Turkey
Marmaris 89 A5 SW Turkey
Marne 65 E2 *Cultural region,* N France
Marne 65 E3 ↔ N France
Maro 108 H4 S Chad
Maroantsetra 112 G4 NE Madagascar
Maromokotro 112 G4 ▲ N Madagascar
Maroni River 51 F2 ↔ French Guiana/Surinam
Maroua 108 G4 N Cameroon
Marquises, Îles 115 *Island group,* N French Polynesia
Marrakech 106 C2 W Morocco
Marrawah 117 F7 Tasmania, SE Australia
Marree 117 E5 South Australia
Marsá al Burayqah 106 G3 N Libya
Marsabit 111 D5 N Kenya
Marsala 71 C8 Sicily, Italy
Marsberg 69 B4 W Germany
Marseille 65 E7 SE France
Marshall Islands 115 ◆ *Republic,* W Pacific Ocean
Marsh Harbour 45 D1 Great Abaco, W Bahamas
Martigues 65 E6 SE France
Martin 73 E6 NW Slovakia
Martinique 45 K5 *French ◇,* E West Indies
Martinique Passage 45 K5 *Channel,* Dominica/Martinique
Marton 119 D4 North Island, NZ
Martos 67 D5 S Spain
Mary 93 D4 S Turkmenistan
Maryborough 117 H4 Queensland, E Australia
Maryland 37 F4 *State,* NE USA
Masai Steppe 111 D6 *Grassland,* NW Tanzania
Masaka 111 C5 SW Uganda
Masan 95 C6 S South Korea
Masasi 111 D7 SE Tanzania
Masaya 43 D5 W Nicaragua
Maseru 112 D6 ● W Lesotho
Mashhad 91 F1 NE Iran
Masindi 111 C5 W Uganda
Masira, Gulf of 91 F5 *Bay,* E Oman
Masqat *see* Muscat
Massa 71 B3 C Italy
Massachusetts 37 G3 *State,* NE USA
Massawa 111 D2 E Eritrea
Massenya 108 G4 SW Chad
Massif Central 65 D5 *Plateau,* C France
Masterton 119 D5 North Island, NZ
Masuda 95 D7 SW Japan
Masvingo 112 E5 SE Zimbabwe
Matadi 112 B3 W Congo
Matagalpa 43 D4 C Nicaragua
Matale 99 E8 C Sri Lanka
Matamata 119 D3 North Island, NZ
Matamoros 41 F3 NE Mexico
Matane 33 F4 Québec, SE Canada
Matanzas 45 B2 NW Cuba
Matara 99 E8 S Sri Lanka
Mataram 101 E8 C Indonesia
Mataró 67 G2 E Spain
Mataura 119 B7 ↔ South Island, NZ
Mataura 119 B8 South Island, NZ
Matā'utu 121 K4 ○ Île Uvea, Wallis and Futuna
Matautu 121 B5 C Samoa
Mataveri 121 C6 Easter Island, Chile
Matera 71 E6 S Italy
Matías Romero 41 G5 SE Mexico
Mato Grosso 51 E6 *State,* W Brazil
Mato Grosso do Sul 51 E7 *State,* S Brazil
Matosinhos 67 B3 NW Portugal
Matsue 95 D6 SW Japan
Matsumoto 95 F5 S Japan
Matsuyama 95 D7 Shikoku, SW Japan
Matterhorn 69 B9 ▲ Italy/Switzerland
Matthew Town 45 E5 S Bahamas
Maturín 51 D1 NE Venezuela
Mau 99 E3 N India
Maui 39 B6 *Island,* Hawaii, USA
Maun 112 C5 C Botswana

Column 6

Mauritania 108 A2 ◆ *Republic,* W Africa
Mauritius 102 ◆ *Republic,* W Indian Ocean
Mawson 122 E4 *Australian research station,* Antarctica
Maya 43 B2 ↔ E Russ. Fed.
Mayaguana 45 F3 *Island,* SE Bahamas
Mayaguana Passage 45 E3 *Passage,* SE Bahamas
Mayagüez 45 H4 W Puerto Rico
Maych'ew 111 D3 N Ethiopia
Maydan Shahr 93 F5 E Afghanistan
Mayfield 119 C6 South Island, NZ
Maykop 79 A8 SW Russ. Fed.
Maymyo 101 A2 C Burma
Mayor Island 119 D3 *Island,* NE NZ
Mayotte 112 G4 *French ◇,* E Africa
Mazabuka 112 D4 S Zambia
Mazatlán 41 D4 C Mexico
Mazury 73 F2 *Physical region,* NE Poland
Mazyr 77 D3 SE Belarus
Mbabane 112 E6 ● NW Swaziland
Mbala 112 E3 NE Zambia
Mbale 111 C5 E Uganda
Mbandaka 112 C2 NW Congo
M'Banza Congo 112 B3 NW Angola
Mbanza-Ngungu 112 B3 W Congo
Mbarara 111 C5 SW Uganda
Mbé 108 G5 N Cameroon
Mbeya 111 C7 Mbeya, SW Tanzania
Mbuji-Mayi 112 D3 S Congo
McAllen 39 F6 Texas, USA
McClintock Channel 35 G3 *Channel,* Nunavut, N Canada
McCook 39 F3 Nebraska, USA
McKinley, Mount 35 D2 ▲ Alaska, USA
McKinley Park 35 D4 Alaska, USA
McMurdo Base 122 C6 *US research station,* Antarctica
Mdantsane 112 D7 SE South Africa
Mecca 91 B5 W Saudi Arabia
Mechelen 60 C6 C Belgium
Mecklenburger Bucht 69 C2 *Bay,* N Germany
Mecsek 73 D8 ▲ SW Hungary
Medan 101 B6 Sumatra, E Indonesia
Medellín 51 B2 NW Colombia
Médenine 106 F2 SE Tunisia
Mediaş 77 B6 C Romania
Medicine Hat 35 G7 Alberta, SW Canada
Medina 91 B4 W Saudi Arabia
Medinaceli 67 E3 N Spain
Medina del Campo 67 D3 N Spain
Mediterranean Sea 80 D4 *Sea,* Africa/Asia/Europe
Médoc 65 B5 *Cultural region,* SW France
Medvezh'yegorsk 79 B3 NW Russ. Fed.
Meekatharra 117 B4 Western Australia
Meerssen 60 E6 SE Netherlands
Meerut 99 D2 N India
Mehtarlam 93 G5 E Afghanistan
Mejillones 53 A3 N Chile
Mek'ele 111 D2 N Ethiopia
Meknès 106 C1 N Morocco
Mekong 101 C4 ↔ SE Asia
Mekong, Mouths of the 101 C5 *Delta,* S Vietnam
Melaka 101 B6 Melaka, Peninsular Malaysia
Melanesia 121 G3 *Island group,* W Pacific Ocean
Melbourne 117 F6 Victoria, SE Australia
Melghir, Chott 106 E2 *Salt lake,* E Algeria
Melilla 106 D1 *Enclave,* Spain, N Africa
Melita 35 H7 Manitoba, S Canada
Melitopol' 77 F6 SE Ukraine
Melle 60 B6 NW Belgium
Mellerud 59 C6 S Sweden
Mellieha 80 B6 E Malta
Mellizo Sur, Cerro 53 A8 ▲ S Chile
Melo 53 D5 NE Uruguay
Melsungen 69 C5 C Germany
Melun 65 D3 N France
Melville Island 35 G2 *Island,* Parry Islands, NW Terr./Nunavut, NW Canada
Melville Island 117 D1 *Island,* Northern Territory, N Australia
Melville, Lake 33 G3 ◎ Newfoundland and Labrador, E Canada

MELVILLE PENINSULA

Melville Peninsula 35 H3 *Peninsula,* Nunavut, NE Canada
Memmingen 69 C7 S Germany
Memphis 37 C4 Tennessee, USA
Ménaka 108 E3 E Mali
Menaldum 60 D2 N Netherlands
Mende 65 D6 S France
Mendeleyev Ridge 123 C3 *Undersea feature,* Arctic Ocean
Mendi 121 B2 W PNG
Mendocino, Cape 39 A2 *Headland,* California, USA
Mendoza 53 A5 W Argentina
Menemen 89 A3 W Turkey
Menengiyn Tal 97 F2 *Plain,* E Mongolia
Menongue 112 B4 C Angola
Menorca *see* Minorca
Mentawai, Kepulauan 101 B7 *Island group,* W Indonesia
Meppel 60 E3 NE Netherlands
Merano 71 C1 N Italy
Mercedes 53 C4 NE Argentina
Mergui 101 B4 S Burma
Mérida 67 C4 W Spain
Mérida 51 C2 W Venezuela
Mérida 41 H4 SW Mexico
Mérignac 65 B5 SW France
Merowe 111 C2 *Desert,* W Sudan Africa
Merredin 117 B5 Western Australia
Mersey 63 D6 ≈ NW England, UK
Mersin 89 D5 S Turkey
Meru 111 D5 C Kenya
Merzifon 89 D2 N Turkey
Merzig 69 A6 SW Germany
Mesa 39 D4 Arizona, USA
Mesopotamia *see* Iraq
Messalo, Rio 112 F4 ≈ NE Mozambique
Messina *see* Musina
Messina 112 D5 NE South Africa
Messina, Strait of 71 E8 *Strait,* C Mediterranean Sea
Mestia 89 G1 N Georgia
Mestre 71 D2 NE Italy
Metairie 39 H5 Louisiana, USA
Metán 53 B4 N Argentina
Metapán 43 B3 NW El Salvador
Meta, Río 51 C2 ≈ Colombia/Venezuela
Métsovo 75 D4 C Greece
Metz 65 F2 NE France
Meulaboh 101 A6 Sumatra, W Indonesia
Meuse 65 E2 ≈ W Europe
Mexicali 41 A1 NW Mexico
Mexico 41 D3 ◆ *Federal Republic,* N Central America
Mexico City 41 E5 ● C Mexico
México, Golfo de *see* Gulf of Mexico
Mexico, Gulf of 28 G3 *Gulf,* W Atlantic Ocean
Meymaneh 93 E4 NW Afghanistan
Mezen' 79 C3 ≈ NW Russ. Fed.
Mezőtúr 73 F8 E Hungary
Mġarr 80 A6 N Malta
Miahuatlán 41 G6 SE Mexico
Miami 37 F7 Florida, USA
Miami Beach 37 F7 Florida, USA
Mianyang 97 E4 C China
Miastko 73 C2 NW Poland
Michalovce 73 F6 E Slovakia
Michigan 37 D2 *State,* N USA
Michigan, Lake 37 D2 ◎ N USA
Michurinsk 79 B6 W Russ. Fed.
Micronesia 115 ◆ *Federation,* W Pacific Ocean
Mid-Indian Ridge 15 *Undersea Ridge,* C Indian Ocean
Mid-Atlantic Ridge 14 *Undersea feature,* Atlantic Ocean
Middelburg 60 B5 SW Netherlands
Middelharnis 60 C5 SW Netherlands
Middelkerke 60 A6 W Belgium
Middle Andaman 99 H5 *Island,* Andaman Islands, India
Middlesbrough 63 E5 N England, UK
Midland 39 F5 Texas, USA
Midland 33 D5 Ontario, S Canada
Mid-Pacific Mountains 15 *Undersea feature,* NW Pacific Ocean
Midway Islands 26 *US* ◇, C Pacific Ocean
Miechów 73 E5 S Poland
Międzyrzec Podlaski 73 G3 E Poland
Międzyrzecz 73 C3 W Poland
Mielec 73 F5 SE Poland
Miercurea-Ciuc 77 C6 C Romania
Mieres del Camino 67 C1 NW Spain
Mi'eso 111 E3 C Ethiopia
Miguel Asua 41 D3 C Mexico
Mijdrecht 60 D4 C Netherlands
Mikhaylovka 79 B7 SW Russ. Fed.
Mikun' 79 D4 NW Russ. Fed.
Mikura-jima 95 G6 *Island,* E Japan
Milan 71 B2 N Italy
Milano *see* Milan
Milas 89 A4 SW Turkey
Mildura 117 F5 Victoria, SE Australia
Miles 117 G4 Queensland, E Australia
Milford Haven 63 C7 SW Wales, UK
Milford Sound 119 A7 South Island, NZ
Mil'kovo 86 I3 E Russ. Fed.
Milk River 35 G7 Alberta, SW Canada
Milk River 39 D1 ≈ Montana, USA
Milk, Wadi el 111 B2 ≈ C Sudan
Mille Lacs Lake 39 F1 ◎ Minnesota, USA
Millennium Island 115 *Atoll,* Line Islands, E Kiribati
Millerovo 79 A7 SW Russ. Fed.
Mílos 75 F6 *Island,* Cyclades, Greece
Milton 119 B8 South Island, NZ
Milton Keynes 63 E7 SE England, UK
Milwaukee 37 D2 Wisconsin, USA
Minas Gerais 51 H7 *State,* E Brazil
Minatitlán 41 G5 E Mexico
Minbu 101 A2 W Burma
Minch, The 63 C3 *Strait,* NW Scotland, UK
Mindanao 101 G5 *Island,* S Philippines
Mindelheim 69 C7 S Germany
Minden 69 B4 NW Germany
Mindoro 101 F4 *Island,* N Philippines
Mindoro Strait 101 E4 *Strait,* W Philippines
Mingäçevir 89 I2 C Azerbaijan
Mingaora 99 C1 N Pakistan
Minho 67 B2 ≈ Portugal/Spain
Minicoy Island 99 C7 *Island,* SW India
Minna 108 E4 Niger, C Nigeria
Minneapolis 39 G2 Minnesota, USA
Minnesota 39 F1 *State,* N USA
Miño 67 B2 ≈ Portugal/Spain
Minorca 67 H3 *Island,* Balearic Islands, Spain
Minsk 77 C2 ● C Belarus
Minskaya Wzvyshsha 77 C2 ⛰ C Belarus
Minto, Lac 33 D2 ◎ Québec, C Canada
Miraflores 41 C4 W Mexico
Miranda de Ebro 67 E2 N Spain
Miri 101 D5 East Malaysia
Mirim Lagoon 53 D5 *Lagoon,* Brazil/Uruguay
Mirjaveh 91 F3 SE Iran
Mirny 122 D5 *Russian research station,* Antarctica
Mirnyy 86 F4 NE Russ. Fed.
Mirpur Khas 99 C3 SE Pakistan
Mirtoan Sea 75 E6 *Sea,* S Greece
Miskitos, Cayos 43 F3 *Island group,* NE Nicaragua
Miskolc 73 F7 NE Hungary
Misool, Pulau 101 G7 *Island,* Maluku, E Indonesia
Misratah 106 F2 NW Libya
Mississippi 37 C5 *State,* SE USA
Mississippi Delta 39 H5 *Delta,* Louisiana, USA
Mississippi River 37 C4 ≈ C USA
Missoula 39 D1 Montana, USA
Missouri 39 G3 *State,* C USA
Missouri River 39 F2 ≈ C USA
Mistassini, Lac 33 D4 ◎ Québec, SE Canada
Mistelbach an der Zaya 69 F6 NE Austria
Misti, Volcán 51 C6 🌋 S Peru
Mitchell 117 G4 Queensland, E Australia
Mitchell, Mount 37 E4 ▲ North Carolina, USA
Mitchell River 117 F2 ≈ Queensland, NE Australia
Mito 95 G5 S Japan
Mitú 51 C3 SE Colombia
Mitumba Range 112 D3 ⛰ E Congo
Miyako 95 G3 C Japan
Miyako-jima 95 G6 *Island,* Sakishima-shotō, SW Japan
Miyakonojō 95 D8 SW Japan
Miyazaki 95 D8 SW Japan
Mizpe Ramon 91 G7 S Israel
Mjøsa 59 B5 ◎ S Norway
Mława 73 E3 C Poland
Mljet 75 C3 *Island,* S Croatia
Moa Island 117 F1 *Island,* Queensland, NE Australia
Moala 121 J5 *Island,* S Fiji
Moanda 112 B2 SE Gabon
Moba 112 D3 E Congo
Mobaye 108 H5 S CAR
Mobile 37 D6 Alabama, USA
Mochudi 112 D6 SE Botswana
Mocímboa da Praia 112 F3 N Mozambique
Môco 112 B4 ▲ W Angola
Mocuba 112 F4 NE Mozambique
Modena 71 C3 N Italy
Modesto 39 B3 California, USA
Modica 71 D8 Sicily, Italy
Modimolle 112 D6 NE South Africa
Moe 117 F6 Victoria, SE Australia
Mogadiscio *see* Mogadishu
Mogadishu 111 F5 ● S Somalia
Mogilno 73 D3 C Poland
Mohammedia 106 C1 NW Morocco
Mohéli 112 F4 *Island,* S Comoros
Mohoro 111 D7 E Tanzania
Moi 59 A6 S Norway
Mo i Rana 59 C3 C Norway
Mõisaküla 59 E6 S Estonia
Moissac 65 C6 S France
Mojácar 67 E5 S Spain
Mojave Desert 39 C4 *Plain,* California, USA
Mokp'o 95 B7 SW South Korea
Mol 60 D6 N Belgium
Moldavia *see* Moldova
Molde 59 B4 S Norway
Moldo-Too, Khrebet 93 H2 ⛰ C Kyrgyzstan
Moldova 77 C5 ◆ *Republic,* SE Europe
Molfetta 71 E6 SE Italy
Mölndal 59 B6 S Sweden
Molodezhnaya 122 E3 *Russian research station,* Antarctica
Molokai 39 B6 *Island,* Hawaii, USA
Molopo 112 C6 *Seasonal river,* Botswana/South Africa
Moluccas 101 G7 *Island group,* Indonesia
Molucca Sea 101 F6 *Sea,* E Indonesia
Mombacho, Volcán 43 D5 🌋 SW Nicaragua
Mombasa 111 E6 SE Kenya
Møn 59 B7 *Island,* SE Denmark
Monaco 65 F6 ◆ *Monarchy,* W Europe
Monaco 65 F6 ● S Monaco
Mona, Isla 45 H4 *Island,* W Puerto Rico
Mona Passage 45 H4 *Channel,* Dominican Republic/ Puerto Rico
Monbetsu 95 G1 NE Japan
Moncalieri 71 A2 NW Italy
Monchegorsk 79 B2 NW Russ. Fed.
Monclova 41 E3 NE Mexico
Moncton 33 F5 New Brunswick, SE Canada
Mondovì 71 A3 NW Italy
Monfalcone 71 D2 NE Italy
Monforte 67 B2 NW Spain
Mongo 108 H4 C Chad
Mongolia 97 D2 ◆ *Republic,* E Asia
Mongu 112 C4 W Zambia
Monkey Bay 112 E4 SE Malawi
Monkey River Town 43 C2 SE Belize
Monóvar 67 F5 E Spain
Monroe 39 H4 Louisiana, USA
Monrovia 108 B5 ● W Liberia
Mons 60 C7 S Belgium
Monselice 71 C2 NE Italy
Montagua, Río 43 B3 ≈ Guatemala/Honduras
Montana 39 D1 *State,* NW USA
Montana 75 E2 NW Bulgaria
Montargis 65 D3 C France
Montauban 65 C6 S France
Montbéliard 65 F3 E France
Mont Cenis, Col du 65 F5 *Pass,* E France
Mont-de-Marsan 65 B6 SW France
Monteagudo 53 B3 S Bolivia
Monte Caseros 53 C5 NE Argentina
Monte Cristi 45 F4 NW Dominican Republic
Montego Bay 45 D4 W Jamaica
Montélimar 65 E6 E France
Montemorelos 41 E3 NE Mexico
Montenegro 75 C3 *Republic,* SW Serbia and Montenegro (Yugoslavia)
Monte Patria 53 A5 N Chile
Monterey Bay 39 A3 *Bay,* California, USA
Montería 51 B2 NW Colombia
Montero 53 B2 C Bolivia
Monterrey 41 E3 NE Mexico
Montes Claros 51 G6 SE Brazil
Montevideo 53 C6 ● S Uruguay
Montgenèvre, Col de 65 F5 *Pass,* France/Italy
Montgomery 37 D5 Alabama, USA
Monthey 69 A8 SW Switzerland
Montluçon 65 D4 C France
Montoro 67 D5 S Spain
Montpelier 37 G2 Vermont, USA
Montpellier 65 D6 S France
Montréal 33 E5 Québec, SE Canada
Montrose 63 D4 E Scotland, UK
Montserrat 45 J5 *UK* ◇, E West Indies
Monywa 101 A2 C Burma
Monza 71 B2 N Italy
Monze 112 D4 S Zambia
Monzón 67 F2 NE Spain
Moonie 117 G4 Queensland, E Australia
Moora 117 B5 Western Australia
Moorea 121 A5 *Island,* Îles du Vent, W French Polynesia
Moore, Lake 117 B5 ◎ Western Australia
Moose 33 C4 ≈ Ontario, S Canada
Moosehead Lake 37 H2 ◎ Maine, USA
Moosonee 33 C4 Ontario, SE Canada
Mopti 108 C3 C Mali
Mora 59 C5 C Sweden
Morales 43 B3 E Guatemala
Moratalla 67 E5 SE Spain
Morava 73 D6 ≈ C Europe
Moravia 73 D6 *Cultural region,* E Czech Republic
Moray Firth 63 D3 *Inlet,* N Scotland, UK
Moree 117 G5 NSW, SE Australia
Morelia 41 E5 S Mexico
Morena, Sierra 67 C5 ⛰ S Spain
Mórfou 80 C6 W Cyprus
Morghab, Darya-ye 93 E4 ≈ Afghanistan/Turkmenistan
Morioka 95 G3 C Japan
Morlaix 65 A2 NW France
Morocco 106 B2 ◆ *Monarchy,* N Africa
Morogoro 111 D6 E Tanzania
Moro Gulf 101 F5 *Gulf,* S Philippines
Morón 45 D3 C Cuba
Mörön 97 D1 N Mongolia
Morondava 112 G5 W Madagascar
Moroni 112 F4 ● Grande Comore, NW Comoros
Morotai, Pulau 101 G6 *Island,* Maluku, E Indonesia
Morrinsville 119 D3 North Island, NZ
Morris Jesup, Kap 123 C4 *Headland,* N Greenland
Morvan 65 E4 *Physical region,* C France
Moscow 79 B5 ● Russ. Fed.
Mosel 65 F2 ≈ W Europe
Moselle 65 F3 ≈ W Europe
Mosgiel 119 B7 South Island, NZ
Moshi 111 D6 NE Tanzania
Mosjøen 59 C3 C Norway
Moskva 93 F4 SW Tajikistan
Moskva *see* Moscow
Mosonmagyaróvár 73 D7 NW Hungary
Mosquito Coast 43 E4 *Physical region,* Nicaragua
Mosquito Gulf 43 G6 *Gulf,* N Panama
Moss 59 B5 S Norway
Mosselbaai 112 C7 SW South Africa
Mossendjo 112 B2 SW Congo
Mossoró 51 I4 NE Brazil
Most 73 B5 NW Czech Republic
Mosta 80 B6 C Malta
Mostaganem 106 D1 NW Algeria
Mostar 75 C2 S Bosnia and Herzegovina
Mosul 91 C2 N Iraq
Mota del Cuervo 67 E4 C Spain
Motril 67 D6 S Spain
Motueka 119 C5 South Island, NZ
Motul 41 H4 SE Mexico
Motu Nui 121 C6 *Island,* Easter Island, Chile
Mouila 112 A2 C Gabon
Mould Bay 35 G2 Prince Patrick Island, NW Terr., N Canada
Moulins 65 D4 C France
Moulmein 101 B3 S Burma
Moundou 108 G4 SW Chad
Mount Cook *see* Aoraki
Mount Gambier 117 F6 South Australia
Mount Hagen 121 B2 C PNG
Mount Isa 117 F3 Queensland, C Australia
Mount Magnet 117 B4 Western Australia
Mouscron 60 B7 W Belgium
Moussoro 108 G3 W Chad
Moyen Atlas 106 C2 ⛰ N Morocco
Mo'ynoq 93 D1 NW Uzbekistan
Moyynkum, Peski 93 G1 *Desert,* S Kazakhstan
Mozambique 112 E5 ◆ *Republic,* S Africa
Mozambique Channel 112 F5 *Strait,* W Indian Ocean
Mpama 112 B2 ≈ C Congo
Mragowo 73 F2 NE Poland
Mtwara 111 E7 SE Tanzania
Muar 101 B6 Peninsular Malaysia
Mucojo 112 F4 N Mozambique
Mudanjiang 97 H2 NE China
Mufulira 112 D4 C Zambia
Muğla 89 A4 SW Turkey
Mukacheve 77 B5 W Ukraine
Mula 67 E5 SE Spain
Mulhacén 67 D5 ▲ S Spain
Mulhouse 65 F3 NE France
Muller, Pegunungan 101 D6 ⛰ C Indonesia
Müllheim 69 B7 SW Germany
Mull, Isle of 63 B4 *Island,* W Scotland, UK
Mulongo 112 D3 SE Congo
Multan 99 C2 E Pakistan
Multinational Stations 122 A3 *Multinational research station,* Antarctica
Mumbai 99 C5 W India
Münchberg 69 D5 E Germany
München *see* Munich
Muncie 37 D3 Indiana, USA
Munda 121 E2 NW Solomon Islands
Mungbere 112 D1 NE Congo
Munich 69 D7 SE Germany
Munster 63 A7 *Cultural region,* S Ireland
Munster 69 B4 NW Germany
Muonio 59 D2 N Finland
Muonioälv 59 D2 Finland/Sweden
Muqdisho *see* Mogadishu
Mur 69 F8 ≈ C Europe
Muradiye 89 H3 E Turkey
Murchison River 117 B4 ≈ Western Australia
Murcia 67 F5 SE Spain
Murcia 67 E5 *Autonomous community,* SE Spain
Mureş 77 A6 ≈ Hungary/Romania
Murgap 93 D4 ≈ SE Tajikistan
Murgap 93 D3 S Turkmenistan
Murghob 93 H3 SE Tajikistan
Murgon 117 H4 Queensland, E Australia
Müritz 69 D3 ◎ NE Germany
Murmansk 79 C2 NW Russ. Fed.
Murmashi 79 B2 NW Russ. Fed.
Murom 79 B5 W Russ. Fed.
Muroran 95 F2 NE Japan
Muros 67 A1 NW Spain
Murray, Lake 121 A2 ◎ SW PNG
Murray River 117 F5 ≈ SE Australia
Murrumbidgee River 117 F6 ≈ NSW, SE Australia
Murska Sobota 69 F8 NE Slovenia
Murupara 119 E3 North Island, NZ
Mururoa 115 *Atoll,* Îles Tuamotu, SE French Polynesia
Murwara 99 E4 N India
Murwillumbah 117 H5 NSW, SE Australia
Murzuq, Idhan 106 F4 *Desert,* SW Libya
Mürzzuschlag 69 F7 E Austria
Muş 89 G3 E Turkey
Musa, Gebel 106 I3 ▲ NE Egypt
Musala 75 E3 ▲ W Bulgaria
Muscat 91 F4 ● NE Oman
Musgrave Ranges 117 D4 ⛰ South Australia
Musoma 111 C5 N Tanzania
Musina 71 D8 Sicily, Italy
Musters, Lago 53 A7 ◎ S Argentina
Muswellbrook 117 G5 NSW, SE Australia
Mut 89 C5 S Turkey
Mutare 112 E5 E Zimbabwe
Muy Muy 43 D4 C Nicaragua
Mwanza 111 C6 NW Tanzania
Mweka 112 C2 C Congo
Mwene-Ditu 112 C3 S Congo
Mweru, Lake 112 D3 ◎ Congo /Zambia
Myadzyel 77 C2 N Belarus
Myanmar *see* Burma
Myanmar 101 A2 ◆ *military dictatorship,* SE Asia
Myingyan 101 A2 C Burma
Myitkyina 101 B1 N Burma
Mykolayiv 77 E6 S Ukraine
Mykonos 75 F6 *Island,* Cyclades, Greece
Myrina 75 F4 Límnos, SE Greece
Myślibórz 73 B3 W Poland
Mysore 99 D6 W India
My Tho 101 C4 S Vietnam
Mytilíni 75 F5 Lesbos, E Greece
Mzuzu 112 E3 N Malawi

N

Naberezhnyye Chelny 79 D6 W Russ. Fed.
Nacala 112 F4 NE Mozambique
Nadi 121 J5 Viti Levu, W Fiji
Nadur 80 A6 N Malta
Nadvoitsy 79 B3 NW Russ. Fed.
Nadym 86 D3 N Russ. Fed.
Náfpaktos 75 D5 C Greece
Náfplio 75 E6 S Greece
Naga 101 F4 N Philippines
Nagano 95 F5 S Japan
Nagaoka 95 F5 C Japan
Nagasaki 95 C8 SW Japan
Nagato 95 D7 Honshū, SW Japan
Nagercoil 99 D7 SE India
Nagornyy Karabakh 89 H2 *Former autonomous region,* SW Azerbaijan
Nagoya 95 F6 SW Japan
Nagpur 99 E4 C India
Nagqu 97 C4 W China
Nagykálló 73 F7 E Hungary
Nagykanizsa 73 C8 SW Hungary
Nagykőrös 73 E8 C Hungary
Naha 95 A8 Okinawa, SW Japan
Nahariyya 91 H5 N Israel
Nahuel Huapi, Lago 53 A7 ◎ W Argentina
Nain 33 F2 Newfoundland and Labrador, NE Canada
Nairobi 111 D5 ● S Kenya
Najin 95 C3 NE North Korea
Najran 91 C6 S Saudi Arabia
Nakamura 95 E7 Shikoku, SW Japan
Nakatsugawa 95 F6 SW Japan
Nakhodka 86 H6 SE Russ. Fed.
Nakhon Ratchasima 101 B3 E Thailand
Nakhon Sawan 101 B3 W Thailand
Nakhon Si Thammarat 101 B5 SW Thailand
Nakuru 111 D5 SW Kenya
Nal'chik 79 A8 SW Russ. Fed.
Nalut 106 F2 NW Libya
Namangan 93 G3 E Uzbekistan
Nam Co 97 C4 ◎ W China
Nam Dinh 101 C2 N Vietnam
Namhae-do 95 B7 *Island,* S South Korea
Namib Desert 112 B5 *Desert,* W Namibia
Namibe 112 B4 SW Angola
Namibia 112 B5 ◆ *Republic,* S Africa
Nam Ou 101 B2 ≈ N Laos
Namp'o 95 A5 SW North Korea
Nampula 112 F4 NE Mozambique
Namsan-ni 95 A4 NW North Korea
Namsos 59 C3 C Norway
Namur 60 D7 SE Belgium
Namwon 95 B6 S South Korea
Nanaimo 35 E7 Vancouver Island, British Columbia, SW Canada
Nanchang 97 F5 S China
Nancy 65 F3 NE France
Nandaime 43 D5 SW Nicaragua
Nanded 99 D5 C India
Nandyal 99 E6 E India
Nangnim-sanmaek 95 B4 ⛰ C North Korea
Nanjing 97 G4 E China
Nanning 97 F6 S China
Nanping 97 G5 SE China
Nansen Basin 123 D4 *Undersea feature,* Arctic Ocean
Nansen Cordillera 123 C4 *Undersea feature,* Arctic Ocean
Nanterre 65 D2 N France
Nantes 65 B3 NW France
Nanumaga 121 I2 *Atoll,* NW Tuvalu
Nanumea Atoll 121 I2 *Atoll,* NW Tuvalu
Nanyang 97 F4 C China
Napier 119 E4 North Island, NZ
Naples 71 D6 S Italy
Napoli *see* Naples
Napo, Río 51 B3 ≈ Ecuador/Peru
Naracoorte 117 F6 South Australia
Narbonne 65 D7 S France
Nares Strait 35 H1 *Strait,* Canada/Greenland
Narew 73 F3 ≈ E Poland
Narowlya 77 D3 SE Belarus
Närpes 59 D4 W Finland
Närpiö *see* Närpes
Narrabri 117 G5 NSW, SE Australia
Narrogin 117 B5 Western Australia
Narva 59 F5 NE Estonia
Narvik 59 D2 C Norway
Nar'yan-Mar 79 D3 NW Russ. Fed.
Naryn 93 H2 C Kyrgyzstan
Nashik 99 D5 W India
Nashville 37 D4 Tennessee, USA
Näsijärvi 59 E4 ◎ SW Finland
Nassau 45 D2 ● New Providence, N Bahamas

◆ Country ● Country capital ◇ Dependent territory ○ Dependent territory capital ⛰ Mountain range ▲ Mountain 🌋 Volcano ≈ River ◎ Lake ⊠ Reservoir

OPOTIKI

Nasser, Lake 106 J4 ◎ Egypt/Sudan
Nata 112 D5 NE Botswana
Natal 51 I4 E Brazil
Natchez 37 C5 Mississippi, USA
Natitingou 108 D4 NW Benin
Natuna, Kepulauan 101 C6 *Island group,* W Indonesia
Nauru 121 G1 ◆ *Republic,* W Pacific Ocean
Navapolatsk 77 D1 N Belarus
Navarra 67 E2 *Autonomous community,* N Spain
Navassa Island 45 D4 *US* ◇, C West Indies
Navoiy 93 E3 C Uzbekistan
Navojoa 41 C3 NW Mexico
Navolato 41 C3 C Mexico
Nawabshah 99 B3 S Pakistan
Naxcivan 89 H3 SW Azerbaijan
Náxos 75 F6 *Island,* Cyclades, Greece
Nayoro 95 G1 NE Japan
Nazareth 91 H5 N Israel
Nazca Ridge 14 *Undersea ridge,* E Pacific Ocean
Naze 95 B7 SW Japan
Nazilli 89 A4 SW Turkey
Nazret 111 D3 C Ethiopia
N'Dalatando 112 B3 NW Angola
Ndélé 108 H4 N CAR
Ndendé 112 A2 S Gabon
Ndindi 112 A2 S Gabon
Ndjamena 108 G4 ● W Chad
Ndola 112 D4 C Zambia
Neagh, Lough 63 B5 ◎ E Northern Ireland, UK
Neápoli 75 E6 S Greece
Neápoli 75 D4 N Greece
Near Islands 35 A1 *Island group,* Aleutian Islands, Alaska, USA
Nebaj 43 A3 W Guatemala
Neblina, Pico da 51 C3 ▲ NW Brazil
Nebraska 39 F2 *State,* C USA
Neckar 69 B6 ⇝ SW Germany
Necochea 53 C6 E Argentina
Neder Rijn 60 D4 ⇝ C Netherlands
Nederweert 60 E6 SE Netherlands
Neede 60 F4 E Netherlands
Neerpelt 60 D6 NE Belgium
Neftekamsk 79 D6 W Russ. Fed.
Negele 111 E4 S Ethiopia
Negev 91 G6 *Desert,* S Israel
Negombo 99 E8 SW Sri Lanka
Negotin 75 D2 E Serbia and Montenegro (Yugoslavia)
Negra, Punta 51 A4 *Point,* NW Peru
Negro, Rio 51 D3 ⇝ N South America
Negro, Río 53 B6 ⇝ E Argentina
Negros 101 F5 *Island,* C Philippines
Neijiang 97 E5 C China
Nellore 99 E6 E India
Nelson 35 H6 ⇝ Manitoba, C Canada
Nelson 119 C5 South Island, NZ
Néma 108 C3 SE Mauritania
Neman 59 E7 ⇝ NE Europe
Nemours 65 D3 N France
Nemuro 95 H1 NE Japan
Nendö 121 G3 *Island,* Santa Cruz Islands, E Solomon Islands
Nepal 99 E3 ◆ *Monarchy,* S Asia
Nepean 33 D5 Ontario, SE Canada
Neretva 75 C2 ⇝ Bosnia and Herzegovina/Croatia
Neringa 59 E7 SW Lithuania
Neris 77 C2 ⇝ Belarus/Lithuania
Nerva 67 C5 S Spain
Neryungri 86 G4 NE Russ. Fed.
Neskaupstadhur 59 B1 E Iceland
Ness, Loch 63 C3 ◎ N Scotland, UK
Néstos 75 E4 ⇝ Bulgaria/Greece
Netanya 91 G6 C Israel
Netherlands 60 D3 ◆ *Monarchy,* NW Europe
Netherlands Antilles 45 G7 *Dutch* ◇, S Caribbean Sea
Nettilling Lake 35 I3 ◎ Baffin Island, Nunavut, N Canada
Neubrandenburg 69 D3 NE Germany
Neuchâtel 69 A8 W Switzerland
Neuchâtel, Lac de 69 A8 ◎ W Switzerland
Neufchâteau 60 D8 SE Belgium
Neumünster 69 C2 N Germany
Neunkirchen 69 A6 SW Germany
Neuquén 53 A6 SE Argentina
Neuruppin 69 D3 NE Germany
Neusiedler See 69 F7 ◎ Austria/Hungary
Neustadt an der Weinstrasse 69 A6 SW Germany
Neustrelitz 69 D3 NE Germany
Neu-Ulm 69 C7 S Germany
Neuwied 69 B5 W Germany
Nevada 39 C3 *State,* W USA
Nevers 65 D4 C France
Nevinnomyssk 79 A8 SW Russ. Fed.
Nevşehir 89 D4 C Turkey
Newala 111 D7 SE Tanzania
New Amsterdam 51 E2 E Guyana
Newark 37 G3 New Jersey, USA
Newbridge 63 B6 C Ireland
New Britain 121 C2 *Island,* E PNG
New Brunswick 33 F5 *Province,* SE Canada
New Caledonia 121 D5 *French* ◇, SW Pacific Ocean
Newcastle 117 G5 NSW, SE Australia
Newcastle upon Tyne 63 E5 NE England, UK
New Delhi 99 D3 ● N India
New England 37 G2 *Cultural region,* NE USA
Newfoundland 33 G4 *Island,* Newfoundland and Labrador, SE Canada
Newfoundland and Labrador 33 G3 *Province,* E Canada
New Georgia 121 E2 *Island,* New Georgia Islands, NW Solomon Islands
New Georgia Islands 121 D3 *Island group,* NW Solomon Islands
New Glasgow 33 G5 Nova Scotia, SE Canada
New Guinea 121 A2 *Island,* Indonesia/PNG
New Hampshire 37 G2 *State,* NE USA
New Hanover 121 C1 *Island,* NE PNG
New Haven 37 G3 Connecticut, USA
New Ireland 121 C1 *Island,* NE PNG
New Jersey 37 G3 *State,* NE USA
Newman 117 B3 Western Australia
Newmarket 63 F7 E England, UK
New Mexico 39 D4 *State,* SW USA
New Orleans 39 H5 Louisiana, USA
New Plymouth 119 D4 North Island, NZ
Newport 63 D7 SE Wales, UK
Newport 63 E8 S England, UK
Newport News 37 F4 Virginia, USA
New Providence 45 D1 *Island,* N Bahamas
Newquay 63 C8 SW England, UK
Newry 63 C6 SE Northern Ireland, UK
New Siberian Islands 86 F2 *Island group,* N Russ. Fed.
New South Wales 117 F5 *State,* SE Australia
Newtownabbey 63 C5 E Northern Ireland, UK
New York 37 G3 New York, USA
New York 37 F3 *State,* NE USA
New Zealand 119 A5 ◆ *Commonwealth Republic,* SW Pacific Ocean
Neyveli 99 E7 SE India
Ngangzê Co 97 B4 ◎ W China
Ngaoundéré 108 G5 N Cameroon
N'Giva 112 B4 S Angola
Ngo 112 B2 SE Congo
Ngoko 108 G6 ⇝ Cameroon/Congo
Ngourti 108 F3 E Niger
Nguigmi 108 G3 SE Niger
Nguru 108 F4 NE Nigeria
Nha Trang 101 D4 S Vietnam
Nhulunbuy 117 E1 Northern Territory, N Australia
Niagara Falls 37 E3 *Waterfall,* Canada/USA
Niagara Falls 37 F2 New York, USA
Niagara Falls 33 D6 Ontario, S Canada
Niamey 108 E3 ● SW Niger
Niangay, Lac 108 D3 ◎ E Mali
Nia-Nia 112 D1 NE Congo
Nias, Pulau 101 A6 *Island,* W Indonesia
Nicaragua 43 D4 ◆ *republic,* Central America
Nicaragua, Lake 43 E5 ◎ S Nicaragua
Nice 65 F6 SE France
Nicholls Town 45 D1 NW Bahamas
Nicobar Islands 99 H6 *Island group,* India, E Indian Ocean
Nicosia 80 C6 ● C Cyprus
Nicoya 43 D6 W Costa Rica
Nicoya, Golfo de 43 E6 *Gulf,* W Costa Rica
Nicoya, Península de 43 D6 *Peninsula,* NW Costa Rica
Nidzica 73 E2 N Poland
Nieuw-Bergen 60 E5 SE Netherlands
Nieuwegein 60 D4 C Netherlands
Nieuw Nickerie 51 E2 NW Surinam
Niğde 89 D4 C Turkey
Niger 108 E3 ◆ *Republic,* W Africa
Niger 108 E4 ⇝ W Africa
Niger Delta 102 *Delta,* S Nigeria
Nigeria 108 E4 ◆ *Federal Republic,* W Africa
Niger, Mouths of the 108 E5 *Delta,* S Nigeria
Nihon *see* Japan
Niigata 95 F4 C Japan
Niihama 95 E7 Shikoku, SW Japan
Niihau 39 A5 *Island,* Hawaii, USA
Nii-jima 95 G6 *Island,* E Japan
Nijkerk 60 D4 C Netherlands
Nijlen 60 C6 N Belgium
Nijmegen 60 E4 SE Netherlands
Nikel' 79 B2 NW Russ. Fed.
Nikiniki 101 F8 S Indonesia
Nikopol' 77 F5 SE Ukraine
Nikšić 75 C3 SW Serbia and Montenegro (Yugoslavia)
Nile 106 I3 ⇝ N Africa
Nile Delta 106 I2 *Delta,* N Egypt
Nîmes 65 E6 S France
Nine Degree Channel 99 C7 *Channel,* India/Maldives
Ninetyeast Ridge 15 *Undersea Ridge,* E Indian Ocean
Ningbo 97 G4 SE China
Ninigo Group 121 A1 *Island group,* N PNG
Nioro 108 B3 W Mali
Niort 65 C4 W France
Nipigon 33 B4 Ontario, S Canada
Nipigon, Lake 33 B4 ◎ Ontario, S Canada
Nippon *see* Japan
Niš 75 D2 SE Serbia and Montenegro (Yugoslavia)
Nisko 73 F5 SE Poland
Nísyros 75 G6 *Island,* Dodecanese, Greece
Nitra 73 D7 SW Slovakia
Nitra 73 D7 ⇝ W Slovakia
Niue 115 *Self-governing* ◇, S Pacific Ocean
Niulakita 121 J3 *Atoll,* S Tuvalu
Niutao 121 J2 *Atoll,* NW Tuvalu
Nivernais 65 D4 *Cultural region,* C France
Nizamabad 99 D5 C India
Nizhnekamsk 79 C6 W Russ. Fed.
Nizhnevartovsk 86 D4 C Russ. Fed.
Nizhniy Novgorod 79 B5 W Russ. Fed.
Nizhniy Odes 79 D4 NW Russ. Fed.
Nizhyn 77 E4 NE Ukraine
Njombe 111 D7 S Tanzania
Nkayi 112 B2 S Congo
Nkongsamba 108 F5 W Cameroon
Nmai Hka 101 B1 ⇝ N Burma
Nobeoka 95 D8 SW Japan
Noboribetsu 95 F2 NE Japan
Nogales 41 B2 NW Mexico
Nokia 59 E5 SW Finland
Nokou 108 G3 W Chad
Nola 108 G5 SW CAR
Nolinsk 79 C5 NW Russ. Fed.
Nome 123 B1 Alaska, USA
Noord-Beveland 60 B5 *Island,* SW Netherlands
Noordwijk aan Zee 60 C4 W Netherlands
Nora 59 C5 C Sweden
Norak 93 F3 W Tajikistan
Norddeutsches Tiefland 73 A2 *Plain,* N Germany
Norden 69 B3 NW Germany
Norderstedt 69 C3 N Germany
Nordfriesische Inseln *see* North Frisian Islands
Nordhausen 69 C4 C Germany
Nordhorn 69 A3 NW Germany
Nordkapp *see* North Cape
Norfolk 37 G4 Virginia, USA
Norfolk Island 115 *Australian* ◇, SW Pacific Ocean
Norge *see* Norway
Noril'sk 86 E3 N Russ. Fed.
Norman 39 F4 Oklahoma, USA
Normandie *see* Normandy
Normandy 65 C2 *Cultural region,* France
Normanton 117 F2 Queensland, NE Australia
Norrköping 59 C6 S Sweden
Norrtälje 59 D5 C Sweden
Norseman 117 C5 Western Australia
Norsup 121 G5 Malekula, C Vanuatu
Northallerton 63 E5 N England, UK
Northam 117 B5 Western Australia
North America 28 *Continent*
North American Basin 14 *Undersea feature,* W Sargasso Sea
Northampton 63 E7 C England, UK
North Andaman 99 H4 *Island,* Andaman Islands, India
North Bay 33 D5 Ontario, S Canada
North Cape 59 E1 *Headland,* N Norway
North Cape 119 C1 *Headland,* North Island, NZ
North Carolina 37 E5 *State,* SE USA
North Dakota 39 F1 *State,* N USA
Northeim 69 C4 C Germany
Northern Cook Islands 115 *Island group,* N Cook Islands
Northern Dvina 79 C4 ⇝ NW Russ. Fed.
Northern Ireland 63 B5 *Political division,* Northern Ireland, UK
Northern Mariana Islands 115 *US* ◇, W Pacific Ocean
Northern Sporades 75 E5 *Island group,* E Greece
Northern Territory 117 D2 *Territory,* N Australia
North European Plain 54 *Plain,* N Europe
North Frisian Islands 69 B2 *Island group,* N Germany
North Geomagnetic Pole 123 A4 *Pole,* Arctic Ocean
North Island 119 B2 *Island,* N NZ
North Korea 95 C4 ◆ *Republic,* E Asia
Northland 119 C1 *Cultural region,* North Island, NZ
North Little Rock 39 G4 Arkansas, USA
North Platte River 39 E2 ⇝ C USA
North Pole 123 C4 *Pole,* Arctic Ocean
North Saskatchewan 35 G6 ⇝ S Canada
North Sea 54 *Sea,* NW Europe
North Siberian Lowland 86 E3 *Lowlands,* N Russ. Fed.
North Taranaki Bight 119 C3 *Gulf,* North Island, NZ
North Uist 63 B3 *Island,* NW Scotland, UK
Northwest Pacific Basin 15 *Undersea feature,* NW Pacific Ocean
Northwest Territories 35 F4 *Territory,* NW Canada
Northwind Plain 123 B2 *Undersea feature,* Arctic Ocean
Norton Sound 35 C3 *Inlet,* Alaska, USA
Norway 59 A4 ◆ *Monarchy,* N Europe
Norwegian Sea 59 A4 *Sea,* NE Atlantic Ocean
Norwich 63 F7 E England, UK
Noshiro 95 F3 C Japan
Nossob 112 C6 ⇝ E Namibia
Noteć 73 D3 ⇝ NW Poland
Nottingham 63 E6 C England, UK
Nouâdhibou 108 A2 W Mauritania
Nouakchott 108 A2 ● SW Mauritania
Nouméa 121 G6 ○ S New Caledonia
Nova Gorica 69 E8 W Slovenia
Nova Iguaçu 51 G7 SE Brazil
Novara 71 B2 NW Italy
Nova Scotia 33 F5 *Physical region,* SE Canada
Novaya Sibir', Ostrov 86 G2 *Island,* NE Russ. Fed.
Novaya Zemlya 79 E1 *Island group,* N Russ. Fed.
Novgorod 79 A4 W Russ. Fed.
Novi Sad 75 D1 N Serbia and Montenegro (Yugoslavia)
Novoazovs'k 77 G5 E Ukraine
Novocheboksarsk 79 C6 W Russ. Fed.
Novocherkassk 79 A7 SW Russ. Fed.
Novodvinsk 79 C3 NW Russ. Fed.
Novokazalinsk 86 B5 SW Kazakhstan
Novokuznetsk 86 E5 S Russ. Fed.
Novolazarevskaya 122 C3 *Russian research station,* Antarctica
Novo Mesto 69 E9 SE Slovenia
Novomoskovs'k 77 F5 E Ukraine
Novomoskovsk 79 B6 W Russ. Fed.
Novorossiysk 79 A8 SW Russ. Fed.
Novoshakhtinsk 79 A7 SW Russ. Fed.
Novosibirsk 86 D5 C Russ. Fed.
Novotroitsk 79 D7 W Russ. Fed.
Novyy Buh 77 E5 S Ukraine
Nowogard 73 C2 NW Poland
Nowy Dwór Mazowiecki 73 E3 C Poland
Nowy Sącz 73 F6 S Poland
Nowy Tomyśl 73 C3 W Poland
Noyon 65 D2 N France
Ntomba, Lac 112 B2 ◎ NW Congo
Nubian Desert 111 C1 *Desert,* NE Sudan
Nueva Gerona 45 B3 S Cuba
Nueva Guinea 43 E5 SE Nicaragua
Nueva Ocotepeque 43 B3 W Honduras
Nueva Rosita 41 E2 NE Mexico
Nuevitas 45 D3 E Cuba
Nuevo Casas Grandes 41 C2 N Mexico
Nuevo, Golfo 53 B7 *Gulf,* S Argentina
Nuevo Laredo 41 E2 NE Mexico
Nui Atoll 121 I2 *Atoll,* W Tuvalu
Nuku'alofa 115 ● Tongatapu, S Tonga
Nukufetau Atoll 121 I2 *Atoll,* C Tuvalu
Nukulaelae Atoll 121 J3 *Atoll,* E Tuvalu
Nukumanu Islands 121 E1 *Island group,* NE PNG
Nukus 93 D2 W Uzbekistan
Nullarbor Plain 117 D5 *Plateau,* South Australia/Western Australia
Nunavut 35 H3 *Territory,* N Canada
Nuneaton 63 E7 C England, UK
Nunivak Island 35 B3 *Island,* Alaska, USA
Nunspeet 60 E4 E Netherlands
Nuoro 71 A6 Sardinia, Italy
Nuremberg 69 C6 S Germany
Nurmes 59 F4 E Finland
Nürnberg *see* Nuremberg
Nurota 93 E3 C Uzbekistan
Nusaybin 89 G4 SE Turkey
Nyagan' 86 D3 N Russ. Fed.
Nyainqêntanglha Shan 97 C4 ▲ W China
Nyala 111 B3 W Sudan
Nyamtumbo 111 D7 S Tanzania
Nyanda *see* Masvingo
Nyandoma 79 B4 NW Russ. Fed.
Nyantakara 111 C6 NW Tanzania
Nyasa, Lake 112 E4 ◎ E Africa
Nyeri 111 D5 C Kenya
Nyima 97 C4 W China
Nyíregyháza 73 F7 NE Hungary
Nykøbing 59 B7 SE Denmark
Nyköping 59 D6 S Sweden
Nylstroom *see* Modimolle
Nyngan 117 G5 NSW, SE Australia
Nyurba 86 F4 NE Russ. Fed.
Nzega 111 C6 C Tanzania
Nzérékoré 108 B5 SE Guinea
N'Zeto 112 B3 NW Angola

O

Oahu 39 B5 *Island,* Hawaii, USA
Oakland 39 B3 California, USA
Oamaru 119 B7 South Island, NZ
Oaxaca 41 E5 SE Mexico
Ob' 86 D3 ⇝ C Russ. Fed.
Oban 63 C4 W Scotland, UK
Ob, Gulf of 86 D3 *Gulf,* N Russ. Fed.
Obihiro 95 G2 NE Japan
Obo 108 I5 E CAR
Obock 111 E3 E Djibouti
Oborniki 73 C3 W Poland
Ocaña 67 D3 C Spain
O Carballiño 67 B2 NW Spain
Occidental, Cordillera 53 A2 ▲ Bolivia/Chile
Ocean Falls 35 E6 British Columbia, SW Canada
Ocean Island *see* Banaba
Oceanside 39 C4 California, USA
Och'amch'ire 89 G1 W Georgia
Ocotal 43 D4 NW Nicaragua
Ocozocuautla 41 G5 SE Mexico
October Revolution Island 86 F2 *Island,* N Russ. Fed.
Ocú 43 G7 S Panama
Odate 95 G3 C Japan
Ödemiş 89 A4 SW Turkey
Odense 59 B7 C Denmark
Oder 69 E3 ⇝ C Europe
Oderhaff 73 B2 *Bay,* Germany/Poland
Odesa 77 E6 SW Ukraine
Odessa 39 F5 Texas, USA
Odienné 108 C4 NW Ivory Coast
Odoorn 60 F2 NE Netherlands
Of 89 F2 NE Turkey
Ofanto 71 E6 ⇝ S Italy
Offenbach 69 B5 W Germany
Offenburg 69 B7 SW Germany
Ogaden 111 F4 *Plateau,* Ethiopia/Somalia
Ogaki 95 F6 SW Japan
Ogbomosho 108 E5 W Nigeria
Ogden 39 D3 Utah, USA
Ohio 37 E3 *State,* N USA
Ohio River 37 D4 ⇝ N USA
Ohrid, Lake 75 D4 ◎ Albania/FYR Macedonia
Ohura 119 D3 North Island, NZ
Oirschot 60 D5 S Netherlands
Oise 65 D2 ⇝ N France
Oita 95 D7 Kyūshū, SW Japan
Ojinaga 41 D2 N Mexico
Ojos del Salado, Cerro 53 A4 ▲ W Argentina
Okaihau 119 C1 North Island, NZ
Okara 99 D2 E Pakistan
Okavango 112 C5 ⇝ S Africa
Okavango Delta 112 C5 *Wetland,* N Botswana
Okayama 95 E6 SW Japan
Okazaki 95 F6 C Japan
Okeechobee, Lake 37 E7 ◎ SE USA
Okhotsk 86 H3 E Russ. Fed.
Okhotsk, Sea of 86 H4 *Sea,* NW Pacific Ocean
Okhtyrka 77 F4 NE Ukraine
Okinawa 95 A8 SW Japan
Okinawa-shoto 95 A8 *Island group,* Nansei-shotō, SW Japan
Oki-shoto 95 D6 *Island group,* SW Japan
Oklahoma 39 F4 *State,* C USA
Oklahoma City 39 F4 Oklahoma, USA
Oko, Wadi 111 D1 ⇝ NE Sudan
Oktyabr'skiy 79 D6 SW Russ. Fed.
Okushiri-to 95 F2 *Island,* NE Japan
Öland 59 D7 *Island,* S Sweden
Olavarría 53 C6 E Argentina
Oława 73 D4 SW Poland
Olbia 71 B5 Sardinia, Italy
Oldebroek 60 E3 E Netherlands
Oldenburg 69 B3 NW Germany
Oldenburg 69 C2 N Germany
Oldenzaal 60 F4 E Netherlands
Olëkma 86 G4 ⇝ C Russ. Fed.
Olëkminsk 86 G4 NE Russ. Fed.
Oleksandriya 77 E5 C Ukraine
Olenegorsk 79 B2 NW Russ. Fed.
Olenëk 86 F3 ⇝ NE Russ. Fed.
Oléron, Île d' 65 B4 *Island,* W France
Olevs'k 77 C4 N Ukraine
Ölgiy 97 C1 W Mongolia
Olhão 67 B5 S Portugal
Olifa 112 B4 NW Namibia
Oliva 67 F4 E Spain
Olivet 65 D3 C France
Olmaliq 93 F3 E Uzbekistan
Olomouc 73 D6 E Czech Republic
Olonets 79 B4 NW Russ. Fed.
Olovyannaya 86 G5 S Russ. Fed.
Olpe 69 B5 W Germany
Olsztyn 73 E2 N Poland
Olt 77 B7 ⇝ S Romania
Olvera 67 C6 S Spain
Olympia 39 B1 Washington, USA
Olympus, Mount 75 D4 ▲ N Greece
Omagh 63 B5 W Northern Ireland, UK
Omaha 39 G3 Nebraska, USA
Oman 91 E6 ◆ *Monarchy,* SW Asia
Oman, Gulf of 91 F4 *Gulf,* N Arabian Sea
Omboué 112 A2 W Gabon
Omdurman 111 C2 C Sudan
Ometepe, Isla de 43 D5 *Island,* S Nicaragua
Ommen 60 E3 E Netherlands
Omsk 86 D5 C Russ. Fed.
Omuta 95 D7 SW Japan
Onda 67 F3 E Spain
Öndörhaan 97 F2 E Mongolia
Onega 79 B4 ⇝ NW Russ. Fed.
Onega 79 B3 NW Russ. Fed.
Onega, Lake 79 B4 ◎ NW Russ. Fed.
Onex 69 A8 SW Switzerland
Ongjin 95 A5 SW North Korea
Ongole 99 E6 E India
Onitsha 108 F5 S Nigeria
Onon Gol 97 F2 ⇝ N Mongolia
Onslow 117 A3 Western Australia
Onslow Bay 37 F5 *Bay,* North Carolina, USA
Ontario 33 B4 *Province,* S Canada
Ontario, Lake 37 F2 ◎ Canada/USA
Ontinyent 67 F4 E Spain
Ontong Java Atoll 121 E2 *Atoll,* N Solomon Islands
Oostakker 60 B6 NW Belgium
Oostburg 60 B5 SW Netherlands
Oostende *see* Ostend
Oosterbeek 60 E4 SE Netherlands
Oosterhout 60 D5 S Netherlands
Opava 73 D5 E Czech Republic
Opmeer 60 D3 NW Netherlands
Opochka 79 A4 W Russ. Fed.
Opole 73 D5 SW Poland
Oporto 67 B3 NW Portugal
Opotiki 119 E3 North Island, NZ

CAR Central African Republic **FYR** Former Yugoslavian Rebublic **NSW** New South Wales **NZ** New Zealand **PNG** Papua New Guinea **Russ. Fed.** Russian Federation **UAE** United Arab Emirates **UK** United Kingdom **USA** United States of America 137

◆ Country ● Country capital ◇ Dependent territory ○ Dependent territory capital ▲ Mountain range ▲ Mountain ⌖ Volcano ∻ River ⊙ Lake ⊠ Reservoir

RUNDU

Portalegre 67 B4 E Portugal
Port Alexander 35 F4 Baranof Island, Alaska, USA
Port Alfred 112 D7 S South Africa
Port Augusta 117 E5 South Australia
Port-au-Prince 45 F4 ✕ E Haiti
Port-au-Prince 45 ● C Haiti
Port Blair 99 H5 SE India
Port Douglas 117 G2 Queensland, NE Australia
Port Elizabeth 112 D7 S South Africa
Port-Gentil 112 A2 W Gabon
Port Harcourt 108 E5 S Nigeria
Port Hardy 35 E7 Vancouver Island, British Columbia, SW Canada
Port Hedland 117 B3 Western Australia
Portimão 67 B5 S Portugal
Portland 37 H2 Maine, USA
Portland 39 B1 Oregon, USA
Portland 117 F6 Victoria, SE Australia
Port Laoise 63 B6 C Ireland
Port Lincoln 117 E6 South Australia
Port Louis 103 ● NW Mauritius
Port Macquarie 117 H5 NSW, SE Australia
Port Moresby 121 B3 ● New Guinea, SW Papua New Guinea
Porto *see* Oporto
Porto Alegre 51 F8 S Brazil
Portobelo 43 H6 N Panama
Portoferraio 71 B4 C Italy
Port-of-Spain 45 K7 ● Trinidad, Trinidad and Tobago
Portogruaro 71 D2 NE Italy
Porto-Novo 108 E5 ● S Benin
Porto Torres 71 A5 Sardinia, Italy
Porto Velho 51 D5 W Brazil
Portoviejo 51 A4 W Ecuador
Port Pirie 117 E5 South Australia
Port Said 106 I2 N Egypt
Portsmouth 37 F4 Virginia, USA
Portsmouth 63 E8 S England, UK
Port Sudan 111 D1 NE Sudan
Port Talbot 63 D7 S Wales, UK
Portugal 67 A3 ◆ *Republic*, SW Europe
Port Vila 121 H5 ● Éfaté, C Vanuatu
Porvenir 53 A1 NW Bolivia
Porvenir 53 B9 S Chile
Porvoo 59 E5 S Finland
Posadas 53 C4 NE Argentina
Posterholt 60 E6 SE Netherlands
Postojna 69 E9 SW Slovenia
Potenza 71 E6 S Italy
P'ot'i 89 G1 W Georgia
Potiskum 108 F4 NE Nigeria
Potosí 53 B3 S Bolivia
Potsdam 69 D3 NE Germany
Pouébo 121 G6 C New Caledonia
Po Valley 71 C3 *Valley*, N Italy
Považská Bystrica 73 D6 NW Slovakia
Poverty Bay 119 E4 *Inlet*, North Island, NZ
Póvoa de Varzim 67 B2 NW Portugal
Powell, Lake 39 D3 ◎ Utah, USA
Poza Rica 41 F4 E Mexico
Poznań 73 C3 W Poland
Pozoblanco 67 D5 S Spain
Pozsony *see* Bratislava
Pozzallo 71 D9 Sicily, Italy
Prachatice 73 B6 SW Czech Republic
Prague 73 ● NW Czech Republic
Praha *see* Prague
Praia 103 ● Santiago, S Cape Verde
Prato 71 C3 C Italy
Pravia 67 C1 N Spain
Prenzlau 69 D3 NE Germany
Přerov 73 D6 E Czech Republic
Prešov 73 F6 NE Slovakia
Prespa, Lake 75 D4 ◎ SE Europe
Preston 63 D6 NW England, UK
Prestwick 63 C5 W Scotland, UK
Pretoria 112 D6 ● NE South Africa
Préveza 75 D5 W Greece
Pribilof Islands 35 B2 *island group* Alaska, USA
Prilep 75 D4 S FYR Macedonia
Prince Albert 35 G6 Saskatchewan, S Canada
Prince Edward Island 33 G5 *Island*, SE Canada
Prince George 35 F6 British Columbia, SW Canada
Prince of Wales Island 35 H3 *Island*, Queen Elizabeth Islands, Nunavut, NW Canada
Prince of Wales Island 117 F1 *Island*, Queensland, E Australia
Prince Patrick Island 35 F2 *Island*, Parry Islands, NW Terr., NW Canada
Prince Rupert 35 E6 British Columbia, SW Canada
Princess Charlotte Bay 117 G1 *Bay*, Queensland, NE Australia
Princess Elizabeth Land 122 D4 *Physical region*, Antarctica
Príncipe 108 E6 *Island*, N Sao Tome and Principe
Prinzapolka 43 E4 NE Nicaragua
Pripet 77 C3 ≈ Belarus/Ukraine
Pripet Marshes 77 C3 *Wetland*, Belarus/Ukraine
Priština 75 D3 S Serbia and Montenegro (Yugoslavia)
Privas 65 E5 E France
Prizren 75 D3 S Serbia and Montenegro (Yugoslavia)
Probolinggo 101 D8 Java, C Indonesia
Progreso 41 H4 SE Mexico
Prokhladnyy 79 B8 SW Russ. Fed.
Prome 101 A3 C Burma
Promyshlennyy 79 E3 NW Russ. Fed.
Prostějov 73 D6 SE Czech Republic
Provence 65 E6 *Cultural region*, SE France
Providence 37 G3 Rhode Island, USA
Provideniya 123 C1 NE Russ. Fed.
Provo 39 D3 Utah, USA
Prudhoe Bay 35 E3 Alaska, USA
Pruszków 73 E3 C Poland
Prut 77 D6 ≈ E Europe
Prydz Bay 122 E4 *Bay*, Antarctica
Pryluky 77 E4 NE Ukraine
Przemyśl 73 G5 SE Poland
Psará 75 F5 *Island*, E Greece
Psël 77 F4 ≈ Russian Federation/Ukraine
Pskov 79 A4 W Russ. Fed.
Ptsich 77 D3 ≈ SE Belarus
Ptuj 69 F8 NE Slovenia
Pucallpa 51 B5 C Peru
Puck 73 D1 N Poland
Pudasjärvi 59 E3 C Finland
Puebla 41 F5 S Mexico
Pueblo 39 E3 Colorado, USA
Puerto Acosta 53 A2 W Bolivia
Puerto Aisén 53 A7 S Chile
Puerto Ángel 41 G6 SE Mexico
Puerto Ayacucho 51 D2 SW Venezuela
Puerto Baquerizo Moreno 51 B7 Galapagos Islands, Ecuador
Puerto Barrios 43 C2 E Guatemala
Puerto Cabezas 43 E3 NE Nicaragua
Puerto Cortés 43 C2 NW Honduras
Puerto Deseado 53 B8 SE Argentina
Puerto Escondido 41 F6 SE Mexico
Puerto Lempira 43 E3 E Honduras
Puertollano 67 D4 C Spain
Puerto Maldonado 51 C5 E Peru
Puerto Montt 53 A7 C Chile
Puerto Natales 53 A9 S Chile
Puerto Obaldía 43 I6 NE Panama
Puerto Plata 45 G4 N Dominican Republic
Puerto Princesa 101 E4 Palawan, W Philippines
Puerto Rico 45 H4 *US* ◇, C West Indies
Puerto San Julián 53 B8 SE Argentina
Puerto Suárez 53 C2 E Bolivia
Puerto Vallarta 41 D5 SW Mexico
Puerto Varas 53 A7 C Chile
Puerto Viejo 43 E5 NE Costa Rica
Pukaki, Lake 119 B6 ◎ South Island, NZ
Pukatikei, Maunga 121 D6 Ѧ Easter Island, Chile
Pukch'ong 95 B4 E North Korea
Pukekohe 119 D3 North Island, NZ
Pula 75 A2 NW Croatia
Puławy 73 F4 E Poland
Pułtusk 73 F3 C Poland
Pune 99 C5 W India
Punjab 99 D2 *Province*, E Pakistan
Puno 51 C6 SE Peru
Punta Alta 53 B6 E Argentina
Punta Arenas 53 A9 S Chile
Punta Gorda 43 E5 SE Nicaragua
Punta Gorda 43 B2 SE Belize
Puntarenas 43 E6 W Costa Rica
Pupuya, Nevado 53 A2 ▲ W Bolivia
Puri 99 F5 E India
Purmerend 60 D3 C Netherlands
Purus, Rio 51 D4 ≈ Brazil/Peru
Pusan 95 C6 SE South Korea
Püspökladány 73 F7 E Hungary
Putorana Mountains 86 E3 ⛰ N Russ. Fed.
Puttalam 99 E7 W Sri Lanka
Puttgarden 69 C2 N Germany
Putumayo, Río 51 C4 ≈ NW South America
Pyatigorsk 79 A8 SW Russ. Fed.
Pyongyang 95 A5 ● SW North Korea
Pyramid Lake 39 B3 ◎ Nevada, USA
Pyrenees 67 F2 ⛰ SW Europe
Pyrgos 75 D6 S Greece
Pyrzyce 73 B3 NW Poland

Q

Qaidam Pendi 97 D3 *Basin*, C China
Qal'aikhum 93 G3 S Tajikistan
Qal'eh-ye Now 93 E4 NW Afghanistan
Qamdo 97 D4 W China
Qarokul 93 G3 E Tajikistan
Qarshi 93 E3 S Uzbekistan
Qasr Farâfra 106 I3 W Egypt
Qatar 91 D4 ◆ *Monarchy*, SW Asia
Qattara Depression 106 I3 *Desert*, NW Egypt
Qaţţâra, Monkhafad el *see* Qattara Depression
Qazimämmäd 89 J2 SE Azerbaijan
Qazvin 91 D2 NW Iran
Qena 106 J3 E Egypt
Qilian Shan 97 D3 ⛰ N China
Qingdao 97 G3 E China
Qinghai Hu 97 D3 ◎ C China
Qinhuangdao 97 G3 E China
Qinzhou 97 F6 S China
Qiqihar 97 G2 NE China
Qira 97 B3 NW China
Qitai 97 C2 NW China
Qizilrabot 93 H4 SE Tajikistan
Qom 91 D2 N Iran
Qo'ng'irot 93 D2 NW Uzbekistan
Qo'qon 93 G3 E Uzbekistan
Quang Ngai 101 D3 C Vietnam
Quanzhou 97 F5 S China
Quanzhou 97 G5 SE China
Qu'Appelle 35 H7 ≈ Saskatchewan, S Canada
Quarles, Pegunungan 101 E7 ⛰ Celebes, C Indonesia
Quartu Sant' Elena 71 A6 Sardinia, Italy
Quba 89 I2 N Azerbaijan
Québec 33 D3 Québec, SE Canada
Québec 33 E5 *Province*, SE Canada
Queen Charlotte Islands 35 D6 *Island group*, British Columbia, SW Canada
Queen Charlotte Sound 35 D6 *Sea area*, British Columbia, W Canada
Queen Elizabeth Islands 35 G2 *Island group*, NW Terr./Nunavut, N Canada
Queensland 117 F3 *State*, N Australia
Queenstown 119 B7 South Island, NZ
Queenstown 112 D7 S South Africa
Quelimane 112 E5 NE Mozambique
Quepos 43 E6 S Costa Rica
Querétaro 41 E4 C Mexico
Quesada 43 E6 N Costa Rica
Quetta 99 B2 SW Pakistan
Quezaltenango 43 A3 W Guatemala
Quilon 99 D7 SW India
Quimper 65 A2 NW France
Quimperlé 65 A3 NW France
Quito 51 B3 ● N Ecuador
Qurghonteppa 93 F4 SW Tajikistan
Quy Nhon 101 D4 C Vietnam

R

Raahe 59 E3 W Finland
Raalte 60 E3 E Netherlands
Raamsdonksveer 60 D5 S Netherlands
Rába 73 C8 ≈ Austria/Hungary
Rabat 106 C1 ● NW Morocco
Rabat 80 A5 W Malta
Rabaul 121 D1 E PNG
Rabbah Ammon *see* Amman
Rabinal 43 B3 C Guatemala
Rabka 73 E6 S Poland
Rabyanah, Ramlat 106 G4 *Desert*, SE Libya
Race, Cape 33 H4 *Headland*, Newfoundland, Newfoundland and Labrador, E Canada
Rach Gia 101 C4 S Vietnam
Racine 37 D3 Wisconsin, USA
Radom 73 F4 C Poland
Radomsko 73 E4 C Poland
Radzyń Podlaski 73 F4 E Poland
Rae-Edzo 35 F5 NW Terr., NW Canada
Raetihi 119 D4 North Island, NZ
Rafaela 53 B5 E Argentina
Raga 111 B4 SW Sudan
Ragged Island Range 45 D3 *Island group*, S Bahamas
Ragusa 71 D8 Sicily, Italy
Rahimyar Khan 99 C3 SE Pakistan
Raichur 99 D5 C India
Rainier, Mount 39 B1 Ѧ Washington, USA
Rainy Lake 33 A4 ◎ Canada/USA
Raipur 99 E4 C India
Rajahmundry 99 E5 E India
Rajang, Batang 101 D6 ≈ East Malaysia
Rajapalaiyam 99 D7 SE India
Rajasthan 99 C3 *State*, NW India
Rajkot 99 C4 W India
Rajshahi 99 G3 W Bangladesh
Rakaia 119 C6 ≈ South Island, NZ
Raleigh 37 F4 North Carolina, USA
Râmnicu Vâlcea 77 B7 C Romania
Ramree Island 101 A3 *Island*, W Burma
Rancagua 53 A5 C Chile
Ranchi 99 F4 N India
Randers 59 B6 C Denmark
Rangiora 119 C6 South Island, NZ
Rangitikei 119 D4 ≈ North Island, NZ
Rangoon 101 A3 ● S Burma
Rangpur 99 G3 N Bangladesh
Rankin Inlet 35 H4 Nunavut, C Canada
Rapid City 39 E2 South Dakota, USA
Räpina 59 F6 SE Estonia
Rarotonga 115 *Island*, S Cook Islands
Rasht 91 D1 NW Iran
Ratan 59 C4 C Sweden
Rat Islands 35 A3 *Island group*, Aleutian Islands, Alaska, USA
Ratlam 99 D4 C India
Ratnapura 99 E8 S Sri Lanka
Rättvik 59 C5 C Sweden
Raufarhöfn 59 B1 NE Iceland
Raukumara Range 119 E3 ⛰ North Island, NZ
Rauma 59 D5 SW Finland
Rāulakela 99 F4 E India
Ravenna 71 C3 N Italy
Ravi 99 C2 ≈ India/Pakistan
Rawalpindi 99 D1 NE Pakistan
Rawa Mazowiecka 73 E4 C Poland
Rawicz 73 C4 W Poland
Rawlinna 117 C5 Western Australia
Rawson 53 B7 SE Argentina
Rayong 101 B4 S Thailand
Razazah, Buhayrat ar 91 B2 ◎ C Iraq
Razgrad 75 F2 NE Bulgaria
Razim, Lacul 77 D7 *Lagoon*, NW Black Sea
Reading 37 G3 Pennsylvania, USA
Reading 63 E7 S England, UK
Real, Cordillera 110 ⛰ C Ecuador
Realicó 53 B5 C Argentina
Rebecca, Lake 117 C5 ◎ Western Australia
Rebun-to 95 F1 *Island*, NE Japan
Recife 51 I5 E Brazil
Recklinghausen 69 A4 W Germany
Recogne 60 D8 SE Belgium
Reconquista 53 C4 C Argentina
Red Deer 35 G7 Alberta, SW Canada
Redon 65 B3 NW France
Red River 39 G4 ≈ S USA
Red River 101 B2 ≈ China/Vietnam
Red Sea 91 A4 *Sea*, Africa/Asia
Reefton 119 C5 South Island, NZ
Refahiye 89 F3 C Turkey
Regensburg 69 D6 SE Germany
Regenstauf 69 D6 SE Germany
Reggane 106 D3 C Algeria
Reggio di Calabria 71 E8 SW Italy
Reggio nell' Emilia 71 C3 N Italy
Regina 35 H7 Saskatchewan, S Canada
Rehoboth 112 B5 C Namibia
Rehovot 91 G6 C Israel
Reid 117 D5 Western Australia
Ré, Île de 65 B4 *Island*, W France
Reims 65 E2 N France
Reindeer Lake 35 H5 ◎ Manitoba/Saskatchewan, C Canada
Reinga, Cape 119 C1 *Headland*, North Island, NZ
Reinosa 67 D1 N Spain
Reliance 35 G5 NW Terr., C Canada
Rendsburg 69 C2 N Germany
Rengat 101 B6 Sumatra, W Indonesia
Rennell 121 E3 *Island*, S Solomon Islands
Rennes 65 B3 NW France
Reno 39 B3 Nevada, USA
Repulse Bay 35 I3 Nunavut, N Canada
Resistencia 53 C4 NE Argentina
Reşiţa 77 A7 W Romania
Resolute 35 H2 Cornwallis Island, Nunavut, N Canada
Resolution Island 33 E1 *Island*, NW Terr., NE Canada
Réthymno 75 F7 Crete, Greece
Réunion 112 H6 *French* ◇, W Indian Ocean
Reus 67 G3 E Spain
Reutlingen 69 B7 S Germany
Reuver 60 E6 SE Netherlands
Revillagigedo, Islas 41 B5 *Island group*, W Mexico
Reyes 53 A2 NW Bolivia
Rey, Isla del 43 H6 *Island*, Archipiélago de las Perlas, SE Panama
Reykjavík 59 A1 ● W Iceland
Reynosa 41 F3 C Mexico
Rezé 65 B3 NW France
Rhein *see* Rhine
Rheine 69 B4 NW Germany
Rheinisches Schiefergebirge 69 A5 ⛰ W Germany
Rhine 60 E4 ≈ W Europe
Rhinelander 37 D2 Wisconsin, USA
Rho 71 B2 N Italy
Rhode Island 37 H3 *State*, NE USA
Rhodes 75 G6 *Island*, Dodecanese, Greece
Rhodesia *see* Zimbabwe
Rhodope Mountains 75 E3 ⛰ Bulgaria/Greece
Rhône 65 E6 ≈ France/Switzerland
Rhum 63 B4 *Island*, W Scotland, UK
Ribble 63 D6 ≈ NW England, UK
Ribeirão Preto 51 G7 S Brazil
Riberalta 53 B1 N Bolivia
Richard Toll 108 A3 N Senegal
Richmond 37 F4 Virginia, USA
Richmond 119 C5 South Island, NZ
Richmond Range 119 C5 ⛰ South Island, NZ
Ricobayo, Embalse de 67 B2 *Reservoir*, NW Spain
Ried im Innkreis 69 D7 NW Austria
Riemst 60 D7 NE Belgium
Riesa 69 D4 E Germany
Riga 59 E6 ● C Latvia
Riga, Gulf of 59 E6 *Gulf*, Estonia/Latvia
Rigestan 93 E6 *Desert region*, S Afghanistan
Riihimäki 59 E5 S Finland
Rijeka 75 B1 NW Croatia
Rijn 60 E4 ≈ Netherlands
Rijn *see* Rhine
Rijssen 60 E4 E Netherlands
Rimah, Wadi ar 91 C4 *Dry watercourse*, C Saudi Arabia
Rimini 71 D3 N Italy
Rimouski 33 E4 Québec, SE Canada
Ringebu 59 B4 S Norway
Ringkøbing Fjord 59 A7 *Fjord*, W Denmark
Ringvassøya 59 C1 *Island*, N Norway
Rio Branco 51 D5 W Brazil
Río Bravo 41 F3 C Mexico
Río Cuarto 53 B5 C Argentina
Rio de Janeiro 51 H7 SE Brazil
Río Gallegos 53 B9 S Argentina
Rio Grande 51 F9 S Brazil
Río Grande 41 D4 C Mexico
Río Grande 53 B9 S Argentina
Rio Grande do Norte 51 I4 *State*, E Brazil
Rio Grande do Sul 51 F8 *State*, S Brazil
Ríohacha 51 C1 N Colombia
Río Lagartos 41 I4 SE Mexico
Riom 65 D5 C France
Río San Juan 43 E5 *Department*, S Nicaragua
Río Verde 41 E4 C Mexico
Ripoll 67 G2 NE Spain
Rishiri-to 95 F1 *Island*, NE Japan
Rivas 43 D5 SW Nicaragua
Rivera 53 C5 NE Uruguay
Riverside 39 C4 California, USA
Riverton 119 A8 South Island, NZ
Rivière-du-Loup 33 E5 Québec, SE Canada
Rivne 77 C4 NW Ukraine
Rivoli 71 A2 NW Italy
Riyadh 91 C4 ● C Saudi Arabia
Rize 89 F2 NE Turkey
Rkîz 108 A3 W Mauritania
Road Town 45 I4 ○ C British Virgin Islands
Roanne 65 E4 E France
Roanoke 37 F4 Virginia, USA
Roanoke River 37 F4 ≈ SE USA
Roatán 43 D2 N Honduras
Robson, Mount 35 F6 ▲ British Columbia, SW Canada
Roca Partida, Isla 41 B5 *Island*, W Mexico
Rocas, Atol das 51 I4 *Island*, E Brazil
Rochefort 60 D8 SE Belgium
Rochefort 65 B4 W France
Rochester 37 F3 New York, USA
Rochester 39 G2 Minnesota, USA
Rockford 37 D3 Illinois, USA
Rockhampton 117 H4 Queensland, E Australia
Rock Sound 45 E2 Eleuthera Island, C Bahamas
Rocky Mountains 28 ⛰ Canada/USA
Roden 60 E2 NE Netherlands
Rodez 65 D6 S France
Rodos *see* Rhodes
Roermond 60 E6 SE Netherlands
Roeselare 60 B6 W Belgium
Roi Et 101 C3 E Thailand
Rokiškis 59 F7 NE Lithuania
Rokycany 73 B5 W Czech Republic
Roma 117 G4 Queensland, E Australia
Roma *see* Rome
Roman 77 C6 NE Romania
Romania 77 B6 ◆ *Republic*, SE Europe
Rome 71 C5 ● C Italy
Romny 77 E4 NE Ukraine
Rømø 59 A7 *Island*, SW Denmark
Ronda 67 C6 S Spain
Rondônia 51 D5 *State*, W Brazil
Rondonópolis 51 F6 W Brazil
Rønne 59 C7 E Denmark
Ronne Ice Shelf 122 B4 *Ice shelf*, Antarctica
Roosendaal 60 C5 S Netherlands
Roosevelt Island 122 C6 *Island*, Antarctica
Roraima 51 D3 *State*, N Brazil
Roraima, Mount 51 D2 ▲ N South America
Røros 59 B4 S Norway
Rosa, Lake 45 E3 ◎ S Bahamas
Rosalia, Punta 121 C5 *Headland*, Easter Island, Chile
Rosario 53 C5 C Argentina
Rosario 53 C3 C Paraguay
Rosarito 41 A1 NW Mexico
Roscommon 37 E2 Michigan, USA
Roseau 45 K5 ● SW Dominica
Rosengarten 69 C3 N Germany
Rosenheim 69 D7 S Germany
Roslavl' 79 A5 W Russ. Fed.
Rosmalen 60 D5 S Netherlands
Ross 119 B6 South Island, NZ
Rossano 71 E7 SW Italy
Ross Ice Shelf 122 C5 *Ice shelf*, Antarctica
Rosso 108 A3 SW Mauritania
Rossosh' 79 A7 W Russ. Fed.
Ross Sea 122 C6 *Sea*, Antarctica
Rostock 69 D2 NE Germany
Rostov-na-Donu 79 A7 SW Russ. Fed.
Rothera 122 A4 *UK research station*, Antarctica
Rotorua 119 D3 North Island, NZ
Rotorua, Lake 119 D3 ◎ North Island, NZ
Rotterdam 60 C4 SW Netherlands
Rottweil 69 B7 S Germany
Rotuma 121 I4 *Island*, NW Fiji
Roubaix 65 D1 N France
Rouen 65 D2 N France
Roussillon 65 D7 *Cultural region*, S France
Rouyn-Noranda 33 D5 Québec, SE Canada
Rovaniemi 59 E3 N Finland
Rovigo 71 C3 NE Italy
Rovuma, Rio 112 F4 ≈ Mozambique/Tanzania
Roxas City 101 F4 C Philippines
Royale, Isle 37 D1 *Island*, Michigan, USA
Royan 65 B4 W France
Rožňava 73 E6 E Slovakia
Ruapehu, Mount 119 D4 Ѧ North Island, NZ
Ruapuke Island 119 B8 *Island*, SW NZ
Ruatoria 119 E3 North Island, NZ
Ruawai 119 D2 North Island, NZ
Rubizhne 77 G4 E Ukraine
Rudnyy 86 C4 N Kazakhstan
Rufiji 111 D7 ≈ E Tanzania
Rufino 53 B5 C Argentina
Rügen 69 D2 *Headland*, NE Germany
Ruhr Valley 69 A4 *Industrial region*, W Germany
Rukwa, Lake 111 C7 ◎ SE Tanzania
Rumbek 111 B4 S Sudan
Rum Cay 45 E2 *Island*, C Bahamas
Rumia 73 D1 N Poland
Runanga 119 C5 South Island, NZ
Rundu 112 C5 NE Namibia

CAR Central African Republic **FYR** Former Yugoslavian Rebublic **NSW** New South Wales **NZ** New Zealand **PNG** Papua New Guinea **Russ. Fed.** Russian Federation **UAE** United Arab Emirates **UK** United Kingdom **USA** United States of America 139

◆ Country ● Country capital ◇ Dependent territory ◎ Dependent territory capital ▲ Mountain range ▲ Mountain ℞ Volcano ◈ River ◉ Lake ▣ Reservoir

CAR Central African Republic FYR Former Yugoslavian Republic NSW New South Wales NZ New Zealand PNG Papua New Guinea Russ. Fed. Russian Federation UAE United Arab Emirates UK United Kingdom USA United States of America

141

◆ Country   ● Country capital   ◇ Dependent territory   ○ Dependent territory capital   ▲ Mountain range   ▲ Mountain   ▼ Volcano   ☙ River   ◎ Lake   ▣ Reservoir

NORTH AMERICA

CANADA

UNITED STATES OF AMERICA

MEXICO

BELIZE

COSTA RICA

EL SALVADOR

GUATEMALA

HONDURAS

SOUTH AMERICA

GRENADA

HAITI

JAMAICA

ST KITTS & NEVIS

ST LUCIA

ST VINCENT & THE GRENADINES

TRINIDAD & TOBAGO

COLOMBIA

AFRICA

URUGUAY

CHILE

PARAGUAY

ALGERIA

EGYPT

LIBYA

MOROCCO

TUNISIA

LIBERIA

MALI

MAURITANIA

NIGER

NIGERIA

SENEGAL

SIERRA LEONE

TOGO

BURUNDI

DJIBOUTI

ERITREA

ETHIOPIA

KENYA

RWANDA

SOMALIA

SUDAN

EUROPE

SOUTH AFRICA

SWAZILAND

ZAMBIA

ZIMBABWE

DENMARK

FINLAND

ICELAND

NORWAY

MONACO

ANDORRA

PORTUGAL

SPAIN

ITALY

SAN MARINO

VATICAN CITY

AUSTRIA

BOSNIA & HERZEGOVINA

CROATIA

MACEDONIA

SERBIA & MONTENEGRO
(YUGOSLAVIA)

BULGARIA

GREECE

MOLDOVA

ROMANIA

ASIA

ARMENIA

AZERBAIJAN

GEORGIA

TURKEY

IRAQ

ISRAEL

JORDAN

LEBANON

IRAN

KAZAKHSTAN

KYRGYZSTAN

TAJIKISTAN

TURKMENISTAN

UZBEKISTAN

AFGHANISTAN

PAKISTAN

TAIWAN

JAPAN

BRUNEI

INDONESIA

EAST TIMOR

MALAYSIA

SINGAPORE

BURMA

AUSTRALASIA & OCEANIA

MAURITIUS

SEYCHELLES

AUSTRALIA

NEW ZEALAND

PAPUA NEW GUINEA

SOLOMON ISLANDS

MARSHALL ISLANDS

MICRONESIA